Encyclopedia of
FISH

Encyclopedia of
FISH

JOHN DAWES

with David Alderton and Amy-Jane Beer

Grange
BOOKS

This edition published in 2005 by Grange Books

Grange Books plc
The Grange
1-6 Kingsnorth Estate
Hoo
Near Rochester
Kent ME3 9ND
www.grangebooks.co.uk

ISBN 1-84013-792-4

Editorial and design:
The Brown Reference Group plc
8 Chapel Place
Rivington Street
London
EC2A 3DQ
UK
www.brownreference.com

Editorial Director: Lindsey Lowe

Project Director: Graham Bateman

Editors: Marion Dent, Andrew Stilwell, John Woodward, Virginia Carter

Art Editors and Designers: Tony Truscott, Steve McCurdy

Picture Research: Alison Floyd

Main Artists: Denys Ovenden, Mick Loates, Colin Newman

Production: Alastair Gourlay, Maggie Copeland

Printed in Singapore

Title page: **Hammerhead shark**
Half title: **Clown fish**

Contents

Whale shark

Moray eel

Bitterlings

Introduction

About 70 percent of our planet is covered in water, the overwhelming majority forming the seas and oceans. Perhaps a little surprisingly, freshwater—including that contained in all the major rivers and lakes of the world—accounts for just a tiny fraction of the total: no more than 1 percent.

Many of our seas (and certainly all of our oceans) extend to great depths. They therefore contain vast volumes of water, large tracts of which are as alien to us as the surface of other planets. Many of the life forms they contain are also mysterious and, to a large extent, little known.

Yet fishlike creatures have been living, breeding, and dying in the world's waters for around 480 million years.

Admittedly, these early aquatic organisms were quite different than the fish we know today. They were nevertheless the basal stock from which all backboned animals, including fish, arose.

Today there are over 24,000 different types of fish (some of the latest estimates place this figure close to 29,000), all descended from the ancient fishlike creatures of the middle Ordovician period about 480 million years ago. Over time some have evolved into weird and wonderful shapes and colors to the extent that they now hardly look like fish at all. Others, however, have remained virtually unchanged. They are the so-called "living fossils," the most famous of which are undoubtedly the coelacanths, whose present-day representatives are almost identical to the last fossils known from deposits dating back some 70 million years.

Fish are remarkable creatures. During the course of evolution they have developed physical and behavioral characteristics that have allowed them to inhabit most of the world's bodies of water, except for a few places where no life can possibly exist. They have spread to such diverse habitats as coral reefs, dark abysses, deep caves, thermal springs, arctic waters, seasonal pools, raging torrents, mid-ocean expanses, and numerous other watery worlds. As a result, the forces of evolution have molded fish into myriad configurations that make it possible for them not just to tolerate such conditions but to thrive and breed in them, often in spectacular ways. For example, some fish can fly, others can walk, "talk," spit, drown, break wind, or live out of water; some can even live inside the body cavity of another living organism. It seems that whatever lifestyle we can think of, fish have successfully exploited it.

When it comes to feeding, the range of possibilities is just as diverse. Certainly many fish have more or less straightforward feeding requirements and habits. Sharks, for instance, feed on other animals, hunting them down and generally biting them into swallowable pieces. Yet even among sharks there are important variations, and the largest species—the whale shark and the basking shark—are exceptions. These gentle giants are hunters, but their prey consists mainly of small crustaceans and other invertebrates that they filter out of the water using massive sievelike structures inside their cavernous mouths.

Image of fish in typical pose

Common name Great white shark (white pointer, blue pointer, maneater, Tommy, death shark, uptail, white death)

Scientific name *Carcharodon carcharias*

Family Lamnidae

Order Lamniformes

Size Specimens in excess of 36 ft (11 m) reported, but confirmed data indicates a maximum size of 18–20 ft (5.5–6.0m)

Key features Torpedo-shaped body with conical, pointed snout; teeth of upper and lower jaws very similar and saw-edged—upper teeth slightly broader; top half of body slate-gray to brownish; irregular line separates top half from pure-white lower half of body; lobes of caudal fin more similar to each other than in most other species, but upper lobe a little larger than lower; underside of pectoral fins have blackish tips

Breeding Livebearing species that gives birth to 5–14 young (probably more) after gestation period of up to a year; scars predominantly on pectoral fins of mature great white females suggest males bite females during mating, as in other sharks

Diet Mainly bony fish; also cartilaginous fish (including other sharks), turtles, seabirds, and marine mammals, including dolphins, seals, and sea lions

Habitat Wide range of habitats from surfline to offshore (but rarely midocean) and from surface down to around depths exceeding 820 ft (250 m)—although it has been reported to dive to a depth of over 4,000 ft (over 1,200 m)

Distribution Predominantly in warm-temperate and subtropical waters, but also warmer areas

Status Listed by IUCN as Vulnerable; not listed by CITES; world population sometimes quoted at around 10,000, but true numbers unknown

Name and scientific classification of group

Sizes given in imperial units followed by metric equivalent

Basic description of fish, its life, diet, breeding, and distribution

⊖ *Summary panel presents key facts and figures for each fish.*

At the other extreme, some fish don't feed at all —at least not in the traditional sense. The males of some deep-sea anglerfish, for example, attach themselves by their mouths to the body of a chosen female and spend the rest of their lives as parasites, obtaining all their nourishment in dissolved form from the female.

Some fish have evolved fascinating methods for tracking down their food or attracting food to them. Archerfish, for example, can "shoot down" prey from branches overhanging the water, by spitting at it. Other fish set up "cleaning stations" and attract fish covered in parasites. On arrival of suitable clients, the cleaner fish promptly groom them, picking off annoying surface parasites and thereby obtaining a meal for themselves. In a somewhat perverse variation on this unusual relationship, some noncleaners masquerade as cleaners but actually bite out chunks of fin and flesh from unsuspecting victims that stop by for a clean-up. Other fish have inbuilt fishing rods, complete with "bait," which they use to lure prey within reach. In deep dark waters some of these "fisherfish" go a stage farther and use lights to attract prey.

Over many millions of years fish have exploited the qualities offered by water for breeding purposes. We therefore find a bewildering range of breeding strategies in the fish world. In many species eggs and sperm are scattered into the water and abandoned, but in others the eggs are retained inside the body until the moment of birth. In fact, some fish even nourish their developing embryos almost in the same way as mammals. There are even species that employ in-womb cannibalism, in which the strongest embryos quite simply eat their weaker siblings. And that's not all: In the seahorses and pipefish, it is not the females that give birth, but the males!

Our relationship with fish stretches back thousands of years, with fish forming an important part of the human diet since prehistoric times. Today that relationship continues, sometimes with catastrophic consequences for the fish. History is littered with examples of our insatiable appetite for fish having driven species to the very brink of extinction.

In many other cases it is not commercial fishing that has posed the most serious threat to the continued survival of fish species, but the damage we have done (and continue to do) to our planet, for example, through pollution. Repeated introductions of selected fish species into areas outside their range either to control certain human diseases, such as malaria, or to provide sport for anglers, have also taken their toll among native species. So much so that at the time of writing the status of around 800 fish species is officially considered by the International Union for the Conservation of Nature (IUCN) as being either Vulnerable, Endangered, or Critically Endangered.

As we have become more aware of the need to save these species, numerous conservation programs have been developed and implemented. Happily, some are enjoying considerable success, with stocks recovering, if not to their former levels, at least to within touching distance of relative safety. Other species, however, face a bleak future and will almost certainly be heading for extinction unless we take urgent steps to arrest their decline. For some it may already be too late; for others there may still be a little time. But we cannot afford to wait because the ticket to extinction is, after all, strictly one way.

The Encyclopedia of Fish

IN THIS ENCYCLOPEDIA you will find 69 detailed articles on individual fish species or related groups of species. The subjects have been selected to cover a broad range of types from all corners of the globe. Here you will find familiar fish, such as the great white shark and barracudas, as well as the less familiar, such as headstanders and molas.

They range from fish that occur only in fresh water or that are exclusively marine to those such as the Atlantic salmon that face the challenges of both environments. The *Encyclopedia* starts with a detailed review of the biology and natural history of fish (What Is a Fish?). Then each article starts with a detailed summary panel (see left) that includes an artwork portrait of the fish in question or a representative of a group and a summary of the basic facts, figures, and biology of each fish or group. There follows the main article, which describes the most interesting aspects of the science and natural history of each fish. Dynamic photographs are used throughout to illustrate the text.

The aim of the *Encyclopedia* is to provide an introduction to a variety of fish and their lifestyles; it is hoped that this will stimulate a greater interest in their fascinating hidden world.

WHAT IS A FISH?

Most of us can recognize a fish when we see one, but actually defining a fish is not so easy because many of the criteria we might use also apply to other creatures. For example, fish are creatures that live in water, but then so do many other animals. Fish have scales, but this feature is also found on reptiles such as lizards and crocodiles, as well as on the legs of birds. Even more unhelpful is the fact that many fish, including, for example, whale catfish (family Cetopsidae), walking catfish (family Clariidae), sea catfish (family Ariidae), and antenna catfish (family Pimelodidae)—to name just a few representative families from the catfish order Siluriformes—are totally devoid of scales.

Gills are another fishlike characteristic, but many other creatures, like frogs, toads, newts, and salamanders, also have gills—at least during the early part of their lives. Even some aquatic insects have gills. Fish move by using fins, but fins are not unique to fish, either. Fins are found in squid and cuttlefish, for example, and these animals are mollusks, a group of invertebrate animals (animals without backbones).

Fish have an internal skeleton made either of cartilage or bone. But squid and cuttlefish also have an internal skeleton. So do starfish and their relatives, the sea urchins, which are also invertebrates. Equally, an internal skeleton is a major feature of all the other groups of vertebrates including amphibians, reptiles, birds, and mammals. It begins to appear that a fish has no defining characteristics that makes it unique. Moreover, if all the above points are carefully analyzed, then the almost inevitable conclusion is that there really is no such thing as a fish!

Unusual though this may sound, it is not so far-fetched. Indeed, there are scientists who believe that lumping together all groups, from the lampreys and hagfish through the sharks and their relatives to the bony fish, and calling them all "fish" is the same as saying that all flying vertebrates such as bats, flying lizards, and birds are all birds simply because they can fly. After all, a lamprey and a goldfish are as different from each other as a bat (a flying mammal) is from a chicken. We could therefore even say that the term "fish" is simply a convenient label for referring to an aquatic vertebrate that is not a frog, a seal, a turtle, or any other creature.

A Pragmatic Approach

Therefore it is impossible to state categorically what a fish is or to define the term in such a way that it plugs all possible loopholes and at the same time provides positive

and useful information. In the end the best we can do is draw up a potentially useful list of distinguishing characteristics, but even this is plagued with numerous exceptions to virtually every rule. Nevertheless, it would be impossible to eliminate the word "fish" from our vocabulary. It would also be unnecessary and undesirable. It does, after all, tell us something about the organisms to which it is intended to apply. However, when we use it, we should appreciate that it is a very wide-ranging word indeed.

In practice, whenever the term "fish" is used, it generally refers to aquatic species that can be split into two large groups: the cartilaginous fish (Chondrichthyes)—including sharks, skates, rays, and chimaeras—and the bony fish Teleostomi (Osteichthyes)—including all other species from guppies to sea horses. In addition, this book also includes the jawless fish (Myxini and Cephalaspidomorphi or Monorhina)—hagfish and lampreys.

⊕ *Not all fish conform to the typical fishlike shape! The bizarre-looking leafy sea dragon (Phycodurus eques) looks more like a mass of seaweed. The unusual shape helps it remain concealed when it floats among marine vegetation.*

Characteristics of Fish

Although there are exceptions, it is possible to list the characteristics that, together, allow us to recognize an animal as a fish. They are listed below.

- A braincase and limb (fin) skeleton consisting of cartilage or bone
- Fins, usually—but not invariably—with spines or rays
- Breathing through outward-directed gills covered by an operculum (gill cover), which results in an external slitlike aperture or a series of gill slits
- Bodies usually, but not always, covered in scales
- A swim bladder used in buoyancy control (there are exceptions, as in sharks)
- A sensory organ known as the lateral line running in a head-to-tail direction or another series of sensory pits (again, as in sharks)
- Cold-blooded (poikilothermic)—in other words, the body temperature matches that of the environment (again, there are some significant exceptions, such as tuna, which can raise their body temperature well above that of the surrounding water)

⊕ *Examples of different types of living fish: river lampreys (Lampetra fluviatilis), class Cephalaspidomorphi, feeding on prey (1); tiger shark (Galeocerdo cuvier), class Chondrichthyes (2); regal angelfish (Pygoplites diacanthus), class Actinopterygii (3).*

1

2

3

Evolution of Fish

It is generally accepted that life began in water some 3 billion years ago. For many millions of years after that there appears to have been no major development leading to the emergence of complex organisms. Indeed, it took around 2.4 billion years before the first animals that could be regarded as invertebrates began to evolve.

From then on the pace accelerated, and it only took the relatively short time of about 120 million years before the first vertebrates evolved. These aquatic creatures, known from fossils dating back around 480 million years or so—in other words, from the middle Ordovician Period—were the first fishlike creatures. Although they were very different from their modern-day equivalents, they nevertheless form the basal stock from which not just fish but all other vertebrates subsequently evolved.

The earliest fish were jawless, a feature still retained by some of today's aquatic vertebrates such as the hagfish

⊕ *The limestone quarries of Solnhofen, Bavaria, Germany, have yielded a huge variety of fish fossils. Among them is the Jurassic fish* Gyrodoras circularis, *shown above, which strongly resembles a modern bony fish.*

and lampreys. However, unlike hagfish and lampreys, many of the early species had bony body plates on their bodies, and many of the later types were not eel-like in appearance. Fish with true jaws (known as acanthodians) did not evolve for another 40–50 million years. Some acanthodians were large fish growing to around 6.5 feet (2 m) in length.

The jaws of these giants suggest that they were active hunters, probably prowling ancient waters much as sharks do today. Indeed, the species are often referred to as spiny sharks. They carried spines in front of each fin and between the pectoral and pelvic fins, and the top lobe of the the tail fin was longer than the lower (a condition known as heterocercal), as in modern-day sharks. Most species, though, were quite small. At first, acanthodians lived in marine conditions, but later fossils are found in freshwater deposits. It is from such acanthodians that modern-day fish have arisen, albeit with numerous extinctions along the way. Among the extinctions are the acanthodians themselves; they disappeared after about 150 million years.

The placoderms—named for their bony plates—emerged about 400 million years ago and survived for about 70 million years. Among the placoderms were a group called the antiarchs. They were unusual-looking fish. Most were only about 1 foot (30 cm) long with bodies that were triangular in cross section. Antiarchs had bony plates on their bodies and eyes. The eyes were very small and located very high on the head. The pectoral fins, or at least what appear to be the equivalent of pectoral fins in modern-day fish, had an external skeleton instead of an internal one and looked more like the leg of a lobster than a fin. Antiarchs were probably slow movers that lived on the bottom.

Another group of placoderms, the arthrodires, were probably fast-swimming predators, with the largest types growing to around 20 feet (6 m) in length. Like the acanthodians, the arthrodires probably behaved as sharks do today.

We know very little about the breeding habits of these fish, but in at least one group of placoderms, the ptycodontids, the eggs may have been fertilized internally. Indications that this may have been so are found in the different shapes of the pelvic fins of males and females, with the males having structures that are similar to the claspers found in living male sharks.

The fossil record is incomplete, of course, so some of our interpretations must be based on partial information. Nevertheless, the evidence is sufficiently wide ranging and representative for some major conclusions to be drawn. One is that some fish families have existed, more or less unchanged, for many millions of years up to the present day. For instance, we can say that bichirs (family Polypteridae) have been around for 135 million years or

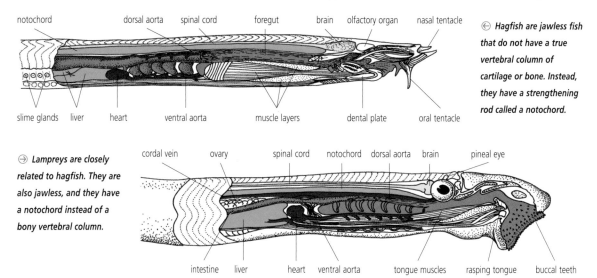

Hagfish are jawless fish that do not have a true vertebral column of cartilage or bone. Instead, they have a strengthening rod called a notochord.

Lampreys are closely related to hagfish. They are also jawless, and they have a notochord instead of a bony vertebral column.

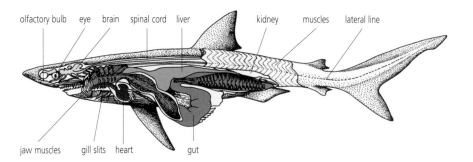

Sharks and rays have a cartilaginous skeleton. All sharks and rays have jaws, but the teeth are not fixed to them. Sharks do not have a swim bladder.

so. Likewise, lungfish (families Ceratodontidae and Lepidosirenidae) have long histories stretching back to Devonian times (400–350 million years ago). Most famous of all the so-called "living fossils" is the coelacanth (*Latimeria chalumnae*). The first genuine remains of the species occur in Devonian rocks, and the last records are in sediments about 70 million years old. It was long assumed, therefore, that the coelacanth had become extinct about that time. But in 1938 a living specimen was caught by fishermen off the Comores in the Indian Ocean. Others have since been caught, and a new species of coelacanth has even been discovered. From examinations of these fascinating fish it appears that the coelacanth has changed little since the time of the last known fossils 70 million years ago.

Fish Biology

The four major groups of fish—the cartilaginous fish, the bony fish, the hagfish, and the lampreys—are very different from each other. Yet they all share at least one thing in common: They all live in water. Therefore they must carry out all their activities—breathing, feeding, breeding, and so on—while submerged. Although the type of water in which fish live varies in its salinity

(saltiness), the biological challenges are similar. However, the responses or solutions to these challenges are met in many different ways.

The Skeleton

Hagfish have no bone cells in their body. Nor do they have a true skull or a vertebral column (backbone). They do, however, have a "trough" in which the brain is cradled. They also have a flexible, rodlike structure (the notochord) that runs all the way along the back. In lampreys the notochord contains a series of paired structures known as arches that are made up of cartilage. Sharks and bony fish not only have braincases and jaws but also a skeleton of cartilage (in sharks) or bone (in bony fish), a backbone divided into individual vertebrae, as well as supports to the fins. Bony fish also have a series of bones that form the gill-cover apparatus.

The Gills

Gills are delicate structures richly supplied with blood vessels that let a fish absorb oxygen from the water and at the same time release waste carbon dioxide from its body. In this way the fish can breathe. All four major groups of fish have gills. However, their arrangement is

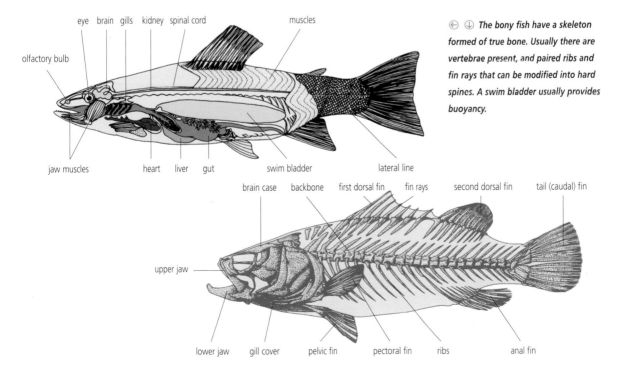

← ↓ *The bony fish have a skeleton formed of true bone. Usually there are vertebrae present, and paired ribs and fin rays that can be modified into hard spines. A swim bladder usually provides buoyancy.*

olfactory bulb

eye brain gills kidney spinal cord muscles

jaw muscles heart liver gut swim bladder lateral line

brain case backbone first dorsal fin fin rays second dorsal fin tail (caudal) fin

upper jaw

lower jaw gill cover pelvic fin pectoral fin ribs anal fin

very different. In hagfish the water enters through the nostrils, instead of the mouth, and passes into muscular pouches that act as gills. The outflows from the pouches join up and leave the body either through a single opening or through up to 16 openings in some species.

In lampreys the incoming water flows through seven ducts, or channels, each one leading to a separate gill opening. The gills are also supported by a cartilaginous structure known as the branchial basket—a feature not found in hagfish.

In sharks and their relatives each gill has its own gill flap connecting with the outside; there are usually five gill flaps, but there are six or seven in the six- and seven-gilled sharks.

In bony fish the gill opens via a single external slit protected by a bony structure known as the gill cover or operculum.

⊕ *Lowland temperate lakes with aquatic vegetation such as water lilies are favored by many freshwater fish species, including carp (Cyprinus carpio), tench (Tinca tinca), and rudd (Scardinius erythrophthalmus).*

The Fins

There are also significant differences in the number and structure of the fins between the groups. The simplest arrangement occurs in hagfish, which only have a caudal (tail) fin. Lampreys have a dorsal (back) fin as well.

Sharks and bony fish have a similar number of fins: one or two dorsal fins, a single caudal (tail) fin, an anal (belly) fin, two pelvic or ventral (hip) fins, and two pectoral (chest) fins. Most bony fish have a single dorsal fin, although some have two dorsal fins. Other species, for example, the salmons, characoids, and some catfish, have a fatty, usually small adipose fin instead of the second dorsal fin. Sharks do not have an adipose fin. Also, in bony fish the bones of the fins—called spines and rays—are visible.

Some Other Features

All four groups of fish have eyes, but in hagfish they are tiny and lack a lens. The shape of the lens in fish eyes is usually spherical—the best shape for focusing under water. In the few species that need to see above and

below the water surface at the same time, like the so-called four-eyed fish (family Anablepidae), the part of the lens responsible for above-water vision is elongated (as in land-living vertebrates), while the parts used for underwater vision are rounded.

Blood is pumped around the fish's body by the action of the heart, as in other vertebrates. However, hagfish have several hearts instead of a single one.

A series of ear canals, known as the semicircular canals, enable fish to hear and maintain their balance. In sharks and bony fish there are three semicircular canals, just as there are in terrestrial vertebrates. In lampreys there are two, and in hagfish there is only one.

Hagfish and lampreys are totally scaleless. Sharks are covered in modified scales usually referred to as dermal denticles, or skin teeth. Dermal denticles give the skin of sharks a rough, sandpaper feel. True scales are typical of the vast majority of bony fish, although quite a few have lost their scales and have evolved scaleless or naked bodies.

Bony fish adjust their position in the water using a saclike structure known as the swim bladder, gas bladder, or air bladder. Gas can be injected into or extracted from the swim bladder, and this in turn controls the buoyancy of the fish. Some bony fish, including some bottom-dwelling species, have lost their swim bladders during the course of evolution. Sharks, lampreys, and hagfish do not have swim bladders.

Sensing the world outside the body is vital in order to survive. One of the most important sensory structures in bony fish is the lateral line organ, responsible for detecting vibrations in the water. It can be seen on the outside of the body or head as a series of pores. Neither hagfish nor lampreys have a lateral line organ, however. In addition to the lateral line organ sharks also have other sensory structures, most notably the ampullae of Lorenzini—an organ that is extremely sensitive to tiny electrical changes. It is often used to detect the presence of other creatures hidden in the sand.

Fish Habitats and Behavior

The vast majority of the water found on Earth is in the oceans and seas. They account for more than 70 percent of the planet's total surface area. By comparison, the amount in freshwater habitats is tiny—about 30,000 cubic miles (125,000 cubic km) spread out over about 1 percent of the Earth's surface. Four-fifths of this volume

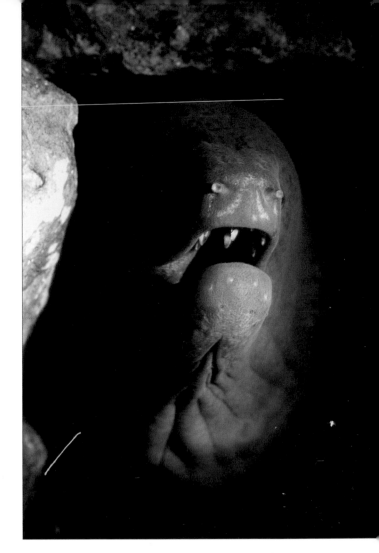

ⓐ *Moray eels are voracious predators that have adopted a skulking lifestyle. They usually hide away in caves, among coral, or in wrecks until an unsuspecting victim comes near, when it is swiftly grabbed.*

is contained in about 40 lakes, such as the Great Lakes of the North American landmass and the rift lakes of Africa. The remaining one-fifth is contained in river systems such as the Nile, Amazon, Yangtze, Mississippi, Colorado, Danube, St. Lawrence, and the thousands of tributaries that feed them.

Fish are adaptable creatures that are found virtually everywhere there is water. The habitats they occupy include the arctic wastes, fast-flowing mountain streams, slow-flowing rivers, tiny mud pools no larger than an elephant's footprint, crystal-clear warm-water reef zones, the open sea, the dark, cold abysses of the world's oceans where no light ever reaches, and the water that flows through some cave systems.

Unusual Lifestyles

Within a particular type of habitat there may be a variety of different fish species, all living their own unique lifestyles, many of which are as unusual as they are fascinating. Some of the pearlfish (family Carapidae), for example, live much of their lives inside the body cavity of sea cucumbers. The bitterlings (family Cyprinidae) live in steams, rivers, and ditches, but their eggs are laid inside the breathing tubes of freshwater mussels. The mudskippers (family Gobiidae) spend several hours each day out of water, feeding and displaying on mudflats. The freshwater hatchetfish (family Gasteropelecidae) and the marine flying fish (family Exocoetidae) live their lives in the surface layers of the water and can actually leave it altogether, flying or gliding through the air for some distance to avoid predators.

Other species move between one type of habitat and another at certain times of their lives. The most famous of these are the salmon and trout (family Salmonidae), some of which migrate long distances from the sea back to the rivers where they were born to breed and (in some species) die. The freshwater eels (family Anguillidae) also migrate to spawn. Most notably, the European eel (*Anguilla anguilla*) undertakes a 4,000-mile (6,440-km) spawning migration from its home rivers to the Sargasso Sea in the western Atlantic Ocean between Bermuda and the West Indies. The American eel (*A. rostrata*) also breeds in the Sargasso Sea, but its migrations take place over a much shorter distance.

The water temperature in polar regions can frequently approach freezing point. Yet some fish not only tolerate such cold conditions but actually live in them most of their lives and even breed there. A range of strategies help fish survive in such cold waters. The blackfin icefish (*Chaenocephalus aceratus*), for example, has its own internal antifreeze system that prevents it from freezing solid.

At the other end of the spectrum some toothcarps or desert pupfish (family Cyprinodontidae) can tolerate water temperatures as high as 104° F (40° C). So, too, can some cichlids (family Cichlidae) and the spangled perch (*Leiopotherapon unicolor*) from Australia, which live in hot springs of a similar temperature. The spangled perch is particularly adaptable, reportedly being able to withstand water temperatures ranging from 41° F (5° C) to 111° F (44° C) and salinities ranging from pure fresh water to pure sea water.

Eat or Be Eaten

Living in such diverse habitats, fish have a vast selection of aquatic food items at their disposal, including other fish. If we were to make a list of foods taken by fish, many would be unsurprising, with aquatic creatures and plants making up the bulk of the menu. However, there are also some surprises on the list.

Flying insects, for instance, are caught by many species of fish. Usually the insects have either landed on the water surface by mistake or have fallen in. Either way, most fish that feed on aerial insects simply pluck them from the water surface. The archerfish (family Toxotidae), however, actually shoot down insects by spitting powerful jets of water at them.

Sharks have achieved notoriety for their attacks on humans. Yet their diet does not normally include us but fish and sea mammals like seals. Perhaps surprisingly, though, the two largest species, the whale shark (*Rhincodon typus*) and basking shark (*Cetorhinus maximus*), are filter feeders that sift small organisms such as shrimplike krill from the water.

Fish are such versatile feeders that some even ingest feces. The best known of these is the scat (*Scatophagus argus*), but many others also indulge in this habit. It is common, for instance, for African barbs (*Barbus* species) to follow hippopotamuses under water, swarming around their anus and feeding on their feces the moment they are produced. Some cichlids also feed on unusual food items: They suck out the eyes of their prey.

Remarkably, some fish do not feed at all—at least, not in the normal sense of the word. The males of some anglerfish (order Lophiiformes) bite into the female, usually on her belly, during the early stages of their lives and never let go after that, in effect becoming parasites. The males derive their nourishment from the dissolved nutrients carried in the female's blood.

Female anglerfish, as well as nonparasitic males, have special appendages on their heads that form fishing rods complete with "bait." Frogmouth catfish (*Chaca* species) also use a lure to catch prey. Some deep-sea fish go a stage further and attract prey using lights. These superefficient hunters have fearsome teeth and hugely elastic stomachs that can accommodate prey of almost any size. Other fish pretend to be something else, such as a leaf or a piece of seaweed, thus enabling them to float undetected toward their chosen prey. Perhaps the best of these camouflage artists are the sea dragons, close

relatives of the sea horses (family Syngnathidae). Their camouflage also helps hide sea dragons from predators.

Breeding Flexibility

Just as fish use many ways to obtain a meal, they also adopt many different ways for breeding. However, there are two main categories: egg laying, in which eggs are released into the water where they are fertilized, and livebearing, in which the eggs are fertilized inside the body of the female, which subsequently gives birth to fully formed young. Within these two broad categories there are numerous variations, including one in which the eggs are fertilized internally and are released after a period of time. Livebearing has arisen in several unrelated groups of fish. For example, it occurs in members of the families Poeciliidae and Goodeidae—small freshwater species—and also in some species of sharks and rays.

Egg-laying methods can vary even in related groups of fish. The splashing tetra (*Copella arnoldi*) lays its eggs on a leaf above water level; the male then splashes them with water until they hatch. Others, like the grunion (*Leuresthes tenuis*), lay their eggs on a beach.

Many egg-laying species scatter their eggs in open water and abandon them, while others build nests and guard the eggs. Some gouramis, for example, the dwarf gourami (*Colisa lalia*) build bubble nests; others like the sticklebacks (*Gasterosteus* and *Pungitius* species) glue

their nest together with secretions from their kidneys. Cichlids lay eggs on stones, leaves, or in caves, and some take protection further by brooding the eggs inside the mouth. This technique is also adopted by the totally unrelated bonytongues (family Osteoglossidae). Annual killifish (family Aplocheilidae) lay their eggs in mud during the rainy season. There they remain when the pools dry up; but when the rains return, the eggs hatch out—often in a matter of hours.

Sex changes are fairly common in fish. Many, like the anemonefish (family Pomacentridae), can change from male to female. Others, like the wrasses (family Labridae), can change from female to male. In some of the groupers (family Serranidae) individuals can be both male and female at the same time. Animals that have both male and female sex organs are called hermaphrodites.

Fish and Man

The relationship between fish and humans has a history stretching back many thousands of years. Cave paintings and fish bones found around prehistoric human settlements testify to it. Sometimes the human

⊕ The dwarf gourami (Colisa lalia) is a bubble-nest builder. The method, which is also adopted by several other species, involves blowing bubbles to form a nest that floats at the surface and into which eggs are then laid.

exploitation of fish and their habitats has been carried out without it adversely affecting overall fish stocks or their environment. However, in many cases the relationship is an overwhelmingly one-sided affair in terms of benefits, with the losers invariably being the fish.

History is littered with incidents of spectacular losses of fish stocks due to overfishing, the dramatic collapse of the herring fishery being one. Some of the most notorious examples of overexploitation, as well as the most unusual, are featured here. Among them are the taking of sharks for their fins, an essential ingredient in the world-famous shark fin soup so highly regarded in the Orient. Another is the devastation of totoaba (*Totoaba macdonaldi*) stocks for their swim bladders—another soup delicacy—but there are many others.

Threatened Species

The totoaba was so persecuted that its numbers dropped to the level where it was close to extinction. Even today, many years after the industry peaked and after vigorous conservation efforts, numbers are so low that it is still classified as Critically Endangered. The totoaba is one of 750 species of fish officially reported by the World Conservation Union (IUCN) as being under threat in the wild. The three highest categories of threat are: Critically Endangered, Endangered, and Vulnerable. About 3 percent of all the species that have been evaluated by the World Conservation Union (just under 50 percent of all known species of fish) fall into one of these categories, giving us serious cause for concern. The table below shows how the numbers have changed between 1996 and 2003, the last available figures at the time of writing.

	1996	2000	2002	2003
Critically Endangered	157	156	157	162
Endangered	134	144	143	144
Vulnerable	443	452	442	444
TOTAL	734	752	742	750

While the number of Endangered species has leveled out between 2000 and 2003, and while the number of Vulnerable species has actually declined during this period, this does not mean that there is any reason to feel overoptimistic. The increase in Critically Endangered species forcefully shows that we need to be as concerned as ever, even more so. The situation is serious and will become even worse if we are unable to reverse the trend.

The Human Factor

Our relationship with fish and other wild animals is not always negative, of course. Indeed, some species, like the blackbird, house sparrow, brown rat, and cockroach, would be less abundant than they are today were it not for their close association with humans (although it appears that numbers of garden birds may now be suffering in some countries as a result of predation by domestic cats). Generally speaking, however, wild plant and animal species tend to be placed under a higher level of threat through their association with humans.

The threats faced by fish include reducing stocks to critically low levels by simply catching too many individuals, habitat destruction caused by projects such as land reclamation, pollution, and interference with the natural ecological balance through the introduction of nonnative species. In the case of migratory species like salmon, sturgeon, and others, changes include dams, reservoirs, river channelization (the diversion of river courses into manmade channels), and other habitat modifications that can present insurmountable hurdles as the fish attempt to reach traditional spawning grounds upriver. In the worst cases local populations, or even species, can be driven to extinction as a direct result.

Often it is not changes in the quality of the water or the migratory routes that pose the greatest risks but the restricted distribution of the species concerned. When the restriction is extreme, as in the case of the Devil's Hole pupfish (*Cyprinodon diabolis*) or the Bandula barb (*Barbus bandula*), the threat is so serious that stringent steps need to be taken to ensure the survival of the species.

Ironically, one of the biggest threats that some fish have to face is posed by other fish. There are countless instances of fish being introduced—intentionally or otherwise—into habitats outside their own natural range. This may be done to cater to a demand for sport angling species, as in the case of trout, or as a means of providing a new source of animal protein for local communities, as in the case of the Nile perch (*Lates niloticus*) introduced into Lake Victoria, one of the African rift lakes, or even to combat disease, as in the case of the mosquito fish (*Gambusia affinis* and *G. holbrooki*) that have been widely introduced for biological control of malarial mosquitoes in many countries.

Sometimes the introduced species, while achieving the original aims, also places native species under threat. This can be through direct predation on native species

⬆ ➡ Two contrasting examples of fishing. Above: a Filipino fisherman with his catch of a devil ray (Mobula japanica), probably destined for the local market. Right: Farmed salmon (Salmo salar) reared in carefully controlled conditions in a Scottish loch—a mass-production technique increasingly adopted for other fish species.

and their eggs, competition for space, competition for food or spawning sites, or quite simply, through having a higher reproductive rate than native species.

Overfishing is also undoubtedly a major factor affecting the future of many species. Some species are placed under such survival pressures that only drastic action, including total or partial bans, can hope to save them from extinction. Species as diverse as tunas (family Scombridae), cods (family Gadidae), and some sharks all fall into this category, but there are many, many more.

Although detailed assessment of the threats being faced by every freshwater and marine species of fish is clearly outside the scope of any commission, the data and information that have been gathered in the compilation of the Red List by the World Conservation Union allow us to make certain overall statements. Consequently, we can conclude, for instance, that an extremely serious deterioration of fish stocks, especially of river-dwelling species, has occurred.

Fish can do nothing to save themselves, but we can. It is therefore our moral responsibility to act in a manner that does not place the survival of other species at risk.

We have failed many times over the years, but we have also enjoyed success, and some species that were heading for extinction are now slowly recovering as a result of conservation measures. Among them are the establishment of areas where the fish are protected and carefully monitored, fishing quotas are controlled, captive breeding and restocking programs are undertaken, the quality of habitats is improved, international laws are enforced, and so on. But we still need to do more.

Hagfish (*Myxine* species)

Common name Hagfish and lampreys

Subphylum Vertebrata (Craniata)

Superclass Agnatha

Classes Myxini (comprising hagfish: order Myxiniformes, family Myxinidae); Cephalaspidomorphi (comprising lampreys: order Petromyzontiformes, family Petromyzontidae)

Size Up to 46 in (1.2 m) in hagfish; up to 36 in (90 cm) in lampreys

Number of species Hagfish: about 50 in 6 genera; lampreys: about 40 in 7 genera

Key features Lampreys: eel-like with 1 or 2 dorsal fins and simple caudal fin; no biting jaws; mouth a disk with horny teeth; 7 gill openings; ammocete larval stage very different from adult; hagfish: eel-like, white to pale brown, with fleshy median fin and 4–6 tentacles around mouth; no biting jaws

Breeding Lampreys: spawn in rivers and streams, freshwater species moving upstream and marine species entering from sea; some with complex life cycles; hagfish: lay a few large eggs at sea

Diet Lampreys: as larvae, particles filtered from water; parasitic adults attach to host fish and feed on blood and tissues; nonparasitic adults do not feed; hagfish: dead or dying fish and sea mammals on seafloor

Habitat Lampreys: seas and rivers; hagfish: seabed

Distribution Lampreys: temperate marine and freshwater; hagfish: mostly temperate oceans and seas (excluding midocean zones) but also cooler, deeper tropical waters

Status Not threatened

↑ *A 24-inch (61-cm) hagfish (Myxine species), showing its elongated, eel-like form, simple fin, and mouth tentacles.*

Hagfish and Lampreys

Myxinidae,
Petromyzontidae

At first sight hagfish and lampreys look like eels. Yet despite this similarity, the relationship between them and their lookalikes is more distant than the relationship between sharks and goldfish.

HAGFISH AND LAMPREYS ARE KNOWN as jawless fish because they lack true jaws (although hagfish do have a biting mechanism). They do not have backbones of cartilage or bone, retaining the pliable notochord instead, and they have no paired fins or limb skeletons, although hagfish have some cartilage rays in the tail fin.

The structures known as semicircular canals located inside their "ears"—which help them maintain their balance—are also unlike those of true fish, birds, amphibians, reptiles, and mammals. Hagfish and lampreys have one or two semicircular canals instead of the three found in other vertebrates. Their gills, too, are different in that they are "back to front," with the gill filaments pointing inward instead of outward as they do in the jawed fish. In addition, their external gill openings consist of pores rather than slits.

Despite the fact that they share many of these features—including a long fossil history that probably extends over 500 million years in the case of hagfish and about 280 million years in lampreys—it would be

⊕ *The jawless mouth and central nostril of a hagfish are surrounded by sensory tentacles, but the animal has no true eyes. The gill openings are simple rows of pores on each flank.*

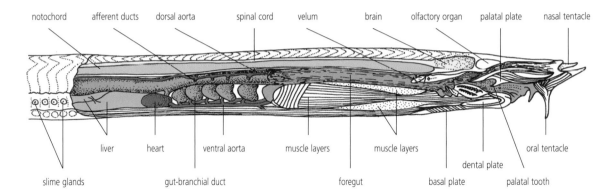

notochord   afferent ducts   dorsal aorta   spinal cord   velum   brain   olfactory organ   palatal plate   nasal tentacle

liver   heart   ventral aorta   muscle layers   muscle layers   oral tentacle

dental plate

slime glands   gut-branchial duct   foregut   basal plate   palatal tooth

wrong to assume that these two primitive fish are intimately related. Most scientists now regard them as quite distinct jawless fish (agnathans) with separate evolutionary histories and classify them in different classes and orders.

Scavenging Hagfish

Hagfish are strictly marine creatures that live and breed in the sea. They are widely distributed, mainly in temperate regions of the world, but not in the midocean zones. They also occur in some parts of the tropics, where they are confined to deeper, cooler waters.

Despite their eel-like appearance hagfish have numerous noneel (and nonfish) characteristics that have served them well over many millions of years. For example, they have four main hearts and two pairs of smaller

⊤ A hagfish has no backbone, and its body is supported by a flexible notochord. In many ways its anatomy is very primitive, but some features, such as the slime glands, are highly developed.

*⊥ Hagfish spend much of their lives doing very little because their low metabolic rate allows them to survive for a long time without eating. This hagfish (*Eptatritus stouti*) is coiled on the seabed off Monterey, California.*

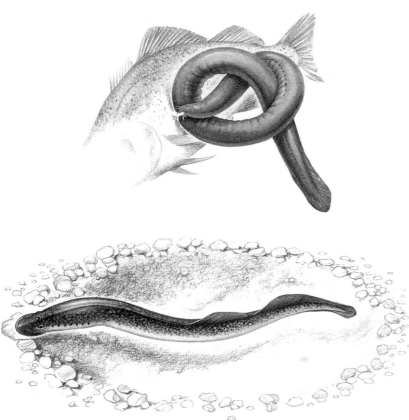

they remain around their meal until it is completely consumed. In the case of a large animal like a dead whale this can take many months and involve thousands and thousands of hagfish. They also feed on dying (rather than dead) creatures, behaving almost as if they were parasites, and they eat small live animals such as marine worms.

Slimy Loops

One of the most remarkable abilities of hagfish is the way they can tie themselves in knots. When a hagfish finds a victim, it rasps a hole in the flank using its special mouth plates and toothed tonguelike structure known as a piston, and literally forces itself into the body cavity. To achieve this, it needs to gain some form of leverage, so once it has grasped the prey with its specially adapted biting tongue teeth, the hagfish loops its smooth, eel-like, slimy body into a knot and slides it forward until it presses against the victim's body. This allows it to either open up the body or tear out a chunk of flesh.

The hagfish can also use its knotting skill as an escape mechanism, particularly when it is

⬆ *A hagfish eating a dead fish by knotting its body for leverage and pushing its way into the carcass to feed from the inside (top). A sea lamprey (Petromyzon marinus) building a nest depression (above).*

hearts. They are not, however, supplied with nerve endings as in higher animals; neither do they have the radial heart muscles that other vertebrates have. Further, the oxygenated water that they take in does not get to the gills via the mouth but through an opening (the nasopharyngeal duct) at the tip of the head. They lack a stomach, and there is no real braincase, the brain being surrounded by a form of sheath. They also have tiny, degenerate eyes without lenses.

All hagfish are scavengers, with a highly developed ability to find food. Vast numbers of hagfish can home in on a dead fish or sea mammal lying on the seafloor. When they do,

combined with huge quantities of slime that can be exuded from its body. By presenting a would-be predator with an extremely slimy knot, the hagfish is quite likely to deter it from pressing home its attack. This ability to produce body knots is also exhibited by some of the moray eels (family Muraenidae).

A hagfish can also rid itself of excessive slime by tying itself in a knot and sliding the knot from one end of its body to the other. The technique is very efficient, yet it does not clear the animal's single nostril of slime. To do this, a hagfish will "sneeze" and force the mucus out with a jet of water.

Hagfish High Fashion

There are countless people around the world who own wallets, briefcases, boots, and even golf bags made from hagfish skin. However, there is not much glamor attached to such a label, so the material is marketed as eel skin or conger eel skin.

The hagfish skin trade arose in the late 1970s in South Korea, where a method of tanning the skin was developed. In a

remarkably short period the technique spawned an industry, with substantial fleets operating off the coasts of Korea and nearby countries. At one time as many as 1,000 boats were in full operation, with catches of around 5 tons per boat per day. Not surprisingly, the hagfish population could not withstand the onslaught, with the inevitable result that catches plummeted in the late 1980s.

Demand for "eel skin" products remained high, though, so the hagfish fleets turned their attentions elsewhere. They targeted the waters off the western U.S. and the eastern coasts of Canada, where hagfish were totally unexploited. Catches, as expected, began to climb once more. Off California, for example, 2,200 U.S. tons (2,000 metric tonnes) of hagfish were caught in 1989 alone.

Exactly what effect continued large-scale fishing—which includes some 2,400 U.S. tons (2,234 metric tonnes) per year destined for human consumption—will have on hagfish populations is unknown. However, it is becoming clear that attention will need to be focused on these rather unappealing creatures if their survival is to be ensured.

Feeding and Fasting Lampreys

Lampreys fall into two groups: parasitic forms and nonparasitic forms. During their larval phase both types spend most of their time buried in soft sediments in freshwater habitats such as streams and rivers, feeding on tiny organisms, debris, and algae that they filter from the water. This phase lasts at least three years. Throughout this period growth is relatively slow; but eventually, when the larva is 3 to 6.5 inches (7.5–16 cm) long—depending on species and conditions—metamorphosis from larva to adult begins.

Slowly the whole structure of the animal becomes transformed into the adult form, with large, functional eyes and a well-developed mouth—although as with hagfish, a lamprey has no true jaws. The changes take between three to six months; and once they are completed, the newly metamorphosed adults either migrate

⊕ *All lampreys are equipped with toothed, suckerlike mouth disks. Parasitic lampreys like these sea lampreys (Petromyzon marinus) use their disks to cling to fish and rasp holes in their skin and flesh.*

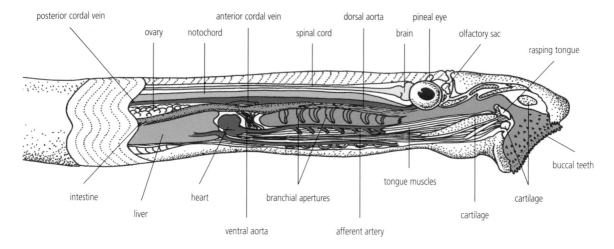

posterior cordal vein · ovary · notochord · anterior cordal vein · spinal cord · dorsal aorta · brain · pineal eye · olfactory sac · rasping tongue · buccal teeth · intestine · liver · heart · branchial apertures · ventral aorta · afferent artery · tongue muscles · cartilage · cartilage

⬆ The anatomy of a lamprey is more "advanced" than that of a hagfish, with tough cartilage in the head and gill regions. Lampreys also have efficient eyes.

out to sea, in the case of marine species, or—in the case of nonmarine species—embark on a free-swimming freshwater existence.

Parasitic lampreys then spend up to two years feeding, growing rapidly, and attaining full maturity. These lampreys attach themselves to their chosen hosts by means of their suckerlike oral disks, rasp open a wound, and either suck the blood or feed on the muscle tissue of their unfortunate victims.

In the course of evolution some species have lost their parasitic feeding habits, and during the adult stages of their lives they do not eat at all. These nonparasitic forms, known as brook or dwarf lampreys, go without food of any kind from the moment they attain maturity until they spawn and die. Not surprisingly, this phase of their life is much shorter than the equivalent phase in parasitic species.

The evolution of nonparasitic lampreys from parasitic forms is well documented. About half the known nonparasitic species can be matched or paired up with equivalent, larger parasitic forms from which they are believed to have evolved. While differences are evident in the adults of each ancestor/descendant coupling—brook lampreys being smaller, with blunter teeth—their larvae are virtually indistinguishable.

As full maturity is attained, further changes take place. Parasitic types stop feeding at this stage, and sea-living species migrate to fresh water. As the process gathers momentum, a whole series of changes begins to indicate (as in salmon) that death is not far away. As the gut shrinks, the teeth begin to degenerate, the fat reserves are used up, and the genital papillae develop. Meanwhile, the spawning urge pushes the adults toward their breeding grounds and to their inevitable death.

Spawning Migrations

Unlike hagfish, which spawn in the sea and lay only a few relatively large eggs, lampreys spawn

Lamprey Invasion

Although lampreys may be eaten and are regarded as a genuine delicacy by some, there is no largescale commercial fishery. Lampreys do, however, have a significant commercial impact because of the devastation that parasitic species can cause in fish farms, or among wild fish stocks exploited for human consumption.

One of the most dramatic and damaging examples of this occurred in the years following the opening of the Welland Canal linking Lake Erie to Lake Ontario in 1828. It resulted in a massive invasion of parasitic lampreys into Lake Erie and, over subsequent decades, from there to the other Great Lakes. As they spread, the lampreys caused enormous damage, particularly to the trout fishery. Expensive control measures and restocking programs failed to solve the problem, and have cost both the commercial and recreational fishing industries vast sums of money in the process.

in fresh water and can lay anything from a thousand (brook or nonparasitic species) to several hundred thousand eggs (parasitic species). The need to spawn in fresh water means that marine species must migrate, sometimes over distances exceeding 600 miles (1,000 km) from the sea in order to breed. It is not known, however, if migrating lampreys return to their river of birth, as salmon do. Whatever the case, marine species have to spend some time in estuaries adapting to freshwater conditions before making the final push upstream to their gravel spawning grounds. Freshwater species may also have to migrate, but over much shorter distances.

In nonparasitic species spawning may occur in groups over a single communal nest that consists of a depression created on the bottom by excited spawners thrashing around. The lampreys may also remove individual stones or pebbles to the edges of the spawning site.

Parasitic species, on the other hand, tend to spawn in pairs. The female attaches herself to a large pebble close to the rim of the nest, and the male then attaches himself to his mate. The pair then release their eggs and sperm amid much thrashing around, which results in most of the eggs being buried in the gravel, where they lie until they hatch some two weeks later. Once spawning has been completed, all adult lampreys die.

Amazing Ammocetes

Upon hatching, the larvae—known as ammocetes—drift downstream until they reach a stretch of river with slow-flowing water and a fine-grained bottom. There they burrow into the silt or mud and begin feeding. The ammocetes look quite different from the adults of their species. Their eyes, for example, are underdeveloped and are covered by skin. The mouth, too, does not bear any adult features. Instead, there is an oral hood leading to the mouth opening itself, and the hood is surrounded by fine tentacles known as cirri. A water current is drawn into the mouth through the combined activity of the pharyngeal, or gill,

pouches and the action of a valvelike structure known as the velum. Mucous secretions then trap food particles, and the beating action of cilia (tiny hairlike structures) moves them down into the body for digestion.

During this phase of their life cycle larval lampreys feed in much the same way as lancelets (Cephalochordata), although the mechanism used to channel water through the pharynx differs. Even so, their filter-feeding, burrow-dwelling characteristics, allied to having an endostyle (a long mucus-secreting groove found in the pharynx), may indicate that there is an ancestral relationship between lampreys and both the lancelets and the sea squirts and their relatives.

Hagfish and Lampreys Compared

Most significant among the many differences that exist between hagfish and lampreys are the following:

Hagfish	Lampreys
Tiny eyes	Well-developed eyes
Several hearts	Single heart
Mouth barbels (whiskers)	No mouth barbels
No dorsal fin	2 dorsal fins
Produce large amounts of slime	Do not produce large amounts of slime
1 semicircular canal in ear	2 semicircular canals
Have teeth on the tongue but not around the mouth	Have teeth both on the tongue and around the mouth (oral disk)
Single nostril at tip of snout, leading into pharynx	Single nostril opening located between the eyes and ending in a blind sac
Juveniles are hermaphrodite but lose one reproductive organ and become single sex	Juveniles are either male or female at any one time but not both
Adults believed not to die after spawning	Adults die after spawning
Newly hatched young are similar to adults	Newly hatched ammocoete larvae look quite different from the adults
Able to tie body into a knot	Not able to tie its body into a knot
Able to "sneeze" to clear slime from nostril	Not able to "sneeze"
5–14 pairs of gill openings	7 pairs of gill openings

Elephant Fish *Callorhynchus milii*

The elephant fish is so named for the distinctive padlike protuberance around its mouth, giving it an elephantlike appearance. In fact, all three species of plow-nose chimaera have this appearance.

Common name Elephant fish (southern beauty, ghost shark)

Scientific name *Callorhynchus milii*

Family Callorhynchidae

Order Chimaeriformes

Size 4 ft (1.2 m)

Key features Two tall triangular dorsal fins present along the back, with a sharp, venomous spine in front of the first dorsal fin; upper lobe of caudal fin is triangular and rather sharklike; very evident protuberance in front of mouth; basic coloration silvery with variable brown markings over body; lives in deep water, coming closer inshore when breeding

Breeding Egg laying; breeds seasonally

Diet Invertebrates, mainly different types of shellfish

Habitat Continental shelf

Distribution Southern Pacific Ocean around New Zealand, breeding mainly along eastern coast of South Island; sometimes caught off North Island; also encountered off coast of Australia, becoming more common moving south from New South Wales down to Tasmania and South Australia

Status Highly vulnerable because of overfishing

THE PROTUBERANCE IS SHAPED SO THAT it folds back both in front of and below the mouth, resembling a plowshare in appearance, which explains why the three members of this genus are collectively known as plow-nose chimaeras.

This distinctive feature has a relatively broad surface area and is equipped with ampullae of Lorenzini, which are electroreceptors. The padlike protuberance acts rather like a scanning device, capable of registering the presence of prey buried in the seabed out of sight. The fish can then use their snouts to dig out their prey. The upper jaw is fused to the head as in other chimaeras, and they rely on bony plates in their jaws to grind up the invertebrates that form the basis of their diet. Unlike batoids but like sharks, chimaeras also have tongues in their mouths.

All *Callorhynchus* species are found in the Southern Hemisphere, with their range extending from the western side of southern Africa eastward across the southern Pacific to the Chilean coast of South America. They have no spiracles on their heads for respiratory purposes, in contrast to rays. Instead, they take in water through their nostrils—and not through their mouths (as in most fish)—which then passes over the gills. The best-known member of the group is the elephant fish (*C. milii*), so-called because of the appendage attaching off its upper jaw, which can also be likened to a trunk. Its ugly appearance explains why (rather ironically) it is also known as the southern beauty, particularly in the Australian parts of its range. Confusingly, one of the other species, *C. callorhynchus*, is also sometimes called an elephant fish. The third species is *C. capensis*, the Cape elephant fish.

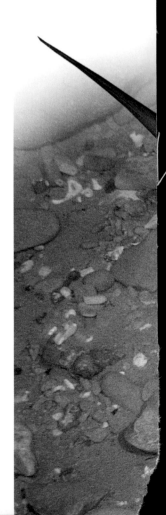

In Deep Waters

Elephant fish live in relatively deep water down to 660 feet (200 m), but in the southern spring they move into shallower areas and at this stage are not found below 130 feet (40 m), where they will spawn. Females lay relatively large eggs, each measuring about 4 inches (10 cm) wide and 10 inches (25 cm) long. They are yellowish-brown in color, which helps conceal their presence on the sandy seabed where they are deposited.

The young develop slowly in their egg cases; they start to hatch from May onward after an interval of between six and eight months. They measure about 4 inches (10 cm) in length at this stage and subsequently develop slowly, often not breeding for the first time until they are five years old. The egg cases themselves, resembling seaweed thanks to the hairs on their surface, are often washed up in quite large numbers in areas close to the spawning grounds, such as Sumner Beach near Canterbury in New Zealand.

Commercial Fishing Pressures

A study carried out between the 1960s and 1980s showed that the reproductive habits of elephant fish were changing in some parts of their range where populations were subjected to the pressures of commercial fishing, such as the Pegasus Bay region off the coast of New Zealand. The growth rates of the young elephant fish increased significantly during this period, by more than 50 percent in some cases, which had the effect of enabling them to mature up to two years earlier. This biological response is a typical reaction that has been documented in other fish—even mammals such as whales when they are heavily hunted, causing their population to plummet. This is a warning that the species is being overexploited and is at risk of becoming endangered.

At present about 1,000 tons (907 tonnes) of elephant fish are landed annually from around New Zealand, and regular catches are also made in Australian waters. It is clear that further studies will be essential to conserve these ancient and distinctive fish. The situation is made more critical because the major fishing period in New Zealand waters coincides with the stage when reproductively mature members of the species are congregating to breed, thus having a potentially serious effect on subsequent generations as well.

⊕ *This female elephant fish, also called the southern beauty or ghost shark, displays the usual coloration of dark marks on a silvery body. It is shown depositing its egg cases on the seabed.*

Tasseled Wobbegong

Eucrossorhinus dasypogon

Wobbegongs are masters of disguise. Lying motionless on the bottom, they can look more like a mass of sponges, encrustations, and seaweeds than sharks.

WITH ITS FLATTENED BODY AND HEAD, irregularly patterned body coloring, masses of elaborate skin flaps or barbels around the mouth, and habit of resting motionless on the bottom for most of the day, it is easy to miss a tasseled wobbegong even from a distance of a few feet.

Unsharklike Sharks

The tasseled wobbegong and its five relatives are true sharks despite their unsharklike appearance. However, they differ from many other sharks in that they do not need to swim incessantly in order to pass oxygenated water over the gills. Like other sharks that spend part of the day on the bottom, such as the zebra shark (*Stegostoma fasciatum*), nurse sharks (family Ginglymostomatidae), angel sharks (family Squatinidae), and the whitetip reef shark (*Triaenodon obesus*), the tasseled wobbegong can pump water through its gill cavity, eliminating the need to be always on the move.

Potentially Dangerous Carpets

Wobbegongs are generally considered to be nonaggressive toward humans. That is not always the case, though, and wobbegong attacks on humans are known to occur. In fact, the tasseled wobbegong is regarded as a "man killer" in Papua New Guinea. However, there are no documented accounts to back this up.

Elsewhere, wobbegongs have definitely attacked humans from time to time. Mostly this comes about when divers do not see the shark because of its excellent camouflage and accidentally step on or disturb a resting fish.

Other attacks have occurred as a direct result of provocation—for example, by waving a

Common name Tasseled wobbegong

Scientific name *Eucrossorhinus dasypogon*

Family Orectolobidae

Order Orectolobiformes

Size Maximum size usually around 4 ft (1.2 m); occasionally reported up to 12 ft (3.7 m)

Key features Flattened body and large, flattened head; numerous ornate skin flaps around the mouth; large mouth located at front of head—not underslung as in most other sharks; body covered in irregular mottled patterns that provide excellent camouflage; fanglike teeth; 2 dorsal fins, approximately equal in size; large pectoral and pelvic fins

Breeding Mating season and duration of pregnancy unknown; number of offspring unknown; embryos obtain nourishment from their yolk sacs during development; may be around 8 in (20 cm) long at birth

Diet Feeds close to the bottom on fish and invertebrates

Habitat Shallow, inland waters down to around 130 ft (40 m)

Distribution Western Pacific Ocean, Northern Australia (from Queensland to Western Australia), Indonesia, Papua New Guinea, and Irian Jaya

Status Listed by IUCN as Near Threatened due to coral-reef habitat destruction

⊕ Their perfect camouflage allows wobbegongs to lie motionless in wait for prey during daylight hours, gulping in any suitably sized unsuspecting victim that swims within range. When darkness falls, they become much more mobile and actively hunt prey, including large crustaceans like crabs and lobsters, or softer-bodied food like squid, octopuses, and fish (including other sharks).

hand in the proximity of a wobbegong's mouth or by pulling its tail. In the first instance the fish may bite not necessarily as an attack but probably more in the form of an instinctive lunge at potential prey. In the second instance it probably does so in self-defense.

In addition to bites based on mistaken identity or reflex action, apparently unprovoked attacks are also occasionally recorded. None has been life-threatening, but some have resulted in nasty injuries due not just to the power of the bite but also the large fanglike teeth that wobbegongs possess.

The Other Wobbegongs

There are six described species of wobbegong distributed over three genera. In addition, there are several undescribed "species." The tasseled wobbegong (*Eucrossorhinus dasypogon*) is the sole representative of its genus.

The genus *Sutorectus* is also monotypic; its sole species is the cobbler wobbegong or cobbler carpet shark (*S. tentaculatus*). Despite being common in Australian waters, this shark is little known. It is presumed to be a livebearer like other wobbegongs. The cobbler wobbegong may attain 6.6–9.8 feet (2–3 m) in length.

Orectolobus contains four known species: the Japanese wobbegong (*O. japonicus*), which grows to over 3.3 feet (1 m) in length; the spotted wobbegong (*O. maculatus*), which can attain around 10.5 feet (3.2 m); the ornate or banded wobbegong (*O. ornatus*), which is slightly smaller; and the northern wobbegong (*O. wardi*), which exceeds 18 inches (46 cm). Both the spotted wobbegong and the ornate wobbegong are known to have attacked humans. Recorded litter sizes for the genus range from at least 12 pups in *O. ornatus* to 37 in *O. maculatus*.

Common name Whale shark

Scientific name *Rhincodon typus*

Family Rhincodontidae

Order Orectolobiformes

Size Around 39 ft (12 m), but may grow to 59 ft (18 m)

Key features Whalelike body with massive, flat head; truncated snout; cavernous mouth with numerous small teeth; body base color grayish with light spots and stripes—the pattern unique to each individual; underside white; 3 distinct ridges along top of body

Breeding Little information available; females may retain fertilized eggs within their bodies until they hatch; up to 300 developing embryos may be held at different stages of development by a single female; newborn whale sharks thought to measure only up to 28 in (71 cm)

Diet Zooplankton, small fish, and other small animals filtered out in vast volumes by the gill rakers

Habitat Both inshore and oceanic waters; found from the surface down to a depth of around 425 ft (130 m)

Distribution Tropical and temperate waters in the Atlantic, Indian, and Pacific Oceans

World Population Unknown

Status IUCN: Vulnerable; Not listed by CITES

Whale Shark

Rhincodon typus

The whale shark is a classic "gentle giant" of the animal world. Approachable and inoffensive, this huge filter feeder is the largest of all living fish.

ACCORDING TO SOME ESTIMATES, THE whale shark can grow to 59 feet (18 m) in length. Most reports, though, place it at around 39 feet (12 m), which still makes it the largest fish in the world. Its closest rival is the basking shark (*Cetorhinus maximus*), which grows to around 33 feet (10 m), but may attain a maximum size close to 50 feet (15.2m).

As a result of their shared large size, docility, and filter-feeding habits, both species are often (as here) mentioned together. This does not, however, mean that they are particularly closely related. In fact, the whale shark belongs to the family Rhincodontidae in the order Orectolobiformes (carpet sharks), while the basking shark belongs to the family Cetorhinidae in the order Lamniformes (mackerel sharks). Both the whale shark and the basking shark are the sole representatives of their respective families.

Approachable Giants

Although both species are enormous, and are true sharks in every aspect of their biology, neither fits into the "vicious" predator image so often associated with most shark species. In fact, both the basking shark and the whale shark are the classic "gentle giants" of the animal world. They are so inoffensive that they can be easily approached by divers who derive enormous pleasure from being able to swim in midocean with these goliaths of the deep that could destroy them in an instant, but never do so.

It is this approachability that, particularly over recent years, has probably contributed to a greater extent than any other individual factor in raising fears about the continued survival of

⊕ *The huge tail of a whale shark powers it through the oceans incessantly in its quest for food.*

the whale shark. To this must be added the species' habit of gathering together in large groups in certain parts of the world. Such activity renders large numbers accessible not only to well-intentioned ecotourists, scientists, and conservationists but also to those whose interest in whale sharks is less benevolent.

Commercial Fishing

It is reported that as many as 1,000 whale sharks were taken by anglers from three Indian villages in just one year. Throughout the Philippines the catch may be even higher. In the region of Jagna in Southern Bohol alone, for example, some 100 whale sharks were caught in 1996, a significant drop from earlier years' catches. A year later the catch was around half, indicating that the local whale shark population was decreasing fast, having earlier disappeared from the former fishing grounds off Pamilacan Island about 12 miles (20 km) south of Bohol.

The exact numbers of whale shark taken on a global, or even regional, scale are

→ Strips of whale shark meat being sun-dried in the Philippines. Despite a ban on fishing for whale sharks, the practice continues.

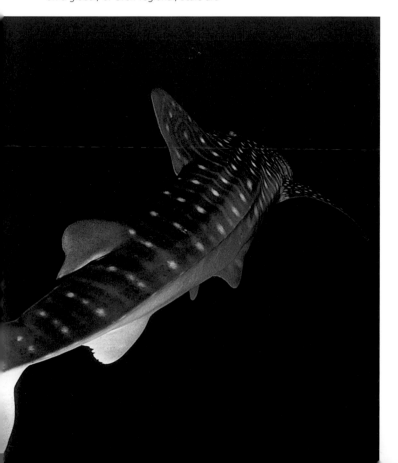

unknown, however. One of the most often quoted reasons for this—as for all other shark species that are caught for commercial purposes—is secrecy within the markets, part of which is alleged to consist of illegally caught fish. Some markets are also accused of failing to publish the relevant statistics.

Therefore, while estimates indicate a world trade in shark and shark products in the region of $240 million, the true scale of the global market is believed to be higher. What percentage of the total world trade consists of whale shark or its products is also unknown.

Traditionally, in the Philippines whale shark meat was first cut into strips and then sun-dried, with most of the meat supplying local markets. However, as demand for fresh shark meat increased from other countries, particularly in the Asian region, fishing activity increased, and catches decreased.

In spring 1998 a ban was imposed on whale shark fishing in the Philippines. Yet, every year since then (up to 2000) significant quantities of meat ranging from just over 1,750 pounds (800 kg) to over 4,400 pounds (2,000 kg) have been confiscated at seaports and airports in the Philippines, demonstrating that illegal fishing is still continuing, although its scale is yet again unknown.

Numerous Questions, Limited Answers

Figures such as the above immediately give rise to a whole host of concerns and questions. Can, for example, the world populations of

One Family or Three?

Although the whale shark is considered by most shark experts as being the sole representative of its family, the Rhincodontidae, some taxonomists include the nurse sharks and the zebra shark (*Stegostoma fasciatum*) within the same family.

Most authorities classify the three genera of nurse shark, each with a single species—the Atlantic nurse shark (*Ginglymostoma cirratum*), the West African nurse shark (*Pseudoginglymostoma brevicaudatum;* also called *Ginglymostoma brevicaudatum*), and the tawny nurse shark (*Nebrius ferrugineus*)—within their own family, the Ginglymostomatidae. The sole species of zebra shark likewise constitutes its own family, the Stegastomatidae.

whale shark sustain such a level of harvesting? Are there, indeed, separate populations, or is there just one single, migratory world population? If it is the latter, then the implications of sustained removal at the level of the three above-mentioned Indian villages, or the lower ones cited for the Bohol region in the Philippines, are even more serious than if there are distinct geographical populations. Even more fundamental, however, are the numerous questions relating to the shark's biology, such as current world numbers, the reproductive rate, the age at which the sharks breed, their growth rate, and their lifespan.

Data on all these issues, however, is woefully limited. Ironically, one of the reasons may be that despite the existence of past and present fisheries, the whale shark has not traditionally been regarded as a major commercially exploitable species. Had this been the case, there can be little doubt that today we would be far more familiar with whale sharks than we currently are.

Clearly, action needs to be taken quickly to obtain such baseline information, while at the same time implementing measures for protecting existing stocks. Study programs are now under way in several countries to gather data, while protection programs have been put in place in a number of regions, including the eastern seaboard of the U.S., the Maldives, the Philippines, and Western Australia.

Hopefully, results from the various studies, plus an expansion of protective measures to embrace other regions populated or visited by whale sharks, will help us understand this magnificent animal better and thus ensure its survival.

Forty-year-old Problem Solved

In 1953 an egg case containing a whale shark embryo was netted at a depth of around 260 feet (79 m) in the Gulf of Mexico. Unusually, though, this large egg had very thin walls when compared with the tough, leathery equivalents of other known egg-laying species of shark. It also lacked the characteristic tendrils (twisted fiberlike outgrowths that permit the egg cases to become attached to seaweeds and other structures) possessed by oviparous species.

Was the whale shark, therefore, an egg layer—or did the unusual egg case indicate a different breeding strategy? Since the find was unique, it fired a debate that lasted for more than 40 years. Then, in 1995 a pregnant female whale shark was caught off Taiwan. It contained 300 embryos in a range of developmental stages. The majority of them were still in their egg cases, but some had already hatched and were therefore close to birth. The whale shark was, thus, shown to be a viviparous (livebearing) species.

⊖ *Divers are dwarfed by a whale shark, attended by remoras swimming near the Ningaloo Reef in Western Australia.*

Tiger Shark

Galeocerdo cuvier

The tiger shark is one of the most dangerous of all sharks. Yet remarkably, it can be hypnotized, becoming limp and inoffensive while in this trance. First, though, it is necessary to roll the shark on its back— a challenging prospect.

Common name Tiger shark

Scientific name *Galeocerdo cuvier*

Family Carcharhinidae

Order Carcharhiniformes

Size Commonly attains a length of 10–14 ft (3–4.3 m) and weighs between 850–1,400 lb (385–635 kg); maximum length reported 24.3 ft (7.4 m) and a weight of over 6,855 lb (3,110 kg)

Key features Snout broad and blunt; large mouth with large serrated (cock's comb) teeth; grayish body with darker vertical bars forming "tiger" pattern; patterning particularly well pronounced in juveniles, but fading with age; white underside; top lobe of caudal fin long and powerful

Breeding Livebearing species in which litter sizes vary between 11 and 82 pups; gestation up to 12–13 months; newborn pups measure 20–40 in (51–102 cm)

Diet Extremely varied—virtually anything edible (see caption right); also swallows an array of nonedible items, including bottles, cans, pieces of metal, rubber tires, money, cloth, sacks of coal, and even explosives; species sometimes described as the ocean's "dustbin with fins"

Habitat From intertidal zone down to depths of around 460 ft (140 m); reported as being able to descend to around 1,000 ft (305 m) or deeper; usually found near the surface and frequently in river estuaries and lagoons; may be found in the open ocean but is not a true oceanic species

Distribution Widely distributed in most tropical and warm-temperate regions, but not found in the Mediterranean

Status Listed by IUCN as Lower Risk near threatened

BESIDES BEING A GENERALLY AGGRESSIVE species, the tiger shark presents a danger to humans because of its indiscriminate tastes when it comes to food. It will eat almost anything edible, and humans fall within this category. Tiger sharks are near the top of the league in terms of recorded attacks on humans, only being outscored by the great white shark (*Carcharodon carcharias*). Although the great white may be responsible for a greater number of attacks, the tiger shark is responsible for more fatalities.

The main reason for this may lie in its form of attack. The great white tends to bite and release its victim, subsequently returning for the second bite, but the tiger shark simply attacks and saws chunks off its prey from the very first bite. There is, consequently, no break between the first and second bites during which the victim could attempt to escape.

Attacks can be launched from below the prey or from the water surface. In the latter case a tiger shark will often lift its head out of the water either to look around for suitable prey or at the moment of impact with its victim. The great white is one of only a small number of other sharks to do this.

Indiscriminate Palate

The tiger shark's great versatility in feeding behavior and wide-ranging tastes mean that it will frequently have hard, indigestible objects in its stomach, for example, turtle shell. When this happens, the shark will regurgitate the inedible item. The ability is not unique to the tiger shark, but it is yet another factor that enables it to feed on such a wide range of items.

⊕ Almost anything the tiger shark can swallow is on the menu, including crustaceans, mollusks, fish including other sharks, sea snakes, turtles, birds, seals and sea lions, whales and dolphins, land mammals from cats to donkeys, carrion, garbage, and the occasional human.

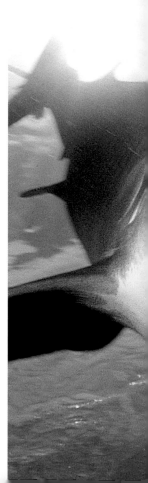

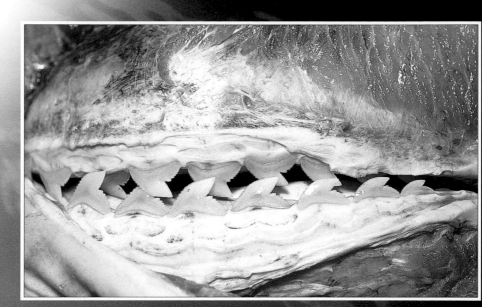

→ Armed with a powerful set of jaws and fearsome, serrated teeth, a large tiger shark can bite through tough shell and bone. No wonder it also takes inedible objects like plastic and lumps of metal.

Taming a Tiger

For all their ferocity, tiger sharks can become limp and inoffensive within a few seconds. All that one needs to do is flip the shark over onto its back. This, of course, presents an almost impossible challenge when faced with a free-swimming and perhaps angry specimen. If the shark is already partially immobilized, however, the task is more achievable.

This is precisely what Dr. Tim Holland of the Hawaii Institute of Marine Biology and his team discovered when the Tiger Shark Research Program was launched during the early 1990s. The program was set up to improve our level of understanding of the tiger shark after a series of fatal attacks on humans had occurred between 1991 and 1993 around Hawaii, renewing interest in the reintroduction of a shark control program despite the failure of a project set up between 1959 and 1976. Tim Holland argued that rather than launch another tiger shark hunt, attempts should be made to learn more about the species, its biology, and its movements. One way in which this could be achieved was by tagging specimens and fitting them with transmitters.

To do this, tiger sharks were caught on baited lines and pulled alongside the research boat. Once secured, basic data like length was obtained, along with a DNA sample. Every shark was then given a numbered tag that would allow it to be identified if recaptured.

To track movements day and night, transmitters needed to be fitted to the sharks by making an incision along the belly, inserting a transmitter, and sewing up the opening. Performing such a task on an angry, thrashing shark would be difficult and dangerous. However, it was discovered that when secured sharks were flipped onto their backs, they went into a kind of trance as if hypnotized. This condition, called tonic immobility, lasted up to 20 minutes, during which time the transmitter implantation could be completed in safety and without undue stress or injury to the shark.

The Albatross Hunter

Tiger sharks hunt mostly at night, but these versatile predators are also active during daylight. One of the best-documented instances of daytime hunting involves the taking of young albatrosses in shallow water around small, sandy Hawaiian islands located in the northwest of the archipelago. From late June to early August the large numbers of young albatrosses hatched on these islands are ready for their first flight. It can be a challenging affair at the best of times, but for the young birds hatched on these low-lying Hawaiian islands the difficulties are even greater than for their counterparts born elsewhere.

Most albatrosses can launch themselves into the air from clifftop perches. On the sandy Hawaiian islands, however, there are no cliffs. The young birds therefore line up close to the shore, face the wind, and flap their wings frantically in their attempts to achieve liftoff. Most manage this difficult maneuver successfully and fly off out to sea where they will spend several years before they return to breed. Some, however, fail to take off properly and may not even make it past the shoreline. They are the lucky ones, since they are still on land and can try again.

Those that manage to take off only to land on the water are the unlucky ones. Waiting for them, sometimes in water less than 3 feet (91 cm) deep, are tiger sharks that gather around the island shallows year after year to feed on the hapless albatrosses that fail to negotiate their maiden flight successfully.

Among the interesting facets of tiger shark behavior the program revealed was that the species may take between two weeks and ten months to return to the same area. This unpredictable timescale could explain why tiger shark control programs have little overall effect on the number of attacks: The individuals responsible for the attacks are not likely to be resident sharks. Instead, there appears to be a constant movement of sharks into and out of an area. As a result, removed specimens are likely to be replaced quickly by newcomers.

The advantages that tonic immobility presents have been exploited both with tiger sharks and other species for a variety of purposes. For example, gut content analysis can now be carried out at the time of capture and without the need to harm or kill the shark.

By "taming the tiger," we have learned a great deal about this impressive species.

Predator Turned Prey

The tiger shark's reputation as an all-consuming predator that is also likely to attack humans has occasionally made it the target of control programs. Some of them have consisted of an active hunt for the species. In Hawaiian operations between 1959 and 1976 nearly 4,700 tiger sharks were killed—yet, the number of shark attacks remained virtually unchanged.

Whether hunted as a means of attempting to reduce risks for humans or for obtaining fins for the lucrative "fin soup" market, the end result is the same: a decline in some local populations. The tiger shark is also targeted as a game fish, for its meat, and as a source of vitamin A, liver oil, and durable leather. It is also the victim of "nontarget" fishing, being caught on tackle meant for species like tuna and swordfish. Despite these pressures, the tiger shark is not believed to be under threat of continued survival as a species.

⊕ *A 10-foot (3-m) tiger shark caught in an antishark net off Durban, South Africa, is hauled aboard. Such measures help protect bathers but take a heavy toll of other marine life, including harmless creatures like turtles.*

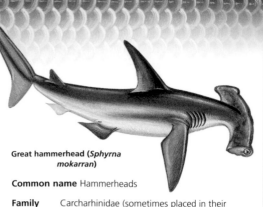

Great hammerhead (*Sphyrna mokarran*)

Common name Hammerheads

Family Carcharhinidae (sometimes placed in their own family, Sphyrnidae)

Order Carcharhiniformes

Number of species 8 or 9

Size Smallest: scalloped bonnethead—3 feet (90 cm); largest: great hammerhead—around 19.7 ft (6 m)

Key features Characteristic and variable lateral lobes on head (the "hammer"); eyes at ends of "hammer"; nostrils widely spaced near outer front extremities of "hammer"; body powerfully muscled; first dorsal fin high and prominent, second very small; pectoral fins small; caudal fin with long, pointed upper lobe bearing a distinct notch, lower lobe small and pointed

Breeding Internal fertilization: nourishment initially supplied by egg yolk; subsequent nourishment via placenta; gestation around 8 months; litter sizes from 6 to over 40 pups, depending on species and size of female

Diet Wide range of prey from open-water and bottom-dwelling bony fish to skates, rays, other sharks (including hammerheads), squid, crustaceans, and sea snakes

Habitat Open and shallow waters, ranging in depth from inshore reefs and near-shore shallows down to around 1,000 ft (300 m) in scalloped hammerhead; most species stay in upper 260 ft (80 m) of the water column

Distribution Widespread in many tropical and warm-temperate regions

Status IUCN lists 5 species as variously under threat

⊕ *The great hammerhead (Sphyrna mokarran) has been known to attack humans. Length to 20 feet (6.1 m).*

Hammerheads Carcharhinidae

Unmistakable and awe-inspiring, hammerheads are among the most intriguing of all sharks. The scientific name for eight of the nine species, Sphyrna, *means "hammer" and is a reference to the fact that the sharks have rather unusual heads.*

THERE ARE EIGHT OR NINE species of hammerhead known, and all have the characteristic head shape that makes this group of sharks immediately recognizable. The head has traditionally been referred to as being hammerlike, but in fact the head shape more closely resembles a "T" than a hammer—although even this is not equally applicable across all species.

Winglike Heads

One feature all species have in common is that they possess lateral extensions on either side of the head. The positioning of the nostrils and eyes, at the edge of these fleshy extensions, is also similar in all species. A third common factor

⊕ *One of the eyes, each of which is situated at the end of the lateral lobes of the head, can be seen clearly in this scalloped hammerhead being cleaned by two king angelfish (Holacanthus passer).*

is that in cross-section the extensions are thin and winglike, with a slightly curved top surface, a flat under surface, and a tapering back edge. They are definitely not hammerlike in cross-section. Indeed, the extensions are so slim that they are hard to make out when viewed end on.

The shape of the "hammer" differs from species to species, a fact that is partly reflected in some of their names. The winghead shark (*Eusphyra blochii*) has long, winglike extensions that can be almost half as long as the body. Then there are the similarly descriptive scoophead (*S. media*) and the mallethead or scalloped bonnethead (*S. corona*).

In the scalloped hammerhead (*S. lewini*) the front edge of the "hammer" has a pronounced indentation in the center. In contrast, as its name implies, the smooth hammerhead (*S. zygaena*) lacks the indentation. In both these "hammers" the front edge is convex, a feature that distinguishes them from the great hammerhead (*S. mokarran*) in which it is almost straight. The smalleye hammerhead (*S. tudes*) has a wide "hammer" with a central indentation similar to that found in the scalloped hammerhead. The back edge is, however, almost straight, and its eyes, as indicated by the name, are relatively small when

compared with those of other hammerheads. In the uncommon whitefin hammerhead (*S. couardi*) the head is similar to that of the scalloped hammerhead. In fact, many taxonomists regard the whitefin simply as a variant of the scalloped hammerhead.

Enigmatic Hammers

As long as hammerheads have been known, one question has repeatedly been asked: What is the function of the "hammer"? Four factors may throw some light on the possible roles of the "hammer," although conclusive proof has not yet been provided for any of them.

Sharks have small, jelly-filled pits known as the ampullae of Lorenzini on their snouts. The ampullae are very sensitive at picking up the weak electrical discharges that living creatures emit. As a result, sharks can detect prey even when it is buried under sand or gravel.

In hammerheads the front edge and front part of the underside of the "hammer" are richly supplied with ampullae of Lorenzini. This suggests it is used in prey location, which in hammerheads often consists of animals that live close to the bottom or buried beneath it.

The widely separated nostrils, one at each end of the front edge of the "hammer," may

Costs and Benefits

Natural selection often produces distinct advantages or benefits in one direction, but may be accompanied by a loss of ability in another. For example, if a fish develops very large, powerful jaw muscles during the course of evolution, they will occupy more space than smaller, less powerful muscles. The larger muscles must be fitted within the skeleton of the head. The question is, where? It can be done by increasing the overall size of the head or creating suitable spaces through the reduction in size of other structures. Either way there are consequences. A larger head results in loss of overall body power despite the increased power of the jaw itself or a loss of streamlining and, consequently, speed through the water.

The body design of a hammerhead presents an excellent example of the balance between costs and benefits. On the one hand, the tall first dorsal and small pectoral fins help the fish hunt for food along the bottom. However, the arrangement provides relatively little lift for the fish as it swims—an important factor for sharks that spend much of their time in open water. This required lift may be provided by the hammer itself because it is winglike in cross-section. It is also believed that the back or trailing edge of the hammer can be adjusted by special muscles located within the hammerhead's jaw, thus giving the fish greater control over its movements.

Within the "hammer" the separation of the nostrils and ampullae of Lorenzini may provide benefits in terms of prey location. Equally, the eyes, located at the ends of the "hammer," may also cover a wider field of vision. However, the cost of this arrangement is that a hammerhead cannot see what lies directly ahead of it unless it swings its head from side to side.

also help in prey location by providing the shark with a wide field over which it can smell potential food items. The field may be widened even further by the side-to-side movement of the head that a hammerhead makes when scanning the bottom in search of prey.

While the ampullae of Lorenzini may enhance a hammerhead's ability to home in on its targets by their electrical discharges, the capability is only brought into play once the shark is relatively close to its victim—about 12 inches (30 cm). However, the nostrils can smell prey at much larger distances, and this, allied to the enhanced visual field provided by the widely separated eyes, may help make hammerheads such efficient hunters.

⊖ *A shiver of scalloped hammerheads, the most abundant hammerhead, at a seamount in the Pacific. Such gatherings may number more than 200 individuals. The reason for these mass congregations is unclear.*

It is also suggested that the winglike shape of the "hammer" provides lift and therefore helps hammerheads stay afloat.

Hammerhead Shivers

If an individual hammerhead is impressive, imagine what 200 or more gathered together looks like, for this is precisely what happens above isolated seamounts in the eastern Pacific. Elsewhere, as off the Natal coast of South Africa, the schools (more correctly known as shivers) tend to consist of around 20–30 individuals—still impressive, but not as dramatic as the much larger Pacific congregations.

Shivers equaling or surpassing the eastern Pacific ones were once also known from the Gulf of California in Mexico, but they were decimated by commercial fishing. Much information regarding hammerheads has been obtained from studies carried out on shivers. They also raised many questions.

Why, for example, should the Mexican shivers contain six times more females than males? Why should they form only during the day and disperse in the evening? Why should they tend to form near the surface? What is the main purpose of these daytime schools?

Mating is probably one reason; but since it is not the main activity observed, and since communal hunting behavior is absent, could there be other, more fundamental purposes, such as safety in numbers? In other words, could the hammerheads be using this type of behavior more as a means of protection against predators like killer whales?

As far as we know, the only species that forms shivers is the scalloped hammerhead, but what natural selection pressures led to the evolution of schooling just in this species?

Some Schooling Clues

Although we do not possess conclusive proof of their purpose, we do have evidence of some of the advantages that schooling provides. We know, for example, that the largest females control the center of the schools, and that they are very dominant over smaller females. Bouts of aggression displays toward the subordinate individuals are therefore common (they can also be directed at other large females as a means of maintaining a "respectful" distance). The displays can include a range of behaviors, from head shaking and sideways body thrusts (shimmying) to upside-down swimming and spiraling through 360° (corkscrewing).

If such displays do not persuade a subordinate female to swim away from the immediate vicinity of a dominant female toward a less central (and hence less favored) location, the larger female may actually hit the smaller one with her chin. There is thus a movement that helps ensure that the fish at or near the center of the shiver are the largest and, consequently, the most "desirable" females; in other words, they are capable of producing more offspring than their smaller competitors.

Mature males also visit a school from time to time, often in search of a female. When this happens, the male will swim straight for the center of the school where the most desirable females are waiting. On approaching a potential mate, the male is usually challenged as an intruder and will respond by tilting his underbelly toward the female. This may be a way of showing the dominant female that he is not an intruding rival but a suitor.

Head-butting Shark

At least one species of hammerhead, the great hammerhead, has been reported as using its "hammer" in a most unusual way to immobilize bottom-dwelling prey like skates and rays. The great hammerhead has evolved the technique of using its hammer to butt and then pin down its prey to the bottom. Having achieved the feat, the shark can then spin around and bite out pieces of the victim's "wings," thus preventing it from escaping and making it considerably easier to devour.

While this behavior has not been documented in any other species of hammerhead, and only rarely in the great hammerhead, the possibility exists that it may be more widespread than our current level of knowledge reveals.

① In the bonnethead or shovelhead (Sphyrna tiburo) the head profile is rounded at the front, resembling a spade, shovel, or bonnet.

If he is accepted by a receptive female, the pair will begin their courtship rituals. As in most other sharks, it involves the male chasing and biting the female. Actual mating does not occur within the school itself but in open water or as the pair sinks toward the bottom. Again as in other sharks, the male will bite the female on one of her pectoral fins, thus partially immobilizing her and helping him achieve an appropriate position from which he can insert one of his claspers in her cloaca and transfer his sperm into her reproductory tract.

After mating has been completed, the male plays no further part in the reproductive cycle. The females, though, will return to the school.

"Caring" Parents

Hammerheads have a pregnancy period lasting around eight months. During this time the embryos initially obtain nourishment from their yolk sac. However, once it has been used up, the yolk sac attaches itself to the uterine (womb) wall of the mother and develops into what is termed a "yolk-sac placenta." From now on, each embryo obtains nourishment from its mother via the placenta, as a result of which it develops into a well-formed, self-sufficient pup by the time of its birth.

As birth approaches, some species of hammerhead shark move into relatively shallow water where they may release as few as six or over 40 pups depending both on the size of the female and of the species. Baby hammerheads are born with their "hammers" folded back against the side of the body, thus making the birth process easier.

After birth the young of some species—notably the scalloped hammerhead—will form schools in shallow-water bays, dispersing at dusk to hunt in the surrounding reefs and returning at daylight. Over a period of several months, from spring to early fall, the number of young may gradually grow until there could be as many as 10,000 young sharks.

There are some intriguing reports from the Red Sea that indicate that the scalloped hammerhead may exhibit parental behavior to an unexpectedly sophisticated level for a shark. In these instances it was noted that schools of young sharks were surrounded by adults in what appeared to be some form of protective "shield." Should this unusual behavior be confirmed as constituting parental care, it would represent an aspect of shark reproductive biology that no one could have predicted from studies undertaken so far.

Common name Basking shark (sunfish)

Scientific name *Cetorhinus maximus*

Family Cetorhinidae

Order Lamniformes

Size Around 33 ft (10 m), but possibly up to 50.5 ft (15.4 m)

Key features Variable color—brown, dusky black, or blue along the back, becoming lighter toward dull white belly; snout pointed; mouth cavernous; skin covered in small denticles and thick layer of foul-smelling mucus; 5 large gill slits, inside which is the food-filtering mechanism consisting of gill rakers; caudal fin typically sharklike, with upper lobe longer than lower

Breeding Internal fertilization followed by a gestation period of around 3.5 years; developing embryos believed to feed on unfertilized eggs during gestation; females thought to give birth to 1 or 2 pups measuring about 5.5 ft (1.7 m) in length (although some estimates indicate up to 50 young in a single batch)

Diet Planktonic invertebrates filtered from water by the gill rakers

Habitat Spotted mainly in inshore and offshore surface waters, but suspected of also inhabiting deeper zones, possibly down to 650 ft (198 m) or more

Distribution Temperate regions of Pacific and Atlantic Oceans, extending—along western coast of American continent—from British Columbia to Baja California; on east coast ranges from Newfoundland to South America, perhaps avoiding Caribbean; in eastern Atlantic ranges from Scandinavia to southern Africa; also found in Mediterranean and Black Sea, eastern Indian Ocean, around Australia, New Zealand, and up to Asian coasts, past Japan and northward

Status Listed by IUCN as Vulnerable for the species overall, but Endangered for the north Pacific and northeast Atlantic population; not listed by CITES

Basking Shark

Cetorhinus maximus

*The basking shark is a true giant of the oceans. Yet, like its even bigger relative the whale shark (*Rhincodon typus*), the basking shark is a harmless plankton feeder.*

THERE IS GROWING CONCERN FOR the long-term prospects of the basking shark. For example, some populations have now declined to the stage where they are being officially listed as Endangered, while the species as a whole is now considered Vulnerable.

Although estimates vary—something that is unavoidable when trying to establish population

levels from direct observations of a widely distributed but dwindling species in the wild—all point to the fact that the species has been going through a serious decline. For example, around the Isle of Man, off the coast of Britain, reported sightings over a seven-year period have indicated that the population in those waters has dropped by around 85 percent.

Another reason for concern is because basking shark fisheries still exist in a number of countries, including Norway, China, and Japan. Furthermore, according to a study carried out by the UK-based Basking Shark Project, as many as 95 percent of all the fish taken by commercial fisheries are females. This is not the result of intentionally hunting females but simply because for unknown reasons the majority of fish found feeding at the water surface are females. The removal of so many females from a population is sure to have serious consequences.

Incomplete Knowledge

It is perhaps surprising that so many gaps exist in our understanding of a species that has been known for some 250 years (the basking shark was first described in 1765). In fact, debate even surrounds basic data such as the actual size attained by basking sharks. Although a length of 33 feet (10 m) is usually quoted, the largest specimen that has actually been measured was around 32 feet (9.8 m) long. However, there are unconfirmed reports of specimens measuring 45 feet (13.7 m), as well as a 1948 report of a specimen measuring 50.5 feet (15.4 m).

It is generally accepted that sexual maturity is attained between the ages of two and four years. This belief is based on growth rings

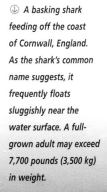

⊕ *A basking shark feeding off the coast of Cornwall, England. As the shark's common name suggests, it frequently floats sluggishly near the water surface. A full-grown adult may exceed 7,700 pounds (3,500 kg) in weight.*

Commercial Uses

In the past the main product of the basking shark commercial fishery was squalene, the oil found in its liver. As much as 75 percent of the liver consists of this oil. An adult basking shark can yield around 1,100 pounds (about 500 kg) of squalene. This high-quality oil was primarily used as a lubricant in engines. Squalene was also used for lighting. Other uses include squalene capsules as a vitamin supplement and as an ingredient in skin moisturizers. In recent years research has indicated that squalene may offer some protection against cancer, which, if proved to be the case, could lead to continuing demand for the oil.

Basking shark meat was also eaten, and its tough skin was tanned and used as leather. Both of these industries have now declined, but demand for its fins (for soup) from Far Eastern markets remains, with 2.2 pounds (1 kg) of dried fins fetching as much as $700. It is estimated that despite fishing bans and restrictions in certain regions, as many as 5,000 basking sharks are still hunted every year, primarily for their fins.

⊕ *A 19th-century engraving showing basking sharks being hunted in the waters around Scotland.*

that occur in the individual bones of the vertebral column—somewhat similar to the annual growth rings in trees. Some experts believe that two such rings are laid down each year. However, since the number of rings is known to decrease toward the tail, current estimates may, in the end, turn out to be only approximate. As things stand at the moment, basking sharks are believed to have a lifespan of around 50 years.

Mating takes place during the summer months, at least in northern European waters and off Iceland, after which the females disappear. Fertilization is known to be internal, and the females are believed to incubate a small number of eggs within their bodies up to the moment of birth. It is suspected that after a gestation period of around 3.5 years, females give birth to fully formed young that measure around 5.5 feet (1.7 m) in length. Some reports state that females give birth to just one or two young, but other reports refer to as many 50 being produced.

There is also disagreement about the volume of sea water filtered by feeding adults. Like the whale shark, basking sharks consume only small planktonic creatures that occur in immense quantities in the surface waters of the oceans. According to the Basking Shark Project, a volume equivalent to a 165-foot (50-m) swimming pool can be filtered each hour, or around 475,500 gallons (1,800,000 l). Another estimate puts the hourly throughput at around 1,850 gallons (7,000 l), and another at just 1,585 gallons (6,000 l) per hour.

Protective Measures

No universal protection program for basking sharks is currently in force, although several national and regional incentives are in place. In the waters surrounding the Isle of Man, for instance, the species has received strict protection since the mid-1990s. This was subsequently extended to full protection in British waters in 1997. New Zealand, too, afforded the species strict protection by banning all target fishing for it in 1991.

Commendable though efforts to protect the species are, they can only at best be marginally effective in global terms, since they only apply to national waters. As a result, any specimens that move into international waters, in other words, outside the traditional 12-mile (19-km) limit, lose the protection and can be

⊕ *When a basking shark feeds, it first gulps in water containing tiny plankton and then sieves them from the water with its comblike gill rakers, which can be seen here between the gill slits.*

fished (usually under quota or international "contra" arrangements). For example, Norway is allowed to harvest sufficient sharks to obtain 98 tons (100 tonnes) of liver per year in exchange for an agreed tonnage of white fish taken from Norwegian waters by other countries' fishing fleets.

Many fisheries have collapsed over the years due to declining populations of basking shark. Demand for the oil has decreased as synthetic or less expensive alternatives have been developed. Nevertheless, the need for protection remains, and the latest listings are likely to reflect more accurately the current status of the species than the previous, rather vague, category of "Insufficiently Known."

Basking Shark "Bytes"

• The basking shark does not have the typical biting teeth of most sharks; instead, it has six rows of tiny teeth in the upper jaw and eight in the lower one; each row bears around 100 teeth measuring around 0.2 inches (0.5 cm)
• The basking shark's diet consists of floating zooplankton that it filters from the water using mucus-covered gill rakers (bristlelike outgrowths of the gill arches)
• Basking sharks have very large livers: it has been estimated that the liver of a 29-foot (8.8-m) specimen weighed around 2,070 pounds (940 kg)—capable of producing about 600 gallons (2,270 l) of oil
• The liver of the basking shark can account for about 25 percent of the total body weight of the fish
• The basking shark is sometimes referred to as the sunfish because of its habit of swimming at the water surface, often with part of its back exposed, as if "sunbathing"; the more common name also refers to this habit of "basking" in the sun

Common name Great white shark (white pointer, blue pointer, maneater, Tommy, death shark, uptail, white death)

Scientific name *Carcharodon carcharias*

Family Lamnidae

Order Lamniformes

Size Specimens in excess of 36 ft (11 m) reported, but confirmed data indicates a maximum size of 18–20 ft (5.5–6.0m)

Key features Torpedo-shaped body with conical, pointed snout; teeth of upper and lower jaws very similar and saw-edged—upper teeth slightly broader; top half of body slate-gray to brownish; irregular line separates top half from pure-white lower half of body; lobes of caudal fin more similar to each other than in most other species, but upper lobe a little larger than lower; underside of pectoral fins have blackish tips

Breeding Livebearing species that gives birth to 5–14 young (probably more) after gestation period of up to a year; scars predominantly on pectoral fins of mature great white females suggest males bite females during mating, as in other sharks

Diet Mainly bony fish; also cartilaginous fish (including other sharks), turtles, seabirds, and marine mammals, including dolphins, seals, and sea lions

Habitat Wide range of habitats from surfline to offshore (but rarely midocean) and from surface down to around depths exceeding 820 ft (250 m)—although it has been reported to dive to a depth of over 4,000 ft (over 1,200 m)

Distribution Predominantly in warm-temperate and subtropical waters, but also warmer areas

Status Listed by IUCN as Vulnerable; not listed by CITES; world population sometimes quoted at around 10,000, but true numbers unknown

Great White Shark

Carcharodon carcharias

The huge great white shark is the perfect hunting machine. It is also many people's worst nightmare. Yet, for all its awesome reputation, this shark has more to fear from us than we have to fear from it.

THE GREAT WHITE IS A SUPREME hunter. It frequents a wide array of habitats and is found at various depths. In terms of dominance and predatory behavior the great white shark is probably rivaled only by the orca or killer whale—a voracious marine mammal.

Long-distance Hunter

The great white is magnificently adapted for its way of life. The shark has a streamlined, torpedo-shaped body and jaws armed with huge teeth that can be replaced by a "conveyor belt" system when lost. Furthermore, a battery of sensors that almost defy human comprehension enable it to detect prey from distances exceeding a mile (1.6 km).

A great white can thus detect the presence of a prey animal like a seal or sea lion and home in undetected—until it may be too late for the selected victim to avoid an attack. When the shark strikes, the first bite can take less than one second. However, in that brief period the following actions occur:

• the snout is lifted
• the lower jaw is dropped
• the upper jaw is pushed forward
• the upper jaw teeth are exposed
• the lower jaw is pushed forward
• the lower jaw is pushed upward
• the lower jaw teeth puncture the prey
• the upper jaw snaps shut.

The hunting technique, involving long-distance detection followed by homing in on the prey, a final burst of speed, and a lightning-fast biting action, has proved exceedingly successful for great whites in their pursuit of

⊕ *Attracted by bait from a boat, a great white shark rears its head out of the water, baring a fearsome, tooth-lined gape to those on board.*

seals and sea lions. It is estimated that about 45 percent of all such attacks are successful, with experienced individuals probably enjoying a success rate as high as 80 percent.

Another technique employed by great whites is called sky hopping. The method consists of the fish raising its head above the water to search around for a suitable victim and is often observed near seal colonies. Around Seal Island in South Africa, and at some other locations, great whites are also known to breach, in other words, jump out of the water during attacks on seals (see box "Breaching Great Whites," page 52).

Poorly Known Breeding Habits

Carrying out field observations on the breeding habits of a generally wide-ranging and potentially dangerous species like the great white presents scientists with a monumental challenge. Even in those cases in which individuals or groups are known to remain within a relatively restricted home range, such observations have, to date, remained elusive.

⊕ *The upper jaw teeth of a great white shark caught off the coast of South Africa. The teeth have sawtoothed edges that help the shark cut large pieces of flesh from its prey.*

We know that fully mature females are larger than males (the largest specimens caught tend to be females), and we know that many females attain sexual maturity when they are approximately 15 feet (4.6 m) in length, with males maturing at around 12 feet (3.6 m). Their age at maturity is estimated to be between 10 and 12 years. We also believe that some "populations" (exactly what constitutes a population of great whites is open to debate)

Wide-ranging Tastes

Although the great white includes pinnipeds like seals and sea lions in its diet, they are generally reserved for colder periods when the shark's preferred food items—mainly large fish—have migrated to warmer regions.

Irrespective of season, the great white shark feeds on a very wide range of prey and carrion. In the Mediterranean, for example, it is reported to include the swordfish (*Xiphias gladius*) in its menu. Quite how a relatively slow-moving species like the great white shark manages to catch such fast-swimming prey, however, is not clear.

Cetaceans (whales and dolphins) also form a regular part of the diet of the great white. They include both slower-swimming species, like some of the larger whales (taken alive or scavenged), as well as fast movers like dolphins and porpoises.

A wide range of bony and cartilaginous fish (including rays, skates, and other sharks) will also be taken, along with turtles, large squid, seabirds, and a whole host of other animals.

⊕ *The sheer size of a great white shark can be judged from this specimen, investigating a diver in a safety cage. Although much photographed and even captured, a great deal of the great white's biology is still not known.*

may congregate at traditional breeding sites. Evidence indicates that mating probably occurs during spring and summer, and that internal fertilization is followed by a gestation lasting up to one year. Males probably bite females during mating; this behavior is well documented in other species.

Following fertilization, the early embryos are released into a chamber that functions as a womb or uterus. There they develop and grow on a diet consisting largely of egg yolk released by the mother into the uterine chamber.

Nourished in this way, embryos grow to a substantial size and may measure around 5 feet (1.5 m) at birth. The total number of young in a single brood varies, with estimates ranging between five and 14.

Survival Threats

Human exploitation has led to a large decline in great white shark numbers. Direct killing by rod and line, harpooning, or chain-line fishing (using long lines baited with numerous hooks) —all primarily to provide sport for anglers and shark products for the curio and other trades— have inflicted significant damage on great white populations. Passive killing, with great whites being accidentally caught in nets and lines set out for other target species, has exerted its own pressure on populations, as have shark nets installed along shark-threatened coastlines to protect bathers.

All such human activities are particularly significant because the great white shark has a 10 to 12-year preadult phase, the female produces only small numbers of pups, and she may produce as few as four to six litters of pups in total during her life.

The extent of the decline and the total number of great whites remaining in the wild are very difficult to quantify. There are several reasons for this, including the diversity of nomadic/homing habits exhibited by the species. Some specimens, for instance, frequent relatively localized home "territories," while others are known to roam over large distances. A further complicating factor is that worldwide the species is relatively scarce.

As a result, although a figure of 10,000 has been cited as an approximate global total, we really do not know how many great whites remain. However, we do know that there are worryingly few, and that they are therefore in desperate need of protection.

Concerned at the decline, several countries and states have, since the 1990s, implemented protection programs based on the so-called

Precautionary Principle. In other words, where doubt exists, it is always better to take steps to protect a species and then modify the action as more data becomes available. The measures range from the banning for sale of all great white shark products to the prohibiting of other directed targeting activities, such as sport fishing or even the active attraction of great whites so that tourists can view them under water.

Further action is, nevertheless, being urged by some conservation bodies that fear the current listing by the World Conservation Union (IUCN) as Vulnerable may not be correct, and that the species may, in fact, already be in the Endangered category.

Breaching Great Whites

Like all open-water shark species, the great white shark tends to launch its attacks either from below or when swimming horizontally just under the surface, often with just its dorsal fin projecting above the water. Prior to or during some of its attacks the great white will also "sky hop." In other words, it frequently raises its head above the water to check on the whereabouts of likely prey.

In addition to these more "conventional" strategies great whites exhibit a third hunting technique known as breaching. Breaching—in which the body is flung partly or completely out of the water—is a behavior more commonly seen in whales and dolphins, and is generally not associated with feeding. In the great white, though, breaching has only been observed during attacks on pinnipeds (seals and sea lions). It is known to occur in several shark populations, but appears to be more closely associated with those found around Seal Island, a small rocky outcrop 8 miles (13 km) off Cape Town in South Africa. It seems that breaching attacks occur more frequently off the western and southern sides of the island where there is sufficient water depth close to the steep rocky shore for vertical attacks to be mounted by the shark.

⊕ *A breaching great white. During a breaching attack both the shark and its victim are carried clear of the water.*

As the shark launches into the attack, it thuds into its victim with such force that its momentum carries both prey and predator clear of the water surface. Once the prey has received the first major incapacitating bite, it is often released. It is then subjected to further attacks while still in the traumatized state produced by the first bite.

Attacks on Humans

Attacks by great white sharks on humans make the headlines worldwide, but the actual number of attacks is extremely low. Of the 50 or so attacks by all shark species that are officially reported each year, only a small proportion of them can be attributed to great whites. Where they happen, it is more likely that the shark mistakes the human for a seal or other prey, rather than identifying the human as a threat or an intruder into its territory. Experiments carried out off Seal Island show that when variously shaped dummies are floated on the surface, great white sharks will go for a seal-shaped dummy more frequently than for, say, one shaped like a square of wood. However, when the dummies are presented as moving targets, the distinction disappears.

A surfer, paddling while waiting for a wave, could therefore be easily confused with a pinniped because from below the overall silhouette against the sky could look, to a shark, like a seal, sea lion, or turtle. Once riding a wave, the surfer could also—irrespective of silhouette—be regarded as a prey animal, since the shape of the moving target will not be quite so important to a great white.

↑ *Although predominantly found in warm-temperate and subtropical waters, the great white may also be found in warmer areas. It is only infrequently encountered in cold boreal regions.*

Longnose Saw Shark

Pristiophorus cirratus

Common name Longnose saw shark (common saw shark, little saw shark)

Scientific name *Pristiophorus cirratus*

Family Pristiophoridae

Order Pristiophoriformes

Size Up to 54 in (137 cm)

Key features Long rostrum (snout or saw) with large pointed teeth separated by one to several smaller pointed teeth; two long barbels on underside of saw; head somewhat flattened, particularly the front half; long, slender body; body color brown or grayish-brown on top, with large, darker blotches; white underside; well-formed fins, but no anal fin

Breeding Females may breed every year or every other year; gestation period lasts about a year; 3–22 pups may be produced in a litter; nourishment during gestation derived from egg yolk; pups 11–14.5 in (28–37 cm) at birth

Diet Predominantly small fish, squid, and crustaceans

Habitat Sandy or muddy bottom preferred, mainly on the continental shelf and slope, but may also enter shallower waters and brackish habitats; depth range from around 130–1,020 ft (40–310 m)

Distribution Southern Australian waters from Western Australia along the south coast to New South Wales; also found around Tasmania; reports from elsewhere may not be accurate

Status IUCN lists as Least Concern

Saw sharks give birth to live young. But how do they manage to do this without the mother suffering serious injury from the sharp teeth that line the saws of her young? Amazingly, baby saw sharks are born with their large saw teeth pointing backward and folded flat against the edge of the saw.

WHEN THE LONGNOSE SAW SHARK was first described scientifically in 1794 by J. F. Latham, it was thought to be yet another sawfish. Sawfish are a similar-looking species belonging to the related group of cartilaginous fish known as rays. That same year four other species of sawfish were also described and placed in the genus *Pristis*.

Among the species described by Latham were the smoothtooth sawfish (*Pristis pectinata*), the southern sawfish (*Pristis microdon*), and the narrow sawfish (*Anoxypristis cuspidata*), all of which can grow to around 20 feet (6 m) in length. Even the fourth species—which later turned out to be the same as the already described east Atlantic sawfish (*Pristis pristis*)—grows to over 8 feet (2.5 m). Compared with the sawfish, the little saw shark is, indeed, small.

That same year Latham probably noticed that the fish he had named earlier was not a sawfish at all but a saw shark and renamed it *Pristiophorus cirratus*. However, the "little" part of the name seems to have stuck. So this species, the largest of the saw sharks, is still sometimes referred to by the most inappropriate name of little saw shark.

Incidental Victims

The longnose saw shark is a predominantly subtropical species that is found south of the equator between latitudes 30° and 40° S. There are some references to its occurrence around Japan, the Philippines, and South Africa, but the accuracy of these reports is unclear. The vast

majority of authenticated reports refer to the species being restricted to southern Australia.

Within this range the species is normally found at depths of between 130 and 1,020 feet (40–310 m). The longnose saw shark is also reported to live in brackish water, which therefore suggests that it occurs in shallow environments, at least during part of its life or at certain times of the year.

The shark's depth range overlaps that of several commercial fisheries in the region. Consequently, the longnose saw shark is caught in considerable numbers, although no specially targeted fishery for the species exists. A second species, the shortnose or southern saw shark (*P. nudipinnis*), which is found in the same region, is also similarly exploited.

Both species have excellent-quality meat. At the present time no studies appear to be under way to assess the effect that the large numbers collected (albeit as a bycatch of other targeted fisheries) may be having on their

overall populations. Despite the lack of data, and despite the fairly high levels at which both species are being commercially exploited, neither of them is believed to be under significant threat.

Look, But Don't Touch

On the rare occasions when divers come into contact with saw sharks, they should treat them with the same caution that they treat all other sharks.

Under most circumstances a saw shark found resting on the bottom will either remain there if left alone or swim away. However, if provoked, it can strike out in self-defense and can cause considerable injury. Unlike other sharks, a saw shark will not bite in defense but will attack its aggressor with a side-to-side slashing action of the tooth-lined saw. The saw has proved to be an effective weapon that has ensured the survival of these fascinating sharks for many millions of years.

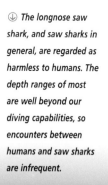

⊕ *The longnose saw shark, and saw sharks in general, are regarded as harmless to humans. The depth ranges of most are well beyond our diving capabilities, so encounters between humans and saw sharks are infrequent.*

Great-Tooth Sawfish

Pristis microdon

Common name Great-tooth sawfish (southern sawfish, freshwater sawfish)

Scientific name *Pristis microdon*

Family Pristidae

Order Rajiformes

Size Overall body length recorded up to 46 ft (14 m)

Key features Flat, narrow snout with well-spaced teeth of matching size around its edges, creating an impression of a saw; evident dorsal and caudal fins; swim like sharks; solitary

Breeding Females give birth to litters of often more than 20 young

Diet Mainly fish; some invertebrates

Habitat Shallow areas of the sea; can also be encountered in estuaries and rivers

Distribution From Africa through the tropical Indo-Pacific region to southeast Asia, north to the Philippines, and south to Australia

Status Listed by IUCN as Endangered

These particular sawfish are often found in rivers, which helps to explain their alternative name of freshwater sawfish, although they are not unique in this respect.

GREAT-TOOTH SAWFISH CAN BE DISTINGUISHED by the positioning of the first dorsal fin (located in front of the pelvic fins on the sides of the body) and also by the enlarged lower lobe of the caudal fin. The saw itself is broad at its base, tapering along its length. Their teeth are large, with between 14 and 22 pairs on each side.

Originally the Australian population of great-tooth sawfish was considered a different species, recognized under the scientific name of *Pristiopsis leichhardti*. Now this description is regarded as a synonym for *Pristis microdon*, which means they are the same species. In 1845 the explorer Ludwig Leichhard discovered this sawfish based on a dead specimen found in the Lynd River, a tributary of the Mitchell River flowing into the Gulf of Carpentaria, thus confirming these rays lived in freshwater areas of Australia. It is now clear that these particular sawfish extend throughout Australia's northern river systems—from the west right across to Queensland—with individuals being found as far as 60 miles (100 km) from the sea, generally in fairly shallow and often muddy waters.

The Longest Sawfish

In some areas small individuals have even been found in ponds where they were left stranded years previously by retreating floodwaters. However, under normal circumstances young sawfish tend to return to the sea as they grow older, although occasionally large specimens are also found in freshwater environments. While great-tooth sawfish typically grow to about 20 feet (6 m), the largest example on record—measuring 46 feet (14 m)—was actually caught in the Chao Phya River in Thailand, some 37

① The great-tooth sawfish is also known as the southern sawfish or freshwater sawfish. Normally it has between 14 and 22 large teeth on each side of its massive saw. Its pectoral fins are high and angular; the first dorsal fin is mostly in front of the pelvic fins, while the caudal fin has a distinct lower lobe.

miles (59 km) from the river's mouth. Sawfish are particularly significant in Thai culture; the saws are often deposited at temples as votive offerings to the gods. This allows scientists to gain valuable insight into both the biology and size of these fish, with records showing saws that measure over 8 feet (2.4 m) in length.

However, the numbers of these shy rays have fallen significantly over recent years, partly as a result of overfishing since they are easily caught in gill nets, and smaller specimens especially may also be hooked on lines. They are heavily hunted as a source of food and also for their saws, which are sold as curios. Furthermore, the inflated prices that are paid in Asian markets for their fins has led to large examples of these sawfish being targeted by fishermen. Habitat changes and pollution have also played a part in their decline.

Unfortunately, great-tooth sawfish may not breed for the first time until they are over 15 years old. Combined with their relatively low reproductive rate, this means that any recovery in their numbers is likely to be slow as a result of many mature breeding individuals having been removed from the population.

In some parts of their range at least, the breeding period is seasonal, tied in with the onset of the rainy season during November and December in the Cape York Peninsula area of northern Queensland. The great-tooth is an "ovoviviparous" species; this means that the

eggs are simply retained in the female's body, and there is no direct connection formed between mother and offspring as they develop. The embryos are nourished instead by the yolk that forms part of their egg. A dozen or more offspring will be born after a period of approximately five months.

Giving Birth

Young sawfish measure approximately 2.5 feet (75 cm) long at birth and emerge with their swords encased in a protective membrane so as to prevent damage to the female's reproductive tract at this stage. This casing is soon abraded and worn off once they start to use the saw to obtain food. In common with many other rays these sawfish are able to adapt their body coloration to match that of their surroundings, so they can vary from sandy shades through yellowish-brown to gray, with their underparts a lighter, creamy shade.

Great-tooth sawfish are slow growing, with a correspondingly long life expectancy of over 40 years. Studies suggest their natural growth rate is about 8 inches (20 cm) in length annually, falling back to about half this figure by the time they reach ten years of age, although their young grow much quicker in aquarium surroundings. Therefore it may be that release plans involving captive-reared stock afford the best opportunity to restore the numbers of these sawfish in some areas.

Marbled Ray

Torpedo
marmorata

The shock from a marbled ray can stun a person badly enough to cause loss of consciousness, though the voltage from it will not kill directly.

Common name Marbled ray (spotted torpedo)

Scientific name *Torpedo marmorata*

Family Torpedinidae

Order Rajiformes

Size Up to 40 in (1 m) in diameter

Key features Large, round disk shape; nostrils and mouth on underside of body; short tail with clearly divided caudal fin; variable marbled appearance; nocturnal by nature; uses its electrical discharge to capture prey

Breeding Viviparous, producing 5–32 pups

Diet Small fish and crustaceans

Habitat Shallow areas of sea grass and on reefs

Distribution From northern waters around the British Isles to the Mediterranean Sea and south as far as the Cape of Good Hope, South Africa

Status Does not appear threatened

IN SOME PARTS OF THE world marbled rays are described as "numbfish." Even so, it seems that the charge they give off is not enough to protect them from large predatory sharks; sharks seem to suffer no significant ill-effects from receiving a shock and prey regularly on them.

The disk shape of marbled rays is large, broader overall when compared with its length. There are two dorsal fins along the back; the first one is shorter than the one behind. Their tails have a basic shape similar to those of sharks, although proportionately shorter in length, with a distinctive caudal fin split into marked upper and lower lobes.

Found over a wide area, the marbled ray is shy by nature; during the day it remains buried and is relatively inconspicuous unless accidentally disturbed on the seabed. These rays easily blend into their background, with only their eyes visible above the sand. Frequenting relatively shallow coastal waters to a depth of nearly 90 feet (28 m), they are sometimes found in brackish estuaries as well. Marbled rays most commonly occur in cooler temperate waters rather than in the tropics.

They ambush their prey of small, bottom-dwelling fish by seizing, then paralyzing them with a powerful electrical charge. Their mouths are relatively small; and because they catch fish bigger than themselves, they can actually choke to death on their victims when they try to swallow them. Their teeth are relatively long and pointed, making it difficult for them to dislodge a fish once it is caught.

⊕ The 40-inch (1-m) marbled ray, also called the spotted torpedo, is found at depths of between 6.5 and 1,215 feet (2–370 m) in the eastern Atlantic from northern Britain to the Cape of Good Hope. It uses its electric organ discharge to stun its fast-moving prey of mainly small fish.

Lengthy Gestation Period

Female marbled rays can have large litters of more than 30 pups. Their gestation period is lengthy compared with other rays, lasting for approximately a year. The female marbled ray only gives birth once every three years and cannot conceive again for two years after producing pups.

Young marbled rays are about 4 inches (10 cm) long at birth. Although their electrical organs are fully developed, they feed largely on crustaceans at first rather than fish. Scientists think that rays can inactivate these organs during the birth process to protect both the mother and her offspring.

Ancient Remedies

Within their range through the Mediterranean Sea these rays were well known to the ancient Greeks and Romans, to whom electricity itself was an unexplained phenomenon. Fishermen learned the danger of coming into contact with these fish when they were pulling in their nets. The shocks generated by these rays were soon used in medicine. Around A.D. 46 the Roman physician Scribonus Largus used these rays for treating migraines and gout.

Treatment took place in shallow water using one or more live rays. The patient was put in direct contact with the fish, with the shock concentrated on the affected part of the body. In the case of gout the patient stood on the ray until the numbness generated by the shocks reached up to the knees. For migraines and other headaches it is likely that the electric shock from the fish had a direct effect on the brainwaves of the person concerned, with the charge being applied to the head in this case.

Using these rays to generate shocks in the treatment of these particular conditions—and even more bizarrely for anal prolapses—is undoubtedly the earliest example of electrotherapy in medicine. It remained fashionable until the late 1600s, suggesting that it was almost certainly beneficial.

Blue Skate

Dipturus batis

The leathery egg cases of the blue skate are often washed up on beaches, entwined with seaweed. Since their origins were unclear, they became known as "mermaid's purses" thanks to their shape, and are still described under this name today.

Common name Blue skate (common skate, gray skate, or flapper skate)

Scientific name *Dipturus batis* (*Raja batis*)

Family Rajidae

Order Rajiformes

Size 9.4 ft (2.85 m)

Key features Large, with long snout; dark olive-gray to brown with numerous pale whitish spots on upper surface of body; underside of body white, with dark spotting, especially pronounced in young fish and males, creating a bluish-gray appearance

Breeding Lays 1 or 2 eggs

Diet Crustaceans, some flatfish

Habitat Coastal zone to 2,000 ft (600 m); lives near the seabed

Distribution Eastern Atlantic, ranging from Iceland and northern parts of Norway down to Adriatic and Mediterranean, extending as far south as Senegal coast

Status IUCN: Endangered in many areas

THE BLUE SKATE IS THE LARGEST species of skate found in European waters, most likely to be encountered in areas where there is a sandy bottom. Here they glide over the surface, with the young feeding especially on crustaceans. However, adults are more opportunistic predators, seeking shoals of mackerel as well as other smaller elasmobranch species such as lesser spotted dogfish (*Scyliorhinus canicula*).

Once fully grown, blue skates rely mainly on their size to avoid predators. They are not very well protected by spines on their upperparts, although a protective layer of up to 18 thorns runs down the tail so they can lash out at close quarters if threatened. Males have more pronounced spines over the snout and on their backs. They also have weak electrical organs running down either side of their tails; their discharge is not strong enough to overcome prey but may be used for courtship purposes.

Mating occurs during the spring, with fertilization occurring internally as in all skates. The male holds the female with his claspers; they have hooks as well as spines, both helping to provide anchorage. The eggs are large, approximately 5.5 by 10 inches (14 x 25 cm), laid singly or in pairs over the summer. They are anchored by the tendrils present at each corner; young skates then hatch about six months or so later. They resemble miniature adults in appearance at this stage, although their bodies are smooth at first, with the hooks and thorns only developing later.

After hatching has occurred, scientists can detect—by the presence of egg cases (called mermaid's purses)—where breeding populations of these skates may be present.

ⓘ *The undulating swimming action typical of skates is here shown by a blue skate. The upper surface can be either olive-gray or brown in color, with a variable pattern of light spots, while the underside ranges from ashy-gray to blue-gray.*

The young may stay together in loose groups; adults also associate in same-sex groups, at least for part of the year in various localities. Some evidence suggests that after hatching, young blue skates will tend to join up to follow larger individuals of their own species, but the reason for this behavior is unclear.

A Smoked Delicacy

Blue skates are fished commercially in significant quantities; their "wings" are sold as a delicacy and often smoked. Heavy fishing during the 20th century has led to such dramatic falls in numbers in various parts of their range that they are now effectively extinct in areas such as the Irish and North Seas and the English Channel through intensive trawling.

Studies in Scottish waters, where individuals were captured, tagged, and released in one area, reveal that these fish are essentially sedentary in their habits. This research also reveals a grim picture regarding recolonization of areas where the species disappeared because of overfishing; over 30 years later in some cases there are no signs of blue skate moving back to these zones.

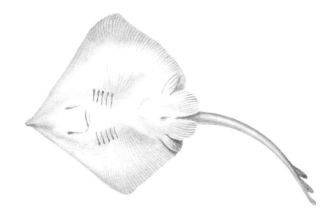

Even worse, blue skate do not reproduce rapidly. Both sexes do not mature until at least ten years old; although females lay up to 40 eggs in a season, they only breed every three years.

While the size of these skates means they can be an attractive challenge for game fishing, angling organizations now actively encourage the conservation of the species by asking their members to return individuals they catch back to the sea. However, it seems likely that more proactive restocking programs will be necessary to restore viable populations of these skates in areas where they were formerly numerous.

⊕ This drawing of the underside of a blue skate shows the very long and pointed snout, the acute outer corners of its triangular-shaped disk, the gill openings, and the projections at the tip of its long, narrow tail.

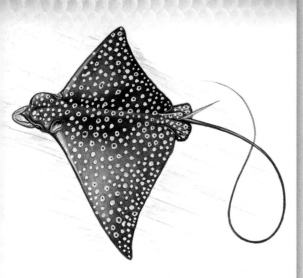

Spotted Eagle Ray

Aetobatus narinari

The tail of the spotted eagle ray is generally long, has a whiplike appearance, and is equipped with relatively inconspicuous stinging spines near the base. Its narrow, trailing tail may be three times as long as its body, although past encounters with sharks may have shortened it considerably.

Common name Spotted eagle ray

Scientific name *Aetobatus narinari*

Family Myliobatidae

Order Myliobatiformes

Size 6 ft (1.8 m), sometimes even larger

Key features Obviously and relatively even whitish or bluish-white spotted patterning over the dark slatey to chestnut-brown upper surface of the body; underparts predominantly white, extending onto the sides of the face; broad, projecting lower jaw; long, narrow tail; active and social by nature

Breeding Females give birth to 4 live young

Diet Mainly clams, oysters, and crustaceans

Habitat Sandy areas relatively near the coast

Distribution Very extensive, found in temperate and tropical areas of the Atlantic off the coasts of both the Americas, Europe, and Africa; also ranges from the Red Sea into the Indian and Pacific Oceans

Status IUCN lists as Data Deficient

SPOTTED EAGLE RAYS GET THEIR name partly from their large size and partly from their graceful movements in water, which are likened to those of a bird of prey in flight. They can swim in a similarly effortless fashion, with their pectoral fins resembling wings, enabling them to soar and turn in the ocean. Eagle rays are widely distributed through both temperate and tropical oceans. Generally they occur quite close to the coast from relatively shallow waters down to depths of 330 feet (100 m); they have also been recorded in river estuaries and even in rivers themselves, notably in the western Atlantic part of their range. However, they are not always sedentary by nature and may migrate over long distances, moving across much deeper parts of the ocean.

There are approximately 21 species that form the family Myliobatidae, with all these stingrays being relatively large in size. In some cases the disk size can exceed 8 feet (2.4 m) and averages about one and a half times their body length. The spotted eagle ray is one of the largest and most commonly encountered members of the group, with the largest recorded specimen measuring 11.5 feet (3.5 m) from one wing tip across the body to the other wing tip. Since it was first described in 1790 from a specimen caught off the coast of the Caribbean island of St. Bartholomew, this species has become known under many different scientific and common names.

The coloration of spotted eagle rays varies through their wide range, and it has

⊖ *This spotted eagle ray shows the typical long snout (flat and rounded like a duck's bill), thick head, pectoral disk with sharply curved, angular corners, whiplike tail instead of a caudal fin, and its pattern of spots. Here it digs for food on the sandy seabed.*

Gliding through the Air

Spotted eagle rays are even able to leap out of the water and glide through the air over some distance—an awesome sight, given their size. As a result, they are often better known as jumping or flying rays around the coast of Australia where they occur. Breaching is most common in the late afternoon as dusk approaches, usually when the water is calm and still. It is thought that this behavior may be linked with the need to obtain more oxygen—the exposure to atmospheric air and the subsequent impact on the surface of the sea improve the intake of this gas via the ray's spiracles and gills. There are also occasions when these rays will leap in this fashion to escape danger, especially if pursued by a shark.

contributed to the confusion surrounding their identity. Although they may occur in temperate areas of the world's oceans, they are most commonly found in tropical waters. Social by nature, spotted eagle rays can be found in large shoals of more than 100 individuals. Its speed and agility help the eagle ray escape from would-be predators like tiger sharks. Their natural athleticism may help explain the large and prominent spiracles that are located behind the eyes and open more vertically than in other species; they help maintain the flow of water over the gills—necessary to meet the ray's respiratory needs.

Spadelike Snout

Spotted eagle rays obtain much of their food close to the seabed, digging here to obtain buried invertebrates, as well as catching other creatures including octopuses and fish. The broad shape of the snout is the reason why this species is also sometimes called the spotted duck-billed ray, with the snout itself acting like a spade to reach clams and oysters buried in the seabed.

Spotted eagle rays are well-equipped to break open the shells of prey with little effort,

⊕ *The bat ray (Myliobatis californica) is a similar species to the spotted eagle ray. Both rays, which are active and sociable by nature, frequently form large schools, like this one in the Galápagos Islands, during the nonbreeding season.*

even those of crustaceans, thanks to the flattened, platelike structure of their teeth. They are formed by the fusion of rows of teeth to create a broader surface better suited to grinding and crushing prey.

Living in groups means that a receptive female will typically mate with several males in about an hour, with the fish pairing together by embracing each other on their underparts to avoid any serious risk of encountering each other's spines. The gestation period is lengthy, even among rays, and lasts for approximately a year, with four pups in a typical litter. In common with other stingrays the eggs of the spotted eagle ray are relatively small and do not contain sufficient yolk to sustain the young pups through to birth.

Therefore, during the gestation period the young will depend on the food supplied by their mother through outgrowths from the uterine lining (called "villi" or "trophonemata") to sustain them. These cords envelop each embryo, not only providing nutrition but also allowing gaseous exchange to take place. The nutriment, called "histotroph," can be either swallowed or taken into the young ray's body through its gill filaments.

Vulnerable Young

Although they are well developed at birth, young spotted eagle rays are especially vulnerable to being seized by sharks at this stage, with the sharks following the birth process closely and seeking to strike when

mother and young are most vulnerable. This may help explain accounts of females producing their young as they leap into the air, possibly confusing sharks in the waters beneath, although scientists do not consider this to be the typical method of giving birth. However, the young themselves are not entirely defenseless because, although they are born with their spines protected in a sheath so as not to sting their mother, the spines become exposed very shortly after birth.

Danger from Spines

Spotted eagle rays are equipped with as many as eight separate stinging hooks at the base of their tail, and they can prove deadly. People who have had the misfortune to be stung by them describe the resulting injury as being immensely painful. Without medical assistance the affected limb may be lost, and fatalities are not unknown, albeit rare. Since spotted eagle rays are actually difficult to approach and swim off if threatened, the risk of being stung without warning by these oceanic giants is actually significantly lower than with other smaller types of stingray.

Diving directly in among a shoal of these fish can be exceedingly dangerous, as is hauling an individual onto a boat—the ray will use its tail like a whip, thrashing around at this stage. The venomous spines themselves can be shed and regrown on an annual basis; a replacement is already evident very close to the site of its predecessor by the time it is shed, so that the ray is not left defenseless. Even if a spine is torn out violently in a confrontation with a shark, for example, it too will normally be replaced.

Spotted eagle rays are also immensely strong—an individual once easily pulled a 22-foot (6.7-m) boat for some distance when it was caught on a line. Rather disconcertingly, these rays are also reputed to utter a sound like a barking dog when hauled from the sea, although this could be explained by the noise of the suction effect of the large disk as the fish writhes around on deck.

Oysters and Clams

The so-called bat ray (*Myliobatis californica*) of the eastern Pacific is a close relative, with habits very similar to the spotted eagle ray. It is also social by nature with massive shoals, numbering thousands of individuals, recorded off the coast of California. In this part of their range these rays are regarded as a serious threat to the oyster beds that are fished commercially. Fishermen attempt to protect these sites by driving stakes into the seabed spaced approximately 6 inches (15 cm) apart in order to exclude the bat rays. The movements of their large pectoral fins can help the rays expose prey buried in the seabed, since their movements will disturb the sand and help expose clams that they can then dig out with their mouthparts.

Manta Ray

Manta birostris

These giants of the ocean can have a wingspan even longer than their body length, measuring some 22 feet (6.7 m). They have inspired fear among sailors down the centuries by circling small boats and leaping above the waves.

Common name Manta ray (giant devil ray)

Scientific name *Manta birostris*

Family   Mobulidae

Order   Myliobatiformes

Size   17 ft (5.2 m); Atlantic mantas are largest

Key features Very distinctive horn-shaped projections (cephalic fins) extend down beneath the eyes; blackish-brown on dorsal surface, with a variable white collar whose patterning allows individuals to be identified; whitish on ventral side of body; active by nature, swimming over long distances rather than concealing itself on seabed

Breeding   Female gives birth to a single young

Diet   Typically feeds on plankton; sometimes small fish

Habitat   Usually in upper reaches of the ocean; sometimes found in estuaries and even in rivers

Distribution Circumglobal in tropical parts of Atlantic, Indian, and Pacific Oceans; ranges as far south as Brazil, sometimes as far north as New England and Georges Bank on eastern U.S. seaboard, although not consistently recorded north of the Carolinas; occurs northward to Redondo Beach, California, on Pacific Coast

Status   Listed by IUCN as Data Deficient

ALTHOUGH MANTAS ARE THE largest of all rays, they feed almost entirely on microscopic plankton that they filter out of the water thanks to the modified structure of their gills. As water is drawn into their large, cavernous mouth, located at the front of the head, and passes over the gills, the arches here filter out microscopic plankton that are then swallowed, going directly into the stomach. The distinctive cephalic fins at the front of the body act like funnels, steering food into the mouth, but are kept curled up when the ray is not feeding. These hornlike projections help explain why this species is also called the giant devil ray. If the manta ray finds a shoal of small fish, they can be sucked into the mouth and swallowed whole. It does have about 270 teeth in its mouth, confined just to the lower jaw.

Frequently encountered on its own, an adult manta ray may be accompanied by groups of smaller pilot fish (*Naucrates ductor*), though occasionally these rays associate in small groups with others of their own kind. They are very graceful in the water, with their name being derived from the Spanish word *manta* (meaning "cloak") to describe the appearance of the ray when it is swimming. Their propulsive power also means they can leap up to 5 feet (1.5 m) out of the sea, not just flying but sometimes even cartwheeling in the air.

Special Courtship Sites

Mating can occur at any stage during the year, with these rays becoming mature once they have attained a wingspan of approximately 13 feet (4 m). At this stage they may congregate in specific courtship sites; one well-known locality

⊕ *This manta ray shows its huge mouth while feeding at the surface of the Red Sea. Mainly a plankton feeder, the manta will take small to medium-sized fish as well.*

is around the island of Yap, part of the federated states of Micronesia in the Pacific Ocean. Researchers there have been able to identify individuals by slight variances in their markings. Whatever her size, the female will only produce a single youngster, which is born after a gestation period lasting around 13 months (395 days). Already well developed at this stage, a young manta ray has a wingspan of over 3 feet (1 m) at birth.

Manta rays are not caught commercially on any scale, although in Mexico the skin of manta rays may be made into an exclusive leather. Their feeding habits, quite apart from their size—they can weigh up to 3,000 pounds (1,360 kg)—largely preclude them from being caught on a rod and line; but when one of these oceanic giants is caught from a boat, the consequences can be unpredictable. There is one record of a 25-foot (7.6-m) motorboat being towed for more than 10 miles (16 km) by a monster manta ray with a wingspan of 22 feet (6.7 m) over a period of five hours. It happened in spite of the crew dropping the anchor as well as shooting and harpooning the ray repeatedly over this period.

The Manta's Companions

Pilot fish are not the only fish that are found living in relatively safety alongside these giant elasmobranchs. Usually they are seen swimming in front of the ray, as if they were guiding it, which is how they got their name. These fish scavenge on food left by the ray. Cleaner fish have also established a temporary but no less remarkable relationship with manta rays. These wrasses (*Labroides* species), conspicuous by their bright colors, occupy specific areas on the reef that manta rays appear to recognize, as they slow down and open their gill slits, allowing the wrasse to dart in and nibble away at parasites that have become established here.

Other fish such as remoras (*Echeneis naucrates*) hitch a permanent ride on the manta ray. Their dorsal fin serves as a suction cup to hang onto the ray's body, frequently either inside the mouth or under the broad pectoral fins of the ray—as they do to inert objects such as ships. They can detach themselves in order to seek food, then reattach themselves using small hooks initially before using their sucker cup, which creates a partial vacuum at the point of attachment to the ray's body.

⊕ A manta ray can leap up to 5 feet (1.5 m) out of the sea, an action that some scientists think shows a cleansing behavior, while others suggest it is part of a mating display.

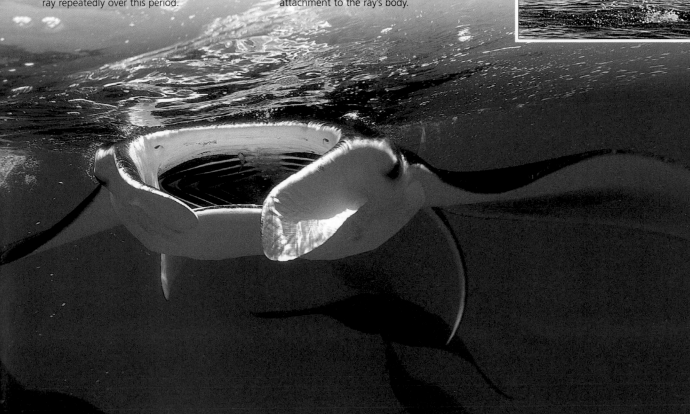

Common name Coelacanth

Scientific names *Latimeria chalumnae, L. menadoensis*

Family Latimeriidae

Order Coelacanthiformes

Number of species 2 known

Size Up to 6 ft (1.8 m) long and weighing up to 210 lb (95 kg)

Form Bluish base color when alive, with light pinkish-white blotches

Breeding Livebearer; a few large eggs, each about 3.5 in (9 cm) in diameter and weighing 10.6–12.4 oz (300–350 g), are released into the oviduct, which acts as a womb for embryos that grow to at least 12 in (30 cm) before birth

Diet Smaller fish

Habitat Cold waters in deep ocean down to more than 330 ft (100 m)

Distribution Cape Province and KwaZulu-Natal (South Africa); Comoro Archipelago (islands between northern tip of Madagascar and east coast of Africa); a related species, *Latimeria menadoensis*, is known from northern Sulawesi, Indonesia

Status Listed by IUCN as Critically Endangered, with little idea of population

Coelacanth

Latimeriidae

The coelacanth was thought to have been extinct for over 70 million years, until one was fished up off the South African coast in 1938.

VERY FEW PEOPLE HAVE EVER seen a coelacanth in the flesh either alive or dead. Yet everyone seems to know about this so-called "living fossil," possibly because of the dramatic story of its discovery. On December 22, 1938, a fishing boat trawling at a depth of around 240 feet (70 m) near the mouth of the Chalumna River, near East London in South Africa, caught a most unusual fish. It was about 5 feet (1.5 m) long, deep metallic blue with iridescent silver markings, and had odd-looking fins. The crew had never seen such a fish before, so on returning to port at East London, they informed Marjorie Courtenay-Latimer, the curator of the local natural history museum.

Perhaps the most peculiar thing about the fish were its fins. The caudal (tail) fin had an extra section protruding from the end. The paired fins had "stems" that looked like limbs, with fin rays fanning out at the edges. There were also two dorsal fins, the rear one being smaller with scales on its stublike base.

Marjorie Courtenay-Latimer wrote to the ichthyologist J. L. B. Smith enclosing a sketch, and on examining the fish, he confirmed that it was a coelacanth. Yet coelacanths were believed to have been extinct for over 70 million years. It was a living fossil.

Fossil Coelacanths

There is a good fossil record of coelacanths stretching back over the past 350–400 million years (Middle to Upper Devonian). They all had the lobed fins, spiny first dorsal fin, and three-part caudal fin of the South African fish. However, the last remaining fossil genus, *Macropoma*, disappeared from the fossil record during the Cretaceous Period (140–170 million years ago), along with all trace of its kind—until the momentous discovery of 1938.

⊙ *The original 1938 specimen of the coelacanth (*Latimeria chalumnae*): the "living fossil" that caused a worldwide sensation when it was discovered off South Africa.*

apparent center of the coelacanth's range.

In 1997, however, Mark Erdman, a scientist on honeymoon in north Sulawesi, Indonesia, identified a coelacanth being taken to the local market. Ten months later he was presented with a second specimen that was still alive, although it died shortly afterward.

These Sulawesi coelacanths seem identical to those from the Comoro Archipelago—from which they are separated by around 6,200 miles (10,000 km)—except for their coloration (they are brown with gold flecks). DNA analysis, however, indicates that they are a separate species: *Latimeria menadoensis*.

⊕ *The ichthyologist J. L. B. Smith poses with the second coelacanth specimen ever found and the first to be preserved intact. Smith devoted a large part of his career to tracking down the coelacanth.*

Present-day coelacanths (*Latimeria* species) are believed to be direct descendants of the genus *Coelacanthus*, which first appears in Permian deposits laid down nearly 300 million years ago. The skeleton of *Latimeria* is virtually identical to that of *Macropoma mantelli*, which lived in the Upper Cretaceous, over 70 million years ago.

Subsequent Finds

Since the first living coelacanth was found in 1938, some 200 specimens have been caught or reported. Nearly all have come from around the Comoro Archipelago, making this the

More recently, another remarkable discovery was made within the St. Lucia Marine Reserve off the northern KwaZulu-Natal coast in South Africa. On October 28, 2000, three divers—Pieter Venter, Peter Timm, and Etienne le Roux—were exploring a submarine canyon in Sodwana Bay when Peter Venter spotted a large fish resting under an overhang. On closer examination he identified it as a coelacanth. Extending their search, the divers found two other specimens. In November of the same year a team of seven divers descended into the canyon and filmed three coelacanths at a depth of 354 feet (108 m). The largest of the fish was

nearly 6 feet (1.8 m) long. It is now believed that this site may hold a viable population of *Latimeria chalumnae*, giving us hope for the future of this most remarkable of fish.

Fascinating Breeder

For a fish considered so primitive, the coelacanth breeds in a most "advanced" way. Rather than releasing sperm and eggs into the water like the majority of other fish (oviparity), it indulges in a reproductive strategy known as livebearing, or viviparity.

Egg-laying (oviparous) fish produce large numbers of eggs; in general, the number is related to the degree of parental care they enjoy. For example, in species like the Atlantic cod (*Gadus morhua*), which abandons its eggs to the elements, a large female can produce as many as 9 million eggs. In sharp contrast, in egg-laying species that practice intense parental care—such as the mouth-brooding cichlids of the African Rift Lakes— the total number of eggs produced by a female is often counted

Living Fossils

While the coelacanth is the best-known fish that can be described as a "living fossil," it is not the only one. For example, the lungfish also fall into this category. However, on examination the term "living fossil" seems to be contradictory. How can a species be "living" if it is a fossil? Fossils, after all, are the remains of now-extinct organisms found in sedimentary rock deposits. Yet coelacanths, while known as fossils in deposits stretching back some 400 million years, are very much alive today.

In purely scientific terms, therefore, "living fossil" has little precise meaning. It is, nevertheless, a term that, over the years, has become widely used and understood by most people. Perhaps the best definition is that coined by Dr. Keith Thomson in his book: *Living Fossil—The Story of the Coelacanth,* in which he states:

"A living fossil is the living representative of an ancient group of organisms that is expected to be extinct (it may for a long time have been thought to be extinct), but isn't."

We can only hope that the coelacanth continues to qualify for the description.

only in tens rather than in thousands.

In livebearing (viviparous) species, in which the eggs and embryos are retained within the female's body, the reduction in the total number of offspring produced can be even more extreme. In the freshwater goodeids, for instance, broods of as few as five individuals are not uncommon.

Fossil evidence has always indicated that ancient coelacanths were livebearers because some Jurassic fossils of adult fish include small immature specimens near the back wall of the abdominal cavity. Proof, however, had to wait for many years. In 1972 a large female was dissected and found to contain 19 very large eggs that had already been expelled from the ovaries. The eggs were some 3.5 inches (9 cm) in diameter: the largest eggs known in fish. Amazingly, they did not have shells; neither did the coelacanth possess any shell-secreting glands. How, therefore, could such large, fluid-filled, unprotected eggs survive if they were released into the water?

⊕ In life the coelacanth swims slowly near the rocky seabed in tropical oceans, where it feeds on small reef fish and cuttlefish.

caught in1973 measured nearly 17 inches (43 cm) in length. These and many other important questions will, no doubt, be unraveled as new discoveries are made.

Finding the Proof

Proof that the coelacanth is viviparous eventually came in 1975, when Dr. Charles Rand of Long Island University and Dr. C.L. Smith of the American Museum of Natural History in New York dissected a female that had been collected in 1962. Not only was she found to be gravid, or pregnant, but she was carrying five large, almost fully developed embryos, each measuring around 12 inches (30 cm) in length. Each embryo still carried its attached yolk sac.

While we now know that the coelacanth is viviparous, there is still a great deal that we do not know about its reproductive biology. It is not clear, for example, how the eggs are fertilized internally, because male coelacanths do not have an obvious mating organ. No one knows how many embryos a female can produce, how long they take to develop, or whether cannibalism occurs between embryos, as in some sharks. Even the size of baby coelacanths at birth is uncertain, although a very young specimen, without its yolk sac,

Present Status

Although it is still not possible to accurately gauge the population levels of coelacanths in their natural habitat, there can be little doubt that at best they are extremely rare. They are therefore categorized by the World Conservation Union (IUCN) as Critically Endangered and in need of protection.

One important protective measure has been taken by the Convention on International Trade in Endangered Species (CITES), which has listed it under Appendix I: a measure that makes all trade in coelacanths illegal. A further measure involves the devising of a simple technique for the safe deepwater release of any specimens accidentally caught by fishermen. Coelacanths released in shallow, warm water invariably die, but the "Deep Release Kit" allows captured specimens to be lowered rapidly in a sack from the warm surface waters to a depth where the water is appropriately cold, and where the fish can release itself safely. At the moment, this appears to be the only way of effectively returning captured coelacanths to the wild.

With regard to the Sodwana Bay population, the fact that it exists within the St. Lucia Marine Reserve already means that it enjoys considerable protection. Nonetheless, legislation is now in place making it illegal to disturb the fish, attempt to collect any specimens, or even locate them and film them without an official permit.

Despite these necessary restrictions, the whole world may in time gain a privileged view of living coelacanths if a planned project gets the go-ahead. The project would involve underwater cameras being installed at appropriate coelacanth sites within the reserve, allowing live pictures of living coelacanths to be be relayed to a special coelacanth website on the Internet.

Australian lungfish (*Neoceratodus forsteri*)

Common name Lungfish

Infraclass Dipnoi

Orders Lepidosireniformes (South American and African lungfish): families Lepidosirenidae (1 sp: South American lungfish, *Lepidosiren paradoxa*) and Protopteridae (4 spp. of African lungfish in genus *Protopterus*); Ceratodontiformes (Australian lungfish): family Ceratodontidae (single sp: *Neoceratodus forsteri*)

Number of species 6

Size From 33 in (85 cm) in *P. dolloi* (spotted lungfish) to over 5 ft (1.5 m) in *Neoceratodus* and over 6.5 ft (2 m) in Ethiopian lungfish (*P. aethiopicus*)

Key features Body elongate with continuous dorsal, caudal, and anal fins; *Neoceratodus* with paddlelike pectoral and pelvic fins and stout body scales; *Lepidosiren* and *Protopterus* with filamentlike pectoral fins, fleshy pelvic fins (filamentlike in *Protopterus*) and smooth scales

Diet Mainly carnivorous, feeding on aquatic animals

Breeding Generally after first rains—before summer rains in Australian lungfish; eggs of African and South American spp. laid in burrows guarded by male, fry have external gills; eggs of Australian lungfish scattered among vegetation, hatch into fry without external gills

Habitat Still pools and deep rivers in Australian lungfish, similar but often shallower waters in other spp.

Distribution Australian lungfish: Murray and Burnett River systems, southwest Queensland, Australia; South American spp: Amazon and Parana River basins; African spp: widespread in Africa

Status Australian lungfish listed in CITES: Appendix II

⊕ *The Australian lungfish (*Neoceratodus forsteri*) grows to a length of up to 5 feet (1.5 m). A native of northeast Australia, it favors deep, slow-flowing water.*

Lungfish

Lepidosirenidae, Protopteridae, Ceratodontidae

Most fish take in oxygen through their gills, but some use other parts of the body as well. The aptly named lungfish have lungs rather like those of land-dwelling vertebrates, and in dry conditions they use them to breathe air.

LUNGFISH HAVE ALWAYS BEEN REGARDED as strange fish to the extent that some people have doubted whether they are fish at all. The reasons for this belief include the way some species have external gills during their larval stages that indicate strong similarities with amphibians (frogs, toads, newts, and salamanders). Lungfish also have limblike pectoral and pelvic fins—features that they share with the coelacanths—strangely joined-up dorsal, caudal, and anal fins, reptilianlike heavy-duty body scales, and of course, lungs.

In fact, when the South American lungfish was first described in 1837, it was believed to be a reptile because of its lung and the nostrils located near its lip. Its scientific name, *Lepidosiren paradoxa*, means it is a "paradox," indicating doubt or confusion. A year or so later the African lungfish was discovered and was regarded as an amphibian owing to its "unfishlike" heart structure. It took some three decades for the reptilian and amphibian connections to be dropped, and the controversy to be resolved.

Ancient Lineage

Fossils of fish that are apparently identical to modern-day Australian lungfish (*Neoceratodus forsteri*) have been found in rocks of around 100 million years of age in New South Wales. This makes it the oldest known species of fish still alive today. It also confers on this species the status of "living fossil," a term that has also been applied to the coelacanth.

Ancient though the Australian lungfish's history may be, that of lungfish in general goes

⊕ *Fragments of its mucous cocoon cling to the skin of this African lungfish (*Protopterus annectens*), dug up during the dry season while estivating in the bed of a dried-up pool.*

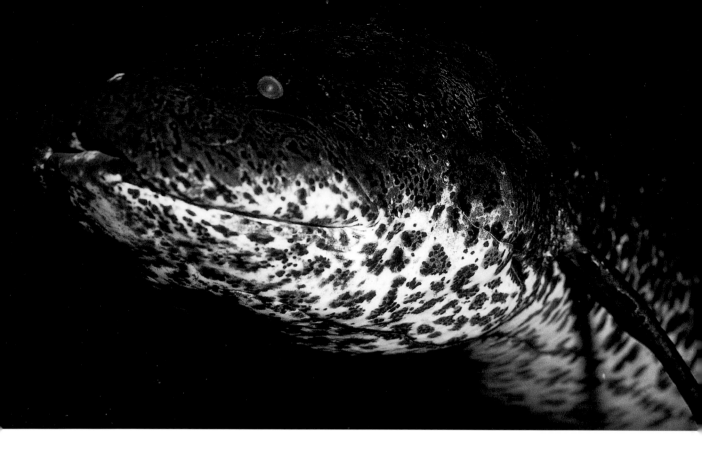

back even further, with Australian-type fossils occurring in Triassic rocks laid down over 200 million years ago. Going even further back in time, fossil cocoons or burrows—some with a lungfish inside—have been found in Permian and Carboniferous rocks, respectively 270 and 350 million years old. However, the heyday of lungfish abundance appears to have been just prior to the Carboniferous, during the Devonian Period—from about 400 to 350 million years ago—when there were many more species (around 100) than the six that still exist today. The earliest species lived in marine conditions, but by the Middle Devonian Period at least some had migrated to fresh water. All living lungfish are strictly freshwater fish.

Just three lungfish families have survived to the present day. Two families, the Ceratodontidae and the Lepidosirenidae, contain a single species each: the Australian lungfish and the South American lungfish, respectively. The remaining family, the Protopteridae, contains four species of *Protopterus* lungfish, all confined to Africa.

Survival Experts

All lungfish are highly adapted for survival under adverse conditions. The most obvious adaptation is the lungs: modified swim bladders surrounded by blood vessels that can absorb oxygen from the air.

Their lungs give lungfish two important survival capabilities. First, they allow the fish to breathe atmospheric air at the water surface, an ability that becomes particularly valuable as their native lakes and rivers begin to dry up with the onset of the tropical dry season. As the water evaporates, the pollutants in the remaining water tend to become more concentrated, and dissolved oxygen levels decrease. Both could eventually kill any fish that relies on the water to supply all its needs, but lungfish survive by breathing air at the surface.

Second, having lungs allows cocoon-building species to breathe atmospheric air while lying dormant in dry lake or river beds. Metabolic adaptations also allow them to control the buildup of waste products inside their bodies. This is a vitally important factor,

⊕ *The Ethiopian lungfish (*Protopterus aethiopicus*) is the largest of the African species, with a maximum length of up to 6.5 feet (2 m). Since its native waters rarely dry up, it can usually survive the dry season without estivating in a burrow.*

particularly in the case of the African and South American species that spend long periods of summer dormancy (estivation) inside cocoons when their ponds dry up. The system of chemical reactions needed for this type of waste control is even in place in the case of the Australian lungfish, which does not secrete a cocoon or estivate.

Sealed Refuge

To construct a cocoon, a lungfish will bite out chunks of bottom mud until it creates a vertical burrow that can extend downward some 10 inches (25 cm) or more. It then slips into the base of the burrow, gradually expanding it until its body can fit in a coiled position with the mouth directed upward. During the process the lungfish's skin produces large quantities of mucus that end up "plastering" the walls of the cavity. As the final remnants of water evaporate from the mud, the mucus hardens to form a tough cocoon, with a breathing tube leading up to the now dry surface of the mud.

Once safely encased, a lungfish will remain in its dormant state until the next rains arrive, which often takes eight months or more. However, laboratory-based experiments have demonstrated that at least one African species, *Protopterus aethiopicus*, can survive in this state of "suspended animation" for up to four years, feeding on its own muscle tissue.

Varied Feeders

Lungfish are predominantly hunters. They do not, however, chase their prey over long distances. They generally prefer to creep up on their victims undetected, particularly at night, and then suck them into their mouths, rather than grabbing them or shaking them to bits like some predatory fish.

Their diet is quite varied and, depending on the size of the individual, as well as the species, can include invertebrates such as snails, worms, and freshwater shrimp or vertebrates like tadpoles, adult frogs, and small fish. Some lungfish also feed on plants, although only as a supplement to their mainly carnivorous diet.

African Lungfish

African lungfish (*Protopterus* species) are elongate in overall body shape and have long filamentlike pectoral and pelvic fins. The range of sizes quoted for the four species varies widely, with some estimates for *Protopterus amphibius* running from 18 inches (46 cm) to 40 inches (1 m) and from 70 inches (1.8 m) to 80 inches (2 m) for the Ethiopian lungfish (*P. aethiopicus*).

African lungfish are the best-known burrow and cocoon constructors, but their tendency and ability to do so varies. The species that most frequently estivates in cocoons is the one usually referred to as "the" African lungfish (*P. annectens*). The Ethiopian lungfish rarely makes burrows and cocoons, probably because this species tends to live in more permanent bodies of water. In the spotted lungfish (*P. dolloi*) females usually leave ponds before they dry up and move—along with immature males—into more permanent water bodies. Mature males remain behind and either reoccupy existing burrows or excavate new ones. They usually rest in the burrows rather than going into a state of dormancy, although they are capable of lying dormant if the water in the habitat evaporates completely. A similar situation seems to apply to *P. amphibius*.

African lungfish depend on their lungs for their survival at all times, not just during periods of estivation. It is estimated that even when oxygen is abundant in the water these lungfish gather about 90 percent of their total oxygen requirements using their paired lungs, raising this to 100 percent during full estivation.

Spawning in African lungfish takes place in burrow-shaped nests excavated by the male. Once the eggs are laid and fertilized, one of the parents—presumed to be the male—stands guard over them and apparently keeps them supplied with oxygenated water, "tail-lashing" around the entrance of the burrow in what has been interpreted as egg-aerating behavior. Confusingly, newly hatched African lungfish fry have external gills, like the young tadpoles of frogs and other amphibians.

Mystery South American

Although the widely distributed South American lungfish (*Lepidosiren paradoxa*) was the first species of living lungfish described, over 165 years ago, it is still surprisingly little known. It has an extremely elongated body, and as in the African lungfish, the pectoral fins are extended into filaments; the pelvic fins, however, are wider with fleshy bases.

The South American lungfish depends on its paired lungs for survival at all times. Its estivation during the dry season is generally partial, with the fish resting in a moist mucus-lined chamber. During the breeding season, which follows the arrival of the rains, males develop external blood-rich "gills" around their pectoral fin bases, which may supply extra oxygen to the water in the burrow where the eggs and young develop, guarded by the male.

Australian Differences

The Australian lungfish, while sharing many characteristics with its African and South American relatives, also exhibits some significant differences. Its body, for example, is considerably stouter and is covered in large, sturdy scales, which are lacking in other lungfish. It also has lobed, flipperlike pectoral and pelvic fins. These features are generally thought to represent a more primitive phase of evolution than that found in either *Protopterus* or *Lepidosiren*. The Australian lungfish also has a single lung, rather than two, and its young do not have external gills and are not protected by either parent. The species also spawns before the rainy season rather than during the rains, like other lungfish.

The Australian lungfish is also unique among lungfish in that it does not build a burrow and does not estivate. Unlike the other species, it depends on its gills rather than its lung for survival; the lung probably acts more as a buoyancy organ than as a respiratory one, like the swim bladder of a more typical fish. Despite this, Australian lungfish can withstand adverse water conditions and can survive for several days out of water, as long as they stay in the shade, and their bodies remain moist.

⊕ *The South American lungfish (*Lepidosiren paradoxa*) is very like the African species, with an elongated body, threadlike fins, and a similar dependence on its paired lungs. This suggests that the two types of lungfish are closely related.*

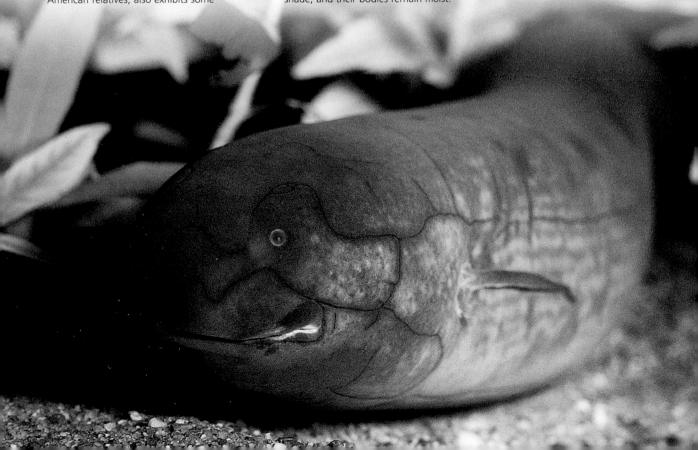

Beluga

Huso huso

The beluga is known throughout the world as the largest of all freshwater fish—and the sturgeon that produces the most highly priced caviar.

THE COLOSSAL BELUGA IS THE largest of all the sturgeons, and indeed the biggest of all freshwater fish. Belugas measuring some 20 feet (6 m) in length are not rare even today, and occasionally giant specimens measuring up to 28 feet (8.6 m) are reported. Such leviathans can weigh well over 2,800 pounds (1,270 kg). If they are female, they can produce up to 7 million eggs at a single spawning. Since the characteristically black eggs form the basis of the most highly prized of all caviars, a single spawn from one of these females represents a sizable fortune.

Long-distance Spawners

Like most of the larger sturgeons, the beluga spends most of its time at sea, feeding mainly on fish such as anchovies, gobies, and herrings. Larger individuals are also reported to take other vertebrates as well, including birds such as

Common name Beluga

Scientific name *Huso huso*

Subfamily   Acipenserinae

Family   Acipenseridae

Order   Acipenseriformes

Size   Up to 28 ft (8.6 m) and 2,865 lb (1,300 kg); typical large specimens up to 20 ft (6 m)

Key features Heavy-bodied profile in adults; younger specimens more streamlined; skin membranes bordering gills fused in throat area; wide mouth and 2 pairs of long barbels on snout; scutes not particularly strong and become worn down and partially lost with age

Breeding   "Fall" race migrates 300 mi (500 km) or more in September–October to upper reaches of rivers; "spring" race migrates in March–April to middle and lower reaches; both spawn around May over pebble or gravel; up to 7 million eggs laid by a large female; fry hatch in about 1 week; adults return to the sea; juveniles generally move out to sea during their first year

Diet   Young beluga feed on invertebrates and small fish; adults feed almost exclusively on fish plus other prey, including waterfowl and, reportedly, seals

Habitat   Mainly close to the surface or in midwater regions over fine sediments, often close to estuaries; moves to deeper water during winter—as deep as 590 ft (180 m) in Black Sea

Distribution Adriatic, Black, and Caspian Seas, and associated river systems

Status   Some populations classified as Endangered by the IUCN; one as Critically Endangered and one as Extinct; CITES Appendix II

⊕ *Bigger than any other freshwater fish, the amazing beluga can rival some of the giant sharks in length and weight. Despite this, it is quite harmless, feeding mainly on small fish.*

waterfowl. However, beluga migrate long distances into fresh water for the spawning season, covering distances of 300 to 380 miles (500–600 km) in the process.

Depending on the timing of the upriver spawning run, two races of beluga can be recognized. The so-called "fall" race enters river estuaries during September and October, and gradually moves upriver during the fall. It overwinters in pits on the river bottom and subsequently swims farther upriver to its spring spawning grounds. The "spring" race does not travel such great distances, preferring to spawn in the middle and lower reaches. This means the fish of this race delay entering the river estuaries until March or April.

Its spawning behavior and choice of egg laying site are similar to those of the Baltic sturgeon, with the eggs being laid on stony riverbeds in fast-flowing water. At temperatures of around 55° F (13° C) the eggs hatch in about a week, after which the larvae take some ten days to begin feeding.

At this early stage in their lives their diet consists of small invertebrates. Gradually, however, the juveniles begin to prey on smaller fish until, eventually, their diet consists almost exclusively of fish. They generally move out to sea during their first year.

Their growth from then on is relatively slow, with lengths of around 40 inches (1 m) being attained after about four years and 80 inches (2 m) after 16 years. Males mature at between 12 and 14 years, while females can take up to 20 years. Individual specimens can then go on to live for over 100 years, undertaking numerous spawning migrations during this time.

Old and Worn

As belugas grow and age, several changes in their body features gradually become apparent. In younger specimens the snout is relatively long and pointed, but this sleek profile becomes considerably blunter and broader with time. The fish's body also becomes much heavier and loses most of its youthful streamlined shape. The fins, particularly the tail fin, also become proportionately smaller in relation to the overall body size. Meanwhile the once-perfect and complete lines of bony scutes extending along the fish's flanks become worn down and incomplete as some of the scutes are progressively lost over time and not replaced.

Caviar Wars

The beluga, along with the two other main caviar-producing species, the Russian sturgeon, or osetra (*Acipenser gueldenstaedti*), and the starred, sevruga, or stellate sturgeon (*A. stellatus*), occurs in the Caspian Sea. Prior to 1991 the Caspian Sea fishery was controlled by the two main caviar producers in the world, the Soviet Union and Iran. Strict management ensured that supplies were guaranteed, and the three sturgeon species enjoyed a respectable level of protection, ensuring their survival.

Among the measures employed was the prohibition of fishing for sturgeon while they were still at sea. This was a crucial part of the conservation program, since maturity is attained during the marine phase of a sturgeon's life (which can be up to 30 years) before it embarks on its first spawning migration into fresh water.

Following the dissolution of the Soviet Union, however, the Caspian Sea coastline acquired three new states: Azerbaijan, Kazakhstan, and Turkmenistan. As a result, the sturgeons living along the coastline have lost much of the protection that they enjoyed during the period of centralized control.

The consequences have been catastrophic for the beluga and its relatives. One of the most serious direct threats comes from poaching along the former Soviet coastline (Iran still maintains strict state control along its own coastline). Economic crises in the region have led to a growth of illegal fishing activities that so far have proved impossible to eradicate.

An indication of the escalating problem in the area can be gained from the numbers of poachers detained by the authorities: 248 in 1994, 280 in 1995, and 623 in 1996. Yet the detention of poachers does not signal success, since it is reported that corruption among river guards responsible for protecting the Volga Delta region is also on the increase. The damaging effects of poaching are also increased by the fishing methods employed, which take fish indiscriminately. They therefore remove not just mature specimens of both sexes but also immature ones, reducing the reproductive potential of future generations.

The situation has now deteriorated to the point at which there is grave concern for the survival of all Caspian sturgeons. Among the measures being taken are temporary fishing bans imposed by the Convention in International Trade in Endangered Species (CITES), along with a compulsory survey of sturgeon stocks, the setting up of strict quotas from 2002, and the implementation of a coordinated management program for all stocks.

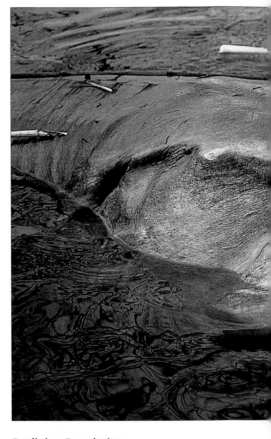

Declining Populations

The beluga has suffered badly from overfishing and from trying to survive in progressively deteriorating habitats. As a result, it is no longer common, and some populations are critically endangered. At least one population (the Italian one) is now believed to be extinct.

Many of the threats to beluga populations can be traced to offshore exploration for oil, which has both direct and indirect effects on the marine environment. They include the physical disruption of the habitat by drilling activities and the laying of pipes for the transport of oil and natural gas, the expansion of oil-allied industries, and unchecked urban growth at oil terminals, with its accompanying problems of sewage production and disposal.

Another threat to the beluga and its relatives is the rapid expansion of factories along the coasts of the former Soviet Union. It is estimated, for example, that well over 1,000

Some idea of the colossal size of the beluga can be gained from this picture of a specimen caught in the Volga Delta region of the Caspian Sea. Beluga are now becoming rare in this region owing to poaching.

new manufacturing outlets have been constructed in Kazakhstan alone. The polluting effects of these industries have added significantly to the already serious pollution problems suffered by the area.

Damming of rivers is also considered a serious threat, since it deprives the beluga of suitable spawning grounds. Even worse, it appears that restocking rivers with breeding belugas has not been possible in recent years in Russia, owing to a scarcity of wild broodstock.

New Targets

The chain reaction effect of beluga declines—and dwindling populations of Russian (*Acipenser gueldenstaedti*) and starred sturgeons (*A. stellatus*) as well—is that other species not normally harvested for caviar are now targeted and their eggs passed off as high-grade caviar. This practice has been confirmed by a test that permits the accurate identification

of a sturgeon species through an analysis of the molecular structure of its eggs. The technique makes it possible to spot cases in which more endangered species are being sold under the name of less endangered ones, thus helping control illegal trade. Vadim Birstein, a scientist who helped develop the test, was also the first chairman of the sturgeon specialist group set up in 1994 to study the status of sturgeon species in the wild. It was as a consequence of this that all sturgeons are now recognized as facing some form of threat in the wild.

The beluga is not considered to be in such extreme danger as the Baltic sturgeon (*Acipenser sturio*) or the short-nosed sturgeon (*A. brevirostrum*). Unlike them, therefore, it is not on CITES Appendix I, which virtually forbids all trade. Nevertheless, it has been on CITES Appendix II since 1998, along with all other sturgeons: a listing that still allows for controlled, monitored trade.

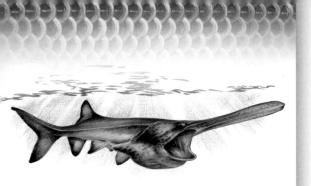

American Paddlefish

Polyodon spathula

*The American paddlefish is the freshwater counterpart of the marine basking shark (*Cetorhinus maximus*): a gentle giant that feeds exclusively on vast numbers of tiny animals.*

Common name American paddlefish

Scientific name *Polyodon spathula*

Family   Polyodontidae

Order   Acipenseriformes

Size   Can attain more than 6.6 ft (2 m) in length and over 100 lb (45 kg) in weight; females larger than males

Key features Body elongate and sharklike with unique "paddle" accounting for a third of total length; cavernous mouth; coloration: slate-gray above, often mottled, shading to lighter tones below

Breeding   Spawns in April and May, producing up to 750,000 large eggs that hatch in about 1 week; fry free-swimming from the outset

Diet   Small drifting invertebrates (zooplankton) and insect larvae

Habitat   Slow-flowing waters such as oxbow lakes and backwaters more than 4 ft (1.2 m) deep

Distribution North America mainly in Missouri River basin and Gulf slope drainage

Status   Designated Vulnerable by IUCN; CITES Appendix II

VARIOUSLY KNOWN ALSO AS THE shovelfish, spadefish, spoonbill, duck-billed cat, shovel-billed cat, or spoonbill cat, the American paddlefish is one of the oddest-looking of all freshwater fish. It is also a big animal that can grow to over 6 feet (1.8 m) long, with an appetite to match. However, it does not hunt down large prey. Instead, it feeds by swimming through swarms of tiny living organisms called plankton with its huge mouth gaping open, and filtering them from the water with its sievelike gill rakers.

The "paddle," or rostrum, accounts for almost a third of the fish's body length and has long been thought to play an important role during feeding. One possibility—especially taking into account its many sensory cells—is that it helps the fish detect and target its food. It could also act as some form of stabilizer when the paddlefish is feeding with its cavernous mouth open, especially against a current. However, paddlefish that have lost the rostrum through injury still manage to feed adequately, so its true role is still uncertain.

Ancient Relationships

Fossil evidence shows that paddlefish have been around since the days of the dinosaurs, so the species can be regarded as a "living fossil." As in sharks, the skeleton is composed of cartilage rather than bone, except for the jaw. The skin is virtually without scales, and the jaw is toothless—but only in adults; young paddlefish have numerous tiny teeth that they gradually lose as they grow. A more obvious difference between juveniles and adults is that juveniles are born without a paddle.

⊖ *The "paddle" of the paddlefish is peppered with sensory cells that may help it detect prey, including a battery of electroreceptors that may be sensitive to the electrical nerve impulses of other animals.*

Paddlefish spawn in spring when the water reaches temperatures of about 55°F (13°C). Each female can produce around 7,500 eggs per pound (450 gm) of body weight, and the large eggs hatch in about a week.

Threats to Survival

Paddlefish were once common in their native waters. However, habitat alteration and pollution have destroyed many of their feeding and spawning areas, and they have also been hit by overfishing. The sharpest decline owing to overfishing occurred during the 1980s, when paddlefish were poached for their caviar to make up for a drop in supplies of sturgeon caviar from Iran, which was at war at the time.

Where the paddlefish is still relatively abundant, it can now be fished on a strict quota basis, which will hopefully conserve natural stocks. Alongside these protective measures, a number of hatchery-based programs initiated since the early 1990s are now producing thousands of juveniles for restocking both existing paddlefish waters and regions such as Pennsylvania, where the species has become locally extinct. Tagging these hatchery juveniles is also leading to a greater understanding of the habits of this fascinating fish, although it will be many years before we know how successfully the restocked fish are breeding in the wild.

Alligator Gar *Atractosteus spatula*

The broad-snouted alligator gar is the giant of its family, as big as an alligator and with a voracious appetite to match.

Common name Alligator gar

Scientific name *Atractosteus spatula*

Family Lepisosteidae

Order Semionotiformes

Size Up to 10 ft (3 m)

Key features Sturdy, cylindrical body with short, round-tipped, broad snout; head resembles that of an alligator when viewed from above; ganoid body scales; "abbreviated heterocercal" tail

Breeding In spring and summer; few details available

Diet Wide range of fish (including other gars), waterfowl, and crustaceans

Habitat Slow-moving backwaters of large rivers, pools, lakes, swamps, and bayous; mainly found in fresh water but occasionally in brackish water or even sea

Distribution From Mississippi basin in southwestern Ohio and southern Illinois southward to Gulf of Mexico from extreme northwest Florida westward to Veracruz in Mexico

Status Not threatened

A FULLY MATURE ALLIGATOR GAR is a hugely impressive fish, and when viewed from above, it certainly lives up to its name. Its relatively short, broad, round-tipped snout gives its head a distinct resemblance to an alligator's head, and it can grow to a truly immense size that is comparable with that of a medium-sized alligator. Add to this its ferociously predatory habits, and its name seems very appropriate.

The alligator gar feeds mainly on fish and crustaceans. Its taste for other fish has resulted in the species being regarded as a menace by many fishers, who accuse the alligator gar of decimating stocks of game fish and even waterfowl (it is reported to be fond of ducks). However, detailed studies of its feeding behavior have shown that the majority of fish species taken are not the game fish that are targeted by human fishers but other types. Nevertheless, the alligator gar is an opportunist hunter that inevitably eats some game fish— including other gars.

There is even a report in an 1820 book by Constantine Rafinesque in which he refers to a struggle between an alligator gar and a five-foot (1.5-m) alligator. The fight apparently ended with the gar cutting the alligator in two and subsequently swallowing it.

Like other gars, it prefers to hang in the water close to the surface and take prey from the upper and middle layers. However, it will also hunt along the bottom, seizing fish and crustaceans, including crabs, and scavenging any scraps lying on the riverbed.

Migrant Breeder

Spawning occurs from midspring to early summer and includes an upriver migration. Few details are available of its breeding biology,

although it is believed to be similar to that of the longnose gar (*Lepisosteus osseus*).

If so, then a single female may spawn with one or more males in a depression that she will have dug in the bottom, laying many thousands of eggs. A large longnose gar is believed to be capable of producing in excess of 77,000 eggs; and since the alligator gar can grow to a much greater size, it can probably produce a lot more eggs. The sticky eggs are heavier than water, so they sink to the bottom, where they are abandoned. Hatching may take a week or more, and the larvae, which are also sticky, remain in the vicinity of the nest until they use up all their yolk.

Once they absorb their yolk, the young gars embark on their predatory careers, taking small aquatic insects and other invertebrates before graduating to small fish. During the early days, and throughout their juvenile phase, alligator gars are themselves eaten by other predatory fish.

This species is also preyed on by humans, particularly in the southern states, where its flesh is prized, and where a small-scale commercial fishery exists for both the alligator gar and the longnose gar. The eggs of many garfish are poisonous, however, and must always be carefully removed from any fish that are to be eaten.

⊕ *Hanging beneath the surface of a pool in the Everglades National Park, Florida, a group of alligator gars lie in wait for anything edible that may swim within range.*

Other *Atractosteus* Species

Common Name	Scientific Name	Size	Habitat
Cuban gar	A. tristoechus	6.6 ft (2 m)	Fresh water
Tropical gar	A. tropicus	49 in (1.25 m)	Fresh water

Bowfin

Amia calva

The bowfin is an adaptable survivor that can live in hostile conditions that would be lethal to most other fish. This has allowed it to colonize a wide range of habitats throughout the eastern U.S.

LIKE MANY OF THE PRIMITIVE FISH, the bowfin has a highly evolved talent for survival. At times, for example, a bowfin can find itself trapped in warm, shallow, and oxygen-deficient water, a situation that would kill most other fish. The bowfin, however, can use its swim bladder as a form of lung. It can take gulps of air at the water surface, draw the air into its swim bladder, and absorb the oxygen into the surrounding network of blood vessels.

In extreme circumstances the fish may go a stage further and burrow into the bottom mud, where it enters a state of torpor, or estivation, rather like that of lungfish. Farmers working land that has been recently uncovered by receding floodwater have even reported plowing up bowfins that have taken refuge in the mud.

Primitive Features

The bowfin has a number of other features that mark it out as a primitive fish. Its skull has a double layer consisting of bone on the outside and cartilage inside. Its skeleton is part bone and part cartilage. Its relatively normal looking tail is actually heterocercal, with the vertebral column extending into the upper lobe in the manner of other primitive fish. Despite such features, however, the bowfin is more advanced than the gars. For example, gars have thick, nonoverlapping ganoid scales, but the bowfin has thinner, overlapping cycloid scales like those of the "modern" bony fish.

Feeding and Breeding

Bowfins prey on a wide variety of animals, including other fish, crayfish, snakes, turtles, leeches, and even rodents. Young bowfins

① Although many of its anatomical features are those of primitive fish, the bowfin has evolved advanced breeding behavior that includes defending its eggs and young against potential predators such as bass and sunfish.

Common name Bowfin

Scientific name *Amia calva*

Family   Amiidae

Order   Amiiformes

Size   Up to 43 in (1.1 m) long and 9 lb (4 kg) in weight

Key features Large head with 2 forward pointing barbels on snout; sturdy cylindrical body with long-based dorsal fin with some 48 rays; cycloid scales; "abbreviated heterocercal" tail

Breeding   In spring; male builds circular matted depression up to 24 in (61 cm) across; female lays up to 30,000 eggs that hatch in 8–10 days; eggs and young defended by male for up to 4 months

Diet   Worms, crustaceans, fish, reptiles, and small mammals; juveniles eat plankton and aquatic insects

Habitat   Lakes, still and slow-moving waters, including swamps; usually near vegetation

Distribution Widespread in eastern North America

Status   Not threatened

cannot tackle such large prey, so they target aquatic insects and their larvae and a variety of planktonic crustaceans.

During the spring spawning season each male migrates to shallow water to construct a nest consisting of a circular depression in the river or lake bed up to 24 inches (61 cm) across. The nests are often constructed close to tree roots or submerged logs, and they are vigorously defended by their builders, each of which may spawn with several females.

A single female can lay up to 30,000 eggs. Hatching takes eight to 10 days, and throughout the incubation period they are defended by the male. After hatching, the young fish form shoals that are protected by the male for several months. Growth is relatively slow, and the fish may not become mature until they are three to five years old.

False-eyed Juveniles

Adult bowfins tend to be dark and drab, but near the base of the top tail fin rays there is a faded eyespot consisting of a black spot surrounded by a yellow to orange halo. This spot is often so indistinct that it is barely visible.

In juvenile bowfins, however, both the eyespot and the halo are brilliantly colored. They stand out beautifully against the duller surrounding colors, forming a "false eye" like that found in many other fish. It acts as a protective feature, since it is believed to draw a predator's attention away from the fish's head. If a juvenile bowfin loses its tail fin as a result of such an attack, the fin may regrow; but if it loses an eye, the consequences would be much more severe. It could even lead to the fish's eventual death from starvation because it would be unable to hunt.

Dragon Fish *Scleropages formosus*

In the Far East the dragon fish is believed to bring health, wealth, and luck to its owners. It is much sought after, and huge sums are paid for the best-quality specimens.

THE DRAGON FISH IS MUCH REVERED by communities of Far Eastern origin based in every corner of the globe. Many western aquarists are also very interested in it, but both its large size and the high prices that adult specimens can command place the dragon fish beyond the reach of most enthusiasts.

The most prized of all are fish with red coloration, but at least two other color forms of the species are known to occur in nature: the silver or green dragon fish and the gold dragon fish. Most of the populations known from Malaysia are of either gold or green-silver dragon fish, while most of the native dragon fish of Indonesia are gold or red. Variations, however, exist within each of the three broad categories, with some types, such as the Sumatran red dragon fish, having a broad dark band along the back. "White" or "black" dragon fish are also occasionally reported from the wild.

Common name Dragon fish

Scientific name *Scleropages formosus*

Subfamily Osteoglossinae

Family Osteoglossidae

Order Osteoglossiformes

Size Up to 35 in (89 cm); usually smaller

Key features Compressed, torpedo-shaped body with pointed head; large eyes and mouth; 2 chin barbels; body covered in large, stout scales; 3 main wild color forms: red, gold, and green or silver

Breeding July–December; 30–90 eggs incubated in mouth of male for 5–6 weeks

Diet Wide range of invertebrates and small vertebrates

Habitat Still or slow-flowing, often turbid or heavily vegetated waters

Distribution Cambodia, Laos, Vietnam, peninsular Malaysia, Philippines, Indonesia (Kalimantan and Sumatra); introduced to Singapore

Status Listed as Endangered by IUCN; CITES Appendix I

The species has also been bred in captivity for many years, producing several color varieties, including one with iridescent scales, sometimes known as the rainbow dragon. None of these varieties, however, can match the value of deep red dragon fish, which can cost many thousands of dollars each.

During the juvenile stages the sexes are almost impossible to tell apart. Once they mature at a length of 18 to 24 inches (45–61 cm), they can be distinguished, but only with difficulty and a lot of experience. Males are slightly slimmer than females, but they have slightly larger mouths. The skin on the chin of a male may also be a little more wrinkled, indicating that this area can be extended to form a nursery pouch for brooding the eggs and young fish.

Surface Feeders

Dragon fish are basically predators on small animals, taking a wide variety of prey ranging from small planktonic crustaceans and aquatic insect larvae to small fish. They feed mainly at or near the surface of still or slow-flowing waters, but like their relatives the arowanas, they have been known to leap up and snatch animals from overhanging vegetation.

Caring Fathers

Dragon fish mature during their third or fourth year, generally spawning for the first time at four years old. Breeding can occur throughout the year, but is at its peak between July and December. Actual mating is preceded by a long period of courtship and bonding that can last two or three months. Each female typically lays some 30 eggs with large yolks, although over 90 have been reported. The male fertilizes the eggs and then picks them up in his mouth. He then broods the eggs for five to six weeks before releasing them, by which time the fry may be nearly 3.5 inches (9 cm) long.

Endangered or Not?

The dragon fish is classified as Endangered by the World Conservation Union because of fear for its continued survival in the wild owing to presumed overcollection. However, the species seems to be quite numerous in parts of Malaysia, and it is possible that the danger of extinction in the wild may be receding.

The red form of the dragon fish is a color variation that occurs naturally in Indonesia, but it is also highly valued by aquarists.

Atlantic Tarpon

Megalops atlanticus

While ranking as the heaviest of all eels, superficially tarpons appear to have little in common with this group. They seem more closely related to other large marine fish sought by sports fishermen, such as tuna or marlin.

Common name Atlantic tarpon

Scientific name *Megalops atlanticus*

Family Megalopidae

Order Elopiformes

Size Up to 8.25 ft (2.5 m)

Key features Elongated, flattened body shape; large eyes; lower jaw extends forward from behind eyes; well-forked caudal fin with a threadlike projection on last ray of dorsal fin; large silvery scales with a slight metallic blue coloration over the back; small, sharp teeth throughout oral cavity; active, lively fish, often congregating in groups where food supply is plentiful, but not a schooling species; frequently leaps out of water

Breeding Spawns in shallow waters; young subsequently develop in brackish or even fresh water. Onset of sexual maturity relatively slow

Diet Carnivorous; primarily fish and cephalopods

Habitat Reef-associated; in fresh, brackish or marine waters; older tarpon sometimes found in rivers

Distribution Western Atlantic, mainly in tropical seas from North Carolina down to Brazil; occasionally recorded farther north up to Nova Scotia; also eastern Atlantic from Senegal to Angola, exceptional occurrences in Portugal, the Azores, and France's Atlantic coast

Status Not under immediate threat

ATLANTIC TARPON ARE BROAD-BODIED IN APPEARANCE, with the typical fin arrangements associated with fish occurring in the open ocean. However, their history reveals that they have an ancient lineage in the fossil record, extending back to the Upper Cretaceous around 130 million years ago. Tarpon enjoyed a widespread distribution then, with their remains having been unearthed in parts of present day Asia, Africa, and Europe. Tarpon still retain one of the key indicators of an ancient ancestry, having so-called "gular plates," which lie between the sides of the lower jaw, close to the skin. This is an anatomical feature that has essentially disappeared from fish of more recent origin.

Eel-like Reproduction

However, the true indicator of the tarpon's affiliations is its reproductive behavior. Spawning occurs at sea; then the young hatch into ribbonlike leptocephali that retreat back to coastal areas where they develop in swampy mangroves and lagoons. They are able to breathe atmospheric oxygen directly, which helps them survive in what can be poorly oxygenated waters. This ability is also found in adult fish, so that they can survive for surprisingly long periods out of water. This also explains why tarpon will roll at the surface of the water, since this movement is thought to be linked to the fish taking in the air that passes directly to its swim bladder. Oxygen from there can then be absorbed directly into the body, with the swim bladder acting like a lung.

The athleticism of these fish, especially when hooked, reveals that they do have a high oxygen requirement. Like some rays, they often

⊖ *It is not uncommon for schools of large tarpon to move into shallow areas on a regular basis, as here in the Florida Keys. They often frequent the same localities. Few fish have a longer potential lifespan, with tarpon being known to live for over 50 years.*

breach the water surface. They are able to jump 10 feet (3 m) vertically and can leap up to twice as far horizontally. This makes them a dangerous prospect to encounter at close quarters, with several fatalities being directly attributable to tarpon. One man was killed outright by a tarpon in Galveston Bay, Texas. It jumped directly onto the boat in which he was sitting, breaking his neck instantly. Other people have drowned after being knocked unconscious and falling overboard after a similar encounter.

Spawning Grounds

Tarpon are slow-growing fish. It is estimated that they will not attain maturity until they are at least seven years old, and perhaps not until the age of 13. Sexual maturity is attained once they are approximately 4 feet (1.2 m) long. The spawning period extends from May to September in waters off the western coast of Florida. This is when adult fish move into the shallows, often choosing localities around a "cay" (a low island or reef) for spawning. Recoveries of young leptocephali suggest that spawning occurs throughout much of the Caribbean region from Trinidad north to the southern coast of the U.S.

Large female tarpon can be incredibly prolific, producing over 12 million eggs each. Undoubtedly it is this huge reproductive capacity that has enabled these ancient fish to remain relatively common. They are a prime target for fishermen, not just for sport but also as a source of food, with their flesh being highly regarded in South America. In addition, the large, reflective, silvery scales of these fish, measuring up to 3 inches (8 cm) in diameter, are used to make jewelry.

⊕ *Tarpon can be found in poorly oxygenated water, since they are able to gulp atmospheric air directly into their swim bladder, from where it can be absorbed into their bloodstream, rather than having to rely on water flowing over their gills to meet their respiratory needs.*

European eel (*Anguilla anguilla*)

Common name European and American eels

Family Anguillidae

Order Anguilliformes

Number of species 15 in 1 genus

Size Typically up to 3.3 ft (1 m)

Key features Snakelike body; crescentlike gill openings on sides of head, broadening into the base of the relatively large pectoral fin; tiny scales evident on body; complete lateral line extending down both sides of head and body; underside of body lightens from golden yellow to silvery as it matures, with upperparts becoming black; have a strong migratory urge when adult, returning to the sea at this stage; otherwise lives often in slow-flowing stretches of fresh water

Breeding Females lay eggs which hatch into larvae that do not resemble adults

Diet Invertebrates and smaller fish eaten in fresh water

Habitat Young hatch in sea; move to fresh water and return to marine environment to breed themselves (behavior described as "catadromous")

Distribution Widely in much of Europe from the far north down throughout the Mediterranean region (European eel); eastern North America from Labrador down to northern South America (American eel)

Status Both groups are numerous, although numbers have declined significantly in some areas

⊕ *The 4.3-foot (1.3-m) European eel (Anguilla anguilla) occurs in fresh water in Europe and North Africa, as well as on North Atlantic coasts from Iceland to North Africa and the Mediterranean and Black Seas.*

European and American Eels
Anguillidae

The breeding cycle of European eels has been a source of mystery over the centuries. The ancient Greek writer Aristotle even suggested that they formed from slime, since the ovary of these fish was inconspicuous when they were caught in fresh water.

LATER IT WAS BELIEVED THAT HORSE hairs, which fell into water, were miraculously transformed into young eels. Even today there are various important aspects of their reproductive biology that have yet to be clearly elucidated.

The first step toward unraveling their remarkable reproductive cycle began in 1763, when an eel larva (called a "leptocephalus") was caught in the sea off the coast of North Wales close to the port of Holyhead. Quite unlike an adult eel in appearance, thanks to its tiny head and ribbonlike, transparent body, it was presumed to be a new species of fish at that time. The suggestion that it could really be an immature eel was not seriously considered until the late 19th century; this was finally confirmed in 1896, when two of these leptocephali, which had been caught relatively close to the Italian coast, completed their metamorphosis into eels in an aquarium.

A major clue to the breeding habits of European eels (*Anguilla anguilla*) came from observing the determination of these fish to go back to the sea, even traveling overland under cover of darkness for part of the journey if necessary. A mature female showing ovarian development was caught at this stage in the Mediterranean Sea off the Straits of Messina that separate Sicily from the Italian mainland. This suggested that breeding took place not in fresh water but in the sea. The belief arose that the spawning grounds for these eels were likely to lie somewhere in the deeper part of the Mediterranean Sea, but in spite of intensive searching, no such locality could be found.

⊙ *At the end of its growth period—9 to 20 years for females, 6 to 12 years for males—the European eel (*Anguilla anguilla*) becomes sexually mature and will travel overland at night in its determination to get to the sea, where it can inhabit deep waters.*

The Sargasso Sea

The mystery of where European eels probably spawned was finally resolved in the early 1920s, using a technique that had been developed for tracking the breeding grounds of cod. Johannes Schmidt, a Danish oceanographer, had previously traced this locality by plotting the sizes of the young fish in plankton samples, concluding that the smallest ones occurred closest to where spawning took place. Applying this technique to the leptocephali of European eels led back to an area lying to the east of the Caribbean—called the Sargasso Sea—located between 20 and 30 degrees N and 48 to 65 degrees W. Further study reveals that conditions in the Sargasso Sea are peculiarly favorable to spawning at depth. The water temperature here is stable, at around 68° F (20° C), warmer at lower levels than elsewhere in the Atlantic.

When Schmidt's method was applied to the American eel (*A. rostrata*), similar results were obtained, confirming that both species bred in

Magnetic Pull

The way in which eels navigate across such remarkable distances —typically traveling perhaps over 4,000 miles (6,400 km) each way in the case of European eels—is still not understood fully. It has been suggested that a rise in water temperature could guide them; but although that might apply to eels originating from British waters, those coming from the Mediterranean would not be able to rely on the same method, since the waters in this region are naturally warmer than would be encountered while crossing the Atlantic.

Eels are also remarkably unresponsive to changes in water salinity, as befits a species moving from salt to fresh water and back again to the marine environment to spawn. They are, therefore, unlikely to rely on salinity changes for navigational purposes. The only other evident physical feature that might act as a guide is the water pressure itself, which obviously increases at greater depths. But here again there are marked discrepancies around the shores of Europe, so that pressure could not serve as a universal guide either. It is much more likely, therefore, that the earth's magnetic field provides the basis for the navigational feats of these eels, whether they are heading from Europe or America to the Sargasso Sea.

the same area. However, the breeding grounds of the American eel lie slightly farther west in the Sargasso Sea, lessening the possibility of coming into contact with their European cousins. Furthermore their breeding period starts earlier, which helps to reduce the possibility of hybridization.

The leptocephali of American eels also develop faster so they complete their journey more quickly, disproving the idea that American and European eels are variants of the same species. There is also an anatomical distinction between these two types of eel. European eels have a body incorporating 115 vertebrae, but the spinal column of the American eel is made up of just 108 of these bones.

The mass migration of eels from Europe's shores, on a journey that requires them to swim for up to 50 miles (80 km) a day, occurs mainly between August and December. Catches of eels returning to the sea at this stage are huge; for example, an eel fishery on Lake Comacchio in Italy reportedly caught around 250,000 fish, weighing just over 322 tons (292 tonnes), on one night in October 1697. While such massive hauls are not made today, the weight of eels caught in some areas during this spawning rush can still be very large; fishermen on Ireland's Bann River made nighttime catches of nearly 40 tons (36 tonnes) in the late 1900s.

The phase of the moon may play a critical role in this mass migration, because eels will move only at night and never when the moon is waxing. How they detect this is a mystery yet to be solved in the field of eel research. If their path is blocked, the migratory instincts of eels are so strong that they will emerge onto land, traveling a quarter of a mile (0.4 km) or more by slithering over grass and earth, around any obstruction, back to the water.

Considering the huge numbers that head to sea simultaneously, very few eels have ever been caught in the sea. Apparently they do not feed on their journey and so cannot be caught with bait of any kind, while their size and shape enable them to pass through trawler nets. Studies may soon be made by satellite tracking, revealing the precise routes that these eels take

⊕ *The European eel (Anguilla anguilla) will eat virtually anything within its environment, even items living out of water such as worms. Here it is shown consuming a shrimp.*

to their spawning grounds; it is believed their journey lasts for four to seven months on average.

Breeding Behavior

Even less is documented about their breeding behavior once they reach their destination. Amazingly no adult eel has ever been caught in the Sargasso Sea, nor have any eggs been obtained there either, to confirm Schmidt's research. Laboratory studies have not been of great assistance either. Attempts to breed these eels successfully, stimulating females with hormones injected into the body to induce spawning, have yielded some fertilized eggs but no success with regards to hatching live leptocephali of either species of Atlantic eel.

What is known from this research is that in spite of being laid in waters down to a depth of 15,000 feet (4,500 m), the eggs themselves do not sink down into the abyss. Instead, thanks to the presence of a tiny volume of oil in each one, they rise up toward the surface and normally hatch within 48 hours. The young leptocephali then drift in the calm, warm waters of the Sargasso, feeding on plankton.

The major reason for the survival of the species is undoubtedly the female's reproductive capacity; a single individual is able to produce

⊙ Eels are frequently caught when they are migrating and mass together in large numbers. Special traps, as shown here, have been devised to catch these fish.

up to 20 million eggs. Massive numbers of leptocephali will be lost, but in spite of the casualties, enough of these tiny specks of life ultimately end up being carried away alive on the currents back to the estuaries that the previous generation left months beforehand. As for the adults, it is generally assumed that they die on their breeding grounds after spawning, unless they revert to a marine existence, living down in the depths of the Sargasso itself, although this is considered very unlikely.

It takes approximately two and a half years for larval European eels to cross the Atlantic Ocean, conveyed by the Gulf Stream and the North Atlantic Current, to reach their destinations. The importance of the current in aiding the movement of leptocephali is shown by the fact that there are no freshwater eels occurring on the Pacific Coast of North America, in the absence of any equivalent currents there. However, there is a major anomaly in that an object can easily be carried by the current right across the North Atlantic from the east coast of the U.S. to Britain in under a year. Therefore it seems strange that the young eels should take so long to complete their journey.

Mysterious Feeding Habits

Another of the unsolved mysteries of eel migration concerns the feeding habits of the leptocephali. It is thought that they do not feed during their journey, partly because none of them have ever been discovered with food in their bodies. In addition their teeth are pointed forward and attached on the outside of their jaws, which would make it difficult for them to grab prey easily. It appears that the teeth do not function primarily as a means of catching prey but rather as a store of calcium. This mineral is critical during the process of metamorphosis to ensure the healthy development of the fish's skeleton. It has been suggested that leptocephali may be able to absorb nutrients through their mouths, using a mechanism similar to that identified in the leptocephali of conger eels (family Congridae).

young eels still retain a primitive attachment to their breeding grounds, remaining in the area for longer than would otherwise be the case, with the result that this increases the time taken to reach their destination.

When they finally arrive at the edge of the continental shelf, they will remain in this area until they have metamorphosed, altering radically in appearance from leptocephalus to a young elver—the so-called "glass eel"—characterized at this stage by their transparent bodies. Their former broad shape is lost, with the elvers resembling short lengths of string. The young eels seem able to monitor their position here, possibly relying on wave movements for this purpose.

Once their transformation is completed, the elvers then head into coastal areas, moving upstream into freshwater areas. They do not feed during this period and effectively shrink in size. Differences in head shape now start to become apparent. Certain individuals are characterized by their very broad head shape, emphasizing the slender shape of their body, whereas at the other extreme some eels have a much more pointed and narrower snout. This now appears to reflect a natural variance in the population, although in the past it served as a basis for splitting them into different species.

Return of the American Eel

There is little dispute that the American eel is a different species from its European relative, although the breeding grounds of both are located in the Sargasso Sea. It is likely that they developed from a common ancestor. American eels do not wander south of the equator, although they have occasionally been recorded as far north as Greenland. The elvers tend to be most commonly encountered in Canadian waters in the spring, where they head in large numbers, becoming progressively rarer through southern parts of the U.S. because they prefer temperate waters. Their route back from the Sargasso Sea is much shorter than that of their European relative, so they only take about a year to complete their journey.

Eel Fairs

Eels have traditionally been caught as a source of food in Europe for over a millennium, with celebratory eel fairs being a long-standing tradition in various parts of Britain, marking the return of the elvers to the rivers after their sea crossing. They were eaten in huge numbers, as were adult eels. However, they need to be prepared carefully because their blood contains an ichthyotoxin that can be harmful to people if it splashes the eyes or enters the mouth accidentally. The eels have to be cooked thoroughly in order to destroy this toxin. They are still popular as smoked fish and also when preserved in aspic, sold then as jellied eels, a traditional delicacy in the East End district of London.

Remarkable Migration

The Atlantic Ocean has grown significantly in width over the millions of years since these eels first evolved, which could explain how this remarkable migration began. At the outset the distance between their freshwater habitats and marine breeding grounds was short, but gradually this distance has increased, forcing the eels to travel farther. It may be that the

Undulated moray eel (*Gymnothorax undulatus*)

Common name Moray eels

Family Muraenidae

Order Anguilliformes

Number of species About 200 in around 15 genera

Size Largest species recorded up to 10 ft (3 m)

Key features Sharp, pointed teeth to grasp small active prey, with a double row of teeth on pharyngeal bones in most species; much blunter dentition pattern for crushing shells in crab-eating morays; some grow to large size and also may be brightly colored; dorsal and anal fins often prominent, but fins reduced to tip of the tail, fusing with caudal fin, in *Gymnomuraena*; tail and head are similar in length; live in lairs rather than in open; often prefer to hunt at night, grabbing unsuspecting prey venturing within reach

Breeding Undocumented but goes through a leptocephalus phase

Diet Carnivorous

Habitat Relatively shallow waters, usually found in warmer seas associated with reefs; at least 2 species venture into fresh water; only 1 species occurs north of the Mediterranean

Distribution Found in all oceans of the world

Status Generally not uncommon

⤴ The 5-foot (1.5-m) undulated moray eel (Gymnothorax undulatus) *lives on rocky reef flats in the Indo-Pacific from the Red Sea and East Africa to French Polynesia, north to southern Japan and Hawaii, south to Australia's Great Barrier Reef, and east to Costa Rica and Panama.*

Moray Eels

Muraenidae

*This family of eels includes some of the most feared members of the entire group, thanks in part to their appearance. Their number also includes the biggest of all known eels (*Thyrsoidea macrura*), which can attain an adult size of over 10 feet (3 m) in length.*

IN GENERAL, MORAYS ARE CHARACTERIZED by their large mouths, normally equipped with prominent, pointed teeth, which help distinguish them from true anguillids (family Anguillidae). In moray eels the teeth may be directed either forward or backward, with the largest often described as canines thanks to their pointed appearance. Moray eels also have a further double row of teeth in the pharyngeal region at the back of the throat.

They represent a large and diverse group made up of approximately 15 genera and about 200 species, and differing widely in their habits. Some of the larger species, such as the giant moray eel (*Gymnothorax javanicus*) that occurs through much of the Indo-Pacific region from the coast of East Africa and the Red Sea across to Hawaii, can represent a danger to unwary divers. However, like other species, it usually only attacks when surprised or threatened at close quarters, preferring to avoid any confrontation by concealing its presence.

Coral Reef Dweller

Giant morays are one of a number of species found on the world's coral reefs, with their shape allowing them to hide away easily in surprisingly narrow, small crevices. These eels are highly adaptable and will adopt artificial retreats, frequently taking up residence in wrecks where holes can provide them with suitable lairs from which they can ambush passing prey. The gray-face moray eel (*G. thyrsoideus*), whose range in the Indo-Pacific extends from Christmas Island north to the Ryukyu Islands lying close to Japan and southward as far as Tonga, is often found in

➔ *As its name suggests, the giant moray eel (Gymnothorax javanicus) can grow to 10 feet (3 m) long, sometimes attacking divers if threatened. It ranges widely from the East African coast across much of the Pacific.*

Divers' Threat

Attacks are often the result of careless curiosity on the part of divers exploring with their hands cavities where a moray eel is lurking out of sight. In addition, trying to kill a moray with a spear gun is difficult, often only resulting in a relatively minor injury; such attempts frequently provide a common reason why divers are then attacked. It is also worth remembering that many lairs chosen by morays may have more than one entry and exit point. So an eel, having been threatened once, may reemerge and attack unexpectedly from a different hole.

this type of environment on reefs. They often occur in pairs and sometimes significantly larger numbers living in the same area.

Adaptable Nature

Some moray eels do not occur in association with reefs but live in much deeper waters. For example, the type specimen of *G. bathyphilus* was taken at a depth of 820 feet (250 m) off Easter Island in the southeastern Pacific. Conversely a few species occur in estuarine surroundings, while the freshwater moray (*G. polyuranodon*) is unique in that it can be found in rivers up to 19 miles (30 km) from the sea, typically at low altitudes. Its adaptable nature is further revealed by its range, which extends throughout the Indo-Pacific region from Sri Lanka and the Philippines via Indonesia to Fiji and Australia. *Echidna rhodochilus* is another member of the group sometimes found in fresh water; it must be handled very carefully if caught, because it can inflict a painful bite.

Aside from their teeth, moray eels have several more passive ways of defending themselves depending on the individual species. The snakelike appearance of these fish has resulted in some species developing similar patterning to mimic that of deadly sea snakes. They include the harlequin sea eel (*Myrichthys colubrinus*), which ranges through the Indo-Pacific from the Red Sea south to the coast of

◑ The black-and-white striped patterning of the zebra moray eel (Gymnomuraena zebra) helps explain its common name. These eels grow to about 5 feet (1.5 m) and have powerful teeth that allow them to crack the shells of crabs and other crustaceans, which figure prominently in their diet.

Mozambique in southeastern Africa and eastward across to the Society Islands in French Polynesia. This eel is characterized by broad black-and-white bands encircling its body, so that it closely resembles the venomous sea snake (*Laticauda colubrina*) in appearance. This type of mimicry confers a degree of protection, deterring attack by potential predators who fear they would be attacking the reptile rather than an eel. As a result, the harlequin sea eel is more conspicuous, frequently seeking food during the day, swimming over the beds of seagrass and sandy areas that are its natural habitat.

The starry moray (*G. nudivomer*) is protected by a toxic covering of mucus over its body, while the flesh of a number of moray eels is toxic. Various species are frequently caught and sold for food through their range, but eating any of these eels is hazardous.

Although often interpreted as a threat gesture by divers seeing morays for the first time, the way in which these fish open and close their jaws repeatedly, revealing their teeth, is not primarily an aggressive gesture but actually aids the flow of water over the fish's gills so it can continue breathing.

Catching Prey

Fish and crustaceans such as crabs feature prominently in the diets of moray eels, although the techniques used to capture prey vary quite widely. The chain moray (*Echidna catenata*) is a species found in the western Atlantic, present in shallow waters including reefs down to a depth of approximately 39 feet (12 m).

Its remarkable hunting technique has been closely studied in the Brazilian part of its range, in the Fernando de Noronha Archipelago off the northeastern coast. It is well equipped to hunt the crabs that feature prominently in its diet. This species has a short, powerful snout with low, blunt, and frequently flattened teeth in the roof of its mouth, allowing these eels to grab and crush the shells of their prey easily. This is a feature of members of this genus that sets them apart from their other sharp-toothed relatives.

⊕ Although it normally feeds on crustaceans, this spotted moray eel (Gymnothorax moringua) is allowing itself to be groomed by a cleaner shrimp (Lysmata species), which helps keep its skin healthy.

The chain moray frequently hunts crabs out of the water at low tide, both locating and catching them by sight, with individual crabs being pursued for distances of up to 16 feet (5 m), although these eels prefer to ambush their prey whenever possible. These morays can survive without problems out of water for up to half an hour, although they frequently return to rock pools as they explore for food; on average they are successful in about half of their attempts. The biggest crabs that they catch can be over three times as large as the width of the eel's head, so they are impossible to swallow whole, unlike smaller prey. Nevertheless, the eel will tear them apart and crush them in its mouth, usually taking just over a couple of minutes to complete this task.

Helping Each Other

Remarkably moray eels, like many other reef fish, may strike up a close association with cleaner wrasse (*Labroides* species) in a strange association in which the normal rules of predator and prey are forgotten. The wrasse, which could provide an easy meal for a hungry moray, actually removes pieces of food from previous meals lodged in the moray's teeth, as well as nibbling off troublesome parasites that may congregate on its body.

These eels will also tolerate brightly colored cleaner shrimp (*Lysmata* species) living alongside them, which perform a similar task. Both these small fish and crustaceans benefit not just from the food provided by the eels but also from the protection that they confer on their smaller companions.

Sense of Smell

Some of the strangest members of the family are the leaf-nosed morays that form the genus *Rhinomuraena*. These ribbon eels are restricted to the vicinity of the Marshall islands, home to *R. quaesita*, and the islands of Ambon and Banda in Indonesia, where *R. ambonensis* is found. They display particularly striking blue coloration on the head, with a sensory barbel on the nose and three similar projections on the lower jaw.

The most obvious feature is the leaflike projections that are also present on the snout, with their large surface area giving these fish considerable sensory input about their surroundings. They may also contribute to the eel's sense of smell, a quite well-developed characteristic in some members of the group.

The posterior nostrils are located just above and in front of the eyes. In many cases the anterior nostrils take the form of small tubes, while the posterior nostrils opening above or just in front of the eyes are simply circular orifices. However, the arrangement varies since the dragon moray eel (*Muraena pardalis*) has two pairs of tubular openings, with the rear pair longer and looking like horns.

A sense of smell is obviously helpful for detecting prey when largely hidden, although, like most predators, moray eels also have good eyesight. Their sense of smell may also have a reproductive function, helping them locate potential mates. Surprisingly, virtually nothing is known about the breeding habits of moray eels even today, including their spawning behavior or where spawning occurs.

Bacterial Infection

Following a bite from a moray eel, the wound often turns septic. That is partly because of the nature of the bite, which can result in a deep puncture wound. As a consequence, anaerobic bacteria can multiply readily in the wound, resulting in a deep-seated infection. Thorough cleaning of the wound after a bite from one of these eels is a vital precaution to prevent potentially serious complications. Morays do not

⊕ *The unusual mottled coloring of the dragon moray eel (Muraena pardalis), shown here in French Polynesia, helps disguise its presence when it is partially hidden among rocks. It is also called the leopard moray eel because of its distinctive patterning.*

have venomous fangs; it is simply the harmful bacteria present in their mouths that are responsible for the resulting infection.

There is absolutely no truth to stories that once they are clamped onto a limb, these eels will not relinquish their grip. They must open their jaws regularly in order to continue breathing by funneling water through the mouth over the gills.

Similarly, the belief that morays are constrictors probably arose mistakenly from the way in which they behave when hauled out of the water on a baited hook. Using their great power, they will try to free themselves by twisting their bodies into a knot. This technique is more commonly used by the fish to prevent octopuses from grabbing at their bodies as they catch these cephalopods.

The risk of eating moray eels depends on the eel's diet. It is probable that those eels that have regularly caught pufferfish pose the greatest threat. The deadly tetrodotoxin seems to accumulate in the eel's body tissues but has no obvious effect on them.

Unfortunately, if a moray whose body contains this toxin is consumed, muscular problems, loss of sensation, and digestive disturbances are all likely to follow. The toxin itself is not destroyed by cooking the fish.

Truth and Legend

Part of the reputation that moray eels have acquired for savagery stems from the days of ancient Rome, with the generic name *Muraena* commemorating Licinius Muraena, who kept these eels as a reflection of his wealth at the end of the second century B.C. This marked the start of a fashionable trend that attracted the interest of Julius Caesar himself. He borrowed 6,000 morays for a banquet from their owner, Gaius Herrius, during which the guests decorated the fish with gems rather than eating them.

Morays were farmed in Rome as early as 92 B.C. However other people took a more sinister interest in keeping these eels, particularly Vedius Pollo, who fed unwanted slaves to his morays as an entertainment for his guests.

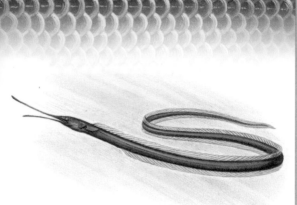

Avocet snipe eel (*Avocettina infans*)

Common name Snipe eels

Family Nemichthyidae

Order Anguilliformes

Number of species 9 in 3 genera

Size Longest species grow to over 3.3 feet (1 m)

Key features Exceedingly slender, long jaws, with upper longer than lower; jaws much shorter in mature males; jaws also diverge along their length; similarly slender body with large eyes; dorsal and anal fins joined with caudal fin; supraoccipital bone absent from skull; others may be as well, including the pterygoid and palatine; inactive, specialized hunter of small invertebrate prey

Breeding Egg laying; spawning is an apparently communal occurrence

Diet Crustaceans; possibly ectoparasites of other fish

Habitat Restricted to marine environment, typically at depths from about 5,250 to 16,400 ft (1,600–5,000 m)

Distribution Widely distributed throughout world's oceans; more common in warmer waters but recorded in the Atlantic as far north as Sable Island Bank off Nova Scotia and between Iceland and the Faeroe Islands

Status Probably not especially rare

 *The 29.3-inch (74.5-cm) avocet snipe eel (*Avocettina infans*) occurs between 165 and 15,000 feet (50–4,570 m) in all oceans north of about 20° S—including the eastern Pacific from Canada's Queen Charlotte Islands down to central Mexico, but excluding the Mediterranean and the eastern equatorial Pacific.*

Snipe Eels

Nemichthyidae

*The characteristic narrow, bill-like mouths of these eels are responsible for their common name. They resemble the bill of the wading bird known as the snipe (*Gallinago gallinago*).*

THIS FAMILY OF EELS IS ANOTHER in which there is marked sexual dimorphism between the sexes once they are mature. It led to adult males being classified as a separate species until their transformation in appearance at this stage was noted. Their jaws shrink dramatically at the onset of maturity, and they develop a short, rather stub-nosed appearance, with a reduced number of teeth in their jaws as well.

Snipe eels are normally found in deep water, but young eels have been observed just 490 feet (150 m) below the surface. Their pattern of dentition is clearly highly specialized and is linked closely with their lifestyle. The entire inside and also the outside of the long jaws of snipe eels are covered with small, backward-pointing teeth. Yet sightings from deep-sea vessels show that these eels are very sedentary in their habits; they lie vertically in the water with their mouths open rather than being active hunters. A study of their stomach contents reveal that deep-sea shrimp form the major component of their diet. It is thought that the long antennae and legs of these shrimp may become wrapped around the teeth, helping the eel secure its prey.

The flexible nature of the snipe eel's jaws help it swallow its prey. Even the jaws of dead specimens can anchor firmly onto a finger. While this highly specialized method of prey capture may not be especially efficient, the likelihood is that snipe eels have a relatively low energy requirement, given their sedentary lifestyle. The shortening of the jaws of males as they mature, combined with the loss of teeth, suggests that they may not live for much longer after this stage. Perhaps they have only one opportunity to participate in spawning, whereas females may do so several times; but their reproductive biology is not understood.

Different Characteristics

Although members of the genera *Avocettina* and *Labichthys* have between 170 and 220 vertebrae, the figure for *Nemichthys* snipe eels is a remarkable 750 or more of these bones. That is because they have a long caudal filament attached to the end of the body, which may serve a protective function. If the filament is damaged or missing, this suggests that another predatory species may have seized the eel, separating part of the filament without injuring its body. While many snipe eels are found in warmer and temperate waters, their range in the Pacific Ocean may extend farther north—one *Avocettina* specimen (christened *A. gilli*) was caught off the Alaska coast in 1890, the only known example of this species.

⊕ *The long snout of snipe eels (*Nemichthys *species) resembles the bill of a bird and explains their common name. Their large eyes help them see well in relatively gloomy surroundings, which suggests that this sense is important to them.*

Peruvian ancovy (*Engraulis ringens*)

Common name Anchovies

Family Engraulidae

Order Clupeiformes

Number of species About 140 species in 16 genera

Size Up to about 16 in (40 cm) long, but most species much smaller

Key features Small, slender, silvery fish, longer and thinner than herring and rounder in cross section; large snout gives chinless appearance; single, tall dorsal fin halfway along body; symmetrical forked tail; single anal fin; small paired fins; highly gregarious schooling fish; migrate in search of food and spawning areas

Breeding Large, floating, oval eggs produced in spring

Diet Plankton or small prey collected on gill rakers or grasped with small teeth

Habitat Mostly marine in tropical, subtropical, and temperate waters; about 15 percent of all species live in fresh or brackish water

Distribution Atlantic, Pacific, and Indian Oceans and some adjoining seas and rivers

Status Generally not threatened, but many species are fished intensively and need careful monitoring; IUCN lists freshwater anchovy as Data Deficient

⊕ *The 8-inch (20-cm) Peruvian anchovy (Engraulis ringens) occurs in the South Pacific from Peru to Chile at depths between 10 and 260 feet (3–80 m); it stays within 50 miles (80 km) of the coast. The fish is a filter feeder, entirely dependent on the rich plankton found in the Peru Current.*

Anchovies

Engraulidae

These small cousins of herring teem in huge shoals in coastal temperate waters of the Atlantic, Pacific, and Indian Oceans. Their distribution is restricted mainly by temperature, but they can tolerate a wide range of salinities—from almost zero to over 42 percent.

THERE ARE AROUND 140 RECOGNIZED species of anchovy, but they are a remarkably conservative group. Even experts would struggle to tell many of them apart at a glance. All are small fish with a slender, torpedo-shaped body. In most New World species the body is almost cylindrical along much of its length, while their Old World cousins tend to be more compressed, bearing a ridge or keel along the front part of the belly like herring (family Clupeidae).

The snout is long and pointed, and projects beyond the lower jaw. The mouth looks large because the upper jaw bones, or maxillaries, are long. In most species they reach at least most of the length of the head, almost back to the gill covers. In comparison the lower jaw is so small that the fish looks as if it has no chin. The eyes are large and placed well forward on the snout, which gives the fish a very wide field of vision—essential when it comes to scanning their three-dimensional habitat for small prey items.

A shoal of anchovies glitters with light reflected from silvery scales. Most are covered from head to tail in neat, silver, cycloid scales, but in members of several genera the body is largely naked with the skin translucent or dark except for a bold silver stripe along each flank.

Anchovy Schools

Anchovies live in large schools. The sight of a thousand or more slender bodies—flickering silver and moving almost as one—is one of the great spectacles of life in the oceans. The precise means by which such schools coordinate their movements are still not fully understood. Anchovies do not appear to communicate by sound, but this does not mean they are silent.

Experiments with underwater microphones over 40 years ago revealed that fast-moving schools emitted pulses of sound that were most intense when the school was veering from side to side. Idling schools were silent. Apparently the sudden bursts of sound are the result of the shock wave that is generated by hundreds or thousands of fish all flexing their bodies against the water at the same moment.

A Varied Diet

Anchovies hunt by two methods—biting and filter feeding. As a general rule, the larger anchovy species hunt smaller fish, and their teeth tend to be well developed. In other species the teeth are very small or absent entirely, and the fish feed exclusively on tiny planktonic animals for which teeth are not necessary. Several species use both methods depending on the availability and concentration of prey. Filter-feeding anchovies have numerous,

very well-developed gill rakers much like those of herring; they sieve particles of food out of the water that is flowing through the mouth toward the gills. The main prey is copepod crustaceans, but anchovies of all species will diversify their diet if their preferred prey is in short supply. Alternative foods include arrowworms, mysid shrimp, and the larvae of fish, mollusks, and polychaete worms. Most of them are hunted at nighttime, whereas copepods are caught during the daytime.

Spawning Time

As a family, anchovies breed all year round in different parts of the world, but single species and populations are more seasonal. For most species spawning takes place well out to sea in spring or summer. At other times of the year they may migrate inland to search for food. The spawning season is long, and females may spawn many times—in some species up to 20

The Real "Jaws"?

Large upper jawbones are one of the distinguishing characteristics of all anchovies, but nowhere is the feature more extreme than in the whiskered anchovy (*Thryssa setirostris*).

This bizarre little fish has an upper jaw over three times the length of its entire head. The bones of the maxillae grow beyond the edge of the mouth, extending like long, gently curving whiskers. They usually reach as far back as the paired pectoral fins, occasionally as far as the anal fin. Quite what advantage the fish gain from these apparently fragile appendages is difficult to imagine.

⊙ *The European, or northern, anchovy (*Engraulis encrasicolus*) is widespread. This shoal was photographed in the Red Sea around a shipwreck, but the species can occur far north in the eastern Atlantic Ocean because of the warming effect of the Gulf Stream.*

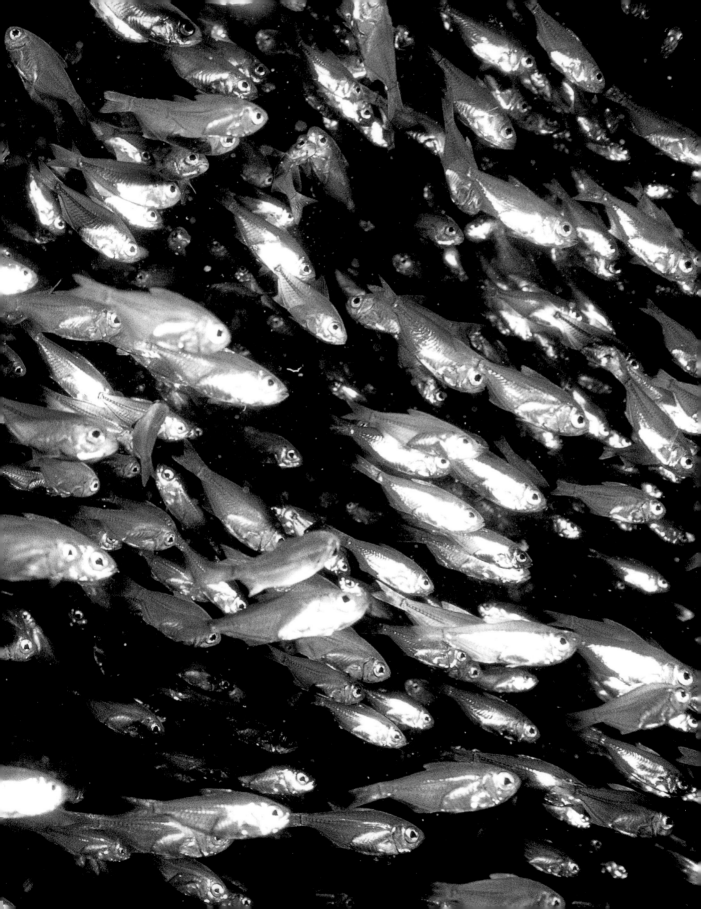

spawnings take place in a single season. Each batch includes a few hundred eggs, and the development and maturation of oocytes in the ovaries goes on almost all year round. The first spawning of the year is triggered by rising sea temperatures.

When the time comes to spawn, schools of anchovies are very large. Males and females spawn simultaneously so that eggs and milt are well mixed in the water. Spawning usually happens in the early part of the night before midnight. This means that the eggs have several hours to disperse under cover of darkness with less risk of the whole batch being eaten by an opportunistic filter feeder. Anchovy eggs are small, transparent, and (unusually for fish eggs) oval in shape. The eggs float close to the surface where the warmth of the sun means the embryos inside develop very quickly.

Anchovy Fisheries

There are major anchovy fisheries in all the world's temperate coastal seas except the northwest Atlantic where the water is too cold to support anchovy stocks. On the European side of the Atlantic the Gulf Stream means that anchovies can live much farther north. In terms of commercial value the most important anchovy species is the Peruvian anchovy (*Engraulis ringens*), which supports the world's largest single-species fishery. Other economically important species are the Argentine anchovy (*E. anchoita*), the northern Pacific anchovy (*E. mordax*), the Japanese anchovy (*E. japonica*), and the European anchovy (*E. encrasicolus*). The ranges of *E. encrasicolus* and *E. japonica* extend as far as western and southern Africa, respectively, and both of these species are fished commercially.

Anchovy fisheries date back at least 1,000 years. Archeologists have found evidence of quite large-scale fishing dating back to the 10th century in places as far apart as Europe and Japan. Often anchovies, sprats, and sardines were fished together, which is still the case in some places today. Sardines (family Clupeidae)

⊕ *A school of European anchovies (Engraulis encrasicolus) being chased by jacks. Anchovies have many predators, but few are as voracious as humans.*

are usually more numerous, but anchovies are more valuable, so pressure on them is greater.

The usual means of capture is in purse-seine nets towed into place by boat and then pulled in from two ends like a giant drawstring bag. Where there are anchovies, there are often commercially important stocks of predators such as mackerel, tuna, hake, and squid. Fishermen have noticed that where these species occur in the same area of the ocean as anchovies, there is distinct vertical stratification. In an effort to stay away from the predators, the anchovies move to shallower depths than they would normally occupy.

Declining Stocks

Anchovy stocks in many parts of the world are in trouble. The status of the European anchovy in the Black Sea is of particular concern. Years of overfishing by Russian and Turkish fleets combined with plagues of comb jellies (*Mnemiopsis leidyi*), which feed on small fish, have decimated stocks. There is evidence that the two subspecies formerly recognized in the region have begun to interbreed once more. Not only will this lead to a reduction in the species' gene pool, it may also mean that future populations will be less well adapted to local conditions.

The majority of the anchovy catch is processed into fish oil, fishmeal, or flavor enhancer for any number of food products. Of the relatively small proportion destined for consumption as whole fish most are preserved by salting. The powerful flavor of preserved anchovies makes them one of those foods that people either love or hate, but even fans of these potent little fish only need to eat small quantities—a small handful of anchovies is enough to flavor a meal for several people.

Humans are not the only animals interested in anchovies. The vast shoals also support an army of other predators, including larger fish, marine mammals, and birds. The population of anchovies that live in the Peruvian Current of the Pacific Ocean not only support a massive fishery, they are also the reason this area has

Anchovies and El Niño

The so-called El Niño Southern Oscillation is a climatic phenomenon that occurs every seven or eight years. During El Niño events prevailing warm winds in the South Pacific reverse their usual movements and disrupt the normal pattern of ocean currents. The result is a warming of usually cold waters off western South America. Carryover climatic effects are felt all around the world, most especially in the Southern Hemisphere.

In a normal year Peruvian fishermen haul up to 14.3 million tons (13 million tonnes) of anchovy from the productive waters of the eastern Pacific. In El Niño years the hugely productive conditions normally caused by the cold water of the Peruvian Current welling up against the continental shelf simply disappear, and stocks of anchovy are reduced to practically nothing. The shortage is disastrous for the local fisheries. It was Peruvian fishermen who first noted the El Niño phenomenon; because the effects were usually first noticed around Christmas, they named it El Niño, from the Spanish for "Christchild."

some of the world's greatest populations of seabirds. They include penguins, shearwaters, gulls, and terns, but the three most important bird predators are cormorants, pelicans, and gannets. These three species depend almost entirely on anchovies for food and are themselves economically important for the production of "guano." Guano is a concentrated mineral deposit formed from the droppings of seabirds deposited on islands and headlands along the coast of Peru, and it is collected in huge quantities for use as fertilizer. It is estimated that the birds create about 1.1 ton (1 tonne) of fertilizer for every 8.8 tons (8 tonnes) of fish consumed—comparable to the efficiency with which industrial fish-processing plants convert fish to fishmeal.

It is estimated that the total catch of Peruvian anchovies by fishermen and birds combined is around 4.4 million tons (4 million tonnes) a year. This amounts to about one-seventh of the world's annual catch, and it all comes from a strip of ocean just 800 miles (1,300 km) long by 30 miles (50 km) wide.

Common name Barbel (European barbel)

Scientific name *Barbus barbus*

Subfamily Cyprininae

Family Cyprinidae

Order Cypriniformes

Size Up to a maximum of 40 in (1.2 m) and weight of 26.5 lb (12 kg) but usually smaller

Key features Pointed snout; underslung mouth with 2 pairs of fleshy barbels; thick lips; scaleless head; smallish eyes set high on sides of head; elongated body, almost cylindrical in cross-section; back slightly curved, but belly flat; all fins well formed; adipose fin absent; greenish-brown coloration on back, turning to golden along the sides

Breeding Spawning from late spring through summer, following short upstream migration to gravelly areas; up to 50,000 sticky, yellowish, poisonous eggs may be scattered over the bottom and abandoned; hatching takes 10–15 days

Diet Bottom-living invertebrates (especially the larvae of two-winged insects), algae, and detritus; may also take small fish

Habitat Flowing rivers with sandy or gravelly bottoms; also found in pools

Distribution From central and eastern England through France and eastward through Europe to Russia; absent from Scandinavia, Ireland, Denmark, and the Iberian Peninsula (populations present in Spain and Morocco are from introduced stocks)

Status Not threatened

European Barbel

Barbus barbus

This is a powerful fish of fast-flowing waters, feeling for food on the bottom with the sensory barbels that give the species its common name.

THE POWER OF THIS FISH, coupled with its relatively large size, make it popular with sport fishermen who seek it out in fast-flowing rivers and weirs.

"Selective" Distribution

Although this species is called the European barbel, it is not native to every country in Europe. For example, it is absent from Italy, Spain, Portugal, and parts of Scandinavia such as Denmark.

Like many large cyprinid species such as carps, the barbel has been introduced into several locations outside its natural range, which extends from England eastward through Europe to Russia. Thus, for example, it was introduced into Lago Banyoles in Catalonia around 1910 and to Morocco from 1926.

Protective Colors

Barbel are bottom-dwelling fish with generally dull coloration. The fins visible from above—the dorsal, pectorals, and caudal—are dark, while the anal and pelvics, only visible from the side, are yellowish-orange. The sides of the body are much lighter than the back.

This coloration and patterning offers barbels two survival advantages: Since they tend to inhabit relatively deep water, they are difficult to spot from the air; from the side, though, they can make themselves visible to other members of the species.

Interestingly, juvenile specimens, which tend to inhabit areas of shallower water often with a gravelly or pebbly bottom, have irregular spotting on the body. This, too, acts as camouflage against attacks from kingfishers, herons, and other fish-eating birds.

⊕ *Well camouflaged from above, the European barbel combs the riverbed for food with its barbel sensors.*

Genetic Double Act

Most fish have their genetic information—the codes that determine everything from shape, color, and even behavior—contained in about 50 tiny structures called chromosomes found in their cell nuclei (see Glossary). At some stage during barbel evolution a fundamental change occurred, as a result of which the number of chromosomes was doubled to 100. This means that each nucleus contains twice as much genetic material.

The doubling of the chromosome number has also been found in two of the European barbel's closest relatives, the Mediterranean, or southern, barbel (*B. meridionalis*), from southern France, northern Spain, Italy, and parts of the Danube basin, and the Po barbel (*B. plebejus*), from Italy, Dalmatia, and Sicily.

Chromosome doubling also occurs in the goldfish (*Carassius auratus auratus*).

Other European Barbels

Although *B. barbus* is known as the European barbel, it is not the only European species in the genus—although it is the only one found in the British Isles. As well as the southern or Mediterranean barbel and the Po barbel there are also several other European species.

The Greek barbel (*B. graecus*) is found in only two lakes: Paralimni and Yliki; it is also found in the Sperchios River. The Euboean barbel, or Petropsaro (*B. euboicus*), is also Greek. It occurs only on the island of Euboea and is listed by the World Conservation Union as Critically Endangered. *Barbus albanicus* is native to Greece and Albania, hence its name. *B. caninus* is found in Italy and Switzerland, while the Turkish, or Thracian, barbel (*B. cyclolepis*) is found not just in Turkey but in surrounding countries as well. The Caucasian barbel (*B. ciscaucasicus*) occurs in the rivers flowing into the Caspian Sea.

The Caspian barbel (*B. brachycephalus*) is unusual not only for its size (up to a maximum of 3.9 feet /1.2 m), but because it occurs in salt water in the Caspian and Aral Seas.

Other European species include the Peloponnesian barbel (*B. peloponnesius*), the Briána (*B. prespensis*) from Albania, Greece, and Macedonia, *B. sclateri* from Portugal and Spain, and *B. tyberinus* from Italy.

Under Threat

The Iberian barbel (*B. comizo*), *B. microcephalus*, from Spain and Portugal, the Mediterranean barbel (*B. guiraonis*), the red-tailed barbel (*B. haasi*), both from Spain, and *B. steindachneri*, from Portugal, are officially listed as Vulnerable. There is, however, a second Iberian barbel (*B. bocagei*), subdivided into several subspecies, which is not on the official World Conservation Union Red List.

Common Carp

Cyprinus carpio carpio

Carp can be extremely longlived fish. The maximum recorded age for a common carp is 47 years.

Common name Common carp (European carp, koi)

Scientific name *Cyprinus carpio carpio*; there are also several naturally occurring varieties regarded as subspecies

Subfamily Cyprininae

Family Cyprinidae

Order Cypriniformes

Size Up to around 4 ft (1.2 m) or more in length and a weight of around 82 lb (37.3 kg) but usually smaller

Key features Heavy-bodied fish; fully scaled body; scaleless head with underslung mouth bearing 2 pairs of barbels; well-formed fins; coloration variable but usually greenish-brown on back fading to yellowish-creamish along belly; ornamental varieties exhibit wide range of colors

Breeding Season extends from spring into summer; over 1,660,000 sticky eggs scattered among vegetation in shallow water; no parental care; hatching takes 5–8 days

Diet Wide-ranging, including vegetation, bottom-living invertebrates, and insects

Habitat Wide range of habitats, particularly larger, slow-flowing or still bodies of water; can tolerate some salt in water; preferred temperature range 37–95° F (3–35° C)

Distribution From its initial central Asian origins the species is now found almost worldwide

Status Although the species *C. carpio* is under no threat of extinction, some populations in a number of countries, for example Austria, Hungary, and Romania, are regarded as Critically Endangered; main causes are decreases in range and decline in habitat quality caused by pollutants and other environmental factors

THE COMMON CARP IS A LARGE, heavy-bodied fish that originated in Central Asia, east of the Caspian Sea. From there, it spread eastward into the Manchurian region of China during the later glaciations of the Ice Age. Then it began spreading naturally westward to the Danube basin and the Black and Aral Seas.

This species is probably the first fish to have been introduced outside its native range by humans. The Romans may have been the first to begin the process, with fish being removed from the Danube and released elsewhere in Europe during the 1st to 4th centuries AD. The fish were usually introduced and cultured for human consumption.

The pace of introductions was irregular for many centuries but picked up during the 20th century, to the extent that the common carp in its various forms is now found virtually throughout the world, except where environmental conditions are too severe for it. This "redistribution" has been so thorough, and the species is found in such numbers, especially throughout Europe, that many people believe the common carp to be a true European fish despite its Central Asian origins.

In many places where the species now occurs, it is exploited as a food or a sport fish. In some countries, though, it is considered a pest, and attempts are repeatedly being made to eliminate it. The fact is that although the common carp is peaceful and tolerant, it can cause great disturbance in its "adopted" range, particularly where large specimens are present in some numbers. A serious potential consequence is that local species of plants and animals can be inadvertently placed under threat of extinction by this inoffensive fish.

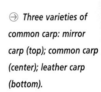

→ *Three varieties of common carp: mirror carp (top); common carp (center); leather carp (bottom).*

Common Carp Splits

Mainly due perhaps to the extremely wide distribution of the common carp, the genus *Cyprinus* is often regarded as being highly variable, and wrongly as monotypic—in other words, containing a single species: *Cyprinus carpio*. In fact, the genus also contains other, lesser known and less widely distributed representatives (see later).

Cyprinus carpio is widely known in three quite different forms:
• The "basic" wild type, which is fully scaled and is usually called the common carp;
• A scaleless, or naked type, the leather carp;
• An almost scaleless type with a few rows of large, reflective scales, called the mirror carp.

In addition, over many years the above characteristics have been bred into ornamental varieties—known as koi—giving rise to some amazing combinations of color and body type. Despite the modifications that all the derived forms have, there are still some common carp characteristics that we can detect in the cultivated descendants, including koi. Among them are a body length of up to 40 inches (1 m) or more, four barbels (two on each side, on the upper lip and the corners of the mouth), and a dorsal fin with a long base. The dorsal fin stretches over a considerable part of the back of the fish. It contains 17 to 22 branched rays, preceded by a strong, toothed spine.

Traditionally, all the cultivated forms have been regarded as varieties of the single species *C. carpio*, or common carp. However, during

the 1990s various studies resulted in the species being subdivided into four subspecies. The common carp is therefore now *C. carpio carpio*, so all the above are now regarded as varieties of this subspecies.

A second subspecies, the Amur carp (*C. carpio haematopterus*) from the Amur basin and surrounding regions, is very similar to the common carp. Like the common carp, it is exploited commercially. However, there are several fin and gill differences that separate it from the common carp; it is also the most resistant of all four subspecies to low temperatures.

Differences in the number of vertebrae (back bones), the number of scales in the lateral line, and in the gill rakers (see Glossary) also separate *C. carpio viridiviolaceus* from Vietnam and southern China from its closest relatives. The fourth subspecies, *C. carpio chilia*, is known from most of the lakes on the Yunnan Plateau in China. However, little detailed data is available on this subspecies.

⊕ A common carp feeding on the bottom using its sensory barbels to detect food. Once food is located, it is sucked into the huge mouth.

Common Carp Cousins

In addition to splitting the common carp species into four subspecies, a number of reviews of the genus carried out during the 1980s and 1990s resulted in its reorganization into no fewer than 14 species (including *C. carpio*). Some, like the common carp itself, are fished commercially, even though they may be small in size, for example, *C. acutidorsalis*, which is found in river mouths in Asia, and *C. multitaeniata* (whose name means "many-striped"), which only occurs in the West River in China. Others are equally, or even more, restricted in their distribution, for example, *C. barbatus*, *C. daliensis,* and *C. longipectoralis*, all of which are only known from Lake Erchai in the Mekong River basin in Yunnan Province, China, or *C. ilishaetomus* from Lake Qiluhu, also in Yunnan. Yet others have descriptive names, such as *C. megalophthalmus*, meaning "large eye," while one, *C. pellegrini*, is a specialized feeder, its diet consisting of plankton.

Two members of the genus are included by the World Conservation Union in its Red List of threatened species. *Cyprinus micristius*, which occurs only in Lake Dian Chi in Yunnan, China, is considered to be Endangered, mainly due to its extremely restricted distribution in the lake, while *C. yilongensis*, known only from Lake Yi-lung (again, in Yunnan Province, China), is now believed to be extinct.

Fish of Many Names

The wide distribution of the common carp (both natural and introduced), plus its natural tendency to vary according to location and environmental conditions, has led to numerous scientific descriptions of "new" species over the years. In total there have been around 74 such descriptions since the original one made in 1758. Gradually, over the years all the descriptions have been reexamined, with the result that 49 have been found to refer to just one species, *Cyprinus carpio*. Further study has resulted in *C. carpio* being split into four subspecies.

Other revisions, and more recent and more accurate descriptions, have meant that the common carp genus, *Cyprinus*, has been narrowed down to 14 species and four subspecies. Only two have common names: the common carp (*C. carpio carpio*) and the Amur carp (*C. carpio haematopterus*). The full listing is: *C. carpio carpio*, *C. carpio haematopterus, C. carpio chilia, C. carpio viridiviolaceus, C. acutidorsalis, C. barbatus, C. daliensis, C. ilishaestomus, C. intha, C. longipectoralis, C. mahuensis, C. megalophthalmus, C. micristius, C. multitaeniata, C. pellegrini, C. yilongensis, C. yunnanensis.*

Little detailed information is available on the three remaining species: *C. intha* from Southeast Asia, *C. mahuensis* from Ma-Hu in Szechwan, China, and *C. yunnanensis*, yet another *Cyprinus* species from Yunnan.

Culinary Carp

In addition to their great popularity as game or sport fish the various cultivated forms of the common carp (except koi) are also in great demand for the table. In fact, so-called "table" carp have been reared specifically for human consumption ever since the Romans began their program of carp introductions.

This tradition was subsequently adopted by European monks who found in the carp a fish that grew rapidly on a wide range of foods, was hardy, delicious to eat, and the perfect alternative to meat on days of abstinence, such as Friday, when meat eating was not allowed.

Many monasteries built their own carp ponds, some of which were so robust and well designed that they are still operational today. Pond carp culture soon became so vital to monasteries that a great deal of time and effort went into improving culture techniques, methods of collecting fish easily, and so on. Many water engineering innovations, some of which are still in existence today, were devised by monks. One of them, the sluice—the gate and channel arrangement used for regulating water flow and for controlling the drainage of ponds—is actually known as a "monk."

In eastern Europe carp is an essential part of the family menu, especially on important days. Many eastern European families therefore eat carp at Christmas instead of indulging in the more western habit of eating turkey.

Numerous recipes are available, many having been passed down from generation to

⬆ *Despite appearances, this common carp is not stranded but is spawning in shallow water.*

Reading the Rings

It is possible to roughly calculate the age of a fish by counting the growth rings in the bones known as otoliths or ear stones. This is similar to the method of calculating the age of trees by counting the growth rings in the trunk. However, unlike a tree, in which a new growth ring is produced every year, the difficulty in using growth ring counts as a way of estimating the age of a fish is that the information can be easily misread. A fish does not simply lay down one growth ring each year; the growth rings are influenced by many factors such as the health of the fish, the kind of habitat it lives in, and the availability of food.

Periods of active growth, when new tissues are being created at a rapid rate, are reflected in the bones. In the case of the otoliths rapid growth results in a light-colored ring of calcium carbonate being laid down. So, since spring and summer are generally the seasons of fastest growth, the period is represented in each otolith as a relatively wide, light-colored zone. Then, as growth slows down during fall and eventually stops altogether during the coldest part of the year, the ring becomes narrower, denser, and darker. In the following spring the cycle begins again.

If a fish remains healthy, finds plenty of food, and does not live in a polluted environment, then growth and no-growth periods will alternate without disruption. In such cases the otoliths will show this in the form of a light-colored, broader ring surrounded by a thinner, darker one produced every year. But if growth stops or is checked during the normal growing season, the fish will not be able to continue laying down its light-colored ring. Instead, it will be forced into the darker-ring phase. As a result, there will be two light and dark rings laid that year. If, instead of one or two, there are several growth interruptions, they will also be reflected in the number of light and dark rings laid down. The longer a fish survives, the greater the likelihood it will experience situations that disrupt its normal growth patterns. Therefore, if an otolith shows, say, 50 rings, it is almost certain that the fish is actually considerably younger than 50 years old.

Applying this knowledge to a famous fish that was once believed to be 223 years old because she had that number of rings, it has now been estimated that the specimen in question (a large female koi known as Hanako) was not this age when she died but much younger. In fact, it is now believed that while ages of 40 to 50 years are quite achievable by carp in ideal conditions, anything in excess of 100 years must be regarded as "overoptimistic."

generation, especially some of the more basic and wholesome ones such as baked carp. Over time, however, as eastern Europeans have settled in other countries, carp eating has spread westward and, along with it, so has the demand for table carp. Recipes have become more westernized, too, with dishes like "Carp Farcie" and "Carpe à la Maitre d'Hotel" now rubbing shoulders with more traditional ones.

Prolific Breeder

In the wild the common carp likes quiet weedy waters, warm conditions (despite its hardiness), and a substratum in which it can root around for its wide-ranging diet of small creatures and vegetation. It can also withstand low levels of dissolved oxygen in the water.

Breeding occurs throughout summer, depending on actual location, in temperatures around 73° F (23° C), with the eggs being scattered among fine-leaved vegetation in shallow water. Spawning is a vigorous and sometimes violent affair, during which some individuals may be injured. The results of such encounters (including loss of scales, skin wounds, and so on) are usually relatively superficial and tend to heal of their own accord in healthy specimens.

The eggs (which can number many hundreds of thousands from a large female) hatch in five to eight days at around 73° F (23° C); the fry become free swimming several days later. Although many factors, like diet and state of health, can affect the total number of eggs that a female produces, a fairly accurate approximation is 100,000 per 2.2 pounds (1 kg) of body weight. Spawnings of well over a quarter of a million eggs are therefore quite commonplace not just in the common carp but in all its cultivated forms as well.

A female measuring as little as 18.5 inches (47 cm), for example, has been found to produce 300,000 eggs in a single spawning. Bearing in mind that adult females can often measure more than twice this length—nearly four feet (1.2 m)—and weigh around 82 pounds (37.3 kg), the species is to say the least highly prolific in the number of offspring it can potentially produce.

Koi Origins

Although nishikigoi—koi for short—have only been with us for something over 200 years, these majestic fish have been developed into so many configurations in this relatively short period that it is easy to lose sight of what,

biologically speaking, a koi, or brocaded carp, actually is. In fact, koi, like the common carp, are members of the species *Cyprinus carpio*. Looking at today's numerous and spectacular koi varieties, it is perhaps difficult to believe that they are all descended from what some describe as a dull, drab, and boring fish.

The first fish that could be genuinely regarded as ornamental varieties of common

carp were developed in the Niigata Prefecture of Japan during the early part of the 19th century. The three main colors usually reported for the early koi are red, white, and yellow.

It is probably the case that these colored fish, which were subsequently bred into other forms, originally arose purely accidentally as the result of spontaneous mutations affecting the color genes in wild common carp stocks. There are accounts of colored carp (red and gray) from an earlier period (around 530 BC); but since these Chinese fish were almost certainly only regarded as food fish, it would be misleading to consider them as genuine koi.

From the early Japanese mutations numerous colorful and attractive varieties have been developed over the years, to the point that today virtually every pond owner will want

The ornamental koi show a much more garish coloration than the wild species but share the same sleek lines and well-formed fins.

to own some of these large, glorious fish at some stage. Even up to the mid-1980s koi keeping tended to be regarded as a rather exclusive end of the pond hobby, basically because the fish were so expensive. Many potential owners were also put off by the names used to refer to the different varieties. It seemed to some as if you needed to learn Japanese before you could attempt to keep koi!

Things have changed dramatically since then. Although Japan still leads the world in the production of top koi bloodlines, other countries, like the U.S., Israel, and Britain, along with fish-producing regions like the Far East, are now producing numbers of koi as well.

Some of these fish may sometimes be less pure in terms of pedigree than those from a long-established Japanese bloodline, but they are colorful and every bit as robust. And they are considerably less expensive than pedigree stock. There is also now a wider variety of competitively priced Japanese koi available.

The result of these changes is that koi keeping has become much more accessible for the general pondkeeper, and this, in turn, has led to a massive surge in interest in these fish from pond owners who would not have considered keeping them in the past. Koi keeping is now an almost worldwide hobby.

Today's koikeepers span a wide-ranging spectrum, from those who are perfectly happy to own purely nonpedigree fish as long as they are attractive and healthy, to those specialists who only keep pedigree koi, or even pedigree specimens of just one variety of koi like the red and white kohaku. Most koikeepers, though, prefer a mixture of fish.

Koi Classification

Koi are classified according to their color, pattern of markings, and type of scales. Within these three broad criteria there are numerous permutations, resulting in well over 100 recognized varieties.

Colors, for instance, are referred to by the appropriate Japanese word; for example, *hi* (red), *sumi* (black), *ki* (yellow), and so on.

→ *Tame koi being hand fed. The koi can exert a powerful suck with its toothless mouth to take in food, which is then ground up by the pharyngeal teeth.*

Therefore, when referring to a fish in which the red markings are particularly good, one would say that its *hi* is of good quality.

Patterns are also referred to in Japanese. For example, a "lightning" or zig-zag pattern is referred to as *inazuma* patterning, while a *tancho* pattern tells us that the fish in question has a red patch in the center of the head. Scalation (the covering of scales on the body) can be complete, in which case it is said to be metallic, or restricted (or almost absent), in which case it is nonmetallic, as in leather and mirror carp, the mirror carp type being referred to as *doitsu* scaling. Other types of scalation can include highly reflective or sparkling patterns (known as *kinginrin* or *ginrin*), or scales that are rather small, revealing the skin in between (called *fucarin* scalation).

When other factors such as overall body coloring are also taken into consideration, it is not surprising, therefore, that a series of major categories, with innumerable subcategories, has been developed over the years for koi.

Mystery "Teeth"

Koi and other carpkeepers occasionally find unusual objects lying on the bottom of their pools. The objects look a little like teeth, but instead of being pointed, they are small, rounded cubes or three-dimensional rectangular structures, some with wrinkles on one of the surfaces. What can the objects be? The answer is that they are pharyngeal teeth, normally located in the throat and used for grinding food particles. Pharyngeal teeth can sometimes become dislodged, and then they are either swallowed or spit out. Either way, they eventually end up on the bottom of the pool.

→ *As its name suggests, the gold ghost koi is a rich golden color. Nevertheless, like other koi, it is still very much a carp. Even ornamental varieties still retain the typical carplike body shape.*

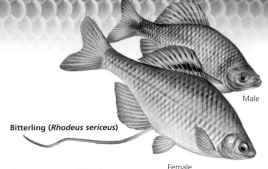

Bitterling (*Rhodeus sericeus*)

Male

Female

Common name Bitterlings

Subfamily Acheilognathinae

Family Cyprinidae

Order Cypriniformes

Number of species About 15 in 5 genera

Size Most species 2.4–4 in (6–10 cm)

Key features Relatively deep bodied (particularly males); largish silvery scales on body; scaleless head; narrow caudal peduncle; all fins well developed, especially dorsal (in males) and forked caudal fin; coloration: most olive-green on back with silvery scales on sides of body; scales suffused with range of colors

Breeding Generally spawn April–June; eggs usually laid inside freshwater mussel

Diet Wide range of small invertebrates taken both from midwater and bottom zones

Habitat Ponds, lakes, and backwaters of lowland rivers with slow-flowing currents, usually over fine-grained substrata and in vegetated areas; may also occur in more open habitats in turbid water

Distribution Subfamily as a whole ranges from mainland Europe to eastern Asia, including Russia, China, and Japan; some species have been introduced into countries outside their natural range—*Rhodeus sericeus*, for example, now found in U.S., Canada, Britain, Italy, Croatia, and Uzbekistan, while *R. ocellatus ocellatus* has been introduced into China, Japan, Fiji, Korea, and Uzbekistan

Status 2 species of bitterling listed by the IUCN as Vulnerable: deepbody bitterling (*Acheilognathus longipinnis*) from central and southern Japan and the Tokyo bitterling (*Tanakia tanago*) from the Kanto Mountains, also in Japan; *A. longatus* from Lake Dianchi, China, is Endangered.

⊕ *Bitterling* (Rhodeus sericeus), *native to mainland Europe and eastern Asia, have an original way of breeding, laying their eggs inside a freshwater mussel. Length to 4.3 inches (11 cm).*

Bitterlings

Acheilognathinae

Many animals hide their eggs to avoid their being eaten by predators, and bitterlings are no exception. What is unusual, however, is the place they choose to lay their eggs.

BITTERLINGS ARE SMALL CYPRINIDS THAT have unusual breeding habits. They share many skeletal characteristics with each other and together form the subfamily Acheilognathinae, which contains five genera with a total of 14 or 15 species: *Acheilognathus* (six species), *Paracheilognathus* (one species), *Acanthorhodeus* (one species), *Rhodeus* (four or five species), and *Tanakia* (two species).

Owing to their fascinating breeding behavior, bitterlings have always attracted interest both from scientists and fish hobbyists around the world. However, relatively few species have become popular as aquarium fish.

The most notable of the ones that have is the Amur bitterling, usually known as *Rhodeus sericeus*. A second species, *R. amarus*, is so similar that it is often confused with its close relative; in fact, it may be a subspecies rather than a full species. *Rhodeus sericeus* is also reported as consisting of two subspecies; *R. sericeus amarus*, found in most of the species's European/Russian range, and *R. sericeus sinensis*, found only on the Yangtze River basin.

Mussel-breeding Fish

During spawning the female bitterling develops a very long egg-laying tube (ovipositor). Males become resplendent in their courtship "dress" of shiny scales and intensified colors.

Once a male has located a suitable freshwater mussel (which he will defend against all rivals), he will display in front of any females that approach and invite them to spawn. When a suitable mate enters the spawning territory and a pair bond is formed, the two fish will hover over the mussel, often with their heads tilted down, closely examining it. The female

⊕ *A female bitterling* (Rhodeus sericeus) *inserting her ovipositor into a mussel shell prior to laying eggs.*

may, in fact, actually stimulate the mussel to open its valves (shells) with her egg-laying tube. As soon as she judges that the mussel has separated its valves sufficiently, she will insert her extended ovipositor—which can measure 2–2.4 inches (5–6 cm) in length—into the exhalant siphon of the mussel (the tube through which it breathes out) and will release a few eggs deep within the space inside the gill chamber of the mussel. The whole process happens so quickly that it is often too fast for the human eye to follow in detail.

When the female has released her eggs and withdrawn the ovipositor, the male will release sperm around the opening of the siphon or tube through which the mussel breathes in (the inhalant siphon). The mussel thus takes in the sperm, and the eggs are fertilized.

Only some 40 to 100 eggs are laid by a female, and due to the mussel's protective shell there is no need for spawns to be larger. Once spawning is completed, the male will either attract other females to his mussel or will abandon it to another male. In this way a single mussel may end up holding up to 200 eggs inside its mantle cavity.

Bitterling eggs develop in the shell for a period of 15 to 20 days. Once they hatch, the fry remain in the mussel for a further few days, until they use up their yolk sac.

Freshwater mussels also derive benefits from their association with bitterlings. Their own larvae (called glochidia) attach themselves to the bitterlings and are dispersed by the fish.

⊖ *The rosy or Hong Kong bitterling (*Rhodeus ocellatus ocellatus*) is a highly adaptable and widely introduced fish which is having a negative effect on some native species.*

Razorback sucker (*Xyrauchen texanus*)

Common name North American suckers

Subfamilies Cycleptinae (part), Letiobinae, Catostominae

Family   Catostomidae

Order   Cypriniformes

Number of species 68 in about 13 genera

Size   From around 6.5 in (16.5 cm) to 40 in (1 m)

Key features Body generally long and relatively slim but highbacked in a few species; head scaleless; underslung mouth and fleshy lips wrinkled or bear papillae except in extinct harelip sucker; no lip teeth; well-formed dorsal fin with long base in buffaloes, quillback, carpsuckers, and blue sucker (*Cycleptus elongatus*); no adipose fin; well-formed tail

Breeding Spring upriver spawning migrations reported for many species; eggs usually scattered in shallow water and often over pebbles or gravel; no parental care reported

Diet Mostly small invertebrates filtered from bottom sediments and "vacuumed up" with fleshy-lipped, suckerlike mouth

Habitat Most species occur in cool running waters, often with rocky bottoms, in small or medium-sized rivers, or in clear pools; some *Catostomus* species prefer shallower mud- or soft-bottomed pools and creeks; a few occur in lakes, swamps, and ponds with muddy, silty, or sandy bottoms

Distribution Majority exclusively in U.S. and Canada; others extend into Mexico; longnose sucker (*Catostomus catostomus*) also in Siberia

World population Some species relatively abundant, but about 40% of sucker species less so

Status IUCN lists nearly 30 species under varying levels of threat or causing concern; at least 2 species driven to extinction over past century or so

⊕ *The razorback sucker (Xyrauchen texanus), once extremely abundant in the U.S., is now in danger of extinction. Length to 36 inches (91 cm).*

North American Suckers

Catostomidae

About 40 percent of all sucker species are considered sufficiently under threat by the World Conservation Union for them to be included on its Red List of Threatened Animals (2003).

IN 1949 A FISHERMAN CAUGHT nearly 7,000 pounds (3,200 kg) of razorback suckers (*Xyrauchen texanus*) in Saguaro Lake in one fishing season. By 1966 there were no razorbacks in the lake. This dramatic decline has been mirrored elsewhere in the species's range, to the point where it is now officially regarded as being in danger of extinction. Two of its relatives, the Snake River sucker (*Chasmistes muriei*) and the harelip sucker (*Lagochila lacera*), have actually been driven to extinction. Such is the plight facing some of North America's suckers.

More Threatened Suckers

In addition, the Modoc sucker (*Catostomus microps*) from the Ash, Turner, and Willow Creeks of the Pit River system in California, the shortnose sucker (*Chasmistes brevirostris*) from Upper Klamath Lake and its tributaries in Oregon and California, and the Lost River sucker (*Deltistes luxatus*) from the Lost River system, also in Oregon and California, are all listed as Endangered. The cui-ui (*Chasmistes cujus*) used to occur in two lakes in Nevada: Pyramid and Winnemucca. However, Winnemucca Lake is now dry, leaving Pyramid Lake as the only remaining refuge for this 27-inch (68-cm) sucker.

Other species are not quite under the same level of threat, though some are officially considered to be Vulnerable, the next category down after Endangered. Yet others face lesser threats, while data on a few is partially lacking. Their full status is not known, and

⊕ *The spotted sucker (Minytrema melanops) inhabits deep pools in rivers. It grows to 20 inches (51 cm) in length and is a popular game fish. The downward-facing, suckerlike mouth for which the family is named is clearly visible. The lips of living suckers are either fleshy or covered in tiny outgrowths called papillae, depending on the species.*

they are considered as being in need of further study before the level of risk can be assessed.

Overall, therefore, the status of North American suckers is far from favorable. Many species undoubtedly face an uncertain future unless the causes threatening their survival are tackled. Many face problems in terms of habitat changes and introduced species, while some face an additional biological risk because they can interbreed with related species.

The razorback sucker—which is not found in Texas despite its scientific name but in the Colorado River basin—has faced a wide range of challenges over many years and typifies the plight of the majestic suckers of the U.S.

The Razorback Story

The razorback sucker is one of the largest suckers found in the U.S. Owing to its size— mostly around 24 inches (61 cm) but up to 36 inches (91 cm)—and its abundance, it not only formed one of the most important parts of the Mohave Indians' diet until the early years of last century but was even used as fertilizer.

It is a long-lived species, with ages over 40 years being common, and with some individuals perhaps living closer to 50 years of age. Sexual maturity is attained between the ages of four and seven, and at an average length of

between 16 to 18 inches (40–45 cm). Upriver migrations may precede spawning, with the timing of the spawning season depending on locality. In Lake Mohave, for example, spawning takes place between November and May. In the Middle Green River, though, spawning occurs between mid-April and mid-May.

Among the most serious threats to the survival of the razorback sucker are three nonnative fish species that have been introduced in different parts of its range. Of particular note are two large North American predatory species introduced to cater to the demands of sport anglers. Both the largemouth bass (*Micropterus salmoides*) and the channel catfish (*Ictalurus punctatus*) soon exerted a damaging effect on resident razorback suckers, to the extent that large populations in lakes and reservoirs were wiped out.

In a less spectacular, but equally effective, manner introduced bait fish species like the red shiner (*Cyprinella lutrensis*), another North American native species, had a profound effect on razorbacks by preying on their young.

While these biological threats are relatively recent in terms of the razorback's existence as a species, another naturally occurring threat was detected as long ago as the 19th century and is still regarded as a

significant contributing factor to the species's decline. This time the danger comes from a nonpredatory, closely related species, the flannelmouth sucker (*Catostomus latipinnis*), with which the razorback sucker freely hybridizes in the wild. Hybridization is so frequent in parts of the razorback sucker's range that it poses a threat of extinction of the affected populations.

Away from such biological factors the main dangers facing the razorback come from habitat alteration. Dams (there are no fewer than 44 in the species's range) and the reservoirs they create constitute major barriers

Protecting the Razorback

Although the decline in the razorback sucker's abundance and its ever-diminishing distribution (it is believed to have shrunk to around 25 percent of its original size) had been known for some time, it was not until the 1980s that official moves to protect the fish began to be implemented in earnest. Indeed, prior to this time some of the activities carried out on rivers inhabited by razorbacks—such as the poisoning of part of the upper section of the Green River in 1962 to create better conditions for trout—were directly detrimental to the species.

During the 1980s some 15 million razorbacks were released in former habitats in Arizona as part of a major attempt at helping wild populations recover. Yet despite these efforts, populations failed to reestablish themselves, largely owing to the presence of the introduced predators.

In 1988 a new program aimed at protecting not just the razorback sucker but also some other native species that were under threat was implemented for the Upper Colorado River. This multifaceted project includes restoration of watercourse flows, habitat development and management, restocking, control of nonnative "sport" species, and a monitoring and research initiative. Other projects include the collection of newly hatched razorbacks from Lake Mohave for rearing in specially allocated protected areas and eventual restocking.

Just how effective these laudable efforts will prove to be in the long term will, however, be determined by all the other complex and hard-to-control factors that have brought this unique species of North American sucker to the brink of extinction.

to spawning migrations. They also remove the tributaries that have traditionally assisted razorbacks in their upriver migrations. Other water-management projects have altered environmental conditions in such a way that they have eliminated seasonal variations in water temperature and flow, and replaced them with more constant, but colder, temperatures and more even water flow throughout the year. Such conditions appear to tip the reproductive balance against the razorback and in favor of some of its competitors.

To a lesser extent pollutants, some of which are believed to affect the razorback's ability to breed, have been detected not only in parts of the fish's range but also in its tissues.

The overall effect of all these factors is that not only are adult razorbacks under direct threat, but perhaps even more worrying is the fact that recruitment—the replacement of adults that die with juveniles from subsequent generations—is running dangerously low. The future does not therefore look hopeful for wild populations of *Xyrauchen texanus*.

Sucker Splits

Three subfamilies of North American suckers are generally recognized: the Ictiobinae, containing two genera and seven species; the Cycleptinae, containing two genera and two species; and the Catostominae, containing nine genera and all the remaining species.

The Ictiobinae contains three species known as buffaloes (*Ictiobus* species), one known as the quillback (*Carpiodes cyprinus*), and two species known as carpsuckers (*C. carpio* and *C. velifer*). They are relatively deep-bodied fish distinguished from other suckers by differences in their fin rays, lateral line arrangement, and most significantly, by the higher number of pharyngeal teeth they have—between 115 and 190, the highest totals found in suckers. The largest species in the subfamily is the bigmouth buffalo (*Ictiobus cyprinellus*), a widely distributed fish that occurs from Hudson Bay down to the south of Louisiana, but which has also been introduced into many areas outside its natural range. It can grow to a length of 40 inches (1 m) and is among the largest of all suckers.

The Cycleptinae have just a single representative on the North American landmass. The blue sucker (*Cycleptus elongatus*) is found mainly in the Mississippi River basin but extends into Texas, New Mexico, and Mexico. It is a small-headed fish with an elegant dorsal fin and blue coloration in adults that beautifully reflects the name of the species. The blue sucker grows to around 36 inches (91 cm). Although still common in certain places, its numbers are declining over much of its range. The only other member of the Cycloptinae is the Chinese sailfin sucker (*Myxocyprinus asiaticus*).

The Catostominae constitutes by far the largest group of suckers, so much so that it is subdivided into two tribes: the Catostomini and the Moxostomatini. The razorback, along with some 28 other species belonging to the genera *Catostomus*, *Chasmistes*, and *Deltistes*, all belong to the first of these tribes. All species have a lateral line that runs the whole length of the body and contains more than 50 scales. The tribe contains all the most endangered species.

Catostomus species in particular, but also others like the razorback sucker, quite readily cross-breed (hybridize) with each other. Interestingly, hybridization is more frequent in watercourses where nonnative species have been introduced, or where the watercourse itself has been changed by human activity. Why this is the case is unclear.

The tribe Moxostomatini contains five or six genera: the chub suckers (*Erimyson* species), which have a stubby body; the hog suckers (*Hypentelium* species), which have a broad head and a tapering body; the redhorse suckers (*Moxostoma* species) with their distinctive red fins; the superficially similar but less vividly colored and aptly named spotted sucker (*Minytrema melanops*); the torrent sucker (*Thoburnia rhothoeca*) and its closest relatives; and the now-extinct harelip sucker. Some systems of classification place the harelip sucker in the genus *Moxostoma* and refer to it as *M. lacerum*, whereas others call it *Lagochila lacera*.

Some of the smallest North American suckers are found in the tribe Moxostomatini. The Roanoke hog sucker (*Hypentelium roanokense*) and the blackfin sucker (*Thoburnia atripinnis*) both grow to 6.5 inches (16.5 cm).

Weather Loach

Misgurnus fossilis

The weather loach gets its curious name because of its ability to sense stormy weather. At the imminent onset of such conditions the fish becomes hyperactive and takes gulps of air from the water surface.

Common name Weather loach (European weather loach, pond loach, weather fish)

Scientific name *Misgurnus fossilis*

Subfamily Cobitinae

Family Cobitidae

Order Cypriniformes

Size Up to a maximum of nearly 14 in (35 cm) but usually a little smaller

Key features Elongated, eel-like body; smallish head with underslung mouth; 5 pairs of barbels; smallish eyes located high on side of head; erectile spine under each eye; sightly rounded dorsal and caudal fins; small anal fin; adipose fin absent; body covered in thick slime; dull light brown coloration with several dark bands extending from behind head to base of caudal fin

Breeding Spawning from April to June among plants in shallow water; egg laying may extend over several weeks with as many as 170,000 eggs reported (although much smaller spawns are more common); hatching 8–10 days; newly hatched larvae have small, ribbonlike external gills that help them breathe in oxygen-poor waters into which they are frequently born

Diet Bottom-living invertebrates, including worms, mollusks, and insect larvae; some plant material may also be eaten

Habitat Mainly lowland still waters like floodplains, backwaters, ponds, and marshes—areas that may have fine-grained bottoms with low levels of oxygen, and that may dry up; usually these habitats also heavily vegetated

Distribution Widely distributed in Europe from France, Denmark, and Holland as far eastward as Caspian Sea; absent from southern areas, British Isles, and Scandinavia

Status Not threatened

ALL *MISGURNUS* SPECIES EXHIBIT THE generalized loach body characteristics, having eel-like, elongated bodies that are almost cylindrical in cross-section. They have a smallish head in relation to the body, a subterminal mouth, and five pairs of barbels. The largest of them are on the upper lip and are known as rostral barbels. Like their relatives the *Botia* loaches, all the weather loaches carry an erectile spine under their eye that they can use as a defensive weapon by shaking the head from side to side.

Of the three species mentioned here, the European weather loach is the most distinctly marked: It has several dark body bands running lengthwise from behind the head to the base of the tail. The body is also covered in a rich mucous layer that makes it feel slimy.

Burping and Whistling

Despite being more distinctively marked than some other loaches, the weather loach is still a generally drab-colored fish that spends most of the daylight hours hiding or buried in bottom sediments with just its eyes (which are located high up on the head) above the surface. (In fact, the weather loach is so at home under the substrate that if the water in its habitat temporarily dries up, the fish can bury itself into mud and aestivate—in other words, go into a period of summer dormancy. It also burrows into mud during particularly cold winter spells.)

As evening approaches, the weather loach becomes more active and sets out in search of its food, which consists mostly of bottom-living invertebrates, particularly worms, mollusks, and insect larvae. It also eats some plant material.

⊘ *Buried in sediments during the day, the weather loach emerges at night to feed on small mollusks on the sandy river bed. Normally placid, it becomes agitated when the atmospheric pressure drops.*

Toward dawn the weather loach returns to its normal daytime activity of doing nothing or very little. However, if the atmospheric (barometric) pressure drops, as it does before a storm, the weather loach leaves its resting place and becomes hyperactive, even if the storm breaks in the middle of the day.

The reason for the unusual bouts of activity is that the drop in atmospheric pressure causes a drop in the pressure of the gas that the weather loach has inside its swim bladder. If the drop in pressure is significant, it can also lower the levels of dissolved oxygen in the water—especially in low-oxygen habitats where the weather loach is commonly found.

These conditions cause the weather loach to rise to the surface to take gulps of air, making slapping or smacking sounds as it does so. It also releases some of its stale or used air in a series of burps. More unusually, it can also "break wind," releasing the air through its anus with a whistling sound!

Oriental Relatives

The dojo, or Chinese or Japanese weather loach (*M. anguillicaudatus*), is widely distributed in northeastern Asia. Like its European relative, it is a peaceful bottom dweller with "weather-forecasting" abilities. It is usually smaller than the weather loach, growing to around 8 inches (20 cm) or slightly larger. Its body patterning is more mottled than in the European species, which has longitudinal bands running along the sides of the body.

Both the dojo and the European weather loach occur in two color forms: the wild type as well as a golden one that has been developed for aquariums.

The third species in the genus, known as the Chinese fine-scaled weather loach (*M. mizolepis*), is only known in its wild form, which is heavily mottled grayish-brown on the back fading to lighter shades along the belly. The Chinese fine-scaled weather loach is similar to the dojo in overall size.

Common name Stone loach

Scientific name *Noemacheilus (Nemacheilus) barbatulus*

Subfamily Noemacheilinae (Nemacheilinae)

Family Balitoridae (Homalopteridae)

Order Cypriniformes

Size Up to 6 in (15 cm); usually about 4 in (10 cm)

Key features Elongated body; front half almost cylindrical in cross-section, becoming flattened side to side farther back; moderately sized head and eyes; eye spine absent; small, ventrally placed mouth with 3 pairs of barbels: 2 on upper lip and 1 at each corner of mouth; tiny nonoverlapping scales on body; well-formed fins, tail fin relatively large and almost straight edged; greenish-brown color along back with irregular patches, fading to lighter colors along sides of body; yellowish belly

Breeding Unusually, both sexes may develop nuptial tubercles (see Glossary) on pelvic fins (more prominent in males) during breeding season (from April to June in most areas); breeding adults may gather at spawning ponds; as many as 80,000 eggs may be laid by large females in 2–3 batches; eggs usually scattered among plants or stones; some reports indicate that eggs may be deposited in a cavity and may be guarded by female; hatching takes about 14–16 days; young may take 2–3 years to mature

Diet Mainly bottom-dwelling invertebrates; may also feed on fish eggs and some plant matter

Habitat Mainly central and upper reaches of flowing watercourses with clear waters of varying chemical composition but relatively pollution free and with generally high levels of dissolved oxygen; also found in ponds, quarries, and lakes; also occurs in vegetated waters; frequently found over rocky or pebbly substrata but may also occur over fine-grained sediments

Distribution Widely distributed from Ireland, where it was introduced, eastward through Europe all the way to China, with a few notable exceptions

Status Not threatened

Stone Loach *Noemacheilus barbatulus*

The stone loach can thrive in acidic or alkaline conditions. It can even live in brackish water. However, what it cannot tolerate is poor water quality or low oxygen levels: Its presence in a river is therefore a sign that the water is "healthy."

THE EXTREMELY WIDE RANGE OF WATER conditions that this small species can tolerate is no doubt one of the reasons why it is found from the British Isles all the way to eastern China. It was originally absent from Ireland but has been introduced there. It is still absent from the Iberian Peninsula, Greece, central and southern Italy, and the northern parts of Scotland, Sweden, and Norway.

Extra Oxygen Supplies
It is not clear if every population is equally tolerant of varying water chemistry conditions, though most, if not all, cannot tolerate polluted water or water in which the oxygen level is low. The need for oxygen is reflected in the fact that the stone loach is usually found in flowing water, often in the middle or upper reaches of watercourses where the concentration of dissolved oxygen is highest. It can also occur in ponds or larger bodies of more or less standing water, but then it is usually found close to the source of incoming water or else in the tributaries or runoffs from these habitats.

Under unfavorable environmental conditions, such as in turbid water caused by heavy rains, the stone loach can use its gut as an additional breathing organ, the rich blood supply helping it extract oxygen from the water. However, this is only a device that is brought into use to enable the fish to survive temporarily under such conditions; it is not used when oxygen levels are more normal.

Strict Bottom Hugger
The stone loach is a strict bottom dweller, preferring stretches of streams that are strewn

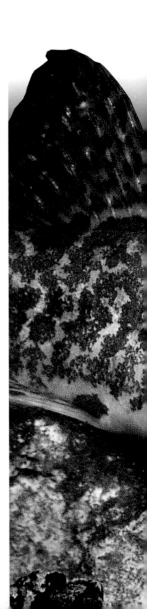

with stones or pebbles, hence its name. Nevertheless, it can also be found in heavily vegetated watercourses with muddy or fine-grained bottoms.

The daylight hours are usually spent hiding among plants or under stones. As evening approaches, the stone loach leaves its hiding place and sets off in search of food. This consists primarily of small invertebrates, including crustaceans, worms, aquatic insect larvae, and nymphs; it may also consume fish eggs and some plant material.

Its elongated cylindrical body, with which it swims in a snakelike manner, allows the stone loach to get into tiny cracks and holes from which it can extract its prey. Three pairs of downpointing mouth barbels help it feel and "taste" its prey during its night forages.

Three-pronged Attack

In the past the stone loach was gathered in substantial quantities for human consumption; its flesh is considered by some to be extremely tasty. Now, however, the practice is much restricted, although the species is still highly regarded by gourmets in certain parts of its range.

Perhaps more significant are the numbers caught for use as bait fish by anglers. Also, in areas where trout (*Salmo* species) occur, either naturally or as introduced stocks, the stone loach is heavily preyed on by the trout.

Despite this "three-pronged" attack on its numbers, plus the effects of pollution in parts of the range, the stone loach is still abundant overall, although some local populations are believed to be declining.

The stone loach inhabits areas of fast-flowing water with stony or gravel bottoms, which it mimicks with its coloring. Hiding during the day, it feeds under cover of darkness at night.

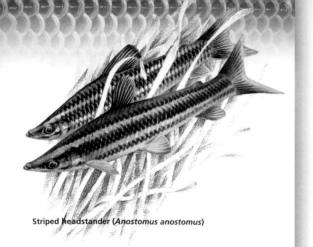

Striped Headstander (*Anostomus anostomus*)

Headstanders
Anostomidae

Headstanders get their common name from the fact that many of them orientate themselves with their heads pointing obliquely downward, giving the impression they are standing on their heads.

DIET PLAYS AN IMPORTANT PART in the orientation of some fish. Many headstanders feed on small aquatic invertebrates and on plants, organic debris, or detritus lying on the bottom. To reach such food items more effectively, the fish often feed in a "nose-down" position.

Some more specialized species, such as the funny-mouthed or gold-ringed anostomid (*Synaptolaemus cingulatus*), have elongated, fleshy-tipped and upturned snouts that they use to feed almost exclusively on insects that hide among rock crevices or submerged logs. Others, like the peculiar-mouthed or big-mouthed anostomid (*Sartor respectus*) feed on algae or sponges.

At first sight it might appear that the upwardly directed mouth that many species of headstanders possess does not quite suit the lifestyle of fish that do not feed at the water surface. However, this is not correct. In fact, the upwardly turned mouth is perfect for fish that swim at an oblique, head-down angle and include in their diet items like small invertebrates that live on the vertical stems and undersides of leaves of aquatic plants. The food the fish eat is located above their heads in just the same way that food is located above the heads of surface-feeding fish.

Two-way Split
Most headstanders have elongated bodies that are almost cylindrical in cross section. They also have distinctive, tubelike nostrils

Common name Headstanders

Subfamilies Anostominae, Chilodontinae

Family Anostomidae

Order Characiformes

Number of species Anostominae: 128 in 10 genera; Chilodontinae: 5 in 2 genera

Size From 3.2 in (8 cm) to 16 in (40 cm)

Key features Most species have elongated body, cylindrical in cross section; notable exceptions: high-backed headstander (*Abramites hypselonotus*) and spotted headstander (*Chilodus punctatus*); head with extended snout ending in small mouth, often with fleshy modifications; in leporins the teeth and lip arrangement creates a "hare lip" effect; mouth upturned in some species, e.g., members of genus *Anostomus*; eyes large; fins well formed; adipose fin present in all species; body patterns include vertical bands, spots, and longitudinal bands

Breeding Information lacking; spawning migrations upriver may occur; eggs scattered, often among vegetation, and abandoned; hatching takes several days

Diet Plants, including algae; some species feed on insects and other invertebrates

Habitat Variety of waters with medium to strong current; vegetation is often preferred; rocks and clefts are headstander habitats, as well as "blackwater"

Distribution Widely in tropical South America

Status Not threatened

⊕ *The 4.7-inch (12-cm) striped headstander (Anostomus anostomus) lives in the Amazon and Orinoco basins. It is usually found head-down in well-oxygenated waters. It is a member of the subfamily Anostominae.*

⊕ *The spotted headstander (Chilodus punctatus) is a member of the subfamily Chilodontinae. About 4 inches (10 cm) long, it is widely distributed in northeastern South America.*

on their snouts. An exception to the elongated, torpedo shape is found in the high-backed headstander (*Abramites hyselonotus*), which is relatively deep bodied. Nevertheless, it has the unmistakable bone and mouth characteristics that identify it as a member of the family Anastomidae.

More specifically, it bears the distinctive bone arrangement of the maxilla (upper jaw) and the premaxilla (the bone directly in front of it) that identifies it as a member of the same subfamily as the striped headstander (*Anostomus anostomus*), the striped leporin (*Leporinus striatus*), and over 100 other species in the Anostominae. In all the species the maxilla is much smaller than the premaxilla.

In contrast to this large group, there is a small one consisting of just five species in two genera, in which the situation is reversed. These fish have a larger maxilla than premaxilla. Nevertheless, they still share a sufficiently high number of characteristics to be included in the headstander family, albeit in their own subfamily, the Chilodontinae.

The best-known species in this small group is the spotted headstander (*Chilodus*

punctatus). The spotted headstander and its nearest allies are classified within a different family by some authorities.

Little-known Hare Lips

There are about 70 species of leporins (*Leporinus* species) in the family. The name of the genus means "young, or little, hare" and refers to the fact that they all have a mouth resembling a "hare lip." This is caused by a cleft (or space) at the tip of the snout, with two prominent teeth completing the visual effect. At around 16 inches (40 cm) the black-lined leporin (*Leporinus nigrotaeniatus*) is one of the biggest species in the Anostomidae.

The group is the least known in the family, and there is much debate concerning both the validity of certain names and the total number of species. Identification is difficult because there is great variation within the genus. Some species have spots, others have vertical bands, yet others have longitudinal band patterns, and some have neither spots nor bands. Adding to the confusion, a single species may show considerable variation in patterning.

ⓐ *The appropriately named black line headstander (Chilodus gracilis) comes from the Amazon region. It grows to about 4.7 inches (12 cm).*

Marbled hatchetfish (*Carnegiella strigata*)

Common name Freshwater hatchetfish

Family Gasteropelecidae

Order Characiformes

Number of species 9 in 3 genera

Size From 1 in (2.5 cm) to 3.2 in (8 cm); aquarium-reared specimens slightly larger

Key features Body with pronounced chest enlargement and keel; head with flat top, upwardly directed mouth; large eyes; dorsal profile straight to dorsal fin; all fins well developed; pectoral fins extremely large; all species have silvery scales on side of body; several species have dark central body line extending to caudal peduncle

Breeding Eggs scattered among roots of floating plants and among vegetation and abandoned; hatching takes 1.5 days

Diet Mostly insects; also aquatic invertebrates

Habitat *Carnegiella* in small streams and creeks; *Gasteropelecus* and *Thoracocharax* in open waters

Distribution Panama in Central America; South American countries except Chile

Status Not threatened

⊕ *The marbled hatchetfish (*Carnegiella strigata*) occurs in the Guyanas and Amazon River basin. Although a few other fish species can glide out of water, only hatchetfish use propulsive force to move through the air. Length to 1.4 inches (3.5 cm).*

Freshwater Hatchetfish

Gasteropelecidae

When confronted by a predator, hatchetfish can leap from the water and fly a short distance to safety by flapping their extended winglike pectoral fins.

IN THE UNENDING STRUGGLE FOR survival fish have evolved countless ways of finding food or avoiding being another animal's next meal. Some blend in with their surroundings, and others escape from enemies by using their speed to swim to safety. In the case of the freshwater hatchetfish, however, they simply disappear! Freshwater hatchetfish (family Gasteropelecidae) are also sometimes known as flying characins—a direct reference to the technique they employ to escape predators: They fly, using their pectoral fins as wings.

Unique Body Shape

The pectoral fins are long and winglike, and arise from a point just behind the gill covers. The leading (front) edge is strong and slightly curved, and the whole fin is usually held pointing upward and backward at a slight angle. The chest is extremely deep but is very narrow in cross-section, like a keel. The shape, which starts in the chin area, extends all the way toward the tail and creates in the process the hatchetlike appearance for which the fish are famous.

The dorsal profile is straight, or nearly so, from the tip of the snout all the way back to the dorsal fin, which is set well back along the body. The mouth is directed upward, and the eyes are large.

Together, these features help adapt hatchetfish to a life spent living just under the water surface, picking off any insects that fall in. But the added bonus is that they enable hatchetfish to fly. The fish can generate sufficient thrust with their powerful chest muscles to propel them free of the water

⊕ *A silver hatchetfish (*Gasteropelecus levis*) showing clearly the characteristic body shape that gives the fish its common name.*

surface and then fly through the air by flapping their pectoral fins.

The ability to fly varies from species to species, the age of a fish, water conditions, and wind strength. However, in still water and wind conditions a fully adult hatchetfish can fly for some 65 to 100 feet (20–39 m) at a height of up to 4 inches (10 cm) above the water surface.

Clearly, a target that disappears from view at the last moment is extremely confusing to a potential predator, and the fact that the hatchetfish is able to then fly some distance away from danger before landing back in the water makes it an extremely effective method of protection. Even modest distances of a few yards are frequently enough to escape the attentions of a predator, particularly in the dark-stained waters in which hatchetfish often live.

Splitting the Hachets

There are only three genera of freshwater hatchetfish: *Carnegiella*, *Gasteropelecus*, and *Thoracocharax*, with a total of nine species. None is fished for food; they are too small and bony. However, all are collected for home aquariums where hatchetfish have been popular ever since the first specimens of

marbled hatchetfish (*Carnegiella strigata*), spotted hatchetfish (*Gasteropelecus maculatus*), and giant hatchetfish (*Thoracocharax securis*) were imported from the wild in 1910.

The "Other" Hatchets

In addition to the nine species of freshwater hatchetfish, several other fish are referred to as hatchets. Among the freshwater species two belong to the genus *Chela*: the Asian hatchetfish (*Chela caeruleostigmata*), also known as the leaping barb, and the Indian hatchetfish (*C. laubuca*), better known as the Indian glass barb. Both species are cyprinids—members of the family Cyprinidae, which includes the carps and minnows, and are therefore not related to the "true" freshwater hatchetfish. The third freshwater species, the elongate hatchetfish (*Tripostheus elongatus*), is related, however, since it is also a characoid and therefore belongs to the same order.

All the other 10 hatchetfish are marine and belong to the family Sternoptychidae. They occur in deep water and some carry intriguing names, such as the half-naked hatchetfish (*Argyropelecus hemigymnus*) and the lovely hatchetfish (*A. aculeatus*).

Tigerfish (*Hydrocynus goliath*)

Common name African tetras

Family Alestidae

Order Characiformes

Number of species Around 110 in 18 genera

Size From 0.8 in (2 cm) to 4.5 ft (1.3 m); most within range of 2–4 in (5–10 cm)

Key features Body elongate and compressed, some species with hump behind head and deeper body, e.g., African moonfish (*Bathyaethiops caudomaculatus*); mouth armed with pointed teeth; fins well formed; forked caudal fin in all species; coloration variable, usually includes bright silvery sides to body; many possess black blotch or streak on caudal peduncle

Breeding Spawning late spring to early fall; eggs scattered over bottom and abandoned; hatching from15 hours to 6–7 days, e.g., tigerfish eggs hatch in 15–22 hours, while Congo tetra (*Phenacogrammus interruptus*) eggs take 6 days or more

Diet Predatory; larger species feed on other fish; smaller ones on insects and other aquatic invertebrates; plant material also eaten

Habitat Fresh waters from streams and pools to large lakes, e.g., Lakes Chad, Albert, Turkana, and Malawi

Distribution Tropical Africa

Status Not threatened

⊕ *At 4.5 ft (1.3 m) in length and a weight of 110 pounds (50 kg) the tigerfish* (Hydrocynus goliath) *is the biggest member of the family Alestidae. This large, streamlined fish with fanglike teeth is a voracious predator of the Zaire River.*

African Tetras Alestidae

The best known of the African tetras is the Congo or blue Congo tetra from the areas around the Congo River, which was first introduced to aquarists in 1950.

THE VORACIOUS, FANG-TOOTHED TIGERFISH (*Hydrocynus goliath*) of the Zaire River looks nothing like the vast majority of fish commonly referred to as tetras. It is much bigger and heavier, and if anything, it appears to have more in common with its better-known cousins, the highly predatory piranhas.

There are at least six species of tigerfish, or water dog, but some are so similar that only an expert could tell them apart. The similarity does not end with appearance: Tigerfish also share an appetite for flesh that is evident just by looking at them. They all have powerful streamlined bodies, with a large forked tail that can propel them forward at enormous speed—speed that is too fast for most prey animals to escape from. Once grasped by the large, fanglike teeth there is no escape, especially since the teeth of the upper jaw alternate with those of the lower, forming a superefficient trap once prey is seized.

By contrast, most tetras are tiny fish between 2 to 4 inches (4–10 cm) long. The delicate orange-red dwarf tetra (*Ladigesia roloffi*) grows to 1.2–1.6 inches (3–4 cm), and the even smaller adonis tetra (*Lepidarchus adonis*) only reaches 0.8–1 inch (2–2.5 cm) in length. They are so small and delicate that their skeleton shows through their flesh. However, the silversides or African silver tetra (*Alestes baremoze*) can grow to about 12 inches (30 cm).

Popular Congos

The most popular and best known of the African tetras is the Congo or blue Congo tetra (*Phenacogrammus interruptus*) from the areas around the Congo River. It is the males that have contributed most to the species' lasting popularity, with their large, reflective greenish-

⊕ *A shoal of Congo tetra (*Phenacogrammus interruptus*). These attractive fish are peaceful and tolerant, making them good aquarium inhabitants.*

blue scales above and below a broad central band of glistening golden scales. In addition, mature males have impressive high dorsal fins and long ray extensions in the center of the caudal fin. They are shoaling fish that are tolerant toward each other, making it possible to keep a large group together in an aquarium.

They are not, however, the only Congo tetras; neither are they the only attractive ones. The redfin Congo tetra (*Micralestes occidentalis*) from Nigeria, for example, has red fins. They stand out spectacularly against the silvery body, as do those of the red Congo tetra (*M. stormsi*) from Ghana. The blackspot Congo tetra (*Phenacogrammus altus*) from West Africa and the yellow Congo tetra (*Hemigrammopetersius caudalis*) from the Congo River tributaries are also impressive fish.

Silversides and Relatives

The family Alestidae is named after the silversides or African silver tetra and its allies belonging to the genus *Alestes*. There are currently 28 species in the genus, but some are so similar to those of other genera, and to each other, that they can be easily confused.

Alestes species are important food fish— the silversides being a good example. It is abundant; it can grow up to 17 inches (43 cm) long and weigh up to 1 pound (450 g). It is also a relatively long-lived species of tetra, with a reported age of around five years.

⊕ A detailed view of the head of the African red-eyed characin (Arnoldichthys spilopterus). Note the large eye.

Red-bellied piranha (*Pygocentrus nattereri*)

Piranhas, Silver Dollars, and Pacus

Serrasalminae

Lurking in the dark waters of the Amazon are voracious fish armed with teeth as sharp as scalpel blades. They can devour any animal in the water in a matter of minutes, leaving just the bare bones.

Common name Piranhas, silver dollars, and pacus

Subfamily Serrasalminae

Family Characidae

Order Characiformes

Number of species About 60 in 13 genera

Size From 6 in (15 cm) to 40 in (1 m)

Key features Body deep and compressed—pronounced in silver dollars; head blunt and massive; lower jaw protruding; sharp cutting teeth in piranhas, grinding teeth in nut and seed-eaters; fins well formed; coloration variable, from shiny and silvery to dull in the pacus and piranhas; some species attractively colored in chest area; fins may be distinctively colored

Breeding Several hundred or even thousand eggs from onset of wet season; eggs scattered or laid in prepared site; may or may not be guarded; spawning in pairs or shoals; hatching takes less than 1 week

Diet True piranhas feed on fish and other prey animals (including reptiles, birds, and mammals), fruits, and seeds; silver dollars eat quantities of leaves; pacus mainly eat fruits and seeds; a few are specialized fin and scale eaters

Habitat From streams and clear water or blackwater rivers to turbid rivers, lakes, and flooded forests

Distribution Widespread in tropical South America

Status Not threatened

⊕ *The fearsome red-bellied piranha (Pygocentrus nattereri) of the Amazon and Orinoco basins grows up to 12 inches (30 cm) in length.*

A SHOAL OF SOUTH AMERICAN piranhas can tear a victim to shreds in a very short space of time. However, a feeding frenzy only happens in certain conditions, such as when the fish are extremely hungry, if their pool is drying up, or if an animal is injured or drowning and therefore struggling to stay afloat. In such circumstances the consequences of an attack are dramatic and final for the victim.

Unfair Press

Like sharks, piranhas are victims of our desire for bloodthirsty news. Most certainly some species can present a serious threat to humans at times, but to depict them as insatiable, vicious killers does these superbly equipped fish an injustice. Many more piranhas are killed by humans than the other way around, for piranhas are popular food fish in the Amazon region. Furthermore, not all piranhas are "killer fish." One of the largest species, *Serrasalmus manueli*, which can grow to around 17 inches (43.5 cm), is harmless to humans.

Many injuries inflicted by piranhas are the result of provocation rather than outright aggression. For instance, injuries are quite common among Amazon fishermen who come into close contact with the fish. The majority of injuries are caused through being bitten by piranhas that are either dumped inside the fishermens' canoes along with the rest of the day's catch or are removed by hand from hooks. The fish, not unnaturally, is fighting for its survival.

⊙ *The razor-sharp, triangular-shaped teeth of a piranha are clearly visible here.*

Piranhas, especially the red-bellied piranha (*Pygocentrus nattereri*), are also killed, dried, varnished, and sold, with their mouth open to show their teeth, as souvenirs to visitors to the Amazon who want to take home a reminder of the "savage" fish they encountered.

Sexing Piranhas

Piranhas are generally regarded as being notoriously difficult fish to sex. Many books, for example, include comments such as: "no external differences between the sexes," "males may be slightly slimmer," or "males may be a little more colorful than females," and so on. Such statements are, however, usually made in aquarium literature and therefore refer to aquarium-reared piranhas.

As far as aquarium piranhas are concerned, the sex of an individual can indeed be very difficult or even impossible to determine. The reason is because aquarists tend to overfeed their fish so that they very quickly begin to lay down layers of fat

⊕ *Harvesting a catch of red-bellied piranhas (Pygocentrus nattereri) in Llanos, Venezeula.*

⊖ *The wimple piranha* (Catoprion mento) *is found in the lower Amazon region. It has an attractive silver-gold sheen to its body.*

reserves—often within days. Under the layers of fat any slight differences between individuals tend to disappear.

In the wild conditions are very different. Most animals—not just fish—go through an annual cycle of "feast and famine." During periods when food is readily available, they put on weight and build up reserves that take them through the leaner periods that invariably follow. In addition, wild fish swim more energetically, and over longer distances, than their aquarium cousins. Therefore, they use more energy and are fitter and slimmer.

Under natural conditions male piranhas have a flat belly profile and females a rounder one. Males are also considerably slimmer than females overall. Males have more intense color, especially around the gills and throat. The differences, while not spectacular, are quite obvious in the wild. They are also only apparent in mature fish. Juveniles are very similar to each other and virtually impossible to separate.

Many-named Piranha

Piranhas are widely distributed and vary in coloration and other features from place to

Perfect Cutting Equipment

When piranhas mount an attack and a feeding frenzy results, it is every piranha for itself. The aim is to eat as much food as it can as quickly as possible. In the process piranhas bite anything, including bone, gristle, and (sometimes) other piranhas. As a result, fish can end up injured and with damaged teeth. A piranha with damaged dentition is not effective. In fact, if the injuries do not heal, it can cost a piranha its life.

Evolution has, fortunately, provided the ideal solution. When a piranha loses or damages one or more of its teeth, it gradually replaces all the teeth on the affected side of the jaw, ending up with a brand new set of lethal biting weapons.

place. Consequently, many species can be easily confused. This means that some are known by a variety of common names. Similarly, piranhas described under different scientific names have eventually turned out to be the same species.

There are over 33 species of true piranha. While not all are as varied or widely known as the red-bellied piranha or the black piranha (*Pygocentrus rhombeus*), many have suffered name confusion over the years. Piranhas range from about 6 inches (15 cm) in the harmless *Serrasalmus irritans* and *Pristobrycon calmoni* to the potentially dangerous blacktail or San Francisco piranha (*Pygocentrus piraya*), from the San Francisco River basin, which at 24 inches (60 cm) is largest of all the true piranhas.

Pacus and their relatives have high-quality flesh. The tambaqui can weigh as much as 66 pounds (30 kg) and is regarded as an important food in tropical South America. Piranhas are only generally fished by riverine people and not by commercial fishermen, however.

Silver Dollar Relatives

There is a third major group in the subfamily. They are often referred to as silver dollars because they have roundish, silvery bodies. Some, like the redhook pacu or redhook metynnis (*Myleus rubripinnis*), can grow to 15 inches (38 cm) or even larger. The hard-bellied silver dollar (*Mylossoma duriventre*) is smaller, although it can grow to around 9 or 10 inches (23–25 cm). Most other species are considerably smaller—particularly those in the genus *Metynnis*, such as the silver pacu (*M. argenteus*) at about 6 inches (15 cm) in length.

The silver dollars are primarily plant-eaters feeding on leaves, seeds and fruits, especially during the rainy season when the forests are flooded and many shrubs and trees produce their fruits and seeds. The association between some silver dollars and trees is so close that fishermen can use the fruit or seeds as bait.

Most species are found in large numbers in flooded forest areas but then tend to

The Nut Crackers

Closely related to the true piranhas are the larger pacus. Some of them, such as the black-finned pacu or tambaqui (*Colossoma macropomum*), grow to lengths of 40 inches (1 m) or more.

Yet despite the closeness of the pacus to the true piranhas, they could not be more different in feeding habits. The teeth of pacus are designed for grinding seeds and cracking nuts. However, since very strong jaws are required in order to crack nuts, bites from pacus can still cause serious injuries. Fortunately, the fish only tend to bite when they are trapped or mishandled, and so it is only fishermen and fish farmers who are likely to be bitten by a pacu.

Fruit-eating Piranhas

The true piranhas—mainly *Pygocentrus*, *Serrasalmus*, *Pristobrycon*, and *Catoprion* species—are beautifully designed predators with huge appetites. Surprisingly, however, their diet can include vegetable matter as well.

Some of the plant material revealed by studies of the gut contents of piranhas enters indirectly from the plant-eating fish that the piranha hunts. However, analyses also show that, in some species—for example, the black piranha—fruits and seeds can account for as much as 10 percent of the total volume of food consumed. Fruits and seeds were the second major food items eaten, only exceeded by fish. So it seems that even these voracious meat-eaters are not totally carnivorous.

Floating Nurseries

As water rises during the wet season in the jungles of tropical South America, large areas of what appear to be grassland break loose from the soil and float. The floating "meadows" can be vast, their size depending on whether they are close to a river channel (where they are smaller) or whether they occur in open flooded plains (where they are larger).

The tangled roots and other submerged structures on the underside of the floating masses create a unique environment that provides excellent shelter for countless creatures, among them baby piranhas and pacus. Pickings are rich in the floating nurseries. The young fish grow rapidly during the high-water season, then when large enough, they move into the less-protected waters occupied by their parents, where they can shoal and feed on larger prey.

disappear into the rivers once fruiting is over, returning only when the rains resume in the following season.

Diverse Breeding Behavior

All members of the subfamily are egg producers, but not all are typical egg scatterers. In the pacus like *Colossoma* and some of the *Serrasalmus* piranhas, for example, eggs are scattered and not guarded. The gold piranha (*Serrasalmus gibbus*) scatters eggs but does not

⊖ *The black pacu* (Colossoma macropomum) *of northern South America is the biggest member of the subfamily Serrasalminae. An important food fish, it is found in most fish markets.*

⊖ *A shoal of black-spot piranhas* (Pygocentrus cariba)*. Growing to around 11 inches (28 cm), this species has a powerful bite that can inflict serious injuries.*

protect them. Spawning occurs over a site prepared by the male, which may decorate it with cut-up pieces of plants.

In other piranhas, the red-bellied piranha, for example, the eggs are laid among trailing tree roots and are guarded, usually by the male. Alternatively, the eggs may be laid in a depression on the bottom once a space has been cleared and any interfering vegetation cut down by the prospective parents.

When spawning occurs between individual pairs in clear water or blackwater (water stained the color of tea) where the fish see each other, color and fin differences often develop between the sexes. This is the case in some of the *Myleus* species. By contrast, some *Mylossoma* species breed in turbid water where visibility is poor or almost nonexistent. Here, pronounced differences between the sexes do not develop, and spawning often happens in large shoals rather than pairs.

Piranhas and their relatives can produce either several hundred or many thousands of eggs depending on the species and the size of the female. Hatching usually takes less than a week. Spawning generally occurs at the outset of the rainy season and may continue for several months.

Walking catfish *(Clarias batrachus)*

Common name Walking catfish

Family Clariidae

Order Siluriformes

Number of species 100 in around 13 genera

Size From 4.7 in (12 cm) to around 4.6 ft (1.4 m)

Key features Elongated body, with some species eel-like; dorsal and anal fins long-based and lack a spine at the front—these fins may be joined to the caudal fin or may be separate; adipose fin usually absent; pectoral fins usually have spine (used in walking), but both pectoral and pelvic fins may be absent; body scaleless; head often flattened and covered in bony plates; eyes range from well formed to tiny or absent; mouth terminal (located at the tip of the snout) with 4 pairs of long barbels in most species (3 in some); modified gills and arborescent and superbranchial organs present in most genera to allow fish to breathe out of water

Breeding Usually at night, at beginning of rainy season, in shallow water; nesting possible but the eggs left unprotected once spawning completed; hatching around 23–30 hours

Diet From small aquatic insects and other invertebrates to fish and small birds

Habitat A wide range of freshwater habitats including lakes, pools, and backwaters; some live in caves or wells

Distribution Widely in Africa, parts of the Middle East, and southern and western Asia; as a food or aquarium fish in other regions—for example, Florida and Hawaii

Status IUCN lists 8 species as under various levels of threat

⊙ *The walking catfish* (Clarias batrachus) *is the best-known member of its family. It is found from India to Indonesia, but has also been introduced elsewhere. Length to 18.5 inches (47cm).*

Walking Catfish   Clariidae

A fish that can walk on dry land and breathe air? Not a biological impossibility for most of the species of walking catfish, which have developed systems that can exploit conditions both in and out of water.

THE ABILITY OF WALKING CATFISH to survive out of water comes about because the gills, or parts of the gills, are specially modified to enable the fish to breathe not just in normally oxygenated water but also in polluted, oxygen-poor conditions. Provided the air is sufficiently humid to keep the gill chamber moist and prevent the scaleless, mucus-covered body from drying out, walking catfish can even survive for a time out of water. They can certainly live out of water long enough for them to walk from one stretch of water to another, using a combination of their pectoral fin spines and eel-like body movements. Walking catfish can also survive periods of drought buried in the mud at the bottom of dried-out pools until the rains return—which may be for several months or more in the hotter, drier areas of their range.

Air-breathing Equipment

All four gills, but particularly the second and fourth, are modified in walking catfish. As well as the normal gill tissue, all the gills have a flap known as the respiratory membrane extending upward into a chamber (the suprabranchial chamber) located above the gills. They also carry a respiratory "fan" that is especially elaborate on the fourth gill arch, whose normal gill tissue is much reduced. Also, parts of the second and fourth gill arches have developed into a finely branched, treelike structure known as the arborescent organ, which is suspended in the suprabranchial chamber.

So while the gills absorb dissolved oxygen from the water in the normal way, the other structures allow walking catfish to absorb oxygen directly from air gulped by the fish at the water's surface. The capacity to breathe in oxygen directly is a major survival tool for the family. If the water in their habitat is polluted or gets too hot, oxygen levels become depleted. Should this happen, walking catfish can switch systems instantly to breathe oxygen from the air. Indeed, some species have become so reliant on their dual-purpose breathing apparatus, they may drown if prevented from breathing surface air from time to time.

The Tree of Life

A walking catfish's arborescent organ, respiratory fan and membrane, and gills perform roughly the same task that lungs do in air-breathing mammals. They are the interface where gas exchange (carbon dioxide for oxygen) takes place. Blood circulates in the fish's body, gradually picking up carbon dioxide. It reaches the arborescent organ and respiratory fan and membrane where the carbon dioxide is released as bubbles through the fish's gill openings, while oxygen is absorbed. Oxygen-rich blood flows from these organs via the superbranchial chamber into the body, where the whole process starts again.

Walking Threat

Walking catfish are widely cultivated as food fish in Africa and Asia. The most popular species is "the" walking catfish, or Asian

⊕ *The walking catfish (Clarias batrachus), also known as the Asian walking catfish, is popular as a food fish. In its albino form it is also kept as an aquarium fish.*

Tree or Labyrinth?

The structure that allows walking catfish to breathe atmospheric oxygen is called the arborescent organ due to its treelike or dendritic (finely branched) nature. In other fish species that take in air at the water's surface, such as the gouramis and their relatives (family Anabantidae), the air-breathing apparatus consists of highly folded plates and is known as the labyrinth organ.

Confusingly, the terms labyrinth organ and arborescent organ are quite frequently used as if they were the same thing. As a result, the walking catfish are often referred to as the labyrinth catfish. However, since the walking catfish do not really have a labyrinth organ, this name should be dropped. More accurately, walking catfish are also referred to as air-breathing catfish.

◉ *This African walking catfish, only partially submerged in shallows in South Africa's Kruger National Park, is probably spawning.*

walking catfish (*Clarias batrachus*), which grows to around 22 inches (55 cm) and is a voracious predator. In the U.S. the albino form of the species became quite popular as an aquarium fish, although less so as a food fish. However, sale of the species is now banned throughout the country, along with all other members of its family, being regarded as "injurious to wildlife."

This is due to the fact that the fish may travel from a polluted water source to a clean one, possibly bringing the pollution with them. There is also concern because walking catfish not only survive where other fish and aquatic creatures may not, but can reproduce rapidly. However, moving from one source of water to another is not always linked to pollution or lack of oxygen. Sometimes it may be due to a lack of food, whose composition in the case of many of the walking catfish is wide ranging and can include insects as well as other fish.

Put all these factors together, and it is evident that walking catfish can present a real threat to native species should they escape and become established in the wild. This in fact is what happened in Florida, where fish that escaped or were released in the period between 1965 and 1967 resulted in most freshwater habitats in the southern half of the state being contaminated by the late 1970s.

Closer to its native waters in Asia, the Asian walking catfish is itself under threat from introduced species such as the much larger African walking catfish (*Clarias gareipinus*), a native of the African Nile and Niger Rivers. It is not just the fear that African walking catfish may replace its Asian cousin that is causing concern, but the fact that these two species can interbreed. Should this become widespread, the genetic integrity of Asian walking catfish could be seriously harmed.

On the other hand, controlled hybridization of the African walking catfish and the large-headed walking catfish (*Clarias macrocephalus*) has been achieved so successfully by aquaculturists that the hybrid has become one of the most popular food fish in countries such as Malaysia and Thailand.

Less Famous Walkers

The *Clarias* genus, containing around 45 species, is the best-known group of the clariids. Little known outside scientific circles are the eel-like species, such as the eel catfish (*Channallabes apus*) and the flathead eel catfish (*Gymnallabes typus*). Two other pink, eyeless species that prefer underground waters are *Horaglanis krishnai*, found in wells around Kottayam in Kerala, India, and *Uegitglanis zammaranoi* from Somalia. The most famous cave-dwelling species is the cave catfish (*Clarias cavernicola*).

① At 4.6 feet (1.4 m) in length and a weight of 132 pounds (60 kg) the African walking catfish (Clarias gareipinus) is one of the largest in its family. It has become very popular as a food fish.

Electric catfish (*Malapterurus electricus*)

Common name Electric catfish

Family   Malapteruridae

Order   Siluriformes

Number of species 11 in 1 genus

Size   From around 4.8 in (12.2 cm) to around 48 in (1.2 m)

Key features Sturdy head; small eyes; fleshy lips; 3 pairs of mouth barbels; nasal or "nose" barbels lacking; no dorsal fin; adipose fin well formed and located near the tail; rounded caudal fin; different degrees and intensity of mottling and body banding

Breeding May spawn in burrows excavated in river banks

Diet   Smaller fish

Habitat   Slow-moving or still waters containing rocks, sunken logs, and roots where the fish can shelter or rest in daylight hours; many preferred waters are tannin-stained (known as blackwaters) or turbid in nature

Distribution Widespread in tropical Africa from western Africa through central regions to the Nile River; individual species may have restricted ranges

Status   Not threatened

ⓣ *The electric catfish* (Malapterurus electricus), *a fierce 4-ft (1.2-m) predator widespread in tropical Africa. The electricity it produces is not only used to stun prey and deter predators but also to navigate and detect prey.*

Electric Catfish Malapteruridae

Often described as large sausages that lie on the bottom doing very little, the electric catfish will knock you back as no sausage can—as unsuspecting humans have frequently found to their cost.

ELECTRICITY GENERATION IS NOT UNIQUE to electric catfish. Numerous fish in many unrelated families employ electricity for various purposes. Many, like the elephantnoses (family Mormyridae), generate weak electrical fields to help them navigate and communicate. At the other end of the electric spectrum the electric eel can produce around 550 volts.

Somewhere in between the weak and the most powerful generators lies the electric catfish, capable of producing bursts of around 350 volts. Such a level of electricity, while not strong enough to kill, is nevertheless powerful enough to stun prey, deter predators, or leave a human hurt or temporarily shocked.

Organic Generator

In electric catfish the organ that generates electricity lies under the skin and occupies an area (on both sides of the body) extending from behind the head to a point approximately in line with the front edges of the adipose and anal fins, ending in a backward-pointing arc. It does not, however, extend into the fins. The organ consists of specialized cells called electrocytes that have evolved from pectoral (chest) muscle cells. The electrocytes are about 0.4 inches (1 cm) in diameter and are stacked on top of each other. One surface of each electrocyte carries a short stalk and is attached to fine nerve fibers. Each stack of cells is enveloped in a jellylike substance and receives a rich blood supply. Each complete organ is, in turn, attached to a large nerve end that arises from the front part of the spinal cord. Because of their orientation and the front attachment of the main nerves the current in the electric catfish's organ flows from front to back.

⊝ *An electric catfish (*Malapterurus electricus) *from Lake Tanganyika, Tanzania. In its mouth is its stunned prey.*

⊕ *Smallmouth electric catfish (*Malapterurus microstoma) *from the northern region of the Zambezi River. Electric catfish hide by day, but at dusk they start to spread out and search for food.*

In addition to the electric organ's function in stunning prey and deterring predators, it also has other functions. It can, for instance, be used in navigation and detecting prey—two activities that do not require the strong pulses that defense and attack demand. In addition, electric catfish use the versatile organ to size up rivals, intruders, and potential mates. However, in the case of a potential adversary it is only employed if other, more moderate, and nonelectrical measures have failed to supply the information or deter the rival.

The longest-lasting discharges the electric organ can generate are the ones used for stunning or hunting; they can last up to 30 seconds and consist of several hundred individual pulses. The pulses are sometimes preceded by a series of weaker ones that the electric catfish may send out to help flush prey into the open.

The Father of Thunder

The properties of the electric catfish were well known to ancient Africans. In fact, the Arabic name for the electric catfish translates as "Father of Thunder." It is also recorded in Egyptian hieroglyphics some 5,000 years old, in which its name translates as "He who had saved many in the sea." It is not clear why the fish was referred to in such terms, although it is known that it was—and still is—used to treat a variety of medical conditions. Reportedly, electric catfish can be placed on the affected part of the body to effect a cure. Quite how this treatment is intended to work is something of a mystery, especially in cases in which live shock-producing fish are used.

Electric Catfish Species

Common Name	Scientific Name	Approx. Size inches (cm)
	M. beninensis	8.8 (22.3)
	M. cavalliensis	4.8 (12.2)
Electric catfish	M. electricus	48 (122.0)
	M. leonensis	6.1 (15.5)
Smallmouth electric catfish	M. microstoma	27.2 (69.0)
	M. minjiriya	40.2 (102.0)
	M. monsembeensis	22.8 (58.0)
	M. oguensis	6.3 (16.1)
	M. shirensis	12 (30.0)
	M. tanganyikaensis	19.1 (48.5)
	M. tanoensis	10.2 (26.0)

All lengths are standard, in other words, measured from snout to base of caudal fin. However, the figure for the smallmouth electric catfish is for the total length—from snout to tip of caudal fin.

How Many Species?

The first electric catfish to be officially described was *Malapterurus electricus,* in 1789. Since it was believed to be the only species in the genus, it became known, quite simply, as the electric catfish. Three other species were subsequently described during the next 90 years, but they all came to be regarded as varieties of the original electric catfish rather than as separate species. The situation remained like this until 1969, when a new species from Central Africa, the smallmouth electric catfish (*M. microstoma*), was described. It was followed in 1987 by the discovery of yet another species, *M. minjiriya*, from West Africa.

It had long been known that electric catfish were not only widespread in Africa, but that they occurred with variable body markings and sizes. However, the differences had not been examined in detail until 2000. When the study was eventually carried out, it was discovered that the electric catfish group consisted of not one, two, or even three species but 11 (see box "Electric Catfish Species"). The main differences between the species are in the overall body length and patterning, the shape and size of the mouth, the tooth arrangement, and the number of vertebrae in the skeleton.

Changing Data

The results of the investigations have opened a whole new chapter in electric catfish history, raising the need for further in-depth studies of each of the new species, especially since some are restricted in their distribution. It has also, of course, changed the distribution map for the electric catfish itself. This species is still the most widespread of all, but many populations of electric catfish once believed to be isolated pockets of *M. electricus* now turn out to be populations of other species. For example, the electric catfish from the Ogôoué basin in Gabon are now known to be the only representatives of the species *M. oguensis.* Similarly, those from the Cavally River on the Ivory Coast are members of the species *M. cavalliensis*, and at least some of the individuals from the Zambezi River basin belong to the species *M. shirensis.*

Little-known Properties

In contrast to the considerable data available on the electrical qualities of electric catfish, disappointingly little is known about other aspects of their biology and affinities.

They are, for example, believed to share some characteristics with the bagrid catfish (family Bagridae), the shark catfish (family Pangasiidae), and the sheatfish (family Siluridae). In fact, the original scientific name for *Malapterurus electricus* was *Silurus electricus*. More research is required on the possible links, however, so the best we can say is that the closest relatives of the electric catfish probably belong to one of the above families.

Of one thing there can be no doubt: Electric catfish are highly aggressive toward each other. They are also keenly predatory, using their electrical equipment to catch prey that they would otherwise be unable to catch largely owing to their lack of speed.

The electric catfish was first imported from Africa into Europe in 1904. It has enjoyed a long history as an aquarium fish, but it has proved impossible to breed the species, or any of its close relatives, in captivity. Details about its breeding season and habits in the wild are also very scarce. It is variously reported to breed during the summer season or during the rainy season. Perhaps both are correct and apply either to the electric catfish in different parts of its distribution or to one or other of the new species that had previously been thought to be variants of the electric catfish.

Intriguing Stories

Breeding is thought to take place in excavated cavities or inside holes in river banks. The holes or burrows measure up to 10 feet (3 m) in length and occur in water ranging between 40 inches (1 m) and 10 feet (3 m) in depth. The electric catfish is reported to form pairs prior to spawning, but no details are available for the other species. However, owing to the former misidentification of species, it is possible that the scant data we have for the electric catfish may also apply to the ten other members of the genus. Intriguingly, one report suggests that the electric catfish may be a mouthbrooder, but this is also unconfirmed.

⊕ *An electric catfish (Malapterurus electricus) showing the color variation and striping sometimes seen in the genus.*

Coral catfish (*Plotosus lineatus*)

Common name Tandan catfish (eeltail catfish, coral catfish, stinging catfish)

Family Plotosidae

Order Siluriformes

Number of species Around 32 in 9 genera

Size From around 4.8 in (12.2 cm) to about 35.4 in (90 cm)

Key features Elongate body, almost eel-like in some genera; flattened or rounded head; 4 pairs of barbels; dorsal and pectoral fins bear a serrated, venomous spine at the front; adipose fin absent; anal and caudal fin joined; top part of caudal fin extends forward along back as a caudodorsal fin with soft rays

Breeding Little known generally; dewfish (*Tandanus tandanus*) well known

Diet Animal matter, including insects, snails, crustaceans, fish, and other invertebrates

Habitat Wide range, from coral reefs through estuaries to rivers; around 50 percent of species strictly freshwater

Distribution Indian Ocean and western Pacific Ocean extending from Japan to Australia

Status IUCN lists Kutubu tandan (*Oloplotosus torobo*) as Vulnerable

⊕ *The coral catfish* (Plotosus lineatus) *grows to about 12 inches (30 cm) and lives at the bottom of reefs and estuaries. In spite of its venomous spines, it is a popular aquarium fish.*

Tandan Catfish · Plotosidae

*Beware of buzzing coral; it has not been colonized by a swarm of bees but a shoal of coral catfish (*Plotosus lineatus*). The "aquatic bees" sting with such severity that it can take months for the wound to heal.*

A WELL-DOCUMENTED ACCOUNT OF SOMEONE being stung by a tandan catfish occurred in 1949. A biologist named A. Herre was stung by a catfish less than 6 inches (15 cm) long that had been lying in the bottom of his boat for about 15 minutes. Assuming the fish was dead, Herre picked it up. Thereupon the fish struggled and stung him on the thumb with one of its pectoral fin spines.

The pain, although considerable, did not prevent Herre from fishing for another half hour or so. However, during this time the pain got worse, as did the swelling—not just of the thumb but eventually the whole hand, wrist, and forearm. The problem became so serious that the swelling had to be medically drained, and Herre was

These black tandan (Neosilurus ater), found in the seas off north Australia, perfectly display the "megafin," in which the caudal and anal fins are joined. The fused fin is a typical identifying feature of tandan catfish.

given a potent morphine painkiller. It took nearly a week for the swelling to go down. Other complications included three days of severe diarrhea and weight loss. After this critical week-long phase almost six months passed before a full recovery was made.

The species responsible for giving Herre such a hard time is the saltwater or coral catfish (*Plotosus lineatus*). It is a particularly beautiful species during its juvenile stages, when it is strikingly marked in dark brown and cream-colored stripes running from head to tail. The stripes disappear with age, and the fish become uniformly dark.

Joined Tandans

Not all members of the family are sea going; nor are they all as dangerous as the coral catfish. In fact, the genus *Tandanus*, which contains about 12 species, inhabits a range of habitats, from fully marine through estuarine to fresh water. The most typical species, the dewfish (*Tandanus tandanus*), is, like the majority of its relatives, strictly a freshwater species. Unlike the coral catfish, it is not easily alarmed and is therefore less of a threat, although its venom is probably just as potent.

Like all the tandan catfish, the dewfish has joined caudal and anal fins. Although there is

⊕ *The toothless catfish (Anodontiglanis dahli) is a native of northern Australian rivers. The pointed head and almost eel-like body give rise to yet another description of fish in the family: eeltail catfish. The dorsal fin has serrated, venomous spines that protect the catfish from predators.*

no adipose fin, the top front end of the caudal fin extends some way forward along the back of the body. This extension is regarded as a second dorsal fin (it contains rays and is therefore quite unlike an adipose fin) and is often referred to as the caudodorsal fin. The joined "megafin," allied to the elongated body form and the four pairs of well-formed mouth barbels, have given rise to yet another name for the Plotosidae: the eeltail catfish.

⊕ *Juvenile coral catfish (Plotosus lineatus) bunch together in a ball for protection while they are still small and vulnerable, and their stinging abilities have not fully developed.*

Dewfish Breeders

The dewfish is the one of the few members of the family in which breeding behavior is understood. The male excavates large, circular nests, some measuring up to 40 inches (1 m) in spring and summer, usually in the sandy or muddy substrata of freshwater estuaries or rivers. There may be large numbers of small rocks and coarse gravel around the edge of the nests, and the insides may also be filled with gravel, stones, and vegetation. A male will seek out a female and chase or drive her to the completed nest. Upward of 20,000 eggs may be laid by a single medium-sized female. After laying, the male takes up nest-guarding duty. Hatching takes about one week, but the male may guard the site for up to 18 days.

In the coral catfish, a marine species, eggs may be laid during summer, either in a nest or in rock crevices. Either way, the nest and the eggs are protected by the male, and hatching takes 7 to 10 days.

"Bumblebee" Balls

Juvenile coral catfish regularly come together to form tight balls, sometimes consisting of hundreds of specimens, with each fish's head pointing toward the center. The balls are capable of moving in one direction or another as if they were a single organism, earning themselves the nickname of "catfish going to church," an imaginative tag coined by Australian Aboriginal children.

Another name used for the colorful, ball-making juveniles is the bumblebee catfish because of their color (although the light stripes are not yellow, as in bumblebees, and the stripes run from head to tail rather than vertically), their swimming behavior, and their ability to make buzzing sounds as they swim through the coral reefs.

Upside-down catfish (*Synodontis nigriventris*)

Common name Upside-down catfish (squeakers, squeaking catfish)

Family Mochokidae

Order Siluriformes

Number of species Around 170 in 10 genera

Size From around 2 in (5 cm) to 27.5 in (70 cm)

Key features Normal-headed species have sloping forehead and slightly to moderately pointed snout; mouth on underside of tip of snout; in sucker-mouthed species mouth is broader and more straight-edged with fleshy lips and broad tooth pads; stout cephalic (head) shield found in all, extending to front of dorsal fin along the top and to the base of pectoral fins along the sides and bottom; 3 pairs of barbels (no nasal barbels), ornate in some; dorsal and pectoral fins possess a stout spine at front, can be "locked" in defense; adipose fin large, becoming sail like in normal-headed species

Breeding Few details available; eggs said to be adhesive and laid under cover; no parental care reported; hatching takes about a week; at least 2 species lay eggs among those laid by breeding mouthbrooding cichlids

Diet Small organisms, crustaceans, and plankton; algae scraped off rocks, logs, and submerged vegetation; larger species take small fish

Habitat Prefer slow-moving waters, lakes, and swamps; sucker-mouthed species prefer faster-flowing waters, some in torrents; many spend day hiding under submerged logs and roots or in caves and crevices

Distribution Widespread in most tropical regions of Africa including African Rift lakes

Status IUCN lists Incomati rock catlet (*Chiloglanis bifurcis*) as Critically Endangered

ⓣ *The 4-inch (10-cm) upside-down catfish (Synodontis nigriventris) swims upside down to graze the underside of leaves for algae and tiny animals.*

Upside-down Catfish

Mochokidae

Some mochokids have the habit of flipping onto their backs and swimming around upside down as if they are sick or injured.

UNUSUAL THOUGH IT APPEARS, SWIMMING in an inverted fashion is natural behavior for upside-down catfish. They do not do it all the time, however; even the most famous species of upside-down catfish, *Synodontis nigriventris*, does not spend its whole life inverted, but it does swim in this way more frequently than do any other species in the family.

In fact, the habit is such an integral and frequent part of the lifestyle of *S. nigriventris* that the fish has developed reverse counter-shading (see box "Now You See Me...Now You Don't"). Instead of the normal body shading pattern consisting of a dark back and a lighter belly, this species, whose species name *nigriventris* means "black belly," exhibits the opposite arrangement—a dark underside and a lighter back.

The upside-down swimming habit of the family, and probably that of others which adopt a similar swimming orientation, is not present at birth and may take a few months to develop.

Normal Heads and Suckers

Although the name upside-down catfish is certainly descriptive of some species and has made mochokids famous the world over, the behavior is not exhibited by the majority of members. Indeed, it is possible that more species are capable of squeaking than flipping over, making the alternative name for the family—squeakers or squeaking catfish—probably more accurate if less colorful.

Two distinct groups are identified within the family Mochokidae. The first group contains species that have what are described as "normal" heads. The other group consists of

ⓓ *Swimming close to the bottom, a beautifully marked polkadot squeaker (Synodontis angelicus) shows the sloping forehead and ornate barbels typical of the "normal-headed" species.*

the suckermouthed species; they have flattened heads and, as their common name indicates, sucker-type mouths.

The normal-headed group is the larger of the two, and it contains seven genera: *Acanthocleithron*, *Brachysynodontis*, *Hemisynodontis*, *Microsynodontis*, *Mochokiella*, *Mochokus*, and *Synodontis*—the last genus being by far the largest, with 70 percent of all the species in the family. It is the genus to which the upside-down catfish *S. nigriventris* and its closest relatives belong. The normal-headed group includes the smallest of the squeakers—Payne's synodontis or the African bumblebee catfish (*Mochokiella paynei*), which grows to a maximum size of 2 inches (5 cm),

Now You See Me...Now You Don't

A fish that is uniformly drab will immediately stand out. In normal sunlight the back of the fish contrasts against the darkness of the water below it, making it visible to predators from above, such as seabirds. The lower half of the body, in shade, will also be darker than the bright background created by the sunlight from above, making the fish visible to predators, such as larger fish, approaching from below. Viewed from the side, the light top and darker lower half created by the sunlight striking the uniformly colored body makes it visible to predators at any angle. One of the most common ways that has evolved allowing species to avoid the attentions of predators is the development of a body patterning that helps them become less visible. In fish, reducing visibility by body patterning is achieved in three ways. Some fish have an almost totally transparent body. Others have a reflective body—in other words, one with silvery scales on the flanks. The other method is to adopt countershading on the body: having darker colors on the back fading to light colors along the belly. The effectiveness of each of the methods, or even a combination of them, depends on a number of factors, including the habits of the fish, its surroundings, and the intensity of ambient light.

The majority of fish species exhibit countershading to great effect. The darker colors along the back absorb light waves from above and make the fish appear virtually invisible against the equally dark background of the water or bottom below. Viewed at any angle, ranging from directly above through horizontal to varying angles from below, the dark-to-light body shading provides effective camouflage against the changing levels of light intensity that exist (in reverse) at these orientations. Similarly, from directly below white or light belly colors make the fish hard to see as it blends into the bright background created by light filtering through the sky.

Countershading is a proven, effective survival mechanism. But some fish—such as the upside-down catfish and their relatives—have the opposite color arrangement. In other words, they have dark bellies and lighter colored backs, which would normally make them stand out from every angle. But such fish are designed to swim upside down; and when they do so, the reverse countershading provides the same level of concealment that it affords species that swim in the more "conventional" manner.

⊕ *Upside-down catfish (Synodontis nigriventris) give a spontaneous display of their unusual swimming skills, which from birth take up to eight weeks to develop. This allows them to exploit a food niche other species ignore— algae and other aquatic microorganisms found on the underside of aquatic plants.*

but is usually smaller. It also contains some of the largest, such as the gray synodontis (*Synodontis schall*), which attains 22 inches (56 cm) or more in length, and the black-spotted dusky synodontis (*S. acanthomias)* at around 24 inches (60 cm) in length.

In the normal-headed genera the mouth is located just under the tip of the snout and is surrounded by three pairs of barbels (the nasal or "nose" pair is lacking). In some species the barbels may be quite elaborate: Some bear membranes or flaps, and others are feathery. The head is also protected with a hard body shield that generally extends to the front of the dorsal fin at the top and to the pectoral fins below. This characteristic arrangement is found in both of the mochokid groups.

In the suckermouth species the barbels tend to be short and much simpler in form. Suckermouths also have characteristic broad, flattened mouths with spread-out lips and pads of scraping teeth. Such an arrangement allows them to cling securely to rocks while they are busy scraping food from them. There are only three genera of suckermouth squeakers: *Atopochilus,* which contains seven or so species; *Chiloglanis,* the 34 or so catlets; and *Euchilichthys,* which contains the three false chiloglanis species.

Like normal-headed mochokids, all the suckermouths have well-formed adipose fins. However, the level of development is nowhere near as sophisticated as that shown by their cousins, which exhibit truly magnificent, almost sail-like adipose fins.

Cuckoo Breeders

A most unusual birdlike breeding strategy has evolved in at least two species of *Synodontis,* the even-spotted synodontis (*S.petricola*), which grows to 22 inches (56 cm) or more, and the cuckoo synodontis (*S. multipunctatus*). Both are whitish fish liberally spotted with black, and both occur in Lake Tanganyika in Africa.

The lake is famous for its spectacular mouthbrooding cichlids. In the breeding season the cichlids go through an elaborate courtship ritual that is routinely exploited by the two enterprising catfish species. After mating, the female cichlid takes the eggs into her mouth and incubates them there until they hatch. Following the hatching and release of the fry, the mother will continue taking her young into her mouth for several more days, or even weeks, whenever danger threatens, thus providing them with an exceptionally high level of protection .

The even-spotted synodontis and the cuckoo synodontis synchronize their breeding with that of several of the mouthbrooding

159

cichlids, following them around as they prepare for spawning. Once spawning gets under way, mouthbrooding cichlids become so focused on the job in hand that they tend to ignore almost anything going on around them, and this is precisely what the parasitic catfish have been waiting for.

As soon as some cichlid eggs have been laid, the catfish dive in between the mating cichlids and release some eggs of their own. It is reported that the catfish eat or steal some of the cichlid eggs before laying their own. Whether this happens or not, the female cichlid picks up any eggs that she sees and incubates

them in her mouth whether they are her own or those laid by the *Synodontis* species. It is estimated that *Synodontis* eggs account for as much as 15 percent of the total brood in one population of the mouth-brooding cichlid *Ctenochromis horei*, one of several mouthbrooding cichlid species to be parasitized by the catfish. The developing *Synodontis* eggs

and fry receive the same level of protection as their cichlid broodmates. It has been suggested that newly hatched synodonts may feed on some of the cichlid eggs or fry. If this turns out to be accurate, the benefits of this parasitic breeding strategy are even higher for the catfish. The parallels with the breeding strategy of the feathered cuckoo are clear.

⊕ *Like the bird for which it is named, the cuckoo synodontis (Synodontis multipunctatus) tricks other species into raising and feeding its young.*

Electric Eel *Electrophorus electricus*

The body shape of electric eels explains why they are often called eels, but they are actually members of the New World knifefish order. Since they were first identified in 1729, electric eels have been one of the most feared fish in the Amazon.

Common name Electric eel (electric knifefish)

Scientific name *Electrophorus electricus*

Family   Electrophoridae

Order   Gymnotiformes

Size   Grows up to 8 ft (2.4 m) long

Key features Large throat; cylindrical teeth; no scales on rounded body; no pelvic fins; anal fin extends around end of tail; approximately 240 vertebrae; remarkable regenerative powers if injured; can breathe atmospheric air directly; prominent electrical organs used to kill prey and to defend themselves, as well as for communicating via electrical impulses

Breeding   Courtship and egg-laying behavior unknown

Diet   Carnivorous, including shrimp, amphibians, and fish

Habitat   Confined entirely to fresh water

Distribution Occurring in the Amazon and Orinoco River basins in South America, including Peru, Venezuela, Brazil, and Guyana

Status   Does not appear uncommon

ELECTRIC EELS ARE VERY DANGEROUS creatures. They can inflict severe, and sometimes even fatal, electrical shocks on people. The electrical power generated by their bodies is even powerful enough to kill an animal as big as a horse wading in their vicinity.

The electric organs of these knifefish are made of three separate structures that together occupy approximately 80 percent of the fish's body volume. The organs take the form of white, jellylike areas divided by fibrous partitions. They total approximately half a million electrical plates that combine to give off a parallel discharge, with the output under the control of the central nervous system.

Measuring the Shock

Measurements reveal that electric eels are able to discharge at least 550 volts with a current of 2 amps, which adds up to an output of 1 kilowatt in total. The shock is of a very brief duration, lasting as little as three-thousandths of a second, but the fish can produce as many as 150 shocks of this type per hour with no significant falloff in output.

The effect of the shock is likely to be significantly worsened if any mistaken attempt is made to handle an electric eel, since it will create separate discharges from the electrical organs in different parts of its body.

The range of the shock's effect is widespread in the water, extending for at least 3 feet (1 m) around the fish, serving to stun or kill prey that the eel might otherwise have had difficulty in catching directly. Electrical discharges of this type also serve as a potent defense against would-be predators in these waters, varying from other fish to reptiles and, notably, larger turtles and caimans.

Lower-intensity outputs are also believed to enable these fish to remain in contact with each other, especially since they tend to be nocturnal in their habits; these outputs may also help them navigate in the water. Electric eels are thought to rely on special electroreceptors, typically on the head for this purpose. With no fin on the upper surface of their body, they must depend entirely on the wavy anal fin running along the underside of the body and their sinuous body shape for their mobility.

Intercommunication

Although little is known about their breeding habits, there is no doubt that communication between the sexes is enhanced by the use of electrical organs. Males reveal their presence by emitting regular, relatively far-reaching pulses. In contrast, the pulses given off by responding females are shorter, so a male is able to distinguish when a receptive female is nearby. Their electrical abilities help compensate these knifefish for their poor eyesight; their eyes are very small relative to their body size. This also partly reflects the murky waters in which the fish are frequently found.

Virtually nothing is known about the development of young electric eels, although it is clear that from an early age they will feed on various crustaceans, especially freshwater shrimp, before moving on to larger prey such as fish. The young tend to be quite aggressive toward each other, whereas adult electric eels are more tolerant of others of their own kind. They are not particularly active fish by nature, often resting on the bottom as well as being nocturnal, preferring to hunt after dark.

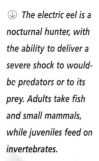

⊕ *The electric eel is a nocturnal hunter, with the ability to deliver a severe shock to would-be predators or to its prey. Adults take fish and small mammals, while juveniles feed on invertebrates.*

Muskellunge (*Esox masquinongy*)

Common name Pikes and pickerels

Family Esocidae

Order Esociformes

Number of species 5 in 1 genus

Size From around 15.5 in (39.5 cm) to about 6 ft (1.8 m)

Key features Elongated body; large, pointed head with distinct duck-billed snout; large mouth with numerous pointed teeth; lower jaw slightly longer than upper; eyes in top half of head; all fins well formed; no adipose fin; pectoral fins close to gill openings; dorsal and anal fins set well back along body; caudal fin forked; body often mottled with irregular streaks; pale belly

Breeding Usually in spring; males arrive at breeding sites before females; cool, shallow waters preferred, underwater vegetation essential; spawning can occur in groups of 1 female and 2 or 3 males; eggs and sperm scattered among vegetation and spread out over several weeks; large female can release up to 600,000 sticky eggs; no parental protection; hatching takes a few days to nearly a month depending on water temperature

Diet Small fish, insects, and other invertebrates during juvenile stages; larger pikes eat amphibians, larger fish, crayfish, small mammals, waterfowl

Habitat Predominantly fresh water but also in brackish conditions; slow-flowing or still waters preferred, especially heavily vegetated and shallow; can be found at 100 ft (30 m); cool water temperatures preferred but not restricted to such conditions

Distribution Widely distributed in Northern Hemisphere but do not occur naturally in northern Norway or northern Scotland

Status Not threatened

⊕ *At 6 feet (1.8 m) in length, the muskellunge (Esox masquinongy) is the longest member of the family Esocidae. This huge North American freshwater predator feeds on a variety of animals, including fish, ducklings, muskrats, and snakes.*

Pikes and Pickerels

Esocidae

Whether 15.5 inches (39.5 cm) or 6 feet (1.8 m) long, pikes and pickerels are fearsome freshwater predators capable of taking prey two-thirds or even half their own size and are themselves regarded as prime game fish throughout their Northern Hemisphere range.

ALL FIVE MEMBERS OF THE family Esocidae are very similar in overall body shape. They have pointed heads with large mouths that extend back to the eye. The lower jaw is slightly longer than the upper jaw, and both are armed with large, sharp, pointed teeth. The body is long and muscular with the dorsal and anal fins located a long way back close to the forked tail.

Perfect Hunting Formula

These lithe, large-mouthed, prong-toothed hunters have a perfect formula for ambushing their prey—they lie and wait blending in with their surroundings until a suitable victim swims by. The body camouflage is so effective, and movements of the pectoral fins so difficult to see, that it is often possible for even a large pike to maneuver into position and drift totally undetected right up to within striking distance of its prey. Before the victim realizes its danger, it is already halfway down the attacker's throat.

Pikes themselves are not safe from these surprise attacks and often regard each other as suitable meals. Consequently, particularly

during the juvenile phase, the young of some species are cannibalistic and regard smaller members of their own species as fair game.

Widely Distributed Hunter

The northern pike (*Esox lucius*) is the most widely distributed member of its family. However, it does not migrate from one region to another but prefers to remain close to the waters where it was born.

Within these restrictions it travels considerable distances and is found in both freshwater and brackish water habitats around the world—but only in the Northern Hemisphere (although not in northern Norway or northern Scotland). This world-famous fish has been introduced into other regions outside its natural range, including Morocco, Tunisia, Madagascar, Algeria, Uganda, Ethiopia, Spain, and Portugal, the last two being among the few European countries in which this pike does not occur naturally. The first northern pike introduction happened in 1185 when English stocks were released into Irish waters.

The northern pike prefers (but is not totally restricted to) cooler waters at very shallow or

⊕ *The highly predatory northern pike (*Esox lucius*) is the heaviest species of pike. Specimens can grow to a weight of 70 pounds (32 kg).*

Pike but Only in Name

The impressive 36-inch (91-cm) blue pike has a perfect snout and finely tuned hunting instincts, but it is not a member of either the pike genus (*Esox*) or the family Esocidae. It is the blue-bodied form of the walleye (*Stizostedion [Sander] vitreum*) and belongs to the same family as darters and perches (Percidae).

Despite the similarity in name and habits, the blue pike is distinguished from its namesakes by having two separate, well-formed dorsal fins—the first of them is located well forward on the body. True pikes have only one dorsal fin on the body, which is located close to the tail.

Once considered a subspecies of the walleye (*S. v. glaucum*), the blue pike was found in two Great Lakes—Erie and Ontario—as well as the Niagara River. However, it is now thought to be either extinct in the wild or almost so.

infections such as tapeworms. In turn they can infect humans if a caught pike, which is considered an excellent though bony food fish, is not thoroughly cooked.

Protein-rich Diet
Most pikes sold for human consumption are caught on a hook and line by anglers who rank

relatively shallow depths, extending down to 100 feet (30 m) at most. It prefers still or slow-moving waters with vegetation where it hides.

Predator and Prey
Adult pikes are loners with a strong territorial instinct that does not allow other adults within their "home" waters. Juveniles are less solitary but are cannibalistic, with larger individuals stalking and feeding on their smaller relations. They are so cannibalistic that it is known that two specimens of equal size choked each other to death because the attacker could not swallow its prey, and the latter was not able to struggle free.

As they grow, pikes change their diet of small fish, insects, and other invertebrates to larger fish, as well as crayfish, newts, frogs, and small aquatic mammals such as water voles, ducklings, and other waterfowl.

For their part, very small or juvenile pikes are taken by other fish as well as predatory aquatic insects (such as dragonfly nymphs), waterbirds, and aquatic mammals such as otters. Adult pikes do not normally fall prey to other fish, but they do suffer from parasitic the species as one of the very best game fish, since a hooked pike will fight until it is exhausted. Unlike some other sport fish that are also caught for eating, pike have proved almost impossible to culture in controlled environments because of their dependence on live fish and their almost total rejection of commercially produced foods.

On their protein-rich diet the northern pike can grow up to 5 feet (1.5 m) long and achieve a weight of 70 pounds (32 kg). However, most specimens are smaller and lighter than this, and females are larger and thicker-bodied than males. Pike grow slowly in adulthood, achieving their maximum length and weight after about 30 years.

⬇ *The northern pike (Esox lucius) is a solitary and highly territorial fish. With its long, flat, duck-billed snout and big mouth filled with large, sharp teeth, it finds small fish easy prey.*

North American Tigers

In addition to the five species of pike discussed here there is a further pike lurking in many North American waters. Although a "true" pike, it is not a "natural" pike but a manmade one.

The tiger muskie, or musky, has attractive, tigerlike stripes along its whole body. It is also a ferocious fighter when hooked—not just its body pattern but its temperament as well contributes to its "tiger" name. The tiger muskie can grow to around 50 inches (1.3 m) in length and weighs over 32 pounds (15 kg). Although it is not the largest or heaviest pike, it is one of the most sought after by anglers because of its fighting spirit.

Tiger muskies were first produced in the 1940s by artificially fertilizing muskie, or muskellunge (*Esox masquinongy*), eggs with northern pike (*E. lucius*) sperm. The resulting hybrids are not only attractively marked but also have more power and ferocity than their parents. Such enhanced qualities are called "hybrid vigor," or "heterosis." Despite this, all tiger muskie males are sterile and most females too, although reportedly some may be fertile and are therefore capable of reproducing.

Thousands of tiger muskies have been introduced into angling waters in many states since the 1940s. Because they cannot reproduce (even if some females are fertile), the stocks must be constantly renewed to maintain population levels. To help keep up numbers, all hooked specimens must be released after capture—a requirement in many tiger muskie areas.

⊙ *Typically, northern pike live in lakes as well as rivers with reedy areas and quiet backwaters (like the one here) where they can hide before ambushing their prey.*

"Traditional" Spawners

Despite their long lifespan, northern pikes mature very early in life—in as little as two to three years—and will spawn every year afterward. Like all its relatives, this species breeds in spring, usually from late March into May, but in more northern parts of the range spawning can extend into July.

It prefers very cool waters for spawning, usually between 41 and 54° F (5–12° C), but it can be as low as 37° F (2° C) and also under ice. While there is some flexibility regarding breeding temperature, the one indispensable

and fixed factor is underwater vegetation. If it is absent, then spawning will not occur.

The males are the first to arrive at the spawning sites, which are often the same spot year after year, in a flooded meadow or other shallow, heavily vegetated habitat. An egg-laden female will often be courted by two or three smaller males, with eggs and sperm being scattered in batches among the vegetation. Each "bout" of egg release lasts one to two hours, with multiple releases spread out over a period of three to four weeks. During this time one large female can release up to 600,000 eggs at a rate of 15,000–20,000 per 2.2 pound (1 kg) of body weight.

The eggs are sticky and adhere to plants, where they remain unguarded by either parent

⊙ *Like its relative the northern pike (Esox lucius), the chain pickerel (E. niger) has the pike family's typical large eyes and long, flat, duck-billed snout. The fish is named after its chain-mail skin patterning; the "links" of the chain are green, while the "space" between is yellowish.*

until they hatch. They will hatch after 23 to 29 days at 43° F (6° C), 12 days at 50° F (10° C), or only 4–5 days at around 64° F (18° C).

Temperature affects not only the speed with which eggs hatch but also how many newly hatched larvae will survive; the figure decreases as the temperature rises.

The degree of crowding is also an important factor, at least where ponds have been stocked with pike fry. In this case the level of cannibalism increases as the degree of overcrowding rises. A similar situation can exist in the wild, where smaller fry form an important part of the diet of their faster-growing relatives.

In addition cannibals grow faster than noncannibals. As the growth rate of cannibals speeds up, so does their appetite. As a result of

this cannibalistic trait, a young northern pike, which can be as tiny as 0.35 inches (0.9 cm) long shortly after hatching in spring, can grow to about 8 inches (20 cm) by the fall.

One, Two, or Three Pickerels?

A beautiful, slim-bodied pike, the redfin pickerel (*Esox americanus americanus*) grows to around 15.5 inches (39.5 cm), making it the smallest member of the family. It is found along the Atlantic Slope drainages of North America from Quebec to southern Georgia. Like all pikes, it is a powerful fish for its size. Its snout is short and broad, and its body has a convex profile, giving it a slightly rounded or humped appearance. As its name implies, some of its fins are red.

The grass pickerel (*E. a. vermiculatus*) grows to around the same size but has a long,

↓ *A grass pickerel (Esox americanus vermiculatus) is very similar to a redfin pickerel (E. a. americanus), but it lacks the reddish fins that give the redfin its name.*

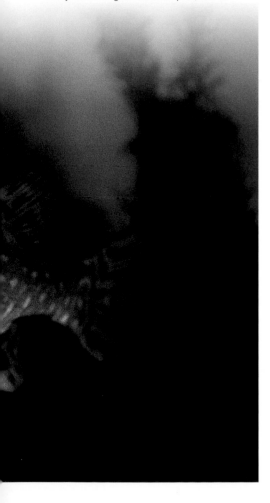

pointed snout, and its body has a flat or concave profile giving it a slightly "sunken" appearance. Its fins are yellowish-green to dusky in color. Its geographical range extends from the Great Lakes northward into Canada, southward to the Mississippi and Gulf Slope drainages, and westward into Texas.

In the part of the Gulf Slope drainage that extends west to the Pescagoula River there is a third pickerel that has characteristics of both the redfin and grass pickerels, and it has amber-colored fins.

"Lunging" Pike

At a length of 6 feet (1.8 m) the muskie, or muskellunge (*E. masquinongy*), is the giant of the pike family. Despite its size, it is not quite as heavy as the largest northern pike, which

Fossil and Giant Pikes

The pike family has been in existence for at least 60 million years. Fossils from sediments of this age (the Eocene) contain bones of a pike—*Esox tiemani*—that lived in Canadian waters. Another fossil pike, *E. papyraceus*, is considerably younger (around 30 million years) and was found in rocks near Bonn in Germany. This species looks very similar to the northern pike (*E. lucius*), whose earliest known fossils are a mere 500,000 years old!

More recent is an account of a "monster pike," called the emperor's pike, because Emperor Frederick II released the fish into the lake from which it was caught. This massive fish was reported to be at least 267 years old, 19 feet (5.8 m) long, and an estimated weight of 350 pounds (160 kg). Disappointingly the emperor's pike proved to be a hoax when a close examination of its skeleton showed that extra bones had been added to the backbone to "stretch" the overall length of the fish to its gigantic proportions!

Another more modestly sized giant was found in Loch Lomond, Scotland. Unfortunately only the head of this northern pike was preserved. It measured just over 12.5 inches (32 cm). Using known body proportions of other pikes, an estimate showed this fish was considerably bigger than the largest-known specimens of the species, but no one knows how large it really was because the body was discarded at the time the specimen was found stranded on the shore.

weighs a maximum of 70 pounds (32 kg). However, it is equally long-lived, with a maximum reported age of 30 years.

Like its relatives, this pike is "built to kill" by using a "lunging" action. It is a master hunter that will also feed on muskrats and snakes as well as the usual family diet of other fish, frogs, and at times crayfish. Ironically, one of its major predators during the earliest stages of life are northern pike juveniles, which hatch a little earlier and are already active hunters by the time the muskellunge fry hatch.

Although overlapping with the northern pike in more northerly parts of its range overall, the muskie is a more southern species that does not extend into the far northern reaches of North America. However, in terms of habitat preferences, hunting techniques, feeding, and breeding behavior, it is a typical pike. In fact, the muskie is so similar to the northern pike in so many of its habits that the two species are even known to interbreed occasionally in the wild where their ranges overlap.

The muskie is one of North America's top sport fish and therefore has been introduced into several areas outside its natural range. It has, for instance, been released along Atlantic drainages all the way down to southern Virginia; it has also been released into some southern and western regions. However, most of the releases have proved unsuccessful.

Chain Pickerel and Amur Pike

The two remaining species of pike are almost equal in size—around 39 inches (1 m) from tip of snout to back edge of tail. The chain pickerel (*E. niger*) is a North American species, while the Amur pike (*E. reichertii*) is found in the Amur River system in northeastern Asia, the only member of the family that does not occur in North America.

The chain pickerel is a long-snouted, slim fish with beautiful chainlike patterning along the body, where the "links" of the chain are green and the "space" between yellowish. The Amur pike does not have a chainlike pattern like its North American cousin, but its entire body and head are covered in many small black spots, giving an alternative common name of black-spotted pike.

The Amur pike is also a chunkier, considerably heavier fish, weighing around 35 pounds (16 kg) when fully grown. In comparison, an adult chain pickerel weighs only 9.4 pounds (4.3 kg). However, both fish are equally efficient stealth-hunters, popular with anglers wanting a fish that is challenging to catch and a valiant fighter once hooked.

⊖ *A fisherman removes a hook from the mouth of a northern pike (*Esox lucius*) that he has caught. It is very popular with sport fishermen, who like the challenge of hooking such a large fish that will fight until it is exhausted.*

Atlantic Salmon *Salmo salar*

Graceful, powerful, awesome, and majestic are just four of the numerous qualities attributed to a fish that is both revered and hunted wherever it is found. A prodigious leaper, it overcomes apparently impossible rapids in its irresistible urge to breed and then it dies.

Common name Atlantic salmon (salmon and many other names)

Scientific name *Salmo salar*

Subfamily/Family Salmoninae/Salmonidae

Order Salmoniformes

Size Extremely variable at maturity but up to 4.9 ft (1.5 m)

Key features Elongated body; pointed snout with rounded tip; large mouth; numerous teeth in both jaws; dorsal fin slightly in front of pelvic fin line; adipose fin present; tail slightly forked; anal fin slightly in front of adipose fin line; pelvic fins on belly; scales very small; fish returning from sea predominantly silver with darker back and white belly; pectoral fins relatively low and behind gill covers; sides have small, X-shaped spots; male's jaw becomes hooked (a kype)

Breeding In fresh water usually between October and January in flowing streams with gravely bottoms; female excavates nests (redds); eggs covered, then abandoned; adults return to sea or home lake; most oceangoing adults die before entering sea, but some (mostly females) survive; eggs hatch after several months

Diet Young fish plankton and small invertebrates, then larger invertebrates; oceangoing adults' diet is squid, shrimp, and fish; landlocked adults eat freshwater crustaceans and fish

Habitat Open sea close to coasts during prespawning phase in migrating populations; deep pools and river stretches in landlocked populations; clear, oxygen-rich, flowing waters preferred by latter; same conditions required for spawning; shallow water preferred by all populations

Distribution Both sides of northern Atlantic Ocean; in the west from northern Quebec in Canada to Connecticut; in the east from Arctic Circle to Portugal, southern Greenland and Iceland to Barents Sea; introduced into many locations, including Australia, New Zealand, Argentina, Chile; some introductions not established

Status Not threatened

THE ATLANTIC SALMON, KNOWN ALSO SIMPLY as the salmon plus many other names, is one of the "classic" species of science and folklore. Its life history has been told and retold over the ages, often wrapped in glamor and romance, as the human imagination has fed on the epic lifestyle of this extraordinary fish.

Unequaled Instincts

In living as they do and in battling heroically (in human terms) to reach the same waters where they were born, Atlantic salmon are driven by biological instincts, which have been bred into their genes over generations. Step by step the forces of evolution have molded the Atlantic salmon into a species that is capable of great feats, with homing abilities that only very few other fish, such as the European eel (*Anguilla anguilla*), can match.

It is these instincts that make the return of the Atlantic salmon to their traditional spawning rivers predictable and exploitable. Thousands are caught each year in nets and traps and on hook and line by anglers as the spawning shoals approach estuaries, in the estuaries themselves, and farther inland once the fish have adapted to fresh water (a major biological feat) and embarked on their upriver migration or run.

During this last stage of their journey the spawners, having fed well at sea and now fat and full of energy reserves, cease to eat. They will fast until those relatively few individuals that survive the stresses of reproduction return to the sea. This process raises fascinating but as yet unanswered questions. If these migrating fish do not feed during this last stage of their

journey, why are most specimens caught by anglers taken during this period of fast? Why does the fish override its instincts and respond to the angler's lure?

From Egg to Adult

After hatching in cool, oxygen-rich waters—the process takes several months and depends largely on water temperature—salmon fry spend up to six weeks among the gravel, absorbing their rich supply of yolk before they embark on their first hunting forays.

During the "postyolk" stage they feed on tiny invertebrates. They will then spend from one to six years as parrs, feeding in fresh water until they are ready to enter the marine phase of their lives. As parrs, growth is slow, only

measuring between 4 and 10 inches (10–25 cm) long by the time they are ready to move out to sea as smolts. Once they do, their growth rate accelerates, partly as a result of a richer diet, which now includes squid, shrimp, and fish; they will also eat some fish during the freshwater stage.

However, not all males migrate to sea. A few stay in rivers where they remain quite small but eventually mature. Those individuals (the vast majority) that migrate spend a further one to four years at sea before they begin their first and probably only spawning run—usually but not always back to their home rivers and often to the same spawning sites where they were born. These marine years are the least known in the life history of the salmon.

⊕ *The Atlantic salmon performs one of the greatest feats of migration and homing in nature, as well as one of the greatest physical feats in the animal world—the return upriver against rapids and waterfalls to its spawning grounds.*

Fish of Many Names

Since it is so widely distributed both naturally and as a result of introductions (dating back to 1864), the Atlantic salmon has acquired numerous common names in many languages.

The English names given to the species, including those attached to various phases of its life cycle as well as to populations, are: bay salmon, black salmon, breeder, caplin-scull salmon, common Atlantic salmon, fiddler, grayling, grilse, grilt, kelt, landlocked salmon, North Atlantic salmon, ouananiche, ouinanish, outside salmon, parr, salmon, salmon peel, sea salmon, Sebago salmon, silver salmon, slink, smolt, springfish, spring salmon, and winnish.

Some of these names are applied to the Atlantic salmon as it goes through its various life stages—from newly hatched fry or alevin to the postspawning phase that returns to the sea. In chronological sequence they are:
• Parr: this phase follows the alevin or fry phase and is distinguished by dark body blotches, called parr marks, on a silvery base.
• Smolt: this term applies to young fish once they lose their parr marks; smolt are silvery with a dark back and represent the stage of downstream migration toward the sea.
• Grilse: adult salmon returning from the sea on their spawning migration.
• Kelt: name given to adults returning to the sea after spawning.

Some of the other names are given to specific types of population of *Salmo salar*. In Canada landlocked populations that cannot migrate to and from the sea but move to and from surrounding rivers to spawn are called ouananiche or ouinanish. Their equivalents in the U.S.—from Lake Sebago and other areas—are called Sebago salmon.

Landlocked populations cannot undertake these journeys, but they retain many of the migratory instincts of their ancestors and will swim upriver when the breeding season starts. These populations (believed to be cut off from the sea after the last Ice Age) consist of smaller fish than the migratory oceangoing ones—the latter grow up to 4.9 feet (1.5 m) in length and weigh over 100 pounds (45 kg).

The Spawning Run
Using a combination of magnetic and oceanic cues along with navigating skills or instincts cued to the stars, salmon that are ready to breed migrate from the open sea toward their home waters many months before they actually spawn. Precisely how they do this is still not fully understood. Nevertheless it is now known that salmon remember features about their home rivers, particularly the water's chemical makeup, which they use to locate the streams where they were born.

This is the general rule. But the altering of river channels through damming, the deterioration of the quality of the water through pollution, or the silting up of traditional spawning grounds due to erosion of the surrounding terrain can all prove insurmountable hurdles. In such cases migrating salmon may divert into new spawning areas; some may also fail to find their way home and end up elsewhere. But generally speaking, homing salmon return to spawn close to where

⬅ This sportsman is fishing for landlocked salmon in these slow-moving waters in the Penobscot River, Maine.

⬇ Salmon alevins, four days after hatching, absorb nutrients from their yolk sacs, which they can depend on for up to six weeks before they begin to hunt for invertebrates. It could be up to six years before they begin to migrate out to sea.

they were born. In the case of physical barriers, such as dams, salmon "ladders" (stepped channels installed in the path of migrating fish) help them overcome such impossible obstacles.

The timing of the upriver migration or run, which is undertaken after a period of time spent in the estuaries gradually adapting to fresh water, varies between regions, with peaks in spring, summer, and fall. Usually the first to arrive are the larger adults, with males tending to arrive before females.

As they move upriver and cease to feed, the males undergo a dramatic transformation. Their coloration becomes intense, and most strikingly their lower jaw lengthens and bends upward in the form of a hook—the kype.

At the spawning grounds females excavate a depression (redd), in shallow water with their tail. Some redds can be quite large—between 10 and 16 feet (3–5 m) in length and 12 inches (30 cm) in depth.

Once the redd is completed, the pair of spawners align themselves upcurrent and come close together. The eggs and sperm are then

released amid much quivering and opening and shutting of jaws. Spawning bouts are repeated over a period of up to two weeks, when as many as 40,000 amber-colored eggs (but usually far fewer), each measuring 0.2 to 0.3 inches (0.5–0.7 cm) in diameter, are released. The female covers up the eggs by vigorously flapping her tail and then abandons them.

During spawning some of the small males, which never left the rivers and matured in fresh water, sneak into the redd and shed their sperm while the larger fish are spawning. If no large male is around, smaller ones can also mate successfully with a large female.

Spawning is a highly stressful activity that involves many factors, starting with the migration to the coasts (often from very large distances) and ending with the release of the last eggs and sperm—and all without feeding. Not surprisingly, the cumulative effects take their toll on spawners, and large numbers die once they use up their last remnants of energy.

Because of the excessive demands that males endure in defending territories and

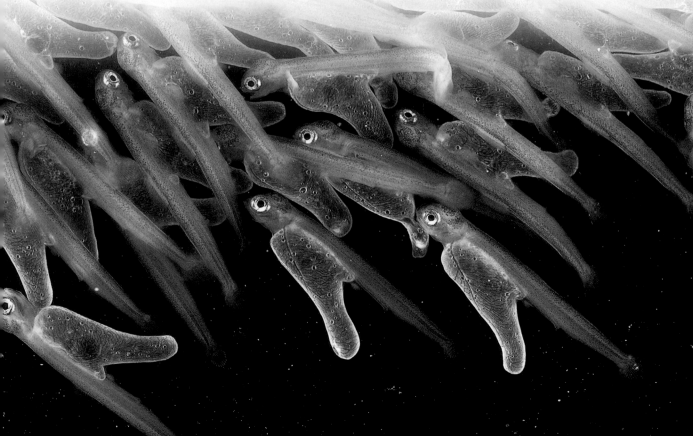

⊕ Estimated to be between two and three years old, this smolt has taken on a characteristic silvery color. At this stage the smolt can begin to adapt to salt water in estuaries.

securing mates, very few get back to the sea; most die after their first spawning season.

The Fittest Females

Larger numbers of females survive from one season to the next, but even for them the percentages are very low. It is estimated that no more than 5 percent of salmon in the U.K.

return for a second season. In the Loire River in France the percentage is even lower—only about 1 percent.

However, calculations made from the dark and light rings that appear on the scales as a fish goes from summer to winter and through spawning show it is possible for some individuals to spawn up to five times.

Although the percentage of repeat spawners is so low, the actual numbers of kelts—fish that migrate downriver to estuaries prior to returning to the sea—can be as high as 25 percent of the total spawning population. However, they are so weak that by the time they reach the estuaries, the number of mortalities is very high.

This sequence of events is a generalized account of the Atlantic salmon's breeding strategy. Considerable variation in this basic pattern exists between populations, rivers, geographical locations, even within individual populations. Over the years this impressive species has revealed many of its secrets but not all. Much still remains to be discovered.

From Capture to Culture

The huge demand for Atlantic salmon—both for the table as well as for angling—has led to the establishment of large farms where the fish are cultured under controlled conditions. In the past natural stocks were fished so extensively that numbers sank to alarmingly low levels. In numerous salmon rivers pollution and dams have also played a part in decimating salmon populations. Once salmon were so plentiful that the supply seemed inexhaustible. Restoring salmon stocks to all their previous haunts is impossible now because of continuing pollution, major changes in river channels, the need for international agreements, and so on.

Culturing them seems to offer a way forward, but the process is complicated. The first country to set up farms was Norway in the 1960s, but now there are farms in many countries.

Production is high despite the difficulties, and more than 200 times more farmed salmon are now available than wild ones. Most of the rearing occurs in cages that are suspended at sea, which has caused great controversy. The farming industry is accused of introducing new diseases, especially infestations of fish lice and gill flukes (two particularly harmful parasites), as well as causing a buildup of organic waste and harmful chemicals in the rearing areas. The risk of genetic damage through the escape of cultured stocks is also causing grave concern, especially those that have had genes from other species inserted into them—for example, from winter flounders (*Pseudopleuronectes americanus*).

This particular debate will continue for many years. Interestingly, in an unexpected twist the Atlantic salmon is benefiting overall because the extremely high production of reasonably priced cultured fish is leading some commercial operations that specialized in wild-caught salmon to close down. As a result, these fish are now at less risk of being netted during their oceangoing phase. Despite the changes, however, the numbers of salmon returning to spawn in rivers continue to decrease year after year. There is still much to be learned about this majestic fish.

Common name Rainbow trout (steelhead, plus many others)

Scientific name *Oncorhynchus mykiss*

Subfamily/Family Salmoninae/Salmonidae

Order Salmoniformes

Size Nearly 4 ft (1.2 m) maximum; some populations, especially some landlocked ones, much smaller and lighter

Key features Elongated body; pointed snout with rounded to blunt tip; large mouth, upper jaw extending beyond eye in large specimens; teeth in both jaws; older males have hooked lower jaw; dorsal fin almost in line with pelvic fins; adipose fin present; tail slightly forked; back edge of anal fin almost in line with adipose fin; pelvic fins on belly, closer to anal than to pectoral fins; pectoral fins immediately behind and below gill covers; variable coloration: steelheads steel-gray and silvery during oceangoing phase changing to rainbow coloring in fresh water; pinkish "rainbow" band runs from cheeks to caudal peduncle; numerous black spots along bluish-black back and down sides

Breeding Behavior like other trout and salmon; breeding season largely dependent on location; egg laying occurs during December in the south, as late as May or June in the far north; eggs hatch after a month depending on temperature

Diet Wide range of aquatic invertebrates and aerial insects; larger specimens also take fish

Habitat Landlocked and other exclusively freshwater populations (rainbows) tolerate conditions from fast-flowing, oxygen-rich streams to still lakes; oceangoing populations (steelheads) travel hundreds of miles out to sea but remain in top 655 ft (209 m) of water column

Distribution Natural range: eastern Pacific coast of North America from Alaska southward to parts of Mexico; introduced into numerous countries

Status Not threatened

Rainbow Trout

Oncorhynchus mykiss

All trout are beautiful creatures, but the rainbow trout is the most impressive of all. Certainly the most colorful of the trout, it lives up to its name with a spectacular range of hues along its flanks. It is also the most widely introduced member of the family as well as one of the most widely introduced of all fish.

THE NATURAL RANGE OF THE RAINBOW trout is the eastern Pacific extending from Alaska south to Mexico. The species has proved such an outstandingly popular food fish and game fish that it is now found virtually all over the world.

Widely Traveled Trout

Many of the introductions have been within the U.S. itself, where the fish is now found in nearly every state. Elsewhere the introductions began in 1877 when North American stocks were taken to Japan. In the same year California stocks of the species were also introduced into New Zealand.

Since then there has been a constant stream of introductions, most of which feature stocks not from the U.S. but from other countries, which now have hugely abundant populations and can serve as possible good sources of stock.

The rainbow trout has proved to be an exceptionally adaptable fish. As a result, a high percentage of introductions have been successful, and many countries now have established populations. The only countries where introductions have failed are Argentina, Indonesia, Mauritius, Zambia, Syria, Iceland, Uruguay, Lebanon, Korea, Tunisia, Iraq, Tahiti, and Thailand. Although this list may seem long, it is nothing compared to the list of successful introductions, which includes over 80 countries across Europe, South America, the Middle East, and Africa. The rainbow trout can be found as far afield as Lake Imanda on the Kola Peninsula in the extreme northwestern corner of Russia.

Along with the wide-ranging introductions is an equally diverse list of around 80 common names for the species. Some of the English-language ones are well known, such as rainbow trout and steelhead trout, but some are not—baiser, coast angel trout, coast range trout, hardhead, kamchatko salmon, Kamloops trout, redband, and summer salmon. A few other names confuse rather than clarify, since they are also used for other species—brown trout and salmon trout are also used for *Salmo trutta*, while silver trout is also used for the sockeye salmon (*Oncorhynchus nerka*).

While the wholesale introduction of the rainbow trout has been almost universally welcomed and has benefited millions of people worldwide, there is always a price to pay for releasing exotic (in other words, nonnative) species into foreign waters—unfortunately paid by species that lose out to the invader in terms of competition for food, space, and spawning areas. In the case of the rainbow trout 25 countries have reported definite or suspected adverse effects on local wildlife, while another 15 countries report its effects as either unknown or probably not significant. Only three countries—Estonia, Ireland, and Papua New Guinea—have reported that the introduction of the rainbow trout has presented no negative side effects.

Kamloops Trout

On their way up the Fraser River migrating trout and salmon come across the mouth of a tributary—the Thompson—that leads to Kamloops Lake. This lake in southern British Columbia, Canada, is home to a special, nonmigrating rainbow trout—or more specifically, two—called Kamloops trout.

One type remains small, attaining a weight of around 4 pounds (1.8 kg) on a diet primarily of aquatic invertebrates and aerial insects. The other type feeds on fish and grows to a weight

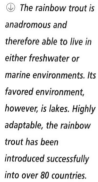

⊕ *The rainbow trout is anadromous and therefore able to live in either freshwater or marine environments. Its favored environment, however, is lakes. Highly adaptable, the rainbow trout has been introduced successfully into over 80 countries.*

of over 44 pounds (20 kg). Kamloops trout have been transplanted to other lakes; here too they can attain impressive weights on a fish-based diet—for example, 50 pounds (22.7 kg) in Jewel Lake, Montana.

Because of the nonmigrating nature of the Kamloops trout as well as their feeding habits, some scientists believe they are sufficiently different from normal rainbows to warrant being regarded as separate species or subspecies. At the moment they are still regarded as *O. mykiss*, but this could change in the future.

Cultured Trout

The rainbow trout is in such high demand both for the table as well as for angling purposes that natural or introduced stocks are unable to satisfy this need on their own. So large-scale farm-breeding operations have been set up, predominantly in temperate regions worldwide.

The outstanding qualities of the species make the rainbow the top choice among cultured trout. For example, rainbow trout grow twice as fast as brown trout (*Salmo trutta fario*), giving them a clear advantage in terms of the food-fish industry. They are also better

⊕ *These rainbow trout display the species' typical coloration—of numerous black spots and a dramatic pinkish "rainbow" running from the cheeks along to the caudal peduncle.*

The Fish from Heaven

Although the natural distribution of the rainbow trout is nowhere as extensive as the nonnatural species introduced into exotic locations, it is sufficiently wide (and takes in sufficiently different habitats) for several forms to have evolved over the years. The difficulty, as with sea (*Salmo trutta trutta*) or brown trout (*S. t. fario*), is in determining if these distinct types are mere strains or subspecies or even species.

A prime example is the impressive golden trout, which is often referred to as the "fish from heaven." The Native Americans, believed to be the first people to discover this gem of a fish, probably coined this name. This particularly striking trout is found in a number of mountain streams in the Upper Kern River basin in southern California. Like most southern trout, this fish from heaven remains small, growing to around 28 inches (71 cm) long, compared to nearly 4 feet (1.2 m) in the normal rainbow trout. Even when transplanted to food-rich habitats, the golden trout never attains either the size or weight of the rainbow (*Oncorhynchus mykiss*); the largest golden trout recorded weighed a little over 11 pounds (5 kg), while a large rainbow can weigh up to 56 pounds (25.4 kg).

Is the golden trout just a strain or form of the rainbow trout or a subspecies or a species in its own right? Some books call it a subspecies (*O. m. aguabonita*), but the latest scientific research says it is a separate species (*O. aquabonita*) with perhaps two subspecies—*O. a. gilberti* from the Main and Little Kern Rivers and *O. a. aquabonita* from the South Fork Kern River.

Prospectors and loggers along with their animals began arriving in the remote Upper Kern River basin in the mid-1800s. They soon transformed the golden trout's home to the point where it was driven close to extinction. It was not until 1978 that federal legislation established the 303,000-acre (122,620-hectare) Golden Trout Wilderness along with a plan to restore the trout's habitat to its former state. The golden trout is now California's official state fish.

⊖ *The Little Kern golden trout (*Oncorhynchus aquabonita gilberti*) is native to the Upper Kern River basin in southern California; the area is now protected as the Golden Trout Wilderness.*

fighters than brown trout when hooked, often doing spectacular leaps into the air; this makes them strong favorites with sport fishermen. Their greater adaptability to water chemistry and temperature conditions also makes them the preferred choice for artificial breeding and rearing.

"Ripe" Trout

Breeding establishments use several methods to maximize their chances of success. The most popular involves the separation of males and females for a time until they are "ripe" following a hormone injection. When ready, the females are removed and their eggs gently squeezed out, using a technique known as stripping that does not damage the fish. Once eggs from a few females have been collected, the same procedure is carried out on the chosen males, and their sperm is spread over the eggs. The egg-sperm mixture is then stirred gently and allowed to rest for about 10 minutes to allow enough time for fertilization to take place. Once washed, the fertilized eggs are then transferred to incubators until they hatch, a process that can take up to one month depending on temperature.

⊖ The rainbow trout is one of the most popular species to be reared on fish farms. Eggs are stripped from the females and mixed with sperm from the males. This mix rests for 10 minutes to allow fertilization to take place.

Successful rainbow trout farms have stocks at every stage of development from "eyed" eggs (in other words, eggs in which the eyes of developing embryos are already visible) to fully mature fish. This allows them to meet a wide range of demands—for example, they are able to supply eyed eggs suitable for stocking waters that do not contain any trout, and adults for stocking angling waters.

The broodstock used on farms usually consists of farmed fish, which reduces the need to take fish from the wild. However, there may be occasions when it is advisable to use wild

⊕ A newly hatched rainbow trout shows the yolk sac on which it depends for nutrition in the first weeks after hatching.

broodstock. For example, if a watercourse already has its own rainbow trout population but the total numbers are low and need boosting, the most sensible course of action is to use some of these residents as a source of sperm and eggs for future restocking of the water—thus not altering the genetic makeup of the population.

The most obvious advantage of this method is that the resident fish will have evolved certain genetic qualities that allow them to survive under the prevailing conditions. Fish or eggs that have been introduced from another river system will not have evolved in the same way; therefore they may not be as well suited.

Releasing rainbow trout into lakes and rivers is not a straightforward process, and a wide range of factors needs to be considered. Among them is the irresistible urge that most rainbows have to migrate downriver and out to sea.

Although humans may be able to mold some of the built-in instincts and characteristics of the rainbow trout, the natural forces that have shaped the rainbow into the remarkable fish that it is are very powerful and will always present new challenges.

Rainbow or Steelhead?

The two most commonly used names for *Oncorhynchus mykiss* are rainbow trout and steelhead trout. At one stage in their lives they look so different from each other that early fish scientists thought they were totally different species. To a large extent the differences are caused by their lifestyles—rainbows remain in fresh water all their lives, while steelheads migrate to sea.

Scientists do not know to what extent the instinct to migrate to sea is genetic, since it appears that all rainbows are capable of adapting to marine conditions. However, some are prevented from migrating because they live in landlocked lakes or watercourses with high waterfalls or other insurmountable barriers.

On returning to their spawning rivers, often from distances of several hundred miles out to sea, steelhead trout are a steel-gray and silver color—hence their name—with the body and tail covered in numerous spots. They are also much larger than their freshwater relatives because of their much richer diet; the largest and heaviest fish reported for the species nearly always are steelheads. It is only when they begin their upriver spawning migration that the coloration begins to change to the more usual rainbow trout hues.

Steelheads enter rivers at all months of the year depending on geographic location and water temperature. Since rivers start warming up much earlier in the south of the range than farther north, southern stocks begin their migrations correspondingly earlier. They also spawn earlier—around December in California compared with May or June in British Columbia.

Even where rainbows and steelheads overlap, each seems to stick to its own kind, with rainbows spawning with rainbows and steelheads with steelheads. This clearly shows that there is a strong genetic influence.

There is also an environmental influence in that the much larger size of the steelheads allows them to excavate nests (redds) and spawn in riverbeds where the sizes of the individual pieces of gravel are too large and heavy for rainbows. They are also able to spawn in faster-flowing waters where rainbows would find it difficult to pair up and spawn.

Whether the observed differences between steelheads and rainbows will lead to the two types drifting so widely apart into separate species that crossbreeding actually becomes impossible—it appears to be still possible at the moment—cannot be predicted but may well happen in time.

Stoplight loosejaw (*Malacosteus niger*)

Common name Barbeled dragonfish

Subfamilies Astronesthinae, Stomiinae, Chauliodontinae, Melanostomiinae, Idiacanthinae, Malacosteinae

Family Stomiidae

Order Stomiiformes

Number of species Around 278 in some 27 genera

Size From about 1 in (2.5 cm) to about 20 in (50 cm)

Key features Elongated to very elongated body; body naked except in 2 species that may have scales or scalelike markings plus a jellylike covering; chin barbel present in most species; mouth typically large; numerous fanglike teeth, very long in many species; adipose fin absent in most subfamilies; snaggletooths and viperfish have an additional adipose fin in front of anal fin; all species have photophores, usually in large numbers, mainly along lower half of body and belly; also photophores at tip of chin barbel and on cheeks in many species; majority are dark-colored, many are black

Breeding Breeding and mating behavior unknown; eggs and larvae planktonic; larvae frequently quite different than adult; most extreme differences found in black dragonfish, whose male and females are also very different

Diet Crustaceans and fish; large prey taken even by modest-sized individuals

Habitat Daily migrations made by many species, rising to shallower depths during night; adults of some species occur at or near surface during hours of darkness, descending to depths in excess of 9,850 ft (3,000 m)

Distribution Atlantic, Indian, and Pacific Oceans

Status Not threatened

⊕ *The 9.5-inch (24-cm) stoplight loosejaw (Malacosteus niger) occurs at depths down to 8,200 feet (2,500 m) in the Atlantic (from Greenland to Scotland), Indian (from the Gulf of Aden to the Bay of Bengal), and Pacific Oceans (China, Australia, and New Zealand east to South America and north to British Columbia).*

Barbeled Dragonfish

Stomiidae

In the deep, dark waters of the world's oceans live a community of creatures that would die if transferred to shallower, warmer parts of the sea—theirs is a hostile environment that humans can visit only for very limited periods of time in the protective shell of a submersible.

IN THE DIM LIGHT BEYOND the reach of the sun's rays these deepwater creatures look as if they belong on another planet. In a way they do, for these cold, dark waters are as alien to humans as the moon or Mars. In the deep these fish tolerate harsh conditions but would never survive if they suddenly found themselves in the sunny, warm, tropical waters of coral reefs.

Weird and Wonderful
Among the many weird and wonderful fish that live in these zones are about 405 species that belong to four families in the order Stomiiformes. One family—the barbeled dragonfish or Stomiidae—contains around 278 species in some 27 genera. The majority of them have a chin barbel that gives the family its overall name. Because of differences in features, scientists cannot agree about the exact relationships between the six groups of barbeled fish that are recognized. Here each is classified as a subfamily, but there will be important changes in the future as new details emerge from ongoing deep-sea exploration.

Snaggletooths
The snaggletooths (subfamily Astronesthinae) consist of around 59 species in five genera. They are scaleless fish that grow to just 12 inches (30 cm) in length. They have large eyes and mouths with teeth that overlap on the outside—the teeth from the lower jaw point upward on the outside of the upper jaw, and vice versa—like crocodiles and alligators.

⊕ *This Sloane's viperfish (Chauliodus sloani), shown here in waters of the South Pacific, is displaying a phenomenon known as bioluminesence—the ability to generate light.*

All fins are well formed, and there is a small adipose fin in all species except for *Rhadinesthes decimus*. Unusually, most snaggletooths also have a second adipose fin located in front of the anal fin along the belly. The tail is distinctly forked; generally the body is long and slim with a pointed, slightly rounded snout. Along the belly there is a row of light-producing cells called photophores.

All species are dark-colored, and many are black, a common feature in deepwater hunters —some snaggletooths are found at depths of 9,850 feet (3,000 m). Despite these great depths, larvae are often found floating at the surface; at night adults migrate into shallower waters, some even very close to the surface.

Snaggletooths mainly eat midwater crustaceans and smaller fish that are unlikely to escape their fanglike teeth. Yet snaggletooths themselves fall prey to larger fish such as tuna and sea mammals like dolphins and whales.

Scaly Dragonfish

The 11 scaly dragonfish or boafish (subfamily Stomiinae) all belong to one genus—*Stomias*. They are much longer-bodied fish than the snaggletooths and look almost eel-like. The fins are set far back along the body, which is covered in a jellylike substance with the exception of the pectoral fins, which, in sharp contrast, are located at the front of the body just behind the gills. The adipose fin is absent.

Scaly dragonfish and snaggletooths also differ in that the former have scales on the body. These scales are six-sided, producing a rather attractive pattern, but are easily shed.

Transforming Vipers and Dragons

While adults of Sloane's viperfish (*Chauliodus sloani*) and the Dana viperfish (*C. danae*) can be told apart, the larvae are very difficult to separate from each other and are also quite different from adults. The larvae are transparent and colorless except for a few pigmented cells near the anal fin in the Dana viperfish; the adults are iridescent blue or darker against an almost-black base color.

Both types of larvae—which hatch from floating eggs—are extremely elongated in body form, round in cross-section, and lack a mouth at first. They are almost identical in every respect except in numbers of muscle blocks and other features that can only be determined by a highly detailed examination. Once they reach a size of around 1.8 inches (4.5 cm), they undergo a transformation into the adult forms, and their eventual differences become apparent. At that point the Dana viperfish develop a short, stiff chin barbel that subsequently disappears in most specimens once they grow to around 2 inches (5 cm) long. In Sloane's viperfish the barbel is soft and remains in most specimens, even fully grown ones.

Although the transformation from larva through juvenile to adult is spectacular in vipers, the most extreme change occurs in the black dragonfish (subfamily Idiacanthinae). If viperfish larvae look very different from the adults, those of the black dragonfish look as if they are extraterrestrial. In the three *Idiacanthus* species the larvae are extremely thin, long, and transparent, which, although making them appear like glassy eels, does not appear very different from the adults' shape. However, the eyes of these larvae are like no others and are mounted at the tips of long stalks that can be almost half the total length of the body.

Although it is not known for certain what exact function these oval-shaped, stalked eyes perform, it is possible that all-around vision is improved—thus assisting the larvae in finding food and avoiding predators. Gradually, as the juvenile stages progress, the stalks are absorbed, with the eyes eventually having a more "normal" position.

Most scaly dragonfish are known only by their scientific names, a little surprising since some of them are particularly descriptive. For example, one of the stockier species—all are slim, but it is a little "fatter" than most—has a very short chin barbel and is called *S. brevibarbatus*, or short-barbeled stomias, while a very slim species with a very long chin barbel is called *S. longibarbatus*, or long-barbeled stomias. The former is one of the smallest scaly dragonfish, around 8.3 inches (21 cm) long; the second is the largest member of the genus at 17.4 inches (44 cm) long.

Viperfish

The viperfish subfamily Chauliodontinae has some nine species in one genus, *Chauliodus*. They vary in size from around 6 inches (15 cm) for the Dana viperfish (*C. danae*) to 14 inches (35 cm) in Sloane's viperfish (*C. sloani*).

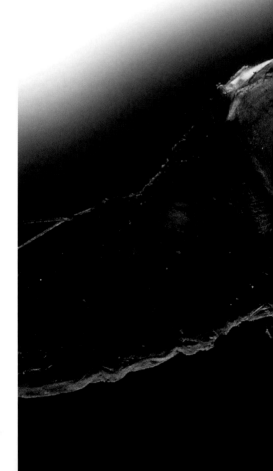

Like their cousins, scaly dragonfish have well-formed eyes, a chin barbel, and a huge mouth—the jaw hinge is located almost as far as the gill covers. These small 12-inch (30-cm) deepwater "eels" are voracious hunters. Their light organ (like snaggletooths) is arranged in the form of two rows of light-producing cells along the belly.

↪ *The black dragonfish (Idiacanthus antrostomus), at 3 inches (7.5 cm) long, is one of the tiniest members in its group. The dark coloring, typical of deep-sea species, helps conceal it from prey.*

The mouth is armed with fanglike teeth whose length gives the collective name for the family. As well as their teeth and slim bodies viperfish are distinguished by their forward-positioned dorsal fin, an adipose fin in front of the anal fin, and (like scaly dragonfish) a jellylike covering on the body. Some species, like Sloane's viperfish, have a very long first dorsal fin ray that loops forward so it lies above the

⊕ *At 14 inches (35 cm) Sloane's viperfish (Chauliodus sloani) is the largest member in its subfamily. It has a slim body and fanglike teeth with a long first ray looping above its mouth.*

mouth. The tip of this ray has a light-producing organ acting as a lure to attract prey toward its cavernous, fearsomely armed mouth. Like their relatives, viperfish also have light-producing organs, or photophores—two rows of large, light-producing cells along the sides, plus an irregular line of smaller photophores in between and a further row along the belly.

Viperfish have a built-in shock absorber—a very long first neck vertebra—to help cushion the impact caused when lunging at prey, as well as controlling prey once the fangs have grasped it. Were the victims small animals, such cushioning would be unnecessary, but viperfish (like their relatives) often catch large prey and hang onto it tenaciously until they swallow it.

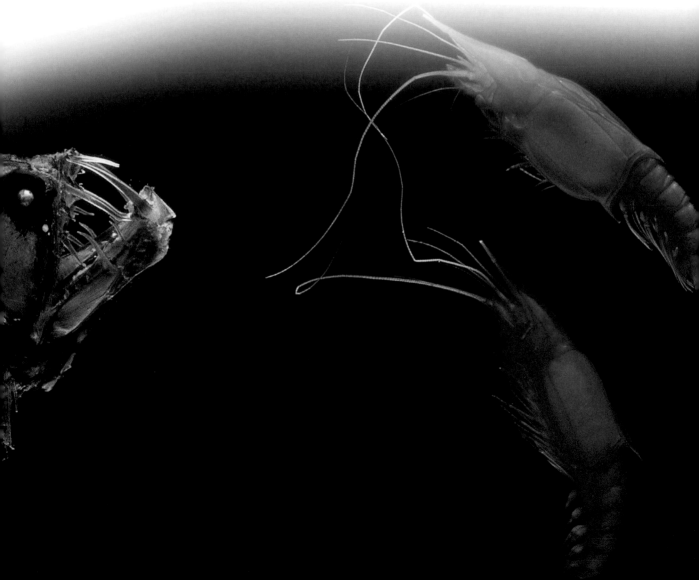

Living Illuminations

Barbeled dragonfish are deepwater specialists, with many species living at depths exceeding 7,870 feet (2,400 m). Remarkably, some of these species, such as the snaggletooth (*Astronesthes gemmifer*), can be collected at the water surface during the night, which shows that in these family members there are large-scale depth migrations during the course of a 24-hour period. Whether collected in one foot of water or several thousand, there is a common link between all these fish—they occur in partial or total darkness.

In common with many creatures that live under such conditions barbeled dragonfish have the ability to generate light—a phenomenon called "bioluminescence," which means "living light" or "living illumination." Bioluminescence does not involve the generation of any heat, as in light bulbs, so it is also referred to as "cold light."

Although details differ between the structures and methods used by living organisms to generate light, all can be grouped under two main categories:

• One type is produced by self-luminous photophores—special structures that generate light through chemical reactions.

• The other type involves "borrowed" light—the organism uses light generated by other creatures, usually bacteria.

Something in the region of between 1,000 and 1,500 species of fish utilize bioluminescence of one of these two types. Barbeled dragonfish use the first type of light, producing it in luminous organs arranged as two longitudinal rows of photophores, sometimes with additional rows in between. Other species also have photophores on the head, at the tip of the chin barbel, and on other parts of the body.

Typically photophores contain light-generating cells (photocytes), whose light may then bounce off a reflector (i.e., a layer of reflective cells) and out through a lens. Other cells can act as a filter, thus changing the color of the light that is emitted.

In the "borrowed" light model the light is generated initially through chemical reactions between a substance (usually luciferin) and the enzyme luciferase as in photophores. However, this reaction does not take place inside the body of the fish itself but within light-producing bacteria. Consequently, the fish can control neither the intensity nor duration of the light, as in self-luminous photophores.

In such species—such as the flashlight or lanterneye fish (family Anomalopidae)—a variety of "controlling" structures like lids have evolved that allow the fish to cover or expose the luminescent bacteria, which are carried in special pouches or cavities that are often found on the fish's cheek.

Light in fish has several uses ranging from communication between members of a species (including sexual and rivalry displays), confusion of a potential predator (by switching a light organ on and off and shifting location when in the "off" position), allowing a fish to camouflage itself against the light coming from the water's surface (helping it disappear when viewed from below), as a lure for attracting potential prey to within range of the jaws, and for tracking prey in the darkness—some scaleless black dragonfish and loosejaws generate red light from organs under the eyes, which they can see, but which any prey animals that can detect only blue or green light cannot.

⊕ *Snaggletooths (Astronesthes* gemmifer*) have light-producing cells (photophores) along the belly. They are also hunters, feeding on crustaceans and small fish, none of which will escape their fearsome, fanglike teeth.*

filifer) from the eastern and southwest Pacific—to extremely long as in the stocky *B. brevis* or the much more elongated *B. pawneei*. Like black dragons and vipers, scaleless black dragonfish change as they go through the larval, juvenile, and adult phases. While some transformations are quite pronounced—like the duck-billed head of the larval scaleless dragonfish (*B. nigerrimus*) changes to an adult's blunt, round head—they are not as dramatic as in the black dragonfish (*see* box p.188).

The three species of black dragonfish also show great differences between the sexes. The tiny males retain some larval characteristics and have few teeth (unusual for a predator). They also remain small, only up to 2 inches (5 cm), probably because they are unable to hunt and feed. But the females are active hunters and continue to grow throughout their lives. The black dragonfish (*I. atlanticus*) reaches 21 inches (54 cm), and the ribbon sawtailfish (*I. fasciola*) slightly less; much smaller is the Pacific blackdragon (*I. antrostomus*) at around 3 inches (7.5 cm). In males the testes take up most of the body; their gut is shrunken and cannot digest food. Scientists think their lifespan is very short, lasting a few months during which they mate and die without feeding at all.

Loosejaws

Loosejaws is an apt description of the 7 or so members of the subfamily Malacosteinae; they have an extremely large mouth that is much longer than the skull itself. Also, there is no membrane between the two halves of the lower jaw; instead, the jaw muscles are enclosed within a sheath or thin layer of tissue.

This arrangement allows the fish to open their jaws to such an extent that they appear to become unhinged when swallowing large prey, a feature that is particularly spectacular in the black or stoplight loosejaw (*Malacosteus niger*). The latter name is apt because one of the two light organs that this species bears on its head (beneath each eye) is red, while the second light organ (behind each eye) is green, suggesting a stop-go traffic light.

Black Dragons

There are two types of black dragonfish—"the" black dragonfish (subfamily Idiacanthinae) and the scaleless black dragonfish (subfamily Melanostomiinae). The former has around 16 genera and 189 species; the latter contains only one genus—*Idiacanthus*—with three species.

As their name indicates, the scaleless, black dragonfish are naked. Like many relatives, most species have a chin barbel that varies from very short or absent—like the sparing (*Bathophilus*

Peregrine ribbonfish (*Trachipterus trachypterus*)

Common name Ribbonfish (dealfish)

Family Trachipteridae

Order Lampridiformes

Number of species 10 in 3 genera

Size From 3.6 ft (1.1 m) to 9.8 ft (3 m)

Key features Elongated body tapering to varying degrees; head generally large; snout either steeply sloping or pointed; large mouth and eyes; dorsal fin extends from head to tail, first few rays generally extended; tail large or small, either with just the upper lobe present or (additionally) with some much-reduced lower lobe rays; tail at sharp angle to body, often perpendicular; anal and adipose fins absent; pelvic fins have very few rays (even just 1) or absent; pectoral fins directly behind gill covers; body naked (scales are easily dislodged); usually silvery, sometimes speckled; some species: distinctive spots along back

Breeding Behavior unknown; eggs and larvae planktonic; egg surface frequently with irregularities such as tiny "pits"; larvae look very different from adults, with numerous filamentlike growths, which gradually disappear

Diet Fish and squid; also crustaceans

Habitat Open ocean at depths ranging from the surface down to 3,300 ft (1,000 m); some species enter brackish water or found close to shore

Distribution Arctic, Atlantic (into the Mediterranean), Indian, and Pacific Oceans

Status Not threatened

ⓘ *The 9.8-foot (3-m) peregrine ribbonfish (Trachipterus trachypterus) occurs at depths down to 1,640 feet (500 m) in the eastern Atlantic from the Mediterranean to South Africa and in the Pacific from Japan south to New Zealand and Chile.*

Ribbonfish Trachipteridae

If a fish swims vertically in the water holding its tail out at right angles to the body, and half of its large tail is missing, the fish may be badly injured or close to death—or it could be a perfectly healthy ribbonfish.

TEN SPECIES OF RIBBONFISH BELONG to the family Trachipteridae. Not all have large tails like the peregrine ribbonfish (*Trachipterus trachypterus*), but they all have what is an odd arrangement—the tail only has one visible lobe, the upper one, although some species can also have a few much-reduced lower lobe fin rays. Another unusual feature is that this single lobe is held out at an angle—almost perpendicularly in some species—to the body.

In addition ribbonfish have a disconcerting habit of orienting themselves vertically in the water, in a head-up, tail-down position rather than the usual horizontal one. When in this position, the tail, which is at an angle to the body, points in the normal, horizontal direction like other fish.

Normally ribbonfish (also called dealfish) are found in deep water—down to 3,300 feet (1,000 m) for the dealfish or blackflash ribbonfish (*T. arawatae*)—and are only rarely caught in nets set out for other species.

Confusing Ribbons

Encounters with live ribbonfish by scuba divers are even rarer, but occasionally they do occur. When they do the divers (even experienced ones) are fascinated, even confused by the fish's features and unique posture in the water. More confusing are the juvenile ribbonfish, which look quite different from the adults; they have numerous filamentlike outgrowths from the fins that make them look very unfishlike.

Variable Shape and Habits

Despite their name, not all ribbonfish have ribbonlike bodies. For example, the 3.6-foot (1.1-m) polka-dot ribbonfish (*Desmodema*

ⓘ *The scalloped ribbonfish (Zu cristatus), shown here near the Virgin Islands in the Caribbean, is a deep-bodied fish that tapers off toward its back end. It is the best known of all ribbonfish because it is commonly found above 300 feet (90 m).*

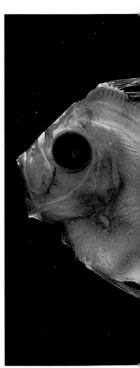

polystictum) is deep-bodied around the shoulder region and only tapers gradually toward the tail. In stark contrast, *Zu elongatus*, one of two species called tapertail ribbonfish—the other is *Trachipterus fukuzakii*—is shallow-bodied with a long, slim, tapering shape and an ultrathin caudal peduncle. This 3.9-foot (1.2-m) species, perhaps the least-known ribbonfish, is found in both the southeast Atlantic and the southwest Pacific.

The second *Zu* species, the scalloped ribbonfish (*Z. cristatus*), is the best known of all the ribbonfish. It is a deeper-bodied species, although it still has the tapering back end and is commonly found at water depths above 300 feet (90 m). Therefore it is more likely to be encountered than most of its relatives.

Like all its family relatives, this species has large eyes and a large mouth that can be extended rapidly to suck in prey at high speed. Its diet, like that of its close relatives, is almost exclusively small fish and squid. A notable exception to this fish-squid menu is the blackflash ribbonfish, which feeds predominantly on crustaceans. This species is

also exceptional because it is the only ribbonfish known to enter estuaries.

King-of-the-Salmon

Native American folklore refers to a fish that leads Pacific salmon back to their home rivers at the beginning of each breeding season. The fish with these remarkable powers is called the "king-of-the-salmon." The scientific name for this species is *Trachipterus altivelis*; it is an impressive silvery-bodied ribbonfish with red dorsal, caudal, and pectoral fins. It grows to around 6 feet (1.8 m) and lives in the eastern Pacific, stretching from Alaska down to Chile.

Like most of the other ribbonfish, the king-of-the-salmon can occur in deep water—down to 2,950 feet (900 m)—and in midocean. Occasionally, however, it is found at the surface close to the shore. It is possible that they are seen or caught coincidentally with salmon as the salmon begin their upriver spawning runs. Therefore this association could have given rise to the legend, but scientifically there is no evidence that ribbonfish and salmon are linked in any way at all.

⊕ *The distinctive spotted pattern along the back of this 3.6-foot (1.1-m) polka-dot ribbonfish (Desmodema polystictum), seen here in Mexican waters, demonstrates how it got its name.*

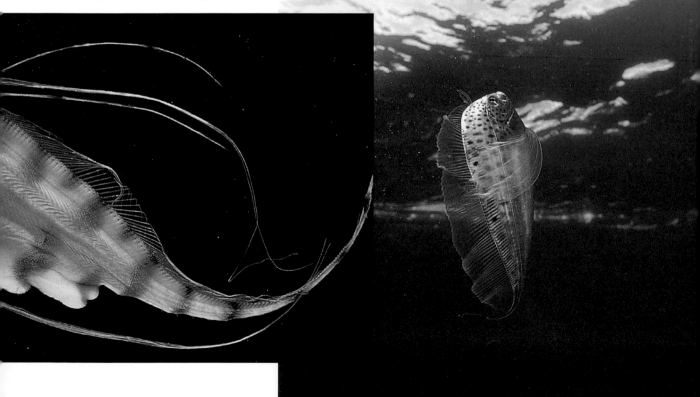

Oarfish

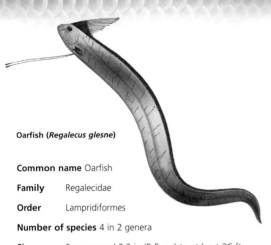

Oarfish (*Regalecus glesne*)

Common name Oarfish

Family Regalecidae

Order Lampridiformes

Number of species 4 in 2 genera

Size From around 2.2 in (5.5 cm) to at least 36 ft (11 m) but probably up to 56 ft (17 m)

Key features Elongated, ribbonlike body; blunt head; large extendable mouth; teeth absent; eyes relatively small; dorsal fin with extremely long base originating above eye and extending to tail; front rays extended ending in small flaps; tail also has extended rays; anal and adipose fins absent; pelvic fins extended with long, paddlelike structures and flap at tips; pectoral fins small and located close to gill covers; body scaleless; silvery blue with dark blotches and streaks; reddish fins

Breeding Behavior unknown; spawning occurs during second half of year; larvae bearing extremely long rays on front of dorsal fin have been collected near surface

Diet Mostly free-swimming, small invertebrates, particularly euphasiids (luminescent, shrimplike crustaceans); also squid and small fish

Habitat Open ocean down to at least 3,300 ft (1,000 m); can also occur at relatively shallow depths but in open water; specimens occasionally washed up on beaches

Distribution All oceans extending into the Mediterranean Sea for one species

Status Not threatened

ⓘ *The 36-foot (11-m) oarfish, or king-of-the-herrings (Regalecus glesne), occurs in the Atlantic (including the Mediterranean), Indo-Pacific, and Pacific Oceans from southern California to Chile. It lives at great depths between 66 and 3,300 feet (20–1,000 m) and feeds on crustaceans, small fish, and squid.*

*Commonly reaching at least 36 feet (11 m) in length, the oarfish (*Regalecus glesne*) is the longest fish in the world. Though not scientifically confirmed, it may grow to more than twice this length—nearly 56 feet (17 m).*

THE OARFISH IS NOT AN ESPECIALLY heavy fish for its length; large specimens can weigh up to 600 pounds (272 kg). This sounds heavy but not for a fish that can be 25 to 36 feet (7.6–11 m) long.

Unlikely Relatives

The oarfish has two close relatives within its genus—*Regalecus russelii* and *R. kinoi*. Both are little known, especially *R. kinoi*. It has been caught off Mexico, and until 2000 scientists believed it was the same species as *R. russelii*. In fact, *R kinoi* is so poorly known that there are no details about its size or biology. Intriguingly its close relative, *R. russelii* from the Indo-Pacific, grows to around 2.2 inches (5.5 cm) in length, much smaller than the record-breaking oarfish.

If further specimens of *R. russelii*, including mature males and females, eventually confirm that this species never grows any longer, there will be some fascinating questions to ponder. For example, are there other species of oarfish still waiting to be discovered, and can they bridge the massive size gap that appears to exist within the genus? If not, how have such differently sized species evolved from a common ancestor? Were there other species of *Regalecus* of varying sizes, all now extinct, leaving only the two extreme ends of what once may have spanned the whole size range?

The only other member of the family—the streamerfish (*Agrostichthys parkeri*)—is not much better known. It is found in the southeast Atlantic, eastern Indian, and southwest Pacific Oceans, grows to at least 9.8 feet (3 m), and is silvery with a rose-colored dorsal fin that has over 400 rays. Since this information is based on only seven specimens, there are enormous gaps in our knowledge of this species.

Pelvic Oars

An oarfish looks nothing like an oar but more like a very long ribbon, with a tuft of extremely extended dorsal fin rays right at the front above the eyes. Another tuft is made up of elongated caudal fin rays at the rear. The tips of the long dorsal rays have skin flaps that look like "oars," but it is the paddlelike flap at the tip of its very long, single pelvic fin ray that looks more like an oar and is responsible for the common name not just of *Regalecus glesne* but all the family.

The oar impression is reinforced by how the fish positions its body and fins in the water—at an angle of around 45°, with the dorsal fin trailing horizontally and providing the main means of power. The pelvic fins are held out in front of the fish to allow the sensitive cells of the flaps at their tip to give advance warning of food in the water. This allows the oarfish time to adapt its breathing, allowing its remarkably extendable mouth to suck in the victim.

Regenerating King-of-the-Herring

Besides being known as the oarfish, *Regalecus glesne* is also called the "king-of-the-herring." This name was used by ancient Norwegians who believed that if an oarfish was harmed, the herring (a valuable food fish since early times) would disappear.

Regenerative powers are also attributed to the oarfish; some may be true, others perhaps a little less so. For example, many oarfish that are caught have missing tails. This happens so often (relatively speaking, since oarfish are only rarely seen) that the tail may be expendable, and the fish can grow another one. Some reports also state that oarfish can lose up to half their body and still regenerate it, as long as the vital internal organs are not damaged.

Tales of Sea Serpents

Ancient mariners frequently told of giant, terrifying sea serpents. Drawings and etchings sometimes show these monsters attacking ships. Were there, or are there, really such creatures, or is it more likely that these monsters are merely large specimens of an inoffensive, unusual fish that features in record books?

⊕ *An oarfish larva is here shown in the waters of Australia's Great Barrier Reef. The larvae are seldom seen in plankton but are very widespread; adults are very rare.*

Goosefish

Lophiidae

The monstrous-looking goosefish, better known to fishermen and seafood fans as "monkfish," are spectacularly ugly. But their cavernous mouth, rows of needle-sharp teeth, bulging eyes, and mottled, strangely ragged-looking skin are all adaptations to an extraordinary way of life.

GOOSEFISH ARE AMONG THE LARGER types of anglerfish, which famously ambush prey by drawing them close with a special lure. The lure is developed from the first of six spines in the first dorsal fin. In the goosefish there is usually a small scrap of flesh, or "esca," at the tip of a long, mobile spine. The lure can be waved gently in a convincing imitation of a scrap of food drifting in the current or twitched to look like a small, darting fish.

All the while the predator itself remains virtually invisible, often partially buried in the sediment. A flat belly allows it to lie closely pressed to the seafloor; with its mottled brownish coloration and the small flaps, or "lappets," of skin around its chin to break up the body outline, the camouflage is practically perfect. When a victim comes within range, the goosefish launches forth, opening its vast mouth so fast that the prey is drawn toward it by the rush of water. Once in the mouth, it is secured with hundreds of finely pointed but very strong teeth and swallowed whole.

Fair Game for a Goosefish

Virtually anything that shows interest in the lure or ventures within gulping distance is fair game to a goosefish. Analysis of stomach contents has revealed the remains of many different fish, including small sharks, large crabs, and even

American goosefish (*Lophius americanus*)

Common name Goosefish

Family Lophiidae

Order Lophiiformes

Number of species 25 species in 4 genera

Size Up to 4 ft (1.2 m) long

Key features Huge, broad head tapers to dorsoventrally flattened body; enormous mouth lined with many hundreds of teeth; lower jaw fringed with small frills of skin; first dorsal fin modified into mobile fishing lure; solitary; nocturnal

Breeding Spawning takes place in spring in deep water, when up to 2.5 million eggs are released in a mass of floating jelly

Diet Carnivorous; mainly other fish attracted by lure and swallowed whole

Habitat Marine; benthic (bottom-dwelling)

Distribution More or less cosmopolitan; in all major oceans and adjoining seas

Status Not thought to be threatened

⊕ *The American goosefish (*Lophius americanus*) can reach lengths of over 4 feet (1.2 m). This grim, voracious predator, found at depths of 330 feet (100 m) in the western Atlantic, will eat anything that comes close to its lure, including fish and all kinds of invertebrates.*

⊕ *The European goosefish (*Lophius piscatorius*) lives close to the seafloor. It is caught by trawlers and prized for its fine flesh.*

diving seabirds. Specimens of goosefish caught in trawlnets nearly always have stomachs crammed full of whatever other fish have been caught in the net. It seems that the close proximity of so many potential prey drives the goosefish—a predator to the last—into a final frenzy of feeding.

Other unusual features of goosefish morphology are the pectoral fins and the gill openings. The pectorals are long and mounted on short, armlike extensions.

Spring Spawning

Goosefish are highly fecund. They spawn in deep water during the spring, and a well-developed American goosefish (*Lophius americanus*) can produce over two and half million eggs at once.

Once fertilized, the eggs develop in a large gelatinous mass that is secreted from the ovaries and looks a bit like frog spawn. Swollen ribbons of this angler jelly float at the surface; these ribbons can be over 2 feet (60 cm) wide and up to 40 feet (12 m) long.

Weird Babies

Larval goosefish are almost as weird-looking as their parents. These youngsters have overly long ventral fins that gradually shrink as they develop. The larvae spend their early lives feeding on plankton near the surface. Then they head for the seafloor when they are about 3 inches (8 cm) long.

Goosefish are found in both shallow and deep water, and the range of depth occupied by a single species is impressive. For example, the American goosefish lives in shallow waters off the Newfoundland coast, but it is also found as deep as 3,300 feet (1,000 m) in tropical waters off Brazil. The closely related European equivalent—*Lophius piscatorius*—occupies depths and latitudes similar to its American cousin on the other side of the Atlantic.

A Good Food Fish

Goosefish are commercially fished under the name of monkfish. The flesh is exceptionally good. It is lean and white with a firm, meaty texture and a delicate flavor. However, because of the fish's unusual shape, the only part that is eaten is the cylindrical tail section. The great head, which constitutes most of the body, is thrown away.

This crab is living dangerously! The structure of the goosefish's head means it is best suited to attacking prey that approaches its lure from above. The fact that the crab has unwittingly come so close is a credit to the angler's superb camouflage and ability to lie quite motionless on the seafloor.

Batfish

Ogcocephalidae

In a group of strange-looking fish, batfish are stranger than most. They appear to have a front and back end from entirely different fish. The front end is greatly flattened and very broad, either circular or triangular in outline, while the back end is a quarter the width and chunky.

Pancake batfish (*Halieutichthys aculeatus*)

Common name Batfish

Family Ogcocephalidae

Order Lophiiformes

Number of species 62 species in 9 genera

Size Up to 14 in (35 cm) long; usually much less

Key features Greatly flattened, pancakelike or boxlike head; large horizontal mouth; narrow body trunk and tail; body supported on large, armlike pectoral fins; solitary ambush predators; prefer "walking" over seabed on modified fins to swimming

Breeding Pelagic larvae similar to those of other anglers

Diet Carnivorous; an ambush predator that takes variety of vertebrate and invertebrate prey, including crustaceans and fish

Habitat Marine; bottom dwelling

Distribution Widespread in all the tropical oceans and many adjoining seas

Status Not thought to be threatened

⊕ *The 4-inch (10-cm) pancake batfish (Halieutichthys aculeatus) is the sole member of its genus. It moves its flattened, scaleless body over the seafloor using its fleshy pectoral and pelvic fins.*

APART FROM THE LARGE EYES bulging up from the top of the head, these unfortunate fish look as if they have been half run over—the front end reduced to a pancake, the back part almost unscathed. Most batfish species are no more than about 8 inches (20 cm) long. However, one species grows considerably larger—the shortnose batfish (*Ogcocephalus nasutus*)—occasionally grows to 14 inches (35 cm).

Batfish have no scales; their body is covered in bony bumps and tubercles that develop in the skin. In *Coleophrys*, *Dibranchus*, and *Halieutopsis* species these are conical in shape, but in *Ogcocephalus* and *Malthopsis* species the bumps are rather more elaborate. Scattered among normal, conical tubercles are larger, star-shaped ones—called "bucklers"—which have a pattern of radiating spines.

Comical Creatures

Fish are often referred to as supreme examples of grace. Not so the batfish. The usual mode of locomotion in these comical little creatures can only be described as an awkward waddle. The enlarged pectoral fins have stout, armlike bases that raise the body from the seafloor. The other ventral fins act as short peg legs, which they use to trundle determinedly over the seafloor, rolling slightly from side to side. Batfish can swim but not terribly well; most of the time they do not move at all. Their lifestyle as ambush predators means that rather than setting out to find food, they sit and wait for it to come to them.

A batfish approached by a diver or other large, threatening animal will remain

⊖ *Like other anglerfish, batfish have a prominent lure, formed from a modified ray of the dorsal fin. The eyes are large and directed upward, to provide the fish with a clear view of approaching prey.*

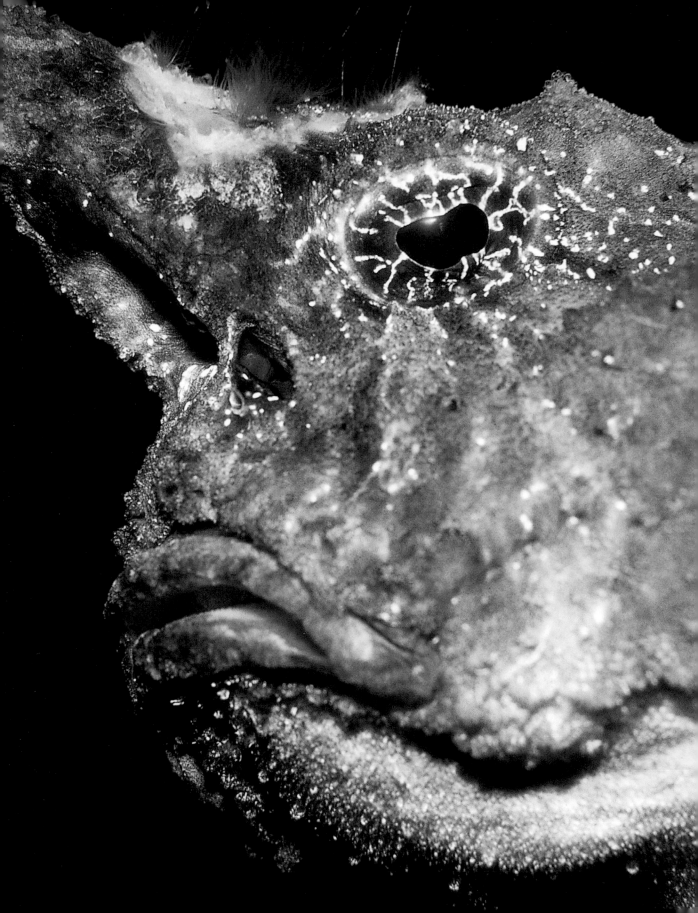

⬅ *The reticulated batfish (Halieutaea retifera) appears rather flat when seen from the side. From above, its front end is completely circular.*

⬅ *The shortnose batfish (Ogcocephalus nasutus) is a shallow-water species sometimes caught and sold as an aquarium novelty.*

motionless, relying on its excellent camouflage to protect it. If prodded, a batfish will try to waddle cautiously away, hugging the seafloor and only swimming as a last resort.

However, there is some evidence to suggest that batfish swim better than is generally imagined. In aquariums they are sometimes seen coming to the surface at night; if this is normal behavior, it may reveal other sides to batfish life that have yet to be properly studied.

Alluring Anglers

Batfish are anglers. They tempt prey animals, usually other species of fish, to come within striking distance with a fleshy lure. The lure, or "esca" as it is more correctly known, is a blob of flesh attached to the end of a retractable fishing rod—the "illicium." As in other anglerfish, the illicium is derived from the first spine of the otherwise vestigial dorsal fin. When not in use, the illicium is drawn back into a special cavity in the batfish's forehead.

In batfish the illicium is shorter than in most other anglers. In order to make the lure especially enticing and perhaps to distract the prey's attention from the danger lurking below, a batfish is able to vibrate the esca. Interestingly, when it comes to deployment of their fishing pole, batfish appear to be left or right handed. When the illicium is extended, the esca can be dangled to the left or the right, but individual fish invariably use only one side.

Typical prey are crabs, shrimp, and small fish that are seized with rows of sharp conical teeth on the jaws and tongue.

Sea Toads

The small but widespread family Chaunacidae includes 12 species of sea toad or coffinfish, thought to be the closest relatives of the batfish, and they are included with them in the suborder Ogcocephalioidei. Sea toads are squat, ugly fish with a large mouth, a small fishing lure, and a swollen body covered with small spines. They are compressed laterally rather than dorsoventrally.

Humpback anglerfish (*Melanocetus johnsonii*)

Common name Deep-sea anglerfish

Families Linophrynidae, Caulophrynidae, Neoceratiidae, Melanocetidae, Himantolophidae, Diceratiidae, Oneirodidae, Thaumatichthyidae, Centrophrynidae, Ceratiidae, Gigantactinidae

Order Lophiiformes

Suborder Ceratioidea

Number of species About 174 species in 11 families

Size Most spp. less than 8 in (20 cm) long; largest sea devils up to 40 in (1 m); males always very small

Key features Most with globular body, lack pelvis fins; fishing lure varied from short stub to elaborate, fleshy growth, usually bioluminescent; solitary

Breeding Dwarf males either free living or parasitic on females; eggs spawned in gelatinous mass; hatch into pelagic larvae

Diet Females carnivorous; prey on other fish and deep-sea invertebrates attracted by luminous fishing lure; free-living males feed on plankton; parasites share resources via blood connection to female

Habitat Marine; pelagic in deep water

Distribution Tropical and subtropical oceans worldwide

Status Little known because habitat so inaccessible

⊕ *Female humpback anglerfish* (Melanocetus johnsonii), *shown here, grow no larger than 7 inches (18 cm), but they dwarf the males, which rarely exceed 1 inch (2.5 cm). The species lives in deep water in tropical and temperate oceans.*

Deep-Sea Anglerfish

Linophrynidae, Caulophrynidae, Neoceratiidae, Melanocetidae, Himantolophidae, Diceratiidae, Oneirodidae, Thaumatichthyidae, Centrophrynidae, Ceratiidae, Gigantactinidae

All of these 11 families of deep-sea anglerfish belong to the suborder Ceratioidea. They differ from other anglerfish in having lost their pelvic fins. They also have the arguable distinction of being among the most magnificently ugly creatures on Earth!

⊕ The silver dots on the skin of this deep-sea anglerfish (Himantolophus species) are bioluminescent organs. They are used in display and are most concentrated in the fishing lure, which glows brightly to attract the attention of prey.

MOST HAVE A BULBOUS BODY, with tatty-looking, knobby, blotchy skin in unlovely shades of black, brown, and olive green. The head is large, and the mouth often gapes to reveal grotesque rows of needle-sharp teeth. The eyes are either large and bulging or small and mean looking. Perhaps it is fortunate that most of these nightmarish creatures are very small.

Ceratioid anglerfish may be the gargoyles of the sea, but they are also extraordinarily successful and diverse—a classic example of how evolution will tinker endlessly with successful adaptations, resulting in an extraordinary number of variations on a theme. When nature creates a design that works, however improbable, it runs with it.

Many of the stranger aspects of anglerfish morphology and ecology are in fact highly practical adaptations to life in an extreme environment. It is an often quoted fact that we know more about the surface of the moon than we do about the depth of the oceans, so it should come as no surprise that creatures that live in the abyssal depths do things differently.

The Original Devil

The largest deep-sea anglerfish, the sea devil (*Ceratias holboelli*), was also the first to be scientifically described; it was the "type" for its genus and family and for the suborder Ceratioidea. This means that the original specimen is the standard by which all others are compared to see if they belong in the same group. The first specimen was discovered washed up on a Greenland beach by Lieutenant-Commander Holboll of the Danish Navy in the mid-1800s. Progress toward understanding the species was slow. Over the next century only 12 further specimens were recorded; most were long dead and in poor condition, having been washed up on land. One of the best examples was found in the stomach of a sperm whale caught by whalers, proving that even the largest anglerfish have predators.

An Important Difference

One important difference between deep-sea anglerfish and other groups such as the goosefish (family Lophiidae) and the batfish (family Ogcocephalidae) is that ceratioids are not bottom dwellers. Most spend their lives hovering in midwater, so they lack the flattened underside seen in other groups.

Deep-sea anglerfish live in almost total darkness. Daylight only penetrates a few hundred feet through sea water. Since most ceratioids live at depths of between a few hundred and many thousands of feet, their world is a sunless one.

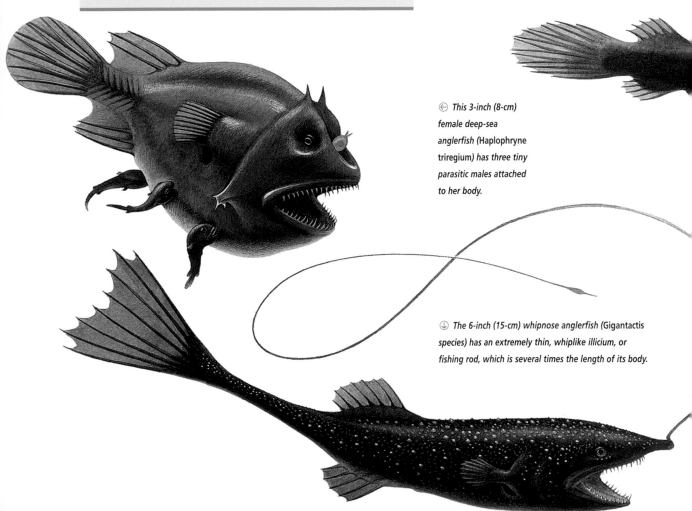

⊖ *This 3-inch (8-cm) female deep-sea anglerfish (Haplophryne triregium) has three tiny parasitic males attached to her body.*

⊕ *The 6-inch (15-cm) whipnose anglerfish (Gigantactis species) has an extremely thin, whiplike illicium, or fishing rod, which is several times the length of its body.*

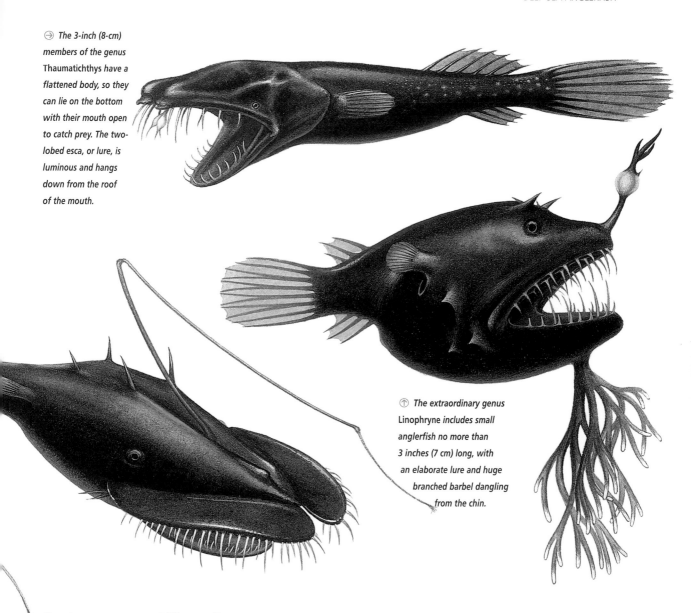

The 3-inch (8-cm) members of the genus Thaumatichthys *have a flattened body, so they can lie on the bottom with their mouth open to catch prey. The two-lobed esca, or lure, is luminous and hangs down from the roof of the mouth.*

The extraordinary genus Linophryne *includes small anglerfish no more than 3 inches (7 cm) long, with an elaborate lure and huge branched barbel dangling from the chin.*

In the 2–3-inch (5–7 cm) Lasiognathus *species the upper jaws expand as a flap on each side. Teeth mounted on the flaps point outward when the flaps are held open. Like most deep-sea anglerfish, these species also have an extremely long, flexible illicium, or fishing rod.*

Different Sizes

Most members of this group are squat fish with a very large head. Deep-sea anglerfish vary in size. The majority are less than 6 inches (15 cm) long, but a few—such as the triplewart sea devil (*Cryptopsaras couesi*) and the giant sea devil (*Ceratias holboelli*)—grow to about 40 inches (1 m). Like toadfish, anglerfish have no ribcage, and the rest of the skeleton is greatly reduced. Not only are the bones very small and simplified, many are barely calcified, and the fish rely mainly on cartilage for support. The

exception to the rule in most species are the jawbones, which are much more substantial although still light by vertebrae standards. Part of the reason for the anglerfish's flimsy skeleton is to improve buoyancy. Anglerfish lack a swim bladder; if it were not for their lightweight bones, they would never get off the seafloor.

The gill openings are modified into small tubes that open just beneath the pectoral fins. The pectoral fins are typically small and rounded or square, with between 12 and 13 rays. The caudal fin of all species has eight or nine rays,

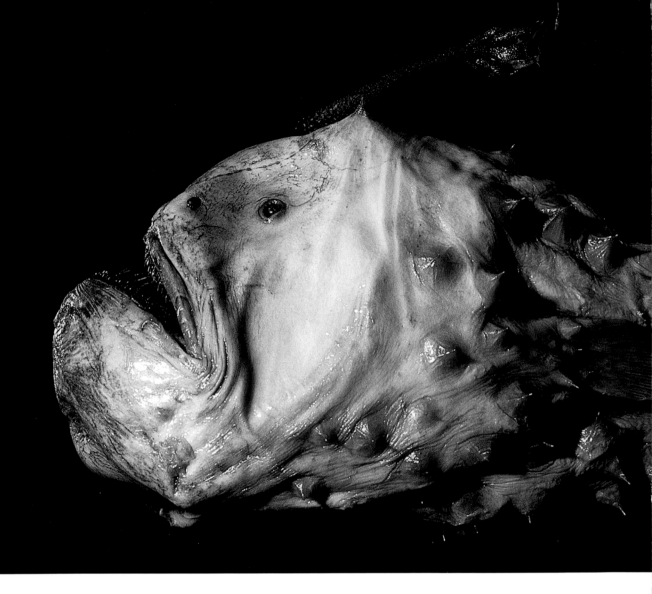

which may be branched or simple. The overall shape of the tail varies from square to round to fan-shaped, but is usually more or less symmetrical. The skin is usually dark brown or black; the body lacks scales but may bear any number of spines, plates, tubercles or other ornamentations. However, compared with the shallow-water anglerfish, ceratioids have little elaborate camouflage. Instead, they rely on the darkness of their deepwater habitat to hide.

The anglerfish's second dorsal fins and anal fin are usually set well back on the body close to the tail. Their size and shape vary, but in most species they contain relatively few, well-spaced rays.

Flashing Fishing Pole

As with other types of anglerfish, it is the first dorsal fin that defines the lifestyle of deep-sea ceratioids. The first dorsal ray grows not from the back but from somewhere near the tip of the snout.

The fin ray is modified into a fishing pole known as the "illicium." This feature can vary from virtually a stout peg to a line several times the length of the fish's body. At the end of the illicium is a lure, known as the "esca," which usually takes the form of a small, fleshy bulb. Often the other rays of the dorsal fin are modified into fleshy, clublike growths, which are called "caruncles."

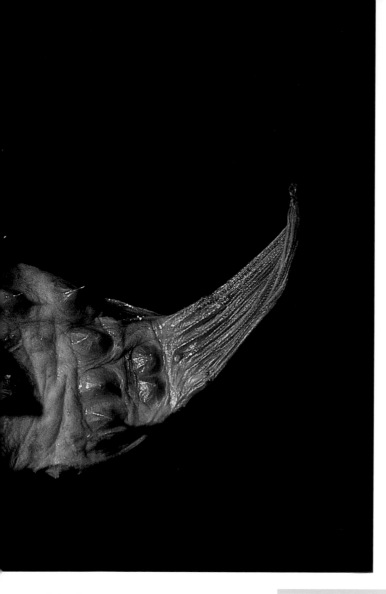

In addition to the bioluminescent lure some deep-sea anglerfish also have their own light-producing organs—such as the large, branching chin barbel of the sea, or net, devils (*Linophryne* species)—that can be made to glow. This light is generated by the fish itself, not by bacteria. It is the result of a chemical reaction involving the protein luciferin and an enzyme called "luciferase" within special cells called "photophores." When the photophores are supplied with oxygen from the bloodstream, they produce light.

Not all deep-sea anglerfish use a bioluminescent lure; it is only the females of most species that hunt in this way. *Neoceratias spinifer*—the sole representative of the family Neroceratiidae—lacks a fishing lure altogether.

A Varied Diet

Deep-sea anglerfish are not fussy eaters. They will eat all kinds of fish as well as crustaceans, cephalopods (squid), and any other deep-sea invertebrates tempted within range by the lure or simply unfortunate enough to venture too close. Once the anglerfish opens its huge mouth, the victim is drawn in on a rush of water and snagged on the untidy rows of wickedly sharp teeth.

The teeth of several deep-sea anglerfish species have taken on nightmarish proportions. For example, in large specimens of some

Bioluminescence

Fishing with a lure is highly effective, but only if potential prey can see the "bait." In several thousand feet of water even the sharpest eyes need a little help.

Anglerfish have a spectacular way of making sure their lure gets noticed—with the help of bioluminescent bacteria they illuminate the esca. Bacterial luminescence is permanent and cannot be produced on demand. So unlike self-luminescent fish, the only way anglerfish can turn their lights on and off is to hide the bacteria from view—by tucking the lure away or closing the pores that open from the tubules in which the bacteria live.

Light Duties

The bioluminescence used by deep-sea anglerfish is not produced by the fish themselves but by colonies of symbiotic bacteria enlisted for the task that live in specially adapted tissues. The fishing lure contains bacteria tightly packed into tiny tubules. In most other fish using bacterial symbionts, the bacteria are one of just three species of *Photobacterium*. However, in ceratioids the bacteria appear more closely related to *Vibrio* species—a group of bioluminescent bacteria that are normally free living. In addition each family of ceratioids appears to have its own highly specific species of *Vibrio* that is not found anywhere else.

Making the Most of Resources

At first it can be difficult to see what possible advantage it is for a species to have dwarf males. After all, in most animals males compete for females to mate with; therefore large size is an advantage. However, in an environment where resources are scarce, males can only grow large at the expense of females—the extra food they need to build and fuel a large body means there is less to help females produce offspring. Parasitic male anglerfish are no more than a means of delivering sperm to the females and do so in the most efficient manner possible under the circumstances.

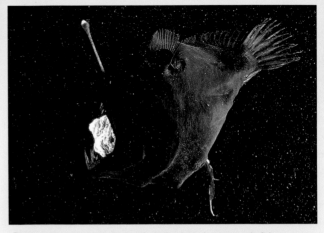

⤉ *Parasitic males are attached to the belly of this deep-sea anglerfish.*

Melanocetus species, measuring just 5.5 inches (14 cm) long, the dozens of teeth in the lower jaw measure almost 1 inch (2.5 cm) long and are shaped like curved needles.

Table Manners

Some female deep-sea anglerfish, such as *Neoceratias spinifer,* even have teeth on the outside of the jaws. They bristle out all around the mouth. Species of *Lasiognathus* (a genus of thaumaticthyid anglerfish) have an

Bizarre Breeding

If the way anglerfish hunt and feed is unusual, their breeding biology is truly bizarre. As previously mentioned, only females hunt using a lure. For many years biologists puzzled over the fact that for certain ceratioid families all the anglerfish examined appeared to be female. Then they noticed many of these females appeared to be infested by small, globular parasites, which it transpired were the males. Their life history is unique among vertebrates.

Parasitic male anglerfish never grow more than a few inches long, often much less. They cannot feed themselves and spend their early adult lives searching for a female. If they do not find one, they die. However, the lucky ones that find a female of the same species use their sharp teeth to bite into her skin. Over the subsequent days and weeks the skin and other tissues of the male fuse with those of his host-mate. His body is nourished by her blood in an arrangement not unlike a mammalian placenta. Quite rapidly most of his organs degenerate. Regulated by hormones in the female's blood, the male becomes sexually mature, and sperm ripen in his testes in time to fertilize her eggs.

The relationship between a parasitic male and his mate is for life—once attached, he cannot survive without her. By taking on one or more parasitic males, the female anglerfish is effectively a self-fertilizing hermaphrodite. She provides the energy and nutrients for the development of both eggs and sperm, and the whole process is under her control.

Nonparasitic Males

Not all male deep-sea anglerfish are parasites. For example, males of the families Oneirodidae, Himantolophidae, and Melanocetidae are small but remain free living. They continue to feed themselves as they did as larvae but only tackle small planktonic prey and never grow very big.

However, unlike the parasitic males of other species, they reach sexual maturity of their own accord and go in search of females in order to breed. They probably find them by sensing pheromones in the water. On finding a

⊕ *The whipnose anglerfish (*Gigantactis vanhoeffeni*) has an extremely long, flexible bioluminescent lure on the end of its fleshy snout and uses it to attract prey. The lure is even shaped like a tiny fish to make it appear more enticing.*

extralarge upper lip that is divided into two flaps fringed with teeth—they rake the water as the mouth closes to scrape the victim into the mouth. The prey is then swallowed whole almost regardless of size.

Both the esophagus and the stomach of anglerfish are highly elastic, and individuals will often consume fish and other prey that are almost as big as themselves—not an option for small-mouthed anglerfish such as whipnoses (*Gigantactis* species).

female, they latch onto her body and fertilize her eggs in a conventional fashion. Just to confuse matters further, some species, such as the fanfin anglerfish (*Caulophryne* species) and the *Leptacanthichthys* species, appear to have both parasitic and free-living males.

Female deep-sea anglerfish are staggeringly fecund. Even small species produce many thousands of eggs in a spawning, and in larger taxa like sea devils (*Ceratius* species) the figure may be several million. The eggs drift toward the surface and hatch into minute larvae that feed on a variety of other plankton. After about two months they return to the depths and develop into juvenile fish.

The sex ratio of young anglerfish is heavily biased toward males. Males need to be abundant, because remaining quite small means they are vulnerable to predation. This also means mature females stand a better chance of being located by a potential mate. Often a large female will carry more than one parasitic male. This is advantageous up to a point; as long as the males do not put too much strain on the female's body, they will give her a more genetically mixed batch of offspring with a better chance of success.

FAMILY BY FAMILY
Caulophrynidae—Fanfin Anglerfish
Fanfin anglerfish are medium-sized ceratioids with a smooth, globular body and spectacular dorsal and anal fins, in which rays almost as long as the body fan out from the back end of the fish. Four species have been described from all major tropical and temperate oceans. Mature males are parasitic on females and grow to less than one-tenth the size of their mates. Juvenile male fanfin anglerfish are the only members of the suborder Ceratioidea to have pelvic fins.

Neoceratiidae—Toothy Sea Devils
The sole member of this family is *Neoceratias spinifer*. Females are unusual in that they lack a fishing lure. Instead, they have an amazing array of needlelike teeth growing inside the mouth and also from the upper and lower lips.

The body shape is much more elongated than other deep-sea anglerfish, presumably an adaptation to a more active form of ambush hunting. Males are dwarf parasites.

Melanocetidae—Black Sea Devils
The single genus *Melanocetus* includes just five known species of black or humpback sea devils. Females grow to around 7 inches (18 cm) long. The head is very large and rounded with a very large mouth. The body tapers sharply behind the pronounced dorsal hump, and the posterior section is about one-third the depth of the head. Males are no more than 1 inch (3 cm) long but live independently of the females.

Himantolophidae—Footballfish
Footballfish are quite large by ceratioid standards. Females grow to 18 inches (45 cm) long. Males reach 1.5 inches (4 cm), which

⊕ A deep-sea anglerfish (Linophryne species) continues to develop inside a large, yolky egg until it is almost adult. This unusual development strategy helps ensure each young fish gets a good start, even when food is scarce.

212

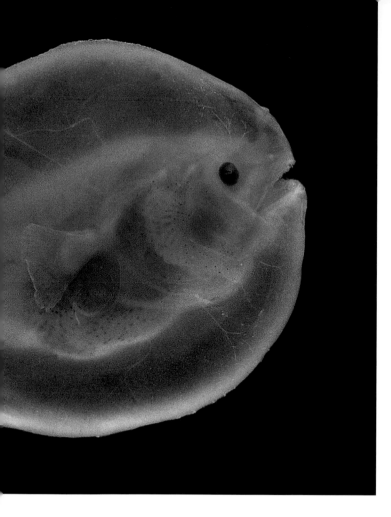

the eye is large. The skin is smooth or covered in small spines. Males are small but free living.

Thaumatichthyidae

The diminutive thaumatichthyid anglerfish have a greatly enlarged upper jaw that overlaps the lower jaw by some distance. So far seven species are known from the Atlantic and Pacific.

Centrophrynidae—Horned Lanternfish

The single species *Centrophryne spinulosa* is known from a few specimens collected in tropical parts of the Atlantic, Pacific, and Indian Oceans. Females are covered in small spines and are about 8 to 9 inches (20–23 cm) long. The body is more elongated than in most other deep-sea anglerfish. Males are dwarf but nonparasitic.

Ceratiidae—Sea Devils

Females of this relatively well-known group are large with distinctive knobby "caruncles," which are located halfway along the back. They are the modified rays of the first dorsal fin. The second dorsal and anal fins are of similar sizes. The mouth is large and almost vertical. Males are dwarf parasites.

Gigantactinidae—Whipnose Anglerfish

Whipnose anglerfish are strange but benign-looking ceratioids. The body is elongated, the head and mouth relatively small. The upper jaw protrudes beyond the lower and bears a fleshy snout; it has an extremely long, flexible fishing rod with a small, fleshy lure at the tip. Several species are relatively recent discoveries, known from just a handful of specimens worldwide.

Linophrynidae—Deep-sea Anglerfish

Female linophrynids carry the largest and most elaborate fishing lures of any anglerfish, but the lure is dwarfed by the huge, multibranched barbel that dangles from the chin like a frond of seaweed and glows in the dark. Its purpose is probably to attract juvenile dwarf males, which become parasitic on the female before reaching sexual maturity.

makes them the largest of all free-living ceratioid males. Female footballfish are almost spherical, with a very short, blunt snout and an extremely elaborate fishing lure.

Diceratiidae—Two-rod Anglerfish

Females of this family are distinguished from all other deep-sea anglerfish in having a double fishing lure. In young specimens especially a second dorsal fin ray emerges just behind the first with its own club-shaped, bioluminescent esca at the tip. Males are free living.

Oneirodidae—Bulbous Anglerfish and Dreamers

The bulbous anglerfish are the largest family of deep-sea anglerfish, with 60 or so species. Females have very small dorsal and anal fins with few rays, but the tail fin is substantial. The mouth is smaller than in most ceratioids, and

Gray mullet (*Mugil cephalus*)

Common name Mullets

Family Mugilidae

Order Mugiliformes

Number of species 75 species in around 17 genera

Size From around 4 in (10 cm) to 4 ft (1.2 m); majority above 8 in (20 cm)

Key features Elongated body; head flattened on top; mouth moderately sized; small teeth or no teeth; fins well formed but no adipose fin; 2 dorsal fins widely separated—first bears 4 spines, second soft rays; pectoral fins close to back edge of gill cover (operculum) high up on body; pelvic fins on front half of belly; anal fin with 3 spines at front; caudal fin forked; blue-green coloration above shading to whitish-silvery along belly; other colors also present

Breeding Spawning summer to fall, or even winter, in seas and estuaries; eggs scattered in open; hatching may only take 1.5 days

Diet Algae, plants, plant debris, tiny free-floating organisms (zooplankton), and organic matter, including small invertebrates sifted from mouthfuls of soft sediments

Habitat Marine, close to coastal waters; many migrate between sea and fresh water, return to brackish or marine environments for spawning

Distribution All tropical, subtropical, and temperate seas

Status Not threatened

ⓐ *The gray mullet (Mugil cephalus) is also known as the flathead mullet. The largest member of the family Mugilidae, it can grow to a length of 4 feet (1.2 m).*

Mullets

Mugilidae

*The gray mullet (*Mugil cephalus*) is a very versatile species: It is a highly prized food fish, it provides sport for anglers, and it is even kept as an aquarium exhibit.*

THE GRAY MULLET (*MUGIL CEPHALUS*) is the best known of the 75 species that make up the family Mugilidae. It is also widely distributed, found in tropical and subtropical seas all over the world. It adapts to marine, brackish, and freshwater conditions, and is found at any depth from the water surface down to nearly 400 feet (120 m). It is so popular in so many countries that it has over 270 common names in languages and dialects all over the world.

The gray mullet is also farmed commercially using freshwater culture ponds in parts of the world such as Southeast Asia. A large fish, it can weigh up to 17.6 pounds (8 kg). Its flesh is sold fresh, frozen, salted, or dried, and its eggs (roe) are sold fresh or smoked.

Mullets in Perspective

Despite minor differences, mullet species generally look quite similar to each other. This can make identification difficult, particularly in the case of wide-ranging species that may vary slightly locally.

Classifying the mullet family in relation to other fish families has caused a certain amount of difficulty over the years. For example, mullets possess two separate dorsal fins; and because the pelvic fins are located in the front half of the belly region, they were once thought to be closely related to the barracudas (family Sphyraenidae) or the threadfins (family Polynemidae). However, a similar arrangement exists in other families, for example, the silversides (family Atherinidae) and their closest relatives like the rainbowfish (family Melanotaeniidae), and it is to these that the mullets are now thought to be closest.

Nevertheless, having other characteristics, like very small teeth or no teeth at all, allied to

long gill rakers that form a sievelike mechanism at the back of the mouth, plus a muscular stomach and a long intestine (absolutely essential when food consists largely of algae and plant debris), means that the mullets have not only a family of their own but an order as well (the Mugiliformes). They are the only family in the order.

Freshwater Mullets

Many species of mullet enter rivers at some stage in their lives. For example, the abu mullet (*Liza abu*) from Iran, Iraq, Turkey, and Pakistan spends most of its life in fresh water. The goldie river mullet (*Cestraeus goldiei*) is widely distributed from the Philippines southward to New Caledonia. It frequents fast-flowing mountain streams and ascends up to around 1,150 feet (350 m) above sea level. Even some of the best-known species, such as the longarm mullet (*Valamugil cunnesius*) and the thicklip gray mullet (*Chelon labrosus*), move between fresh water and the sea at varying stages of their lives, although they spawn at sea.

However, one species—the predominantly North American mountain mullet (*Agonostomus monticola*)—spends the whole of its adult life in a freshwater environment, being found in rivers from Venezuela to Colombia, where it is a popular food fish. Juveniles may occur in the brackish stretches of rivers and streams, however. The mountain mullet migrates into the sea for spawning.

⊕ *The warty-lipped mullet (*Crenimugil crenilabis*) grows to 2 feet (61 cm) and spawns in large groups after dark, usually in shallow lagoons. The fish is of only minor commercial interest.*

Sand smelt (*Atherina presbyter*)

Common name Silversides

Family Atherinidae

Subfamilies Atherininae, Atherioninae ("Old World silversides"), Atheriopsinae, Menidiinae ("New World silversides")

Order Atheriniformes

Number of species Around 165 in 25 genera

Size From 2.8 in (7.5 cm) to 17.5 in (44.5 cm)

Key features Elongated bodies; head pointed or rounded; large eyes; "forehead" slopes upward; dorsal profile straight; mouth located at tip of snout; fins well formed; 2 dorsal fins, no adipose fin; 1st dorsal fin with flexible spines, softer 2nd dorsal; pectoral fins high on side and close to gill covers; tail forked; coloration various shades— green-blue on back in marine species; all have characteristic silvery sides; freshwater species patterned with spots and lines

Breeding Egg scatterers except grunion; spawning season March to April/September; tropical species spawn throughout year; a few, e.g., *Atherinopsis* species like jacksmelt, spawn in winter; eggs scattered over vegetation or substratum; hatching takes several days or longer

Diet Small floating and drifting invertebrates (zooplankton); small fish

Habitat Marine species in shallow seas; freshwater species in streams, rivers, and lakes

Distribution Seas around the globe; some fresh water in North and South America, Australia, and New Guinea

World population Abundant, some under threat

Status IUCN lists 32 species as variously under threat

⊕ *The sand smelt (*Atherina presbyter*) is found in the eastern Atlantic Ocean, mainly around the coasts of Britain, southwest Europe, and North Africa. It grows to about 8 inches (20 cm) in length.*

Silversides

Atherinidae

Silversides are a family of small, silvery fish, one of whose mass shoaling and spawning behavior verge on the truly spectacular. Other species are important commercial food sources.

EACH INCOMING WAVE ON THE high night tide throws a mass of small, writhing silvery fish onto a sandy California beach during a full moon and leaves the fish stranded at the highest point on the shore. As the wave rolls back, it takes another mass of exhausted fish back to sea. The scene has been unfailingly played out for thousands of years: It is the spawning ritual of the grunion (*Leuresthes tenuis*), a member of the family commonly referred to as the silversides (Altherinidae).

Spawning usually occurs between March and August, and is closely linked to the highest tides (the spring tides at full and new moon). Then the high tide reaches farther up the beach than at any other time.

Waiting for the Tide

Millions of grunion crowd the surf line, waiting for the breaking waves to carry them up to the strandline—the highest point reached by the waves. Once there, female grunions rapidly force the back half of their bodies into the soft, wet sand, positioning themselves in an upright position. As this happens, each female is surrounded by a number of males all eager to mate. She quickly releases her eggs under the sand, and the males release sperm around her, fertilizing the eggs. The whole sequence is over in a few seconds, at which point the female wriggles out of the sand and waits, exhausted, until another wave can drag her and the males back into the surf.

The eggs then remain under the sand where they develop into fully formed baby fish over the following two weeks, which is when the next spring tides are due. As soon as the next high tide arrives, all the eggs hatch within

⊖ *Grunions (*Leuresthes tenuis*) spawning en masse on a California beach at night. During the hazardous process many fall victim to predators, including human fishermen.*

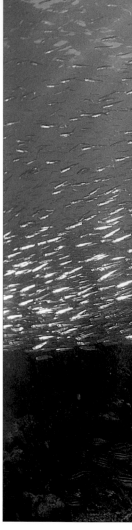

⊕ Silversides shoaling
in shallow water off
Belize in the Caribbean.

⊕ Female grunions dig
the lower parts of their
bodies into the sand and
release their eggs, which
are then fertilized by the
attendant males.

the space of a few minutes, and the young fish are washed into the sea. It will take them about a year to mature, and then they will return instinctively to the beach to breed, just as their parents did. The lifespan of the grunion is about four years. However, it is not known how many actually survive the spawning ordeal.

Commercial Silversides

The grunion is one of nearly 170 species that form an ancient family that evolved between 37 and 50 million years ago. It is the only representative that has evolved the "beaching" spawning strategy. All the other species in the family spawn by scattering their eggs above vegetation or the bottom. Among the other species are some, like the sand smelts (*Atherina presbyter*) and white fish (*Chirostoma* species), that are fished commercially in large numbers in many countries. Sometimes whole fisheries are based on just one species, so great are the numbers in which some silversides occur.

Silversides are sold fresh, dried, or even ground. In some Mediterranean countries, for example, fresh smelts are fried and sold in restaurants. Fresh fish are also sometimes sold as bait. Dried silversides are often sold as pet food, mainly for cats and dogs, although they can also be used for human consumption, especially when soaked. Ground silversides are widely used in the production of fish meal, which is then fed to poultry, pigs, and cattle.

Most family members are primarily marine fish. However, some commercial groups, such as most of the hardyheads (*Craterocephalus* species) of Australia and New Guinea, also occur in fresh water and estuaries. Silversides are about 2.8 and 8 inches (7.5–20 cm) long, but the jacksmelt (*Atherinopsis californiensis*) is about 17.5 inches (44.5 cm) long.

Silversides under Threat

More than 32 species of silversides are believed to be under some form of threat in the wild. In some cases the concern is centered on the lack of data, but in others, as in the highly endangered Murray hardyhead (*Craterocephalus fluviatilis*) from Australia, the threats can be more clearly identified. Topmost are factors like a decline in the number of locations in which the species can be found, or existing populations being separated from each other and therefore not being able to breed.

In two species of Mexican charals (*Poblana* species)—both of which are officially listed by the World Conservation Union as Endangered—the same factors apply but more so, in that all the individuals known to exist are believed to be in single subpopulations. Therefore, if they disappear, so does the species.

Three-spined stickleback
(*Gasterosteus aculeatus aculeatus*)

Common name Sticklebacks

Family Gasterosteidae

Order Gasterosteiformes

Number of species 11 in 5 genera

Size From 2 in (5 cm) to 9 in (23 cm)

Key features Elongated, compressed body, with bony plates
(scutes) running lengthwise; pointed head;
mouth angled upward; eyes relatively large; row
of isolated spines running along back and in
front of soft dorsal fin; number of spines varies
within species, but no spines in Greek nine-spine
stickleback; sometimes pelvic spine and fin
lacking; caudal peduncle slim to very slim;
coloration: variable, especially in males; blue,
green, brown, black, and red (particularly intense
during breeding)

Breeding Female lays eggs in nest built by male; young
hatch 7–10 days later, protected by male

Diet Invertebrates; also fish eggs, larvae, and small
fish

Habitat Pure fresh water through brackish water to fully
marine; vegetated areas (preferably with no
movement or light currents) and fine-grained
bottoms; mostly found in very shallow water, but
some occur down to 180 ft (55 m)

Distribution Widely distributed in Northern Hemisphere

Status IUCN lists Greek nine-spine stickleback (*Pungitius
hellenicus*) as Critically Endangered

*⬆ This 4.3-inch (11-cm) male three-spined stickleback
(Gasterosteus aculeatus aculeatus) constructs a nest from plant
material in which the female will lay her eggs. A male's chest
turns bright red or orange in the breeding season.*

Sticklebacks
Gasterosteidae

*In the Northern Hemisphere the stickleback can easily
be observed in ponds, ditches, or streams. These
small, brilliantly colored prickly fish are usually the
three-spined sticklebacks.*

DESPITE ITS WORLDWIDE FAME, THE THREE-SPINED
stickleback (*Gasterosteus aculeatus aculeatus*) is
the topic of much debate. Along with other
aspects of its lifestyle its feeding and breeding
habits have been studied in great detail for
many years and are quite well known.

Adaptable Stickleback
The three-spined stickleback has a very wide
geographic distribution. In North America it
occurs from Baffin Island and western Hudson
Bay southward to Chesapeake Bay in Virginia,
but not in many central areas except for Lake
Ontario. On the Pacific coast it is found from
Alaska down to Baja California in Mexico. It is
also occurs in Greenland, Iceland, and the
Pacific coast of Asia. In Europe it is found in
most rivers, except large sections of the Danube
River. It also extends into the Mediterranean
and Black Seas and North Africa, from Algeria
to Iran in the Middle East.

This fish is extremely versatile and is found
in a range of habitats from fresh and brackish
water to fully marine conditions—in pure
freshwater shallow streams and ditches to
estuaries and shallow coastal waters to a depth
of nearly 90 feet (27 m). Such fish, which are
capable of living in both fresh and sea waters,
are described as anadromous species.

In view of this stickleback's extensive range
and adaptability to diverse environmental
conditions there are widely differing opinions
on the species as a whole, as well as the nature
of some of its isolated populations.

How Many Three-spines?
One main question, to which no satisfactory
answer has been found, is how many species or

*⬇ The spines on this
adult ten-spined
stickleback (Pungitius
pungitius pungitius) are
clearly well developed.
The ten-spine is one of
two subspecies of the
nine-spined stickleback
(P. pungitius).*

subspecies of the three-spined sticklebacks
exist. The answer is very complex.

When a species is as
widely distributed as the
three-spined stickleback,
it is subjected to different
environmental influences,
such as type and abundance
of food supply, temperature,
quality, speed, depth, and
clarity of water, amount and
type of vegetation, even types of
predator—they can all differ. Also,
isolated populations cannot interbreed.

Separated Populations

Such factors all have an effect on resident fish
that subsequently can evolve along different
paths, so they begin to look and behave quite
differently from one another. If these changes
persist for long enough, or result in very
different characteristics, there will come a time
when separated populations will not be able to
interbreed even if reunited by a natural event
(like two rivers joining up) or for experimental
studies. Thus, over time, a fish that was one
species when it began spreading evolves into
two or more distinct species or subspecies.

This has happened to the three-spined
stickleback to such an extent that scientists are
not sure how many three-spines now exist. For

example, freshwater populations are generally
spotted, with some brown and greenish tones
along the back that fade to silvery on the belly.
However, types that migrate between salt water
and fresh water tend to lack brown tones and
are more bluish-black. This darkening is taken
further, in some isolated populations, in which
males do not develop the same red throat and
chest, green or blue eyes, or brilliant blue-green
body sheen of their close relatives. The length is
also different between freshwater and marine
forms, with the latter growing larger—to 4.3
inches (11 cm) rather than 3.2 inches (8 cm).

Perfect Fathers

During the spring and summer breeding season male sticklebacks develop intense coloration. In the three-spined stickleback (*Gasterosteus aculeatus aculeatus*) this includes a deepening of its existing colors, plus a deep-red throat, chest, and belly. In the nine-spined stickleback (*Pungitius pungitius*) the existing colors all become deeper, with males becoming almost black, particularly when in an aggressive mood. Also, the membranes between the spines of the pelvic fins turn white. As breeding gets under way, the black coloration becomes more restricted—to the underside of the body.

Males establish a territory at breeding time and defend it vigorously. Then they build a tunnel-like nest of strands of vegetation that they glue together with secretions from their kidneys. In the three-spined stickleback the nest is built on the bottom, usually among plants. However, in the nine-spined stickleback it is built a little distance off the bottom among stems of submerged vegetation.

When nest building is complete, males will attract a suitable female by means of spectacular dancing displays. The main factor in a "desirable" female appears to be her plumpness. But not all plump females are full of eggs—some are carrying large internal parasitic tapeworms that make their bellies swell. Assuming the female is able to breed, she will enter the nest and lay up to 600 eggs, leaving the male to fertilize them. Then he will attempt to attract further females until, in the three-spined stickleback, up to 1,000 eggs have been laid and fertilized.

The male stands guard over the eggs until the first hatchlings occur, about 7 to 10 days after laying. The newborns remain close to the nest for a week, protected by their father, before they disperse.

The amount of body armor (plates or scutes) also varies for various populations, even those found within a single country. In Britain, for example, three distinct forms are known. The "trachura" form has scutes running the whole length of the body—from head to caudal peduncle. The "semiarmata" form has incomplete and variable body armor, while the "leiurus" type has no scutes at all. Therefore, do these forms belong to the same species or subspecies—or are they separate species?

Currently the above forms are considered to be members of a single, highly variable

The pointed head, large eyes, and upward angled mouth are clearly visible as this fifteen-spined stickleback (Spinachia spinachia) peeps out from seaweed in Cork County, Ireland. Its alternative name is the sea stickleback.

This pair of three-spined sticklebacks (Gasterosteus aculeatus aculeatus) are about to enter their nest that the male has built on the bottom among plants. Note the male's red breeding color along the underside of his body.

subspecies of the three-spined stickleback—*Gasterosteus aculeatus aculeatus*. Three other subspecies are also recognized. One from Japan, where it is restricted to small freshwater streams, has a slightly smaller head but no common name (*G. a. microcephalus*). The Santa Ana stickleback (*G. a. santaeannae*) is a North American fish found in fresh, brackish, and marine waters. The unarmored three-spined stickleback (*G. a. williamsoni*) from southern California lacks the others' stout body plates; but it, too, is different from the "leiurus" form of the British three-spined stickleback.

All four types are now regarded as subspecies of a single species—*Gasterosteus aculeatus*—but this could change.

Two other species of *Gasterosteus* are also known, but one—*G. crenobiontus* from Romania—has become extinct and was officially listed in 1997. The other is far from extinct. It is the 3-inch (7.5-cm) blackspotted stickleback (*G. wheatlandi*) that occurs in brackish and marine habitats along the Atlantic coastline of eastern Canada and the U.S. from Newfoundland down to Massachusetts. It has been known to enter fresh water, but only rarely, and is found mostly in near-shore areas among vegetation. It is reported that this species lives for only a year, but the three-spined (*G. aculeatus*) lives for three and the nine-spined (*Pungitius pungitius pungitius*) for five.

The Nine-spines

The nine-spined stickleback (*Pungitius pungitius*) may not have nine spines but from six to twelve, so its common name is not really appropriate. Neither is its most widely used alternative name—the ten-spined stickleback. It is one of two subspecies of *P. pungitius* that currently is given the full name of *Pungitius pungitius pungitius*—to distinguish it from *P. p. tymensis*, a smaller, 2.8-inch (7-cm) version found in Japan and the Russian Federation. *P. p. pungitius* is 3.5 inches (9 cm) long.

This Japanese-Russian nine-spined is called the Sakhalin stickleback because of its Russian distribution. It is strictly a freshwater fish, but its more widely distributed relative is also found in fresh, brackish, and fully marine waters. Like the three-spined stickleback, *P. p. pungitius* occurs on both sides of the Atlantic—in the west from Canada down to New Jersey; in the east, all the main drainages of northern Europe and Asia stretching from the U.K. to Korea, Japan, and China. It is also found on the Pacific coast of Alaska and in the Great Lakes basin.

Like the three-spined stickleback, the Amur stickleback (*P. sinensis sinensis*) is interesting in that it grows to different sizes in different habitats—in fresh water it only grows to 2.6 inches (6.5 cm), but in sea water it can reach 3.5 inches (9 cm) in length. The little-known subspecies of the Amur stickleback—(*P. sinensis kaibarae*)—is restricted to freshwater habitats in parts of Japan.

The smoothtail nine-spined stickleback (*P. laevis*), a freshwater species, occurs in England and France; little is known about its life history.

The southern nine-spined stickleback (*P. platygaster*) is a widely distributed European and Asian species that grows to around 2.8 inches (7 cm); it is highly adaptable in its habitats, found in fresh, brackish, and marine waters. Its smaller Central Asian closest relative is the Aral stickleback (*P. platygaster aralensis*), found mostly in the Aral Sea. Almost the smallest stickleback, it measures just 2.1 inches (5.3 cm) in length; it is restricted to freshwater habitats, stretching over a wide part of its Central Asian range, where it is found, largely, in lakes and gentle-flowing bodies of water.

Contrasting North Americans

Two North American sticklebacks look very like the three-spined stickleback—the four-spined stickleback (*Apeltes quadracus*) and the brook

Like all sticklebacks, this nine-spined stickleback (Pungitius pungitius) swims in its preferred habitat of vegetation with little water movement. Its mouth open, it will eat mostly invertebrates, but also fish eggs, larvae, and small fish.

stickleback (*Culaea inconstans*), with three to five spines and four to six spines, respectively.

In the four-spined the dorsal spines are angled in relation to each other, slanting alternately to right and left, with the first two longer than the rest. During the breeding season mature, 2.5-inch (6.4-cm) black males look spectacular—they develop red pelvic fins.

This predominantly marine species occurs near coasts from Canada's Gulf of St. Lawrence to the coastal strip of North Carolina. It is often found in weedy areas and will enter brackish water but rarely into fully freshwater habitats.

In marked contrast, the brook stickleback is a freshwater species that rarely ventures into brackish water but never into the sea. It likes cool, quiet, vegetated waters in ponds, lakes, and backwaters in the northern half of North America. It occurs as far north as the Northwest Territories of the Arctic drainage, spreading south to the Great Lakes and Mississippi River basin, into Montana, southern Ohio, and Nebraska, and east as far as Nova Scotia.

There is also an isolated population in part of the Canadian River that runs through New Mexico—a prime example of the situation mentioned earlier in which the three-spined stickleback could evolve into a new species or subspecies of brook stickleback. Changes are already taking place elsewhere in

Threatened Stickleback

Somewhat better known than some of its closest relatives—but partly for the wrong reasons—is the Greek nine-spined (or ten-spined) stickleback (*P. hellenicus*).

This slender species only grows to around 2 inches (5 cm), and most unusually for a stickleback, it does not have any spines at all! It is a secretive species that lives among the vegetated edges of springs and small rivers in the Sperchios River basin in the central parts of eastern Greece. It is said to bury itself in the bottom mud when escaping from predators.

Unfortunately for this tiny species, its water is also needed by our own species, and as almost invariably happens in such unequal contests, the stickleback is losing out. In fact, its position is so much under threat (it is believed to be now extinct in some parts of its restricted range) that it is officially listed by the World Conservation Union as Critically Endangered.

this species' range, with the population in Alberta and Saskatchewan lacking pelvic fins.

Ultraslim Giant

The largest member of the entire family is the fifteen-spined stickleback (*Spinachia spinachia*) —also called the sea stickleback—which can grow to around 9 inches (23 cm). An eastern Atlantic species, it occurs close to shore along coasts stretching from northern Norway southward to the northern parts of the Bay of Biscay, as well as in the Baltic Sea.

It is an extremely elongated, slim fish with a sharply pointed snout and a very long, thin caudal peduncle. As in most other sticklebacks, the number of spines along the back varies—in this case from 14 to 17. Also just like its relatives, it is the male that builds the nest, often in tidal pools; it consists of seaweed stuck together. Like the nine-spined stickleback, the fifteen-spine builds its nest clear of the bottom.

A single female may lay up to 200 eggs; then, in sharp contrast to other stickleback species, the female dies. The male guards the eggs in typically vigorous fashion.

Armored stickleback (*Indostomus paradoxus*)

Common name Sea horses, pipefish, and allies

Families Syngnathidae (sea horses, pipefish, pipehorses, seadragons), Solenostomidae (ghost pipefish), Indostomidae (armored sticklebacks)

Subfamilies Syngnathidae: Syngnathinae (pipefish, pipehorses, seadragons); Hippocampinae (sea horses)

Order Gasterosteiformes

Number of species Syngnathidae: around 270 in 52 genera; Solenostomidae: 4 in 1 genus; Indostomidae: 3 in 1 genus

Size From 0.95 in (2.4 cm) to 37.4 in (95 cm)

Key features Elongated body (encased in bony rings or star-shaped plates): held upright (sea horses), or horizontal (pipefish, seadragons); long snout (short in armored sticklebacks), small mouth; 1 to 2 dorsal fins, some with spines and soft rays; some species lack pelvic, caudal, anal fins; long, slim caudal peduncle (armored sticklebacks); varied coloration: muted browns to bright colors; sometimes patterned body or dark bars on fins

Breeding Male carries eggs in belly pouch or mass of spongy tissue (sea horses); female carries eggs in pouch formed by pelvic fin (ghost pipefish)

Diet Invertebrates, worms, and other bottom-dwellers

Habitat Shallow coral reefs, seagrass meadows above 165 ft (50 m) depth or to 310 ft (95 m); some in brackish estuaries; armored sticklebacks in still or slow-moving fresh water, leaf litter on bottom

Distribution Widely distributed in tropical, subtropical, and warm temperate regions of Atlantic, Indian, and Pacific Oceans, and Indo-West Pacific; also Myanmar, Cambodia, Thailand, Mekong Basin

Status IUCN lists 45 sea horse and pipefish species as under threat; sea horse species: 19 Vulnerable, 1 Endangered; pipefish species: 5 Vulnerable, 1 Critically Endangered

⊕ *This 1.2-inch (3-cm) long armored stickleback (*Indostomus paradoxus*) can leap out of the water.*

Sea Horses, Pipefish, and Allies

Syngnathidae, Solenostomidae, Indostomidae

We call sea horses quaint and delightful and often do not even think of them as fish. Yet they are beautiful examples of evolution, resulting in creatures ideally adapted to their environment.

SEA HORSES DO NOT LOOK LIKE FISH AT ALL. THEY STAND upright in water, their head at the top and tail at the bottom. In the closely related pipefish the head is at the front and the tail at the back. In sea horses the head points forward, as in normal fish, so that it sits at right angles on top of the body rather than in line with it.

Unfishlike Fish

These are not the only unfishlike characteristics that these remarkable creatures have. The tail, for example, does not have a fin but is a long, rounded extension of the body (the caudal peduncle), used to hold on to plants, just like monkeys on land. Sea horses do not have pelvic fins, and their small pectoral fins look like ears; their long snout makes them look horselike, hence their name. The single dorsal fin has flexible rays and is located halfway down the body, pointing backward (not upward as with other fish). They use this fin for swimming; it acts like a caudal fin in more conventional fish.

Sea horses have bony plates, not scales, on their bodies—a protective body armor that makes sea horses hard-to-swallow prey. In atypical fashion it is the male sea horses that become pregnant and give birth, not the females. Sea horses are truly unfishlike fish.

Not-so-faithful Breeders

It was thought sea horses paired for life, but loyalty only exists between some pairs depending on species and other factors; in the pot-bellied sea horse (*Hippocampus abdominalis*) there is little loyalty, for example.

⊙ *Like all sea horses, this colorful slender sea horse (*Hippocampus reidi*) has the typical pronounced snout, small mouth, and upright position in the water. Sea horses acquired their name from the horselike appearance of the snout.*

Record-breaking Discovery

Depending on which classification or book is consulted, there are as few as 32 species of sea horse—or as many as 120. To them must now be added a new one that was described in 2003.

It is Denise's pygmy sea horse (*Hippocampus denise*)—a record-breaker in that it is the smallest sea horse species known to science. Fully grown males measure just 0.9 inches (2.2 cm), with females being only slightly larger, about 0.95 inches (2.4 cm). Sexual maturity can be reached when the fish are only 0.6 inches (1.6 cm) in length.

According to its discoverer, zoologist Sara Lourie (who also codescribed the species with J.E. Randall), this tiny species lives deeper within coral heads than most other species, which could help its survival in the wild. It is also a more active species than other small sea horses, which makes its name "Denise" most appropriate, since it is derived from the Greek and means "wild or frenzied."

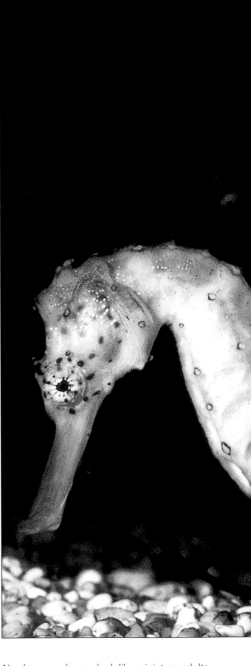

⊕ The World Conservation Union has classified the Knysna sea horse (Hippocampus capensis) *as Endangered. It occurs in the Knysna Lagoon west of Port Elizabeth, South Africa.*

When courting begins between a potential breeding pair, the female looks fuller than the male—he then develops a swollen belly pouch to show his readiness to mate. After a graceful display of "dancing" and entwining of tails, the pair face each other and bring their bellies close together. As the male opens the top of his abdominal pouch, the female transfers some eggs into it, and then he fertilizes them. Depending on age, size, and species, a female can produce up to 1,570 eggs (usually considerably fewer, often less than 100), which the male incubates. Two to four weeks later he gives birth, a process that can last up to 12 hours or more.

Newborn sea horses look like miniature adults. They are totally ignored by their father, so they have to fend for themselves from the start.

Similar, but Different

In their closest relatives—pipefish, pipehorses, and seadragons—the males also brood their eggs in special belly pouches, or spongy tissue under the tail, eventually giving birth.

However, in the pipefish the body is aligned in the more conventional way, with the head and snout directed forward, the tail directed backward, and the dorsal fin directed upward. In the seadragons (such as *Pycodorus* and *Phyllopteryx*) and the pipehorses (such as *Solegnathus* species) frequently the head and tail are held at an angle that lies somewhere between a sea horse and a pipefish.

Both the seadragons and pipefish have the same sort of snout that sea horses have. They also lack pelvic fins, and their pectoral fins lie close to the head and, in many species, have the appearance of ears. Along with other features, such as body casing, this means that currently pipefish, pipehorses, seadragons, and sea horses are all regarded as members of a single family (Syngnathidae) but belonging to

⊕ *A pair of long-snouted sea horses (Hippocampus guttulatus) perform their graceful courtship display by "dancing" and entwining their tails.*

Seaweed-imitating Dragons

There are three members of the pipefish that bear no resemblance to their other relatives. In fact, one looks so much like a clump of floating seaweed that it is frequently impossible to clarify that it is a fish at all. Indeed, the camouflage of the leafy seadragon (*Phycodurus eques*) is so effective that neither its predators nor its prey are even aware of its presence. Therefore predators miss a possible meal, while prey do not know that they are being hunted until it is too late.

The weedy seadragon (*Phyllopteryx taeniolatus*) also gives a good impression of a seaweed, but perhaps not quite so effectively—although its young are next to impossible to spot among bottom vegetation. The ribboned seadragon (*Haliichthys taeniophorus*) looks a little like a very slim, nonupright sea horse with tufts of seaweed growing out of its body. Of the three seadragon species it is the least developed (in terms of leafy growths) and, at 12 inches (30 cm) in length, probably looks more like a single, long frond of seaweed than a clump.

Like all members of the family Syngathidae, the seadragons are male brooders. The eggs are embedded in soft, spongy tissue that runs from just below the belly along the lower edge of the caudal peduncle. A large male can carry up to 300 eggs for up to eight weeks. When the young hatch, they look more or less like miniature replicas of their parents, and they are able to fend for themselves after the first few hours. Both the leafy and weedy seadragons have been bred in captivity.

two separate subfamilies—Syngnathinae (pipefish, pipehorses, and seadragons) and Hippocampinae (sea horses). However, this situation may change after further study.

Ghostly Relatives

Closely related to both the sea horses and the pipefish are the ghost pipefish, which make up the family Solenostomidae. There are only five species in the family, ranging in size from about 2.4 inches (6 cm) in the armored pipefish (*Solenostomus armatus*) to 6.7 inches (17 cm) in "the" ghost pipefish (*S. cyanopterus*).

Like their namesakes, the pipefish, *Solenostomus* species, hold their bodies in the normal way—that is, horizontal, with their head pointing forward and their tail back. However, they can be easily separated from the other pipefish because they have two dorsal fins, a large tail, and large pelvic fins. As a result, they are better swimmers than their relatives. Their body armor, too, is different and consists of large, star-shaped bony plates.

The pelvic fins (totally lacking in sea horses and pipefish) serve a very important purpose in the ghost pipefish. In females they form a pouch in which she carries her eggs until they hatch. However, in the sea horses and pipefish the developing eggs are carried in the belly pouches of the males.

was no dispute. The actual relationship of this family to other armored fish families has been hotly contested for years, however. Even its scientific name reflects this—"paradoxus"—a paradox being something that is contradictory or apparently absurd, but that may be true.

The discovery and subsequent naming of two further species in 1999 did little to resolve the situation. And so the controversy carries on to this day. Most scientists take the view that the three armored sticklebacks belong within the same order as the sticklebacks, along with sea horses, pipefish, seadragons, and ghost pipefish, but in a group of their own—the infraorder Indostomoida.

These elongated, slender fish only measure around 1.2 inches (3 cm) in length; but unlike their relatives, which are all marine, they are restricted to fresh water. They are shy, retiring fish that inhabit still or slowly flowing waters. They spend most of their time hiding and hunting in the thick layers of leaf litter that line the bottom of streams, lakes, ditches, canals, and swamps, where they feed on small, slow-moving invertebrates such as worms.

One species—"the" armored stickleback—is known primarily from Lake Indawgyi in Myanmar (formerly Burma) but may also extend into Cambodia. *Indostomus crocodilus* (no common name) is known only from a blackwater stream in Narathiwat Province, Thailand, while *I. spinosus* (no common name) has a wider distribution in the Mekong Basin.

Very little is known about the biology and, particularly, the breeding habits of these intriguing little fish, although the armored stickleback occasionally is available for home aquariums. Thanks to this some important information has emerged over the years. We know, for example, that this species is among the very few fish that can actually raise and lower its head. We also know that it frequently rests on the bottom with its body aligned at a steep, upward angle, and that it creeps up on worms—using its pectoral fins to move forward and then turning at very fast speed to snap up its prey.

Controversial Sticklebacks

In the world of family relationships fish are no different than other animals or even humans. Sometimes scientists argue about how different species are related. The armored stickleback (*Indostomus paradoxus*) is an excellent example of such a debate.

Until 1999 it was the only known member of its family (Indostomidae)—of this fact there

⬆ *At 6.7 inches (17 cm) long the ornate ghost pipefish (Solenostomus paradoxus) is the largest species in the family Solenostomidae. It inhabits the shallow coral reefs in Indonesia.*

⬅ *This male leafy seadragon (Phycodurus eques) displays the leafy growths typical of its genus. They provide very effective camouflage as it hunts for prey in coral reefs near Kangaroo Island, Australia.*

The Sea-horse Trade

Although it is difficult, perhaps impossible, to state accurately just how many sea horses are caught and traded worldwide, it is safe to say that the figure is over 15 million each year. Sea horses are fished, both as targeted species (that is, they are specifically sought out and collected) or as bycatch (that is, they are caught accidentally in nets set out for other fish). Either way, for many years now there has been mounting concern for the continued survival of at least some species of sea horses, pipefish, and pipehorses in the wild.

There are three main markets for sea horses—traditional Chinese medicine (TCM), ornaments (or curios), and home aquaria. Of them the TCM market is the largest by far, with dried sea horses being sold either whole or in powdered form. Whole sea horses are generally used in tonics and other health-associated drinks, while powdered sea horses are used in a wide variety of medicines designed to treat numerous ailments and illnesses—from asthma to thickening of the arteries or even for broken bones.

⬇ *This red-and-yellow banded pipefish (Dunckerocampus pessuliferus) swims in the normal horizontal position, with head pointing forward and tail back. This male (in Indonesian waters) is carrying eggs in a belly pouch on his abdomen.*

These popular remedies have spread around the world, and they now are sold outside China in countries such as the Philippines, Indonesia, India, the U.S., U.K., and other countries that have an Asian expatriate community. It has been estimated that across Asia some 45 tons (40.8 tonnes) of dried sea

Sea Horses Under Threat

Together the 45 or so countries that trade in sea horses account for between 3 and 15 tons (2.7–13.6 tonnes) of fish every year. This translates into many millions of individual specimens and has led to concern about their status in the wild. No fewer than 19 are now officially listed as Vulnerable by the World Conservation Union, and one—the Knysna, or Cape, sea horse (*Hippocampus capensis*)—is considered Endangered. (Below are sea horses (*Hippocampus* species) for sale for traditional Chinese medicine use in Sabah, Malaysia.)

Among the pipefish five species of *Solegnathus* are also listed as Vulnerable, while the river pipefish (*Syngnathus watermeyeri*) is Critically Endangered.

In the case of the Knysna sea horse, which is found west of Port Elizabeth in Cape Province, South Africa, tourism and pollution have put the species at risk. Tourism is responsible for creating pressure on the estuary around Knysna Lagoon, where freshwater floods have caused heavy die-offs among the resident sea-horse population (these sea horses cannot tolerate low salinity). Increasing levels of pollution also mean that even captive-bred specimens cannot be released into the waters, so restocking is not possible. However, if attempts to control conditions in the natural habitat are successful, the release of captive-bred specimens may be possible in the future.

The situation facing the river pipefish is even worse. This species is restricted to tidal areas of just three South African rivers: Kariega, Kasouga, and Bushman's. This extremely small distribution means that the species is at high risk from external influences like pollution, flooding, loss of its seagrass-bed habitat, or disease. Furthermore, this pipefish appears to have a very short breeding season. Therefore anything that upsets weather or water conditions during this time could pose a threat to the survival of the species.

horses are imported annually. In terms of actual numbers of specimens this probably represents over 15 million individual sea horses.

Large numbers are also sold as curios or ornaments, mainly (but not exclusively) in vacation areas near the sea. Sea horses of all sizes are used and sold—incorporated into anything from a keyring to a lamp base.

In contrast, live sea horses are mainly destined for home aquaria. Past estimates suggest that many hundreds of thousands were caught specifically for this purpose. However, studies carried out in recent years indicate that the numbers are more likely to be a few tens of thousands; this does not mean that only these numbers are caught alive. Many more may be collected and subsequently sold for TCM and curio purposes.

In a global attempt to protect all species of sea horse the Convention in International Trade in Endangered Species of Fauna and Flora—known as CITES—agreed in the fall of 2002 to put all *Hippocampus* species on their Appendix II list. This agreement came into effect on May 15, 2004, which means that special permits have been required to sell and buy sea horses since this date. It is not a ban on trade, but it does mean that trade in these species is now monitored and controlled.

A further and important development in recent years is the considerable increase in the numbers of sea horses being bred in captivity especially for the marine hobbyist. Many thousands of these captive-bred sea horses (consisting of several species) are now being produced in a number of countries, including Australia, Ireland, and the U.K., for sale worldwide. Therefore the future of sea horses now appears to be more promising, although the problem of large numbers being caught accidentally still continues.

→ *Here in waters off southeast Australia a "pregnant" male short-snouted sea horse (*Hippocampus breviceps*), carries his eggs in a belly pouch. In two to four weeks' time he will give birth to live young, a process that lasts up to 12 hours or more.*

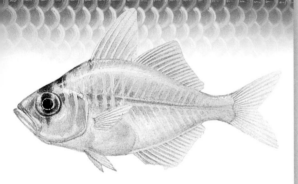

Highfin glassfish (*Parambassis lala*)

Common Name Asiatic glassfish

Family Ambassidae (Chandidae)

Order Perciformes

Number of species About 49 in 8 genera

Size From 1 in (2.5 cm) to 12 in (30 cm)

Key features Body ranging from oval to more elongated and usually compressed; head pointed, with upward-directed mouth at tip; eyes large; all fins well formed; dorsal fin has pronounced notch, front part with hard spines, back part with soft rays; anal fin not notched but with spiny front part and soft-rayed back part; tail forked; some species almost transparent, with skeleton showing; body frequently has irregular vertical dark bands; larger species frequently silvery

Breeding Males of some species use a zigzag display to entice female; pairs of many species scatter eggs among vegetation and abandon them; in Indian glassfish male builds a nest and guards eggs for about 24 hours until they hatch and then guards young; iridescent glassy perchlet (*Parambassis apogonoides*) reported to be a mouthbrooder in which males incubate eggs

Diet Most species feed on invertebrates; some also take smaller fish; *Paradoxodacna piratica* is a specialized feeder on fish scales

Habitat All waters from clear mountain streams, swamps, ponds, rivers, and lakes to brackish and marine conditions

Distribution Widespread in Asia and Oceania

Status Not threatened

⤒ *Like several other species of glassfish, the highfin glassfish (Parambassis lala), also called the Indian glassfish, is a popular aquarium species. Length to 1.2 inches (3 cm).*

Asiatic Glassfish Ambassidae

The astonishing glassfish are famous for the way the muscles of some species are completely transparent, like glass. Despite this, they seem to work as well as the solid-looking muscles of other fish, and they enable glassfish to move around with as much agility as other species.

THE GLASSFISH ARE AN ASIAN family ranging in size from about 1 in (2.5 cm) in species like *Gymnochanda flamea* and *G. limi* to 8 to 12 inches (20–30 cm) in Commerson's glassy perchlet (*Ambassis ambassis*) and the giant glassfish (*Parambassis gulliveri*). All the fish in the family are known as glassfish, although not all are glasslike. Some, like the giant glassfish, are silvery bodied and not particularly transparent. However, since they belong to the same family as the truly transparent or glassy species like the highfin glassfish or glassy perchlet (*Parambassis lala*), they carry the same common name.

Some species, like *G. flamea,* are little known; this fish has only ever been collected from one locality. Others, by contrast, are very well known. For example, the Indian glassfish has been popular in home aquariums since about 1905.

A Case of Mistaken Identity

More accurately, it should be said that we have been familiar with the fish for all this time, although knowing its true identity is a different matter. Traditionally, the Indian glassfish, with its beautifully transparent body, bright fin edges, and broad and fine dark body bands, has been known by the scientific name *Chanda ranga* and later as *Parambassis ranga*. However, it now appears that the fish familiar to aquarists for so many years is not *Parambassis ranga* at all but the highfin glassfish or glassy perchlet (*P. lala*). The "true" Indian glassfish (*Parambassis ranga*) is a larger fish that grows to about 3.2 in (8 cm) and is nowhere near as transparent or glasslike.

Aquarium Favorites

Because of their unusually transparent bodies several glassfish have become well established in the aquarium hobby. Leading the way is the highfin glassfish, a small, peaceful shoaling species that is reasonably easy to maintain, especially with modern-day aquarium diets and equipment. In its natural range in India and Myanmar it predominantly occurs in ditches, ponds, and pools, although it is also known to extend into brackish waters.

Owing to its small size, the species is not fished commercially and is harvested exclusively for home aquariums. The duskyfin glassy perchlet or Wolff's glassfish (*P. wolffii*) and Commerson's glassy perchlet or glassfish, both of which can grow to over 8 inches (20 cm), as well as the longspine glassfish (*Ambassis productus*) at 6 in (15 cm), are also available as aquarium fish; the former is actually bred in captivity specifically for the purpose.

Less common is the 1.6-inch (4-cm) delicate-looking filament-finned glassfish (*Gymnochanda filamentosa*), which has long, extended rays in the back part of the dorsal and anal fins. This scaleless species is a challenging one in terms of aquarium maintenance. Another rarely seen aquarium species is the Himalayan glassy perchlet (*Parambassis baculis*), which grows to about 2 inches (5 cm). It is slightly larger and more elongate than the highfin glassfish but looks quite similar overall.

⊕ *Transparent* **Ambassis gymnocephalus** *glassfish shoaling among soft coral in the Red Sea off Egypt.*

Sharksucker (*Echeneis naucrates*)

Common name Remoras and allies

Families Echeneidae (remoras), Rachycentridae (cobia), Coryphaenidae (dolphinfish)

Order Perciformes

Number of species Echeneidae: 8 in 4 genera; Rachycentridae 1 species; Coryphaenidae 2 in 1 genus

Size From about 12 in (30 cm) to 6.9 ft (2.1 m)

Key features All species elongate; remoras and cobia have flat heads; male dolphinfish have pronounced forehead or crest; eyes large; mouth large; remoras have 2 dorsal fins, the first modified into a sucker; cobia has a long-based, soft dorsal fin preceded by 6–9 isolated short spines; dolphinfish have exceptionally long-based dorsal and anal fins; all other fins well formed, with tail deeply forked in dolphinfish; coloration variable in remoras, ranging from uniform to dark and light longitudinal bands in live sharksucker and cobia; dolphinfish brilliantly colored in metallic hues

Breeding Eggs scattered in open water and abandoned; larvae of cobia and dolphinfish have spines on their gill covers

Diet All predatory, with remoras feeding mainly on scraps of food from their hosts' meals; cobia and dolphinfish feed on fish, squid, and crustaceans

Habitat All found in open water, with remoras and cobia also in shallower waters in the company of large creatures, including—in the case of remoras—sharks, billfish, and turtles; cobia ranges from the surface down to nearly 4,000 ft (1,200 m); dolphinfish often shelter close to, or beneath, floating objects

Distribution Widespread in the Atlantic, Indian, and Pacific Oceans

Status Not threatened

⊕ *The sharksucker (*Echeneis naucrates) *is the largest of the remoras, growing to a length of about 43 inches (1.1 m).*

Remoras and Allies

Echeneidae, Rachycentridae, Coryphaenidae

The weird-looking remoras save energy and enjoy a steady supply of food by attaching themselves to bigger animals. Their favorite "hosts" include sharks and sea turtles, but remoras have even been found hitching rides through the ocean on the hulls of boats.

THE REMORAS ARE OPEN WATER predators—but with a difference. They do not chase after their prey in the manner of marlins, sharks, tunas, or other hunters. Instead, remoras save their energy by allowing themselves to be carried to their food by larger marine creatures such as sharks, manta rays, turtles, or even mammals like dolphins.

Unique Dorsal Fin

The mechanism that makes this possible is the remora's uniquely designed dorsal fin. Instead of helping the fish swim, the fin forms a muscular sucker that allows it to stick onto the body of its hosts. This feature, as well as the way they obtain food, is so fundamentally important to remoras that even young specimens only 1.1 inches (2.7 cm) in length have fully formed suckers.

During the course of evolution several fundamental changes have occurred to the dorsal fin of remoras. First, it has migrated forward and now lies on top of the head. In most bony fish the dorsal fin consists of spines or rays that project upward when the fin is extended. But in remoras the spines have changed dramatically. Instead of being hard, sharp, pointed, and unbranched—as in other fish—they have split sideways and now form a series of ridges or blades (lamina) that are aligned across the top of the head in the form of an oval disc. There can be as few as ten or as many as 28 lamina, depending on the species. Surrounding them and forming the walls of this oval structure is a fleshy edge.

⊕ *Remoras attach themselves to their hosts with a highly modified dorsal fin, shown here, that forms a sucker.*

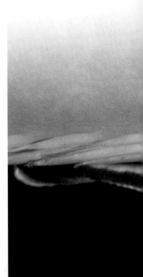

When the disc is pressed against something—usually another fish—and the blades are moved (like the slats in a Venetian blind), the partial vacuum created sticks the remora onto the chosen surface. To release, all the remora must do is realign the "slats" and release the vacuum.

The remoras' hosts appear to be either unaware of their passengers or—more likely—simply tolerate them. They cause no damage and would be impossible to shake off anyway. Remoras are very persistent and do not easily give up once they have targeted a suitable host.

It does not seem to matter to remoras which way around they cling to their host. They may attach themselves sideways, upside down, or the right way up. The main thing is to be carried along until the host catches or finds a meal, at which point the remoras release their hold and feed on bits of flesh scattered by their often messy feeding benefactors.

Remoralike Cobia

The cobia (*Rachycentron canadum*) is the only representative of its family (Rachycentridae). It looks superficially like a remora but grows larger—up to 6.6 feet (2 m). Quite unlike the remoras, though, the cobia does not have a suction disk. Instead, it has six to nine very short spines running from just behind the head to the front of the long-based dorsal fin. The spines are not joined by a membrane and therefore do not form a real fin.

Cobias are frequently seen accompanying large fish like manta rays (a favorite host of the remoras). Indeed, the association is so strong that sport anglers fishing for cobia often track manta rays. In addition to being a target for sport anglers, the cobia is fished commercially. It has fine flesh and is sold fresh, smoked, or frozen, usually in local markets.

Nondolphin Dolphins

There are two species of dolphinfish (*Coryphaena* species) that together form the family Coryphaenidae. Both the common dolphinfish (*C. hippurus*), which grows to about 6.9 feet (2.1 m) and a weight of about 88 pounds (40 kg), and its smaller relative, the 4.3-foot (1.3-m) Pompano dolphinfish (*C. equiselis*), are open-water specialists. They are ocean hunters capable of maintaining high speeds over extended periods. They may also frequent coasts and, unusually, are attracted to floating objects like boats and floating mats of reeds.

In both species the males in particular develop a pronounced bony hump or crest on the head that distinguishes them from females. It is this feature that gives them their common name. Remarkably for large species, dolphinfish only live for four or five years.

The valuable flesh is sold fresh or frozen, and significant commercial fisheries exist, primarily for the larger common dolphinfish but also to a lesser extent for its smaller relative. Both species are important game fish.

⊕ *The sharksucker (Echeneis naucrates) is found in tropical parts of the Atlantic, Indian, and west Pacific Oceans. The one here has attached itself to the ventral (lower) part of its host. Note the sharksucker's flattened head.*

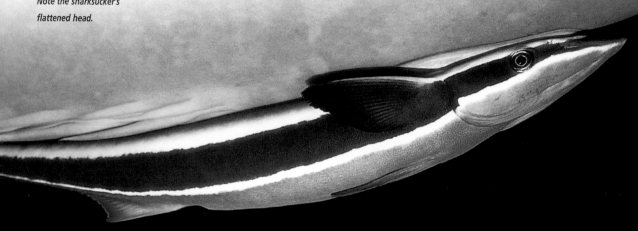

Largescale archerfish (*Toxotes chatareus*)

Common name Archerfish

Family   Toxotidae

Order   Perciformes

Number of species 6 in 1 genus

Size   From about 6 in (15 cm) to 18 in (46 cm)

Key features Body deep and flattened from side to side, although less so in primitive archerfish; head sharply pointed with flat top; large mouth directed upward at an angle; eyes very large and close to top of head; top of body forms straight line from tip of snout to front of dorsal fin; dorsal and anal fins have a few spines at the front, followed by soft, branched rays; tail, pectoral, and pelvic fins well formed; all species except primitive archerfish basically silver bodied with dark bands or blotches along top half; primitive archerfish lacks the bold black blotches; dorsal and anal fins may be dusky with some yellow, particularly in smallscale archerfish

Breeding Very few details available, but largescale archerfish reported to lay between 20,000 and 150,000 eggs, in either fresh or brackish water

Diet   Mainly insects and other invertebrates, frequently, but not always, knocked off foliage with water drops; also smaller fish; largescale and common archerfish eat some plant matter

Habitat   Predominantly marine, but all species spend periods in fresh water, especially the smallscale, primitive, and western archerfish—these species frequently found in swamps and streams, often with overhanging vegetation; common and largescale archerfish typically found in brackish mangrove swamps and estuaries

Distribution From India to the Philippines, Australia, and Polynesia

Status   Not threatened

⊕ *At 16 to 18 inches (40–45 cm) in length the largescale archerfish (*Toxotes chatareus*) is the largest member of the family.*

Archerfish

Toxotidae

Archers use bows and arrows to shoot their targets, or prey in the case of hunters. In tropical swamps there are fish that also shoot down their prey, but by spitting drops of water instead of firing arrows. They are the astonishing archerfish.

MANGROVE-DWELLING ARCHERFISH (*TOXOTES* SPECIES) normally feed off flying insects and other small creatures that fall into the water or graze from the surrounding mangrove vegetation that exists in their natural habitat. But with their large eyes forever turned skyward, archerfish are always on the lookout for unwary tasty morsels that land near the water surface.

When they spot a suitable victim, they shoot it down by spitting jets of water at it with such force that the impact knocks the prey into the water. One gulp later, and the prey is gone. The water jet is produced by pressing the tongue onto the grooved roof of the mouth. As the tongue makes contact with the groove, it creates a tube. Then the fish closes its gill covers, causing the pressure inside the mouth to rise. This, in turn, forces water into the tube and out of the mouth in a thin jet.

Refractive Skills

Remarkable though the "archery" skill may be, it would be impossible to achieve without the fish's ability to compensate for the refraction (bending) of light that occurs when it passes from air to water and vice-versa. When a stick is dipped into water, a "kink" appears where it enters the water, and the part of the stick that is below the surface appears to bend upward.

The optical illusion is caused by the greater "bending power," known as the refractive index, of water compared with air. The result is that although you can still see the part of the stick under water, it is not really where you see it, since what you are seeing is the "bent" or refracted image. Now imagine being under water and looking up at an angle toward

⊕ *One of nature's most impressive and unusual hunting strategies: An archerfish spits a well-aimed jet of water at an insect in an attempt to knock it off the foliage and down to the waiting fish. Archerfish can hit targets up to 5 feet (1.5 m) away.*

the surface. What you see above the water is not exactly where it appears. It has been displaced by the light as it "bends" on its way from water to air in a similar way as the tip of the stick was "bent" as it was dipped into the water—but in reverse.

Archerfish can make allowances for the bending light rays as they target insects above the water. Their aim may not always be perfect, but they still manage to catch plenty of insects using their unique hunting method.

The Family

There are six species of archerfish, all Asian or Australian in origin. The common or banded archerfish (*Toxotes jaculatrix*) has been known as an aquarium fish for over 100 years. It grows to 12 inches (30 cm) but is usually smaller, making it suitable for moderate to large-sized aquariums where, if the design is appropriate, its shooting abilities can be witnessed.

The western archerfish (*T. oligolepis*) is less well known. It is a smaller species that is believed to grow to about 6 inches (15 cm). Originally, the species was reported from the Fitzroy, Isdell, May, and Meda River systems in the Kimberley region of northwestern Australia, as well as from some streams in Papua New Guinea and Indonesia. Recent reports, however, indicate that its Australian distribution is now restricted to parts of the Fitzroy River.

In terms of its biology very little is known.

For instance, like other archerfish, it is likely to feed on insects and have the ability to shoot them down, but there are no documented details about this or its broader dietary habits. We have no information about how it breeds.

If our knowledge of the western archerfish is scant, we know even less about *Toxotes blythii* from Myanmar. We know virtually nothing of its diet and even less about its biology and the length it attains.

The three remaining species, the largescale archerfish (*T. chatareus*), the smallscale archerfish (*T. microlepis*), and the primitive archerfish (*T. lorentzi*)—a rather rare species—are all better known. The primitive and smallscale archerfish are quite small (about 6 inches/15 cm), but the largescale archer grows to about 16 to 18 inches (40–45 cm).

The two largest species and the smallscale archerfish are fished commercially, but not widely. Most of the catches are destined for small local markets where they are sold fresh. The two largest species, the largescale archerfish and the common archerfish, are the ones most popular as aquarium fish.

Butterflyfish Chaetodontidae

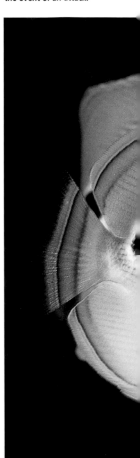

Copperband butterflyfish
(*Chelmon rostratus*)

Common name Butterflyfish

Family   Chaetodontidae

Order   Perciformes

Number of species About 128 in 11 genera

Size   From 3 in (7.6 cm) to 12 in (30 cm); most species
4.7–10 in (12–25 cm)

Key features Body flattened from side to side and usually
quite deep; head pointed, particularly in species
that extract food from crevices or polyps; small
mouth at tip of snout; dorsal fin with spiny front
section and soft-rayed back; anal fin with 3–5
spines at front; all fins well formed; body scales
extend onto both dorsal and anal fins; most
species brightly colored, often with vertical bands;
eye frequently hidden by a vertical band or patch;
false eyes or eye-spots common on either body or
back lower edge of the dorsal fin; many species
develop night colors that differ from the day
ones; colors of juveniles frequently different

Breeding Eggs released into water and unprotected; hatch
in 18–30 hours; larvae have distinctive bony
plates during free-swimming planktonic stage,
which may last from a few weeks to several
months

Diet   Most feed on small invertebrates, coral polyps or
tentacles, zooplankton, algae, or fish eggs; some
species very specialized feeders

Habitat   Mainly found in water less than 65 ft (20 m)
deep, mostly on coral reefs; some species in
rubble zones and water down to 656 ft (200 m)

Distribution Tropical and subtropical Indo-Pacific plus warm-
temperate Atlantic

Status   Five *Chaetodon* species listed by IUCN as
Vulnerable: yellow-crowned butterflyfish
(*C. flavocoronatus*), Easter Island butterflyfish
(*C. litus*), Marley's butterflyfish (*C. marleyi*),
oblique butterflyfish (*Prognathodes obliquus*),
robust butterflyfish (*C. robustus*); main factor
threatening survival is their restricted distribution

⤴ *The 8-inch (20-cm) copperband or beaked butterflyfish
(Chelmon rostratus) is found in the Indian and Pacific Oceans.*

*No coral reef is complete without its colorful
butterflyfish and their close relatives, the angelfish.
Darting around singly, in pairs, or in shoals, these
"living jewels" have fascinated us for generations,
although the first humans who set eyes on them were
more interested in how good they were to eat.*

BUTTERFLYFISH ARE FOUND IN MOST tropical and
subtropical regions of the world, as well as in
some warm-temperate oceans. Over 90 percent
of all species, however, are found in the Indo-
Pacific. There are 11 genera of butterflyfish,
with about 128 species in total.

Specialists of the Reef

The vast majority of species are intimately
associated with shallow-water reefs, with most
being found in water less than about 50 to
66 feet (15–20 m) deep. Some species,
however, are found in deeper water. The Indian
butterflyfish (*Chaetodon mitratus*) has been
found in rubble zones at depths of over 220
feet (68 m). The brown-banded butterflyfish
(*C. modestus*), which, as its name indicates, is
one of the more modestly colored species, has
been collected at a depth of 623 feet (190 m)
off Hawaii. The threeband butterfly
(*Prognathodes guyanensis*) from the Caribbean
region has been found at 656 feet (200 m).

Generally, butterflyfish have a "home
range" within which they tend to remain. Most
are not territorial, but a few certainly are—
vigorously defending their home patch against
all comers. Notable among them are the
orange-face butterflyfish (*C. larvatus*), the two
triangular butterflyfish (*C. triangulum* and *C.
baronessa*), and the chevron butterflyfish (*C.
trifascialis*). The last-mentioned is probably the
most aggressive of all butterflyfish. In an
experiment carried out on the Great Barrier
Reef, Australia, one male attacked a model of a
threadfin butterflyfish (*C. auriga*) so vigorously
that he lost some of his scales in the process.

⤵ *The large, eyelike
spot near the tail of the
foureye butterflyfish
(Chaetodon capistratus)
helps draw predators
away from the fish's
more vulnerable head in
the event of an attack.*

Juvenile Colors

During their juvenile stages butterflyfish go through a color phase in which they may look quite different from adults. Sometimes the difference can be so marked—as in the foureye butterflyfish (*Chaetodon capistratus*)—that it is impossible to tell that the two individuals are simply different color phases of a single species.

In the foureye butterflyfish small juveniles up to 1.2 inches (3 cm) have broad brown body bands. They also have two false eyes (eye spots): one on the caudal peduncle and one above it in the back bottom part of the dorsal fin. Once they grow beyond this size, the body bands begin to narrow, and the top eye spot begins to disappear. By the time they reach adulthood, there are no body bands except for the head band, which runs from the top of the skull through the eye to the chin. Even then, it is much lighter than in juveniles. The top eye spot disappears completely as well, and the

Butterfly or Angel?

At first sight, butterflyfish and angelfish look very similar. They occur together on most reefs and also share a number of other characteristics. Until the mid-1970s the similarities led to both groups being placed in the same family, the Chaetodontidae.

Yet there are distinct differences between butterflyfish and angelfish. The most easily observed is the presence of a stout spine on the cheek (the preopercle) in angelfish. This led to the two groups being allocated separate subfamilies within the Chaetodontidae. Further study led to the conclusion that these and other differences were so significant that butterflyfish and angelfish are now regarded as separate families: the Chaetodontidae and Pomacanthidae, respectively.

One of the most notable differences is the presence of an "armor-plated" larval stage (the tholichthys) in butterflyfish. Angelfish do not go through such a larval phase, although their larvae possess spiny scales. Furthermore, although the juveniles of both butterflyfish and angelfish can look very different from adults, the actual patterning and range of colors in butterflyfish are much closer to those of the adults than they are in angelfish.

The two groups also have different diets. Butterflyfish feed on a range of creatures, of which the most important are hard coral polyps, small invertebrates, tubeworms, and zooplankton. Angelfish tend to feed on sponges, sea squirts, soft corals, and seapens.

now light-colored body develops thin stripes running at an angle backward from the middle of the body to the top of the back, as well as on the belly. Although the color transformations from juvenile to adult are quite dramatic, they are even more pronounced in angelfish.

Since many butterflyfish can be kept quite easily in home aquariums, enthusiasts have been able to document many of the color changes that occur in the species, thus making a genuinely important contribution to our knowledge of the biology of butterflyfish. No aquarist, however, has been able to witness at first hand the unusual larval stage that butterflyfish go through.

It is known as the tholichthys stage, and it begins when the floating eggs hatch some

18 to 30 hours after being laid. The tiny larvae that are released are covered in tough, bony plates that gradually disappear over a few weeks or a few months depending on the species. During the early stages larval butterflyfish spend their time swimming and feeding among the plankton in the surface layers of the sea. Once they begin to change into the postlarval, or juvenile, form they move onto the reefs where they will spend the rest of their lives.

Ever-popular Butterflies

Butterflyfish (and angelfish) are still caught in small numbers for local human consumption. Many more, however, are encountered outside their home ranges, where they are enjoyed by marine aquarists the world over on account of their dazzling colors and body patterns, their unusual, flitting motion—which has helped earn them their common name—and their interesting lifestyles.

⊝ The pincerlike mouth of the crown, or Eritrean butterflyfish (Chaetodon paucifasciatus), enables it to pick tiny food items from the crevices in rocks and coral.

⊝ A shoal of raccoon butterflyfish (Chaetodon lunula) feeds along a reef off Hawaii. The rather gaudy colors of butterflyfish make it difficult for a predator to pick off an individual fish when they are swimming tightly together this way.

Hidden Eyes and False Eyes

Many butterflyfish have a dark band running from the top of the head through the eye and down to the chin. The band is often narrower than the eye; but where that is the case, the iris of the eye has dark sections that coincide with the width of the band, bordered by light-colored areas that match the color of the head. Other species do not have a band, but their eyes are surrounded by large dark patches. Whatever the arrangement, the end result is the same: The eye is hidden from view, helping protect it from attack.

Many butterflyfish go a stage further and have one or more eye spots on the body, on the dorsal fin, or at the base of the tail. False eyes help draw attackers away from the front end of the fish to less vital parts of its body. So although the butterflyfish may be injured in an attack, it might be able to regenerate the damaged tissues. It could not regenerate a real eye. Another advantage may be enjoyed by species with false eyes near the backs of their bodies. If a predator is launching an attack, it may aim just in front of its target to make allowance for the victim's escape dash. But if the "eye" is at the back end, and the predator aims just "in front" of its target, it is actually aiming behind it, because it dashes off in the opposite direction!

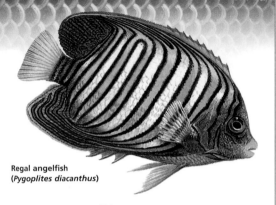

Regal angelfish
(Pygoplites diacanthus)

Common name Angelfish

Family Pomacanthidae

Order Perciformes

Number of species About 85 in 7 genera

Size From 2.4 in (6 cm) to 24 in (60 cm)

Key features Body strongly flattened from side to side and usually quite deep; head blunt to slightly pointed, more so in juveniles; small mouth located at tip of snout; bone in front of gill cover carries a stout spine; dorsal fin has spiny front section and soft-rayed back section; anal fin has 3 spines at the front and soft-rayed back section; all other fins well formed; striking coloration in many species, particularly in pygmy angels; juveniles often have completely different coloration and body patterning than adults

Breeding Eggs released into water while spawning above the reef and then abandoned; hatching may take 18–30 hours; larvae have spiny scales (but not bony plates) and are planktonic for a while

Diet *Centropyge* species feed mainly on algae; *Genicanthus* species prefer zooplankton; most other species feed on sea squirts, sponges, soft corals, sea pens, other invertebrates, and algae

Habitat Most species found on shallow-water tropical reefs; a few, such as the masked angelfish, are found in deeper water; angelfish are very rarely found in open sandy areas

Distribution Widely distributed in all tropical seas, with nearly 90 percent of species in Indo-Pacific

Status Resplendent angelfish is listed as Vulnerable by IUCN largely because of its restricted distribution in waters around Ascension Island in southeastern Atlantic

⊕ *The regal angelfish (*Pygoplites diacanthus*) of the Indo-Pacific grows to about 10 inches (25 cm) in length. Often found near caves, it feeds on sponges and other small invertebrates. It may appear in shoals or solitarily.*

Angelfish

Pomacanthidae

Often confused with similar-looking butterflyfish, angelfish are gloriously colorful coral reef fish that are remarkable for the way they change their colors and patterns as they grow. The differences can be so striking that young and adults look like different species.

ANGELFISH ARE AMONG THE MOST visible fish on tropical reefs, along with butterflyfish. Most species are found in shallow, warm waters about 65 feet (20 m) deep or less. Some are less frequently encountered by reef divers, however, mainly because they occur in deeper water or have restricted distribution.

The masked angelfish (*Genicanthus personatus*) is an example of this, being found in waters from about 60 feet (18 m) down to 275 feet (84 m). While only relatively few specimens are spotted on reef dives, that may simply be because they are rare at such depths. The resplendent angelfish (*Centropyge resplendens*), on the other hand, is truly rare and only occurs around Ascension Island in the southeastern Atlantic.

Sex-reversing Angels

The Japanese angelfish (*Centropyge interruptus*) is unusual among its genus because males can be distinguished from females. The males have a bluer head than females, which have an overall orange face, and there are also some fin differences between the sexes. The Cocos, or yellowhead angelfish (*C. joculator*), and the resplendent angelfish are two other species in which the sexes can be separated from each other on fin and color differences.

Like some other "pygmy angelfish," the Japanese angelfish is capable of changing sex; it is a protogynous hermaphrodite, in which females are able to change into males but not vice-versa. The changes can apparently occur under either the "harem" situation, in which a dominant male controls several females, or when adults occur in pairs. In either case

⊕ *The aptly named lemonpeel angelfish (*Centropyge flavissima*) is a brilliantly colored species that feeds mainly on the algae encrusting rocks and coral.*

females are capable of changing sex, usually over a period of two or three weeks, when the male is removed.

Other *Centropyge* species in which such changes have been reported include rusty pygmy angelfish (*C. ferrugata*), lemonpeel angelfish (*C. flavissima*), Herald's angelfish (*C. heraldi*), keyhole angelfish (*C. tibicen*), and pearl-scaled angelfish (*C. vrolikii*). Among the closely related *Genicanthus* species the Japanese swallow (*G. semifasciatus*) and the masked angelfish have also shown sex reversal.

Spawning displays

Spawning in angelfish occurs mainly over the summer months and (at least in some species) consists of eggs generally being released on a daily basis. Although a harem-controlling male will spawn with just one female at a time, he will nevertheless spawn with every female over a period of some eight to ten minutes.

Eggs and sperm release are preceded by a spectacular open-fin display by the male some distance off the bottom, to which one of the females (or the single female) responds by swimming up to him. As she approaches, the male will nuzzle the female's belly. This is followed by a short, high-speed swim during which both eggs and sperm are released, followed, in turn, by a dash back to the relative safety of the reef by the spawning pair.

The eggs float up to the surface, where they drift among the plankton and hatch. The larvae have spiny scales but not the bony plates of the thorichthys larvae that are characteristic of the butterflyfish (family Chaetodontidae).

What Is a Pygmy Angelfish?

Members of the genus *Centropyge* are often referred to as pygmy angelfish. The label certainly describes the smallest species, such as the flameback angelfish (*C. aurantonotus*), orange or Fisher's angelfish (*C. fisheri*), multicolor pygmy angelfish (*C. multicolor*), blackspot angelfish (*C. nigriocellus*), and resplendent angelfish. They are all, relatively speaking, pygmies, since they only attain a length of about 2.4 inches (6 cm).

However, the largest species in the genus, such as the bicolor angelfish (*C. bicolor*), blacktail or Eibl's angelfish (*C. eibli*), and the Japanese angelfish, all grow to about 6 in (15 cm) long. This makes them significantly larger than some other "nonpygmy" angels like the conspicuous angelfish (*Chaetodontoplus conspicillatus*), barred angelfish (*Centropyge multifasciata*), and purplemask angelfish (*Centropyge venustus*). So although the label "pygmy angelfish" has its uses, it should not be taken too literally.

Delinquent Angels

Once angelfish larvae begin to grow, they descend to the reef where they will spend the rest of their lives. There the young of many species—especially those of the genera *Holacanthus* and *Pomacanthus*—develop very distinctive colors and patterns quite unlike those of the adults. However, through the constant observation of developing juveniles until they became adult, it was possible to determine that they were individuals of the same species. Through such long-term observation it has been possible to trace the development of many angelfish species from earliest stages to the adult. In fact, we know that individuals go through a series of changes, each with fairly unique features.

One of the most interesting aspects of the difference between adults and juveniles is the way in which they react to each other. Every

The emperor angelfish (Pomacanthus imperator) is one of several species of angelfish in which the juveniles (below) look significantly different from the adults.

adult angelfish recognizes other adult angelfish of its own species. Males, in particular, represent a threat to each other, and rivals of most species constantly attempt to exclude all potential competitors for females from their territories.

Yet the behavior of adults toward juveniles is considerably more tolerant. It seems as if they recognize that the small, brilliantly colored individuals present no threat. The juveniles, for their part, have no apparent respect for their elders and seem to ignore the basic "rules" of angelfish behavior. What is unclear is whether adult angelfish are capable of identifying their juveniles as nonthreatening, immature members of their own species, or whether they simply consider their juveniles as belonging to another species and consequently no threat.

A Possible Explanation

Immature individuals of most species are normally incapable of breeding, although there are a few exceptions. If juveniles were colored similarly to adults, then reproductively active, mature individuals (particularly males) would be involved in never-ending displays and disputes

Most of them would be totally pointless because they would be directed at nonreproductive juveniles. They would also be exhausting and debilitating because juveniles normally far outnumber reproductively active adults. The unnecessary waste of energy could soon result in a loss of condition in the adults, with a consequent loss in their ability to breed. If, on the other hand, nonbreeding juveniles look completely different from reproductive adults, the energy that can be conserved and redirected toward productive courtship and spawning is considerable.

Following this line of reasoning, it is possible to see how similar solutions to the common problem may have arisen in totally unrelated species that also have differently

The Japanese swallow (Genicanthus semifasciatus). This specimen is beginning to show the color changes that occur as a female changes into a male.

colored young, for example, in some wrasses (family Labridae). Energy is a valuable asset that needs to be conserved, while the top priority for any animal is reproduction and perpetuation of the species. Thus it appears that in some species in which adults and juveniles live in close proximity, evolution has brought about the necessary mechanisms to solve the problem.

Unhealthy Eating?

Despite its "angelic" name, the Japanese angelfish is anything but angelic in its feeding habits. In at least part of its range it feeds on the feces of planktonic-feeding reef fish, primarily damselfish and fairy basslets. This is not the only food it eats, however, because it will also take a variety of algae and other edible material, and actually has quite a broad diet compared with many of the family.

In fact, many animals feed on feces. Feces contain a lot of half-digested food that is rich in proteins and other nutrients; and since the digestion process has already begun, the nutrients are sometimes easier to absorb than the nutrients in raw foods. The microorganisms in the feces that might cause disease are often killed by exposure to sea water, and in any case the microorganisms and parasites that can occur in the feces of different species may not be dangerous to the angelfish. Even if there is a risk, to the Japanese angelfish it is clearly a risk worth taking.

Scarlet hawkfish (*Neocirrhites armatus*)

Common name Hawkfish

Family Cirrhitidae

Order Perciformes

Number of species 30–35 in 12 genera

Size From about 2.8 in (7 cm) to 24 in (60 cm); possibly up to 39 in (1 m)

Key features Body moderately elongated; head slightly to sharply pointed; mouth from small to moderately large; large eyes; dorsal fin with 10 spines in the front section and soft rays behind; spines with hairy looking tufts (cirri) on tips; all fins well formed; coloration variable but often bright

Breeding Single male mates with a harem of several females; eggs released into the water during nightly spawnings and abandoned

Diet Most species feed on crustaceans and other invertebrates; many species also take smaller fish

Habitat Mainly shallow-water rocky and coral reefs, especially where there are long-branched hard corals; most species at depths of less than 80 ft (25 m), but dwarf hawkfish ranges to depths of 150 ft (46 m)

Distribution Widely distributed in tropical zones of the Atlantic, Indian, and Pacific Oceans, with most species occurring in the Indo-Pacific

Status Not threatened

⊕ *The scarlet hawkfish* (Neocirrhites armatus) *is found in the Pacific Ocean, where it frequents reefs and submarine terraces. It is highly predatory and grows to about 35.5 inches (90 cm).*

Hawkfish

Cirrhitidae

Named for its habit of pouncing on prey like a hawk, a hawkfish also has what seems to be a tuft of hair on the tip of every dorsal fin spine. The unlikely adornment appears to have no obvious function but makes it one of the world's few "hairy" fish.

THE HAWKFISH ARE GENERALLY TOUGH, colorful, adaptable species. As a result, some have become popular among aquarists, from whom a great deal of our knowledge has come. Not all species are suitable for aquariums, however. The giant hawkfish (*Cirrhitus rivulatus*) from the eastern central Pacific, for example, can grow to 24 inches (61 cm) and a weight of 9.3 pounds (4.2 kg) and is thus not a good home aquarium subject.

Aquarium Observations

In sharp contrast, the dwarf or falco hawkfish (*Cirrhitichthys falco*) from the western Pacific only grows to a maximum of 2.8 inches (7 cm) and is a colorful, excellent choice for a home aquarium. Also popular and easy to keep is the longnose hawkfish (*Oxycirrhites typus*). It is not quite as colorful as the dwarf hawkfish but makes up for that with its extremely elongated pointed snout and attractive and intricate body patterning. It is also the only hawkfish that has been bred in aquariums, and it is the only one that produces sticky eggs rather than free-floating, nonsticky ones.

Breeding hawkfish in captivity presents a considerable challenge, and a great deal still needs to be learned and observed about both breeding behavior and the conditions under which breeding occurs. However, other aspects of hawkfish behavior are routinely seen in an aquarium and have been well documented by enthusiasts.

Among them is the "hawklike" behavior responsible for the family name. Predators—whatever the species—must be constantly on the lookout for a meal. When hunting,

⊕ The longnose hawkfish (Oxycirrhites typus) grows to about 5 inches (13 cm) in length. It is the only species in which males can be distinguished from females—males have black edges on the anal and caudal fins.

hawkfish choose a suitable vantage point, usually on a coral branch or some similar underwater structure, and then "sit up" on the tips of their pectoral fins, surveying their home patch. When a suitable victim approaches, they launch themselves into a swift swoop and seize their prey—in other words, like a hawk does. Although they are not built for speed over long distances, hawkfish have powerful muscles that project them forward in an amazingly rapid short burst of speed. Added to the swift lunge is the fact that the victim is unaware of the impending attack, so the hawkfish's success rate is fairly high.

Harem Breeders

A typical breeding unit of hawkfish consists of a dominant male and some two to seven females. The arrangement is referred to as a harem. Should the male be removed for some reason, for example, by a predator or through natural death, one of the females will then change sex and become the dominant male. Such female-to-male sex changes are examples of a process called protogynous hermaphroditism, which is known in a number of families of fish. It is also known to occur in reverse (but not in hawkfish), when it is called protandrous hermaphroditism.

Generally speaking, hawkfish spawn as darkness approaches. At such times the dominant male will visit each of his females and will spawn with whichever is ripe or responsive. Spawning consists of the pair swimming up into the water column and releasing sperm and eggs at the same time. The eggs then float away and hatch out into planktonic larvae. The whole procedure is repeated on a nightly basis.

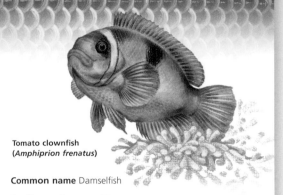

**Tomato clownfish
(*Amphiprion frenatus*)**

Common name Damselfish

Family Pomacentridae

Order Perciformes

Number of species About 335 in 28 genera

Size From about 1.6 in (4 cm) to 14 in (36 cm); most species 3.2–4.7 in (8–12 cm)

Key features Body relatively deep; almost cylindrical in many midwater plankton feeders; some species quite elongate; head often blunt in species living near bottom, less so in midwater species; mouth usually small; eyes relatively large; dorsal fin with long base and hard spines along most of length; tail forked; coloration ranging from bright in anemonefish to subdued in many more mobile swimmers; juveniles of drab species often colorful

Breeding Eggs laid on precleaned surface, usually under cover or close to base of host anemone; Garibaldi nest is patch of red algae; intense courtship by male precedes egg laying; in some, e.g., *Chromis* and *Dascyllus*, single male may spawn with several females; eggs guarded mainly by male; hatching takes 2–7 days depending on species

Diet Mainly small invertebrates; many species also feed on algae; a few feed on coral polyps

Habitat Mostly shallow water on or near coral reefs; some live on sandy or rocky bottoms at less than 65 ft (20 m); a few *Chromis* species occur down to 330 ft (100 m); a few species found in fresh water and brackish mangroves and estuaries

Distribution All tropical seas and some warm-temperate regions, such as off California and around Australia and New Zealand

Status Three damsels listed as Vulnerable by IUCN: St. Helena chromis (*Chromis sanctaehelenae*), St. Paul's Gregory (*C. sanctipauli*), St. Helena Gregory (*Stegastes sanctaehelenae*)—all have extremely restricted mid-Atlantic ranges, leading to high risk of extinction from natural and human-made causes

*⊕ The western Pacific tomato clownfish (**Amphiprion frenatus**) is an anemonefish—a species that hides among anemones. Length to 5.5 inches (14 cm).*

Damselfish

Pomacentridae

Sex changes, stunning colors, life among deadly tentacles, gardening skills, and a host of extraordinary names characterize a group of fish found on every coral reef in the world, and a few other habitats besides. They are the damselfish—among the best-known of all "tropical" fish.

MOST DAMSELFISH, OR DAMSELS, LIVE close to the bottom in rocky, sandy, or coralline zones. Some, however, including many *Chromis* species, spend much of the daytime in large shoals in midwater. There they feed by picking off plankton carried in by the water currents, often some distance above the coral.

Despite spending so much time in midwater, even these damselfish are linked to the reefs, because at the slightest hint of danger they dive into the shelter provided by the coral heads and crevices. They also retreat to the relative safety of the reef at night.

Some damsels, like those belonging to the mainly black-and-white dominoes and humbugs (*Dascyllus* species), are not strictly midwater species, but neither are they strict bottom huggers. They live in shoals and tend to keep close to branching corals, such as those belonging to the genera *Acropora*, *Stylophora*, and *Porites*. They usually hover a little distance above the individual coral heads, face the current, and feed on small free-swimming or floating invertebrates. Some species also associate with anemones. Either way, like their *Chromis* cousins, they can retreat into the safety of the corals at lightning-fast speed.

Clownfish or Anemonefish?

The most famous association with anemones involves the clownfish. Despite their name, there is nothing clownlike about them. In fact, they are quite aggressive rather than comical. They frequently swim in a jerky, undulating manner, which some people consider comical, and most species have bold, contrasting colors

*⊕ The aptly named four-striped damsel (*Dascyllus melanurus*) is a shoaling species that keeps close to corals into which it can dive when danger threatens.*

that usually include broad white bands against a yellow, orange, red, or brown background. Both these features have contributed to the clownfish label.

However, the second name by which the colorful species are known—anemonefish—is far more accurate, since the most typical feature of their lifestyle is that they form close associations with sea anemones. In fact, the association is so close that if anemonefish are separated from their hosts, they will quickly fall prey to one or other of the numerous fish-eating hunters of the reef. With few exceptions—for example, the cheek spines of the most aptly named spine-cheek anemonefish (*Premnas biaculeatus*)—anemonefish exhibit neither the defenses, speed, nor camouflage protection that many other reef fish have. They

Two-way Protection

Anemonefish clearly benefit from the stinging defenses of their anemone partners. But do the anemones derive any benefit from the association? Anemones without fish associates seem to thrive in good numbers. However, it is possible that anemones with fish in residence survive in better shape.

Anemonefish become highly territorial and aggressive when they are within the safety of their host's tentacles, and they can give a painful nip with their strong teeth. In defending their territory, which consists of the anemone and its immediate surroundings, anemonefish may also protect their hosts. They are often observed driving away fish much larger than themselves that may be intent on eating the anemones. They may also help keep the tentacles clean.

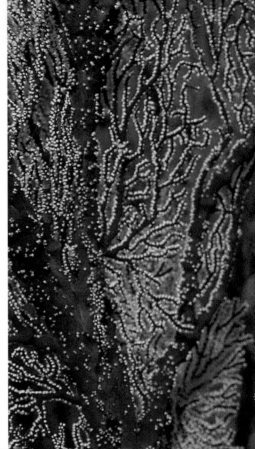

therefore make easy targets if caught out in the open. One solution to a life-threatening situation is to find a bodyguard and remain very close to it day and night. That is precisely what anemonefish belonging to the genera *Amphiprion* and *Premnas* do. The chosen bodyguard is an anemone, usually a large one.

Anemones look like graceful, colorful, many-petalled flowers but are in fact graceful, colorful, many-tentacled animals. Nor are they as harmless or defenseless as they seem. Their waving tentacles are packed with powerful stinging cells called nematocysts that are fired the moment anything, such as a fish, brushes against them. The venom from the stinging cells is used to subdue small prey by paralysis before swallowing it. The venom also paralyzes small intruders or gives an unpleasant "keep off" warning to larger ones.

The challenge for anemonefish, therefore, is how to shelter among the potentially lethal weapons without falling victim to them. Incredibly, they have evolved a mechanism that allows them to do so without stimulating the host anemone to fire its stinging cells. There appear to be two components to an anemonefish's immunity. First, the jumpy, undulating swimming movements of the anemonefish somehow appear to appease the anemone, as if telling it that the fish producing the movements is neither prey nor predator. Second, chemicals produced in the body mucus

⊕ *Males of the colorful Garibaldi (*Hypsypops rubicundus*) choose patches of algae as their territories and defend them vigorously against rivals.*

Sex Changes among the Tentacles

In birds and mammals the sex of an individual is determined at the moment an egg is fertilized. But in fish an individual's sex is often determined by environmental conditions such as the temperature and chemical nature of the water, or even social factors. In anemonefish the presence or absence of a dominant female influences the sex of other fish in the group. The largest fish in a group living among the tentacles of a host anemone is always female, and she keeps the group together by enforcing a strict social "pecking order." The hierarchy is linked to body size, with the largest female bullying those beneath her, which in turn harass smaller members of the group.

There may be six of more fish in the group, but apart from the biggest they are all males of varying maturity. But if the female is killed or removed, the largest male changes sex over a period of days and becomes the dominant female. The amazing change is possible because as the fish develop into subadults, they have both male and female sexual organs in an undeveloped state. As long as a dominant female is around, her presence inhibits the development of the female organs in other fish, and only male tissues develop.

somehow accepts the anemonefish' presence. The anemonefish can therefore swim among the host's powerful tentacles even when there are predators around. Such is the protection that when the breeding season arrives, anemonefish lay their eggs on the rock on which the anemone is attached and as near the base of the anemone's body as possible.

Gardening Damsels

While anemonefish are closely associated with their host anemones, other damselfish are tied to their algal "gardens." The profusion with which the algal mats grow is not, however, a result of any particular gardening skills on the part of the fish. But because they establish a territory and defend it vigorously against intruders, some of which consist of algae-eating species, the algae are not grazed so intensively as elsewhere and therefore grow more luxuriantly. The damselfish also graze on the algae but do not consume sufficient quantities to keep the growth in check.

The algae gardens serve another purpose besides acting as a food supply. Because the size of the patch will depend significantly on the male's ability to defend his territory, larger algal patches are generally associated with the more vigorous males, in other words, the ones that can attract most females and are likely to be more successful during the breeding season.

In addition to repelling rivals and intruders, algal-gardening damselfish males physically remove crawling intruders, including—in the case of larger species—sea urchins and starfish. Some invertebrate intruders do not eat just algae but fish eggs as well. Therefore, by expelling them, the damselfish achieve two distinct aims: preservation of their algal mats and their eggs.

While many of the algal-tending damselfish are small or relatively small—for example, *Stegastes* species only grow to a maximum of 4.7 to 5.1 inches (12–13cm)—the stunning golden-orange Garibaldi (*Hypsypops rubicundus*) from the eastern Pacific Ocean can reach 12 inches (30 cm) or more in length.

⬆ *A golden damselfish (Amblyglyphidodon aureus) carefully tends its eggs laid on coral in the Andaman Sea.*

of the anemonefish appear to send out a similar message to the host anemone. Remarkably, the chemicals are similar to those produced by the anemones themselves, preventing the tentacles from firing their stinging cells as they rub against each other.

The combined effect of the two messages that anemonefish transmit is that the anemone

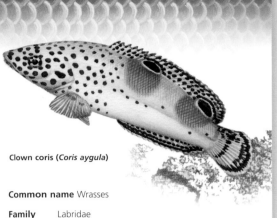

Clown coris (*Coris aygula*)

Common name Wrasses

Family Labridae

Order Perciformes

Number of species 450–500 in more than 60 genera

Size From about 1.8 in (4.5 cm) to over 8 ft (2.5 m); majority of species 6–8 in (15–20 cm)

Key features Mostly relatively elongated, with some, such as cleaner wrasses, slim and almost cylindrical in cross-section; many larger species deeper-bodied; head usually pointed; extendable jaw; forward-pointing front teeth, usually with gap between; all fins well formed; front part of dorsal and anal fin have hard, unjointed spines (more in dorsal than anal), followed by soft, branched rays; body scales cycloid; coloration very diverse and usually much more intense in males than females

Breeding Spawning occurs in pairs or shoals; males and females swim together from the reef toward surface, releasing eggs and sperm into water; eggs float to the surface, where they hatch

Diet Predatory; smaller species feed primarily on invertebrates; larger species also feed on other fish; specialized feeders include cleaner wrasses that feed on external parasites of other fish; some larger wrasses feed on toxic organisms such as seastars, urchins, boxfish, and seahares

Habitat Tropical, temperate, and subarctic coastal waters, preferring rocky and reef habitats

Distribution Widely distributed in the Atlantic, Indian, and Pacific Oceans and most seas, including the Mediterranean and Red Sea

Status IUCN lists 6 species as under various levels of threat

⊕ *The clown coris* (Coris aygula) *feeds mainly on hard-shelled invertebrates such as mollusks and sea urchins. It is sometimes caught commercially and as a game fish. The specimen shown here is a juvenile, complete with false eyes on its fins. Length to 4 feet (1.2 m).*

Wrasses

Labridae

Wrasses are the second most numerous family of marine fish after the gobies (family Gobidae). They range from species no bigger than your little finger when fully mature to species over 8.2 feet (2.5 m) long that weigh as much as two grown men.

WITH SO MANY GENERA AND species in the family Labridae there is considerable debate about how it should be split up, with various taxonomists suggesting different numbers of subfamilies and tribes (subdivisions of subfamilies). However, there is no definitive way at present to separate the different groups of wrasses, so they are included together here.

Wrasses are among the most varied of all fish in terms of size, shape, and lifestyle. Yet, despite obvious differences, there are a few characteristics that link wrasses together. For example, the jaws can be extended forward during displays and feeding. There are gaps between the teeth, and the front ones in each jaw point forward—particularly obvious in the tuskfish (*Choerodon* species). The scales have a smooth back edge and are known as cycloid. Most species also have the unusual habit of burying themselves in the sand at night or when they feel threatened. Most remarkably, the majority of species change sex.

Cleaning Services

Some wrasses have an unusual form of behavior. They become "cleaners" of other unrelated fish, flitting around them and even entering their mouths and gill chambers on occasions to remove parasites. This activity is carried out by juveniles and also the adults of some of the smaller wrasse species, notably the appropriately named cleaner wrasses (*Labroides*).

There are five species in the genus. The smallest is the redlip cleaner wrasse (*L. rubrolabiatus*), which measures about 3.5 inches (9 cm), and the largest is the bicolor cleaner wrasse (*L. bicolor*) at 5.5 inches (14 cm).

⊕ *Forward-pointing front teeth are a feature of wrasses, and they can be seen clearly in this harlequin tuskfish (*Choerodon fasciatus*).*

Sex-change Specialists

The sex of many fish can change depending on circumstances. In some groups, such as anemonefish, individuals go through a male phase before becoming female; they are described as protandrous (or "first-male") hermaphrodites. In the reverse case, in which juveniles develop into females before eventually becoming males, the fish are known as protogynous (or "first-female") hermaphrodites. There is also a third possibility, in which a fish can be both male and female at the same time! Some of the groupers or sea basses are like this and are known as functional or synchronous hermaphrodites.

Wrasses can be either protandrous or protogynous hermaphrodites, most of them being the latter. The massive humphead or Napoleon wrasse, for example, starts as a female and develops into a giant, awe-inspiring male with a huge hump on its head, which accounts for one of its common names.

The way they do it involves "soliciting" by both the cleaners and the clients. The cleaners advertise their services by adopting a particular swimming posture and display above their selected cleaning station—a patch of reef over which they position themselves. The display is recognized by fish needing to be relieved of the irritation caused by parasites. Somehow they need to convey a message to the cleaners that they will not attack them. They do so in a variety of ways, such as gliding slowly over the cleaning station with fins extended, holding their mouth open, positioning their body at an angle, or changing color.

The end result is a mutually satisfying situation for both cleaners and clients. The cleaners obtain a nutritious meal, while the clients rid themselves of troublesome parasites. Cleaning stations soon become well known among reef visitors, and it is not unusual for lines to build up at the most popular ones.

The best-known cleaner wrasse is the 4.5-inch (11.5-cm) bluestreak cleaner wrasse (Labroides dimidiatus). Here a male solicits a female during courtship.

All cleaner wrasses are slim-bodied and colorful fish with small, pointed mouths—the ideal size and shape for picking off small parasites, even from awkward places.

Cleaner wrasses can feed on small aquatic creatures, just like many other wrasses. However, their speciality lies in the ready food supply presented by the parasites on other fishes' bodies. The challenge they face is how to get the food without themselves becoming food for predatory, parasite-carrying fish.

Initial Phases and Terminal Phases

Wrasses change sex as they mature (see box "Sex-change Specialists."). As they grow, the young fish go through what is known as an initial phase. The colors of initial phase fish are generally quite dull. Most fish in the phase are females, but in some species they also include males. Such males are indistinguishable from the females and are known as primary males. It is only during spawning that their colors become more intense and allow them to be distinguished from females.

After a certain time, depending on species, the primary males will adopt full male coloration and finnage, thus entering the terminal phase. Females that eventually develop into males bypass the primary male phase entirely becoming, instead, fully colored and functional secondary males.

In some ways primary males are the equivalent of the "satellite" or "sneaker" males found among the sunfish. Such males, being similarly colored to females, are not seen as rivals by the secondary or terminal phase males, which are dominant and therefore are the ones

Now You See Me, Now You Don't

While wrasses are among the most frequently seen fish on a reef during the day, they are conspicuous by their absence at night. Some of the larger species can be found resting under ledges or in caves. But where do the smaller individuals and species go at night? It is as if they disappear.

They are still around, in fact, but they seek safety by burying themselves in the sand as darkness falls, only venturing out again once dawn breaks. This defense behavior may not guarantee them total safety, since some night-time prowlers can detect buried food by smell or electrical sensitivity, but it does provide considerably more protection than most other forms of shelter.

The reef is not just a dangerous place at night. The day brings its own threats from predators. At such times many wrasses simply do what they do at night: bury themselves at lightning-fast speed and emerge some time later when the coast is clear.

that establish territories and spawn. However, as a dominant male pairs up with a female and they rise in the water to scatter eggs and sperm at the peak of the upward spawning dash, a primary male may rush in and release his own sperm in the vicinity of the eggs.

Interestingly, primary males, while being much smaller than their secondary or terminal phase counterparts, have very large testes and can release vast quantities of sperm. As a result, and despite the fact that they cannot normally get as close to a female as the dominant male, sneakers (also referred to as streakers, furtive males, or cuckolders) can fertilize up to one third of all the eggs released by a female in each spawning bout.

⊕ *As night falls, a razor wrasse (Cymolutes lecluse) prepares to bury itself in the sand as a means of protection against predators.*

Yellowstripe barracuda (*Sphyraena chrysotaenia*)

Common name Barracudas

Family	Sphyraenidae
Order	Perciformes
Number of species	25 in 1 genus
Size	From about 12 in (30 cm) to 6.7 ft (2.1m); at least half of all species grow to over 39 in (1 m)
Key features	All species elongated with pointed head and forked tail; mouth large with numerous, powerful fanglike teeth; lower jaw slightly longer than upper jaw; large eyes; two widely separated dorsal fins; most fins except tail relatively small; lateral line well developed; coloration usually includes dark blue on back, shading to silvery along the belly; body often attractively marked with vertical bands; fins may be colored
Breeding	Spawning usually occurs in groups in open water; eggs scattered and abandoned; few other details known
Diet	Almost exclusively fish, including smaller barracuda and squid; many smaller species also regularly eat shrimp
Habitat	Frequently found near the surface but may descend to depths of about 330 ft (100 m); may be found close to shore, in harbors and lagoons, or in open seas; young may enter brackish water around estuaries and mangroves
Distribution	Widespread in tropical and subtropical Atlantic, Indian, and Pacific Oceans
Status	Not threatened

⊕ *At 12 inches (30 cm) in length the yellowstripe barracuda (Sphyraena chrysotaenia) of the Indo-Pacific and Mediterranean is a relatively small species.*

Barracudas

Sphyraenidae

In some parts of the West Indies, and elsewhere, barracudas are feared even more than sharks—and with some justification, because these superbly built predators can use their fearsome teeth to quickly tear their victims to shreds.

BARRACUDAS ARE OFTEN REGARDED IN THE same vein as piranhas or sharks—fierce predators to be avoided by humans at all costs. Yet not all barracudas are dangerous, and even the ones that are must often be provoked into attacking by invading their territory or disturbing them. In fact, there are more harmless species of barracuda among the 25 that make up the genus and family than dangerous ones.

Nor is it only small species like the 12-inch (30-cm) yellowstripe barracuda (*Sphyraena chrysotaenia*) or red barracuda (*S. pinguis*) that are harmless. One of the largest species, the Guachanche barracuda (*S. guachancho*)—a widely distributed Atlantic species that can grow to 6.6 feet (2 m) and is usually found in shoals—presents no threat to humans.

The similar-sized great barracuda (*S. barracuda*) from the Indo-Pacific and Atlantic can definitely be dangerous. It can weigh up to 110 pounds (50 kg). It rarely attacks humans; but when it does, it can inflict serious injury with just one bite from its powerful jaws and sabrelike teeth. It is also very fast, capable of bursts of speed of almost 70 miles per hour (110 km/h)—nearly 40 feet (12.2 m) per second!

Among the other feared species is the third giant of the genus, the Guinean barracuda (*S. afra*) from the eastern Atlantic. The species can grow to 6.7 feet (2.1 m) and weigh as much as a great barracuda. Like the great barracuda, it is also a much sought-after game fish, owing to its power and fighting qualities. Indeed, for all their reputation, barracudas have more reason to be fearful of humans than the other way round. Not only are barracudas caught for sport, but some species are fished commercially.

⊕ *Looking every bit as menacing as it is, a great barracuda (Sphyraena barracuda) shows its huge, tooth-lined jaws. The species grows to about 6 feet (1.8 m) and is a voracious feeder on fish. It has also been known to attack human divers if disturbed.*

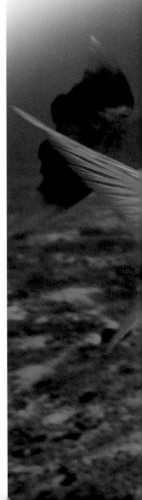

Most barracudas feed on other fish, the range of fish species taken being extremely wide and including smaller barracudas, squid, and their relatives. Occasionally large species will also feed on shrimp, but they more commonly feature on the menus of the smaller species. Lone barracudas may single out victims and then catch them using their superior speed. Schooling barracudas sometimes herd prey into a tight shoal before picking off individual victims.

Predator Turned Prey

Barracudas may be formidable killers, but they are themselves also regarded as prey by other fish at different stages of their lives. Sharks and rays, for example, will eat barracudas, as will large dolphinfish (*Coryphaena hippurus*). Even the 39-inch (1-m) bastard halibut (*Paralichthys olivaceus*), which is one of the large-tooth flounder family, and therefore just an outsized flatfish, preys on the red barracuda (*S. pinguis*).

In the sea it is often a case of a small fish being eaten by larger fish, and sometimes the small fish are just the young of species that the larger fish have good reason to fear.

ⓦ *A school of chevron barracudas (*Sphyraena putnamae*). Note the long, streamlined body with the dorsal and anal fins set well back on the body—typical features of fast-moving, predatory fish.*

**Atlantic mackerel
(*Scomber scombrus*)**

Common name Mackerels and tunas

Family   Scombridae

Order   Perciformes

Number of species About 54 species in 15 genera

Size   From about 8 in (20 cm) to 15 ft (4.6 m)

Key features Body spindle shaped and almost cylindrical in
                cross-section; head pointed; large eyes halfway
                between back of upper jaw and top of head; first
                dorsal fin with hard spines; both fins fit into
                grooves when folded back; pectoral fins with
                hard leading edge; finlets behind second dorsal
                and anal fins extend to base of tail; tail lunate
                with hard, stiff leading edge; 2 keels on either
                side of caudal peduncle; scales very small; most
                species have blue backs and silvery bellies;
                bonitos usually have longitudinal stripes on body;
                mackerels usually have spots or dark streaks on
                upper half of body

Breeding   All are egg scatterers; a northern bluefin tuna
                weighing 600–660 lb (270–300 kg) can produce
                10 million eggs in a single spawning; skipjack
                tuna may breed all year in tropics; others such as
                northern bluefin have narrow spawning seasons;
                southern bluefin tuna may spawn only once in a
                lifetime; hatching may take as little as 3 days

Diet   Mostly smaller fish, squid, and crustaceans; some
                smaller species also sift zooplankton

Habitat   Open water, frequently near surface but some
                down to about 820 ft (250 m); a few, notably the
                albacore, may descend to about 1,970 ft (600 m)

Distribution Widely distributed in tropical and subtropical
                seas; some species are restricted, such as the
                Monterey Spanish mackerel, which is endemic to
                the northern part of the Gulf of California

Status   IUCN lists 5 species as variously under threat,
                including the southern bluefin tuna as Critically
                Endangered

⊕ *The Atlantic mackerel (*Scomber scombrus*) is one of the
world's most important commercial fish species. Many thousands
of tons are caught each year. Length to 24 inches (60 cm).*

Mackerels
and Tunas

Scombridae

*In the mackerels and the tunas evolution has produced
fish that are superbly designed for an entire life spent
on the move at high speed in the warm surface layers
of the ocean.*

UNLIKE AIR, WATER IS DENSE, and it offers a great
deal of resistance to any animal swimming
through it. This, in turn, uses up relatively large
amounts of energy. It is therefore of great
benefit to aquatic animals if they can find ways
of reducing the amount of energy they need to
use when moving around.

Designed for Speed

In the tunas and some of their closest relatives,
the mackerels, with which they form the family
Scombridae, the solutions to the problem are
close to perfection. The body, for instance, is
spindle-shaped—in other words, it tapers at
both ends. As a result, the front end cuts
through the water with maximum efficiency,
while the narrow back end allows water to flow
over it with minimum drag or resistance.
Because the body is almost cylinder-shaped, the
streamlining effect is produced all around it.

   None of the bones of the jaw projects
outward, enhancing the streamlined effect. The
eyes are also located deep in their sockets and
present almost no obstacle to the smooth flow
of water over them.

   The two dorsal fins are small, the first
containing stiff, narrow rays that can stand up
to the force of the water. When folded
backward during high-speed swimming, both
the fins fit into grooves and offer no water
resistance. The pectoral fins have a particularly
strong leading edge and will not collapse even
at the high pressures created by the water
when the fish are swimming at speed. The
finlets behind the dorsal and anal fin allow
water to flow freely between them. The tail is

⊕ *Pacific mackerel
(Scomber japonicus)
shoaling off California.
The species inhabits
warm and temperate
waters and is also found
in the Atlantic and
Indian Oceans. It is an
important food fish in
parts of Asia.*

tall, rigid, and narrow—the perfect structure for high-speed and long-distance swimming. The slender caudal peduncle has two sharp-edged keels on each side. They help the side-to-side tail swings cut through the water with maximum ease. Just as important, the body scales are very small, reducing drag further.

Finally, the swimming style of the tuna has also evolved characteristics that make it ideal for a constantly roaming lifestyle, accentuated by short, high-speed bursts of speed. First, the main swimming muscles are set deep inside the body and are arranged alongside the spinal column. (In most fish the muscles are located just under the skin.) In tunas the flexing of the deep muscles produces little, if any, detectable

⬆ The 6.5-foot (2-m) yellowfin tuna (Thunnus albacares) is distinguished by its long anal and second dorsal fins, small, yellow finlets behind the dorsal and anal fins, and yellow body markings.

movement on the body surface; in other words, the body of a tuna does not flex during swimming as it does in other fish.

The overall effect is that, while the tail swings from side to side, the body itself remains more or less rigid. This means it can cut through the water with minimum resistance. This swimming technique is so typical of tunas that it is referred to as thunniform swimming.

Warm-blooded Fish

Fish are described as cold-blooded, or poikilothermic. The first term is inaccurate because although fish that live in cold water have cold blood, those in warm water have warm blood. In reality, a fish's blood is the same temperature as the surrounding water.

At least, this is true of most fish. But there are a few species, such as larger tunas and some sharks, that can maintain the temperature of their blood and muscles several degrees warmer than the surrounding water. They generate heat from within their bodies. Therefore they are not cold-blooded; they are warm-blooded, or endothermic.

This feature helps the muscles work much more efficiently regardless of water temperature. By being able to produce muscle heat, warm-blooded fish can move with equal ease in either cold or warm water—a clear advantage when chasing prey through differing

water depths (and temperatures) or when traveling over large distances, as tuna, billfish, and some sharks do.

For example, the northern bluefin tuna (*Thunnus thynnus*) can maintain its muscle temperature between 82 and 91° F (28–33° C) whether the temperature of the surrounding water is 45° F (7° C) or 86° F (30° C). While not all species of tuna can match this feat, some, like the yellowfin (*T. albacares*) and the skipjack tuna (*Katsuwonus pelamis*), which can "skip" over the surface in pursuit of prey, can maintain a body temperature some 5–7° F (3–4° C) above that of the surrounding water.

Tunas and Allies

Of the 54 species in the family Scombridae one, the butterfly kingfish (*Gasterochisma*

The "Wonderful Net"

The remarkable bloodflow arrangement that allows a tuna to generate body heat is known as the *rete mirabile*, which means "the wonderful net." It is a network of blood vessels that functions in a very special way.

In fish the blood carries oxygen to the muscles and other organs, and picks up waste carbon dioxide and heat generated by muscle contractions. Then it returns to the heart and, from there, to the gills. Here it releases the carbon dioxide and picks up a fresh supply of oxygen, but it also loses the heat that it has picked up. So in most fish the blood that travels back into the body from the gills via the main blood vessel called the dorsal aorta is at the same temperature as the ocean water.

In tunas and other warm-blooded fish, however, the cold blood leaving the gills does not run into the dorsal aorta. Instead, it goes into large blood vessels that run just under the skin and, from there, toward the main muscles that lie deeper in the body. As it flows inward through a network of small vessels, it meets warm, deoxygenated blood coming out of the muscles through other small vessels. The incoming and outgoing blood vessels run very close to each other in the *rete mirabile*, so the cooler, incoming blood picks up some heat from the warm, outgoing blood. In effect, the network acts as a heat exchanger that ensures the blood supply to the major muscles is always warm.

melampus), is usually put in its own subfamily (the Gasterochismatinae). The remaining species are grouped in the subfamily Scombrinae. The remaining members of the family can be separated into five distinct groups or tribes.

The first consists of two genera of mackerels, with seven species, among which is the widely known, and eaten, Atlantic mackerel (*Scomber scombrus*). The second tribe has two species, the shark mackerel (*Grammatorcynus bicarinatus*) and the double-lined mackerel (*G. bilineatus*).

A third tribe consists of two genera of Spanish mackerels, *Acanthocybium* and *Scomberomorus*, with about 19 species; among them is the extremely elongated wahoo (*A. solandri*), a highly prized game fish that can grow to 8.2 feet (2.5 m). The bonitos consist of four genera and eight species, and include the Atlantic bonito (*Sarda sarda*), which grows to about 3 feet (90 cm) and is important both as a game fish and a food fish.

Finally, there are the tunas, containing five genera and 17 species. Among them is the largest member of the family, the northern

The southern bluefin tuna (Thunnus maccoyii) has been fished so intensively that it is listed as Critically Endangered.

or curried in many countries. Such is the demand for northern bluefin tuna in Japan that the species is now cultured in open-sea pens. This helps reduce pressure on some wild stocks but not enough to allay fears for the long-term commercial survival of the species. The same is true of the albacore (*T. alalunga*).

The fate of the southern bluefin tuna (*Thunnus maccoyii*) is much worse; it is now Critically Endangered. Unless adequate protection measures are taken, it is estimated that the total world population of the species could be as low as 500 individuals by the last two decades of the 21st century.

The Monterey Spanish mackerel, or Gulf sierra (*Scomberomorus concolor*), is also listed as Endangered by the IUCN through a combination of restricted distribution (it is only known from the northern part of the Gulf of California) allied to commercial overfishing. The bigeye tuna (*Thunnus obesus*) from the Indian and Pacific Oceans is considered Vulnerable. Overfishing is the main factor in its decline.

bluefin tuna (*Thunnus thynnus*), one of the world's most important food and game fish.

Declining Stocks

Owing to their size, their firm, tasty flesh, their abundance, and their prodigious fighting qualities, tunas and mackerels have long been top food fish and game fish. Despite high demand, though, many species are still found in large numbers. For example, the Atlantic mackerel is very abundant, particularly in summer, when it becomes a major part of numerous commercial fisheries, especially, but not exclusively, in the Mediterranean.

For many years the northern bluefin tuna was also found in vast numbers. Tending to school according to size, gatherings of the largest specimens frequently included massive fish measuring 13 to 15 feet (4–4.6 m) in length and weighing up to 1,500 pounds (685 kg). Today large specimens still occur but in much smaller numbers, since continued pressure from overfishing has caused serious declines in many populations.

Tuna flesh is eaten raw (as in Japanese sashimi), steamed, fried, grilled, smoked, salted,

The Butterfly Kingfish

The butterfly kingfish (*Gasterochisma melampus*) looks very much like a tuna, but it has a feature that is found in the swordfish and billfish of the families Xiphiidae and Istiophoridae but not in tunas: It is a heat-generating organ consisting of specialized eye muscles. By keeping the eye and brain at a temperature several degrees higher than the surrounding water, the organ allows the fish to hunt in the cooler, deeper layers of the open ocean.

Although the butterfly kingfish is similar to the billfish in this respect, it uses a different set of eye muscles to generate the heat. But since it is unique among the tunas in being able to produce "eye heat," as well as in some other features, it is not considered a typical tuna. In fact, some scientists believe that it does not belong in the family at all.

The butterfly kingfish is widely distributed in most temperate waters in the southern hemisphere, being found down to depths of about 660 feet (200 m) and water temperatures as cool as 46–50° F (8–10° C). It grows to about 5.4 feet (1.65 m) and is considered a good game fish. It is not, however, purposely caught for food.

Atlantic blue marlin (*Makaira nigricans*)

Common name Swordfish and marlins

Families Xiphiidae (swordfish), Istiophoridae (billfish, marlins, sailfish, spearfish)

Order Perciformes

Number of species Xiphiidae: 1 species; Istiophoridae: 11 in 3 genera

Size From about 6 ft (1.8 m) to 16.4 ft (5 m)

Key features All species elongate with a sword or bill: shortest in shortbill spearfish (*Tetrapturus angustirostris*); in swordfish sword is flattened from top to bottom and has sharp edges; in all other species sword is round in cross-section; body almost cylindrical in cross-section; eyes well formed; swordfish lack jaw teeth; dorsal fin narrow based in swordfish and long based in others; sail-like in sailfish; pelvic fins absent in swordfish, narrow but present in others; caudal peduncle has 1 keel on either side in swordfish and 2 keels in others; tail stiff, narrow, and well forked; coloration blackish fading to light brown or gray in swordfish; blue-black on back, shading to silvery flanks in marlins and relatives; some species have vertical blue stripes

Breeding Generally occurs in relatively shallow water; single female may be courted by 1 or more males; millions of eggs produced in a single spawning

Diet Mainly fish, squid, and crustaceans

Habitat Open waters, including midocean; some species also frequent coastal waters; most remain in warmer surface waters above the thermocline

Distribution Most tropical and subtropical waters

Status IUCN lists swordfish and Data Deficient

⬆ *At about 16.4 feet (5 m) maximum length the Atlantic blue marlin* (Makaira nigricans) *is one of the largest and most impressive of the billfish. It ranges through temperate and tropical seas worldwide, usually in open waters.*

Swordfish and Marlins
Xiphiidae, Istiophoridae

*The cheetah is the fastest land animal, capable of running at 65 miles per hour (105 km/h). Yet the black marlin (*Makaira indica*) has been recorded swimming at up to 80 miles per hour (130 km/h) through the high-resistance medium of water that makes any kind of movement difficult. It is an amazing feat.*

WHILE THE BLACK MARLIN IS THE fastest fish in the world, it is not the only outstanding sprinter. It has several relatives also capable of producing great bursts of speed, if not quite so fast. The Atlantic blue marlin (*M. nigricans*) can produce sprints of nearly 50 miles per hour (80 km/h), while the swordfish (*Xiphias gladius*) can generate speeds of 56 miles per hour (90 km/h). Like mackerels and tunas (family Scombridae), these high-speed predators are capable of great pace and sustained swimming activity due to a complicated blood circulation system that allows them to maintain their body temperature some degrees above that of the surrounding water.

Family Differences

The swordfish and its allies are members of a group of 12 species known until recently as the billfish (family Xiphiidae). Today they are considered as members of two separate families. The swordfish is now in the family Xiphiidae by itself, and the remaining 11 species, comprising the marlins, sailfish, and spearfish, form the billfish family, the Istiophoridae.

While all 12 species have elongated, streamlined shapes and a beak, sword, bill, or spear, there are distinct differences between the swordfish and the remaining 11 species. The most significant of them are that the swordfish's "sword" is flattened with sharp edges, while that of other species is round; adult swordfish do not have any jaw teeth, while adult billfish do; the swordfish has neither pelvic fins nor the bones that would normally support them, while

⬇ *The swordfish (*Xiphias gladius*), found in worldwide temperate and tropical seas, is placed in a family of its own, the Xiphiidae. The sword is formed from the elongated snout.*

all the others have both pelvic fins and girdles; the swordfish has a narrow-based dorsal fin, unlike the billfish; and the caudal peduncle of the swordfish has one keel on either side, while in the billfish there are two.

Open-water Hunters

The swordfish and its relatives are open-water fish frequently found long distances from land. However, many species, including the swordfish, are also found near coasts, and a few, most notably the black marlin and the Atlantic sailfish (*Istiophorus albicans*), frequent shallower habitats like reefs.

In the open sea all species tend to stay in the upper layers. There the water is warm, particularly in tropical zones, often reaching a temperature of 68° F (20° C) or more. Below the warm surface layer the temperature of the water drops dramatically—by as much as 1.8° F (1° C) every 33 feet (10 m) or so in some places. The zone where the temperature starts to drop is called the thermocline.

Therefore, by tending to swim above the thermocline, billfish are technically warm-water species (see box "Hot-headed Fish"). In this relatively narrow band some species travel great distances both in their day-to-day lives and when spawning. Swordfish, for example, tend to migrate northward and southward during the warmer months of the year and back to warmer waters as fall approaches. They also migrate long distances to spawn in the Sargasso Sea in the western Atlantic.

Feeding is largely restricted to the upper layers of the water column, although some species, like the swordfish, will also descend to the bottom layers. The main food items consist of fish, crustaceans, and squid.

Stunning Weapons

The sword possessed by the 12 members of the group is not, as some accounts suggest, used in "sword fights" between rivals or to spear large prey or to attack boats. If the first of these was true, there would be very few "undamaged" swordfish and marlins around. If prey was speared, the billfish would be faced with the challenge of removing it from the sword before eating it. It is almost certainly not a technique employed when hunting relatively small prey. However, there are several eye-witness reports of marlins spearing large prey and then shaking it free before swallowing it. Most frequently, the sword is used to either stun or thrash prey to death before it is consumed.

There are documented accounts of swordfish ramming boats and piercing their hulls. There are even examples of hull boards with swords impaled in them; in one example the sword penetrated the wooden hull to a depth of 22 inches (56 cm). More intriguingly, whales have also been found with swords or bills piercing their thick blubber.

However, it is very doubtful that these examples prove swordfish and their relatives attack in this way. We must take into account, for example, the high speed at which the fish are capable of swimming. If a swordfish or marlin comes across a boat or whale blocking its path when travelling at full speed, especially through slightly murky water, it is very doubtful that it will be able to take evasive action.

Reluctant Shoalers

The swordfish and its relatives tend to be loners, although the Mediterranean spearfish is often found in pairs. Additionally, schools of about ten Indo-Pacific blue marlins (*Makaira mazara*) are fairly common, but they are generally smaller individuals; larger specimens are usually solitary animals. The Indo-Pacific sailfish (*Ictiophorus platypterus*) also forms small groups, consisting mainly of similarly sized individuals. The Atlantic sailfish is thought to be the most frequent shoaler of all, with groups of three to 30 or more individuals being reported.

Despite their generally solitary habits, members of both families undertake migrations and come together as pairs or breeding groups during the spawning season. Whether breeding occurs in the southern Sargasso Sea (as in the swordfish) or in shallow coastal waters off Florida (as in the Atlantic sailfish), similar overall patterns of behavior apply.

Tasty Predators

Of all 12 sword-billed species the swordfish is by far the most widely caught by commercial fisheries. It is considered a great delicacy throughout its range but particularly so in the Mediterranean. Since it is a powerful fighter and can grow to nearly 15 feet (4.6 m) and a weight of over 1,430 pounds (650 kg), it is also regarded as a major sport or game fish.

The same goes for many of the marlins and their relatives, all of which are fished commercially to varying degrees except, perhaps, the smallest member of the group, the roundscale spearfish (*Tetrapturus georgii*), which grows to about 6 feet (1.8 m) and a weight of some 53 pounds (24 kg). The largest member of the genus is the striped marlin (*T. audax*), which can grow to about 13.8 feet (4.2 m) and a weight of 970 pounds (440 kg). The flesh of the striped marlin is highly valued for Japanese sashimi and sushi (raw fish) recipes.

One of them consists of a single female being accompanied either by a single male or two or three, but rarely more. This occurs in water ranging from the surface down to about 250 feet (75 m) depending on species, and at water temperatures in the 68–86° F (20–30° C) range—although a depth of 660 feet (100 m) has been reported for the Atlantic sailfish.

The eggs are scattered and abandoned. As many as 40 million have been recorded for the black marlin and 29 million for the swordfish. Yields from some of the slighter-bodied species like the Atlantic sailfish may be more modest. Nevertheless, a 74-pound (33.4-kg) female is reported to have produced 4.8 million eggs in three separate batches during a single season.

Fertilized eggs are tiny—less than 0.04 inches (0.1 cm) across. In the swordfish they hatch into larvae that measure about 0.2 inches (0.4 cm). By the time they reach 0.4 inches (1 cm), they already have a well-formed sword and are efficient miniature predators of plankton. However, at such a small size these future superhunters of the open oceans are, themselves, preyed on by a large number of other fish. Indeed, during their juvenile stages swordfish and marlins are on the menu of all other open-water hunters, including mackerels, jacks, sharks, even other billfish.

Causes for Concern

The majority of swordfish and marlins are eaten well before they reach maturity. Once nearing full size, though, they have few enemies and can cope with most...except one. Humans present the greatest threat to the continued survival of billfish, just as we do to so many other species that share our planet.

We catch billfish for game and food but we do not really know how many specimens can be taken without harming overall stocks. Few detailed studies have been carried out, but one that was—on the Atlantic white marlin—gives cause for serious concern. According to it, the numbers of the species may have declined by as much as 77 percent between 1966 and 1991. Further, catches between 1991 and 1993 were

lower than those expected if the population was renewing itself naturally. This could indicate that the species faces serious danger if remedial steps are not taken. And this is a fish that takes a modest 1.4 to 4.4 years to double its population through breeding (assuming there are sufficient adults of breeding age). Most of the marlins and relations also double their populations in the same time, but for two species, the Indo-Pacific blue marlin and the swordfish, the minimum population doubling time is thought to be between 4.5 and 14 years. Such a long time span could have serious consequences if numbers became decimated.

The second threat we pose is more indirect. As we poison the world's fresh waters and oceans with countless pollutants, some are taken in by aquatic creatures and accumulate in their body tissues. When the creatures are eaten by other animals, they also take in the toxins. But since a predator eats numerous prey animals in its life, it also takes in and accumulates higher levels of poison—and so on up the food chain. Top predators like swordfish therefore end up with very high levels of toxic substances in their bodies.

One of the most lethal toxins is mercury, which in high doses presents a serious threat to the health of the animals that carry it in their tissues as well as those that eat them. Levels of mercury are now so high in some stocks of swordfish and marlins that human health

warnings have been issued in certain regions, urging people to eat the fish only occasionally and, preferably, less frequently than once a week. What the future holds for the swordfish, its relatives, and all other aquatic life forms is impossible to gauge; but if we do not take steps to address the issues urgently and effectively, it could be very bleak indeed.

⬆ The striped marlin (Tetrapturus audax) grows to a length of 10 feet (3 m). It is found in both open seas and inshore waters in the Indo-Pacific, where it feeds on fish and squid.

Hot-headed Fish

Like the larger species of tunas and some sharks, the swordfish and its allies can maintain a muscle temperature above that of the surrounding water. They can also maintain the temperature of their eyes and brain above that of the water, using a special form of heat generation and conservation known as regional endothermy.

Heat is generated when muscles contract. In the swordfish and its relatives one particular set of eye muscles is capable of generating large quantities of heat without contracting. The heat-generating cells that make up the muscles contain special structures involved with energy production; they also have oxygen-storing compounds, something that is typical of cells with a high level of activity.

When the special eye muscle cells are stimulated by impulses from the central nervous system, they respond by generating heat, which keeps both the eyes and the brain warm. It is believed that the higher temperatures allow swordfish and billfish to hunt more effectively in cold water, since the warmth permits both their eyes and brains to function at peak efficiency regardless of the temperature of the surrounding water.

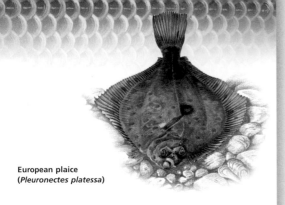

European plaice
(*Pleuronectes platessa*)

Common name Flounders

Families Bothidae (lefteye flounders),
Pleuronectidae (righteye flounders)

Subfamilies Bothidae: Bothinae and Taeniopsettinae;
Pleuronectidae: Pleuronectinae, Rhombosoleinae,
Poecilopsettinae, and Paralichthodinae

Order Pleuronectiformes

Number of species Bothidae: about 157 in 20 genera;
Pleuronectidae: nearly 120 in about 44 genera

Size From 1.4 in (3.5 cm) to 8.5 ft (2.6 m)

Key features Asymmetrical, oval-shaped bodies; head with
both eyes on same (top) side; front edge of
dorsal fin located above or in front of eyes; all
fins separate from each other; pelvic fins
asymmetrical in lefteyes, symmetrical in
righteyes; coloration: top side heavily patterned
in many species; capable of rapid color changes

Breeding About 2 million eggs released

Diet Invertebrates; larger species also take fish

Habitat Nearly always marine; Bothidae: tropical and
temperate zones; usually over fine-grained
bottoms; shallow or relatively shallow waters,
normally above 330 ft (100 m); Pleuronectidae:
tropical, subtropical, temperate, and (almost)
arctic zones; usually over fine-grained bottoms;
depths above 660 ft (200 m); some species may
enter brackish water

Distribution Atlantic, Indian, and Pacific Oceans;
Pleuronectidae: also Arctic Ocean

Status IUCN lists Atlantic halibut (*Hippoglossus
hippoglossus*) as Endangered and yellowtail
flounder (*Limanda ferriginea*) as Vulnerable

↑ *The bony ridge of this 40-inch (1-m) European plaice
(*Pleuronectes platessa*) is visible behind its eyes. Lying flat on the
rocky bottom of very shallow brackish or marine waters, it hunts
for its favorite mollusks at night.*

Flounders

Bothidae, Pleuronectidae

*The righteye flounders, with few exceptions, have both
eyes on the right side of the head and are most
familiar to us on our plates. Of course, the reverse is
true of the aptly named lefteye flounders.*

TOGETHER THE LEFTEYE FLOUNDERS (FAMILY Bothidae)
and their right-eyed counterparts (family
Pleuronectidae) account for nearly 280 of the
690 or so species that make up the order of
flatfish (Pleuronectiformes). At around 157
species the lefteye flounders are the largest of
the families. The righteye flounders, with 120
species, rank third, being slightly outnumbered
by the tonguefish family (Cynoglossidae), at
around 135 species in just three genera.

Fish on the Menu

Most of the best-known species that are fished
commercially for food are righteye flounders,
but there are also some familiar types not just
among the lefteye flounders but also members
of other families (see box).

Usually flatfish are caught in trawl nets
over fine-grained bottoms at varying depths
depending on species and time of year. Some,
such as the Atlantic halibut (*Hippoglossus
hippoglossus*), can be found at great depths—
from around 165 feet (50 m) down to around
6,560 feet (2,000 m). The Pacific halibut

⊕ *The eyed flounder
(Bothus ocellatus) is
found in the Indian and
West Pacific Oceans.*

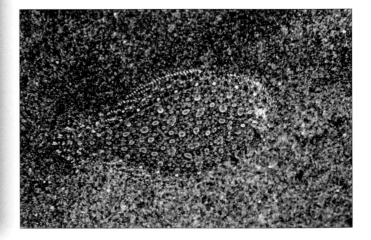

(*H. stenolepis*) does not extend to such great depths but can still be found at around 3,610 feet (1,100 m). Both fish are highly commercial and are usually caught at considerably shallower depths than their maximum.

In the past the Atlantic halibut has been fished very heavily, to such an extent that now the World Conservation Union officially lists it as Endangered. With dwindling stocks and the continuing high demand for this excellent food fish, several experimental projects aimed at rearing the species under controlled conditions have met with some success.

The commercial breeding of European plaice (*Pleuronectes platessa*) is far better established, and important quantities of farmed stocks are now available. It is not endangered, and demand has led to captive rearing.

Soles are also popular food fish, with the lemon sole (*Microstomus kitt*) and Dover sole being particularly highly regarded in international cuisine. However, the Dover sole enjoyed by European diners is quite distinct from that consumed in the U.S. The European Dover sole is *Solea solea*, which can grow to 24 inches (60 cm). It is not a member of the Pleuronectidae or Bothidae (the two families discussed here) but of the Soleidae (discussed under "Soles"). In the U.S. the American Dover sole is *M. pacificus*, a larger fish at around 30 inches (76 cm); it is a member of the Pleuronectidae along with the lemon sole, itself a sizable fish at 26 inches (65 cm) long.

Undoubtedly, the leading species is the European plaice, a northeastern Atlantic species that can grow to around 40 inches (100 cm), weighs around 15.5 pounds (7 kg), and can live for up to 50 years. Few people, though, ever get to see any specimens even closely approaching this size, weight, and age.

⬆ *The European plaice (Pleuronectes platessa) is distinguished by the orange spots on one side of its body, while the other side is characteristically pale. Plaice tend to move from relatively shallow water to deeper water as they grow older.*

The vast majority seen in food markets are less than half this size and are nowhere near the age limit for the species. This species is the most important flatfish in Europe and is sold both fresh and frozen in large quantities.

Adult European plaice can be found in waters as deep as 650 feet (200 m). Although adults can also be found in very shallow water, most of the specimens encountered in such habitats are small. Few, if any, small individuals are ever encountered at depth.

Other Popular Flounders and Friends

While the species mentioned above are among the best-known and most popular flatfish that are eaten in many countries, numerous other species (belonging to several families) are also consumed, some in large quantities. In fact, there are probably more members of this order that are regarded as food fish than of most others. The brill (*Scophthalmus rhombus*), for example, is a 30-inch (75-cm), 16-pound (7.2-kg) European, Mediterranean, and Black Sea member of the family Scophthalmidae, with a broad body and delicate flesh that is popular mainly (but not exclusively) in the more northern European regions.

Another member of this family, the topknot (*Zeugopterus punctatus*), is even more northern in its distribution and is popular in Britain and parts of Scandinavia.

The dab (*Limanda limanda*) is also a predominantly northern Atlantic species. It can grow to 17 inches (42 cm) and weighs around 2.8 pounds (1.3 kg). The flounder (*Pleuronectes flesus*) is longer and heavier, and extends further south to the Moroccan coast and into the Mediterranean and Baltic Seas. Both are members of the family Pleuronectidae that enjoy considerable popularity.

Along the Pacific Coast of the U.S. many species of flatfish are taken both as game and food fish. They include the Pacific sanddab (*Cithraichthys sordidus*) and the California flounder (*Paralichthys californicus*) from the large-tooth flounder family (Paralichthyidae)—plus several members of the righteye flounder family, including the rex sole (*Glyptocephalus zachirus*) and the petrale sole (*Eopsetta jordani*). In the more northern regions the rock sole (*Lepidopsetta bilineata*) is fished in large numbers, while the English sole (*Parophrys*

The Fishing Flatfish

All flatfish are predators and tend to ambush their prey. However, the angler flatfish (*Asterorhombus fijiensis*) in the family Bothidae takes matters a significant step further and actually fishes for its food. It has a form of built-in fishing rod with a bait or lure that, through the remarkable process of "parallel" evolution, closely resembles the "rod and lure" arrangement found in the angler fish (order Lophiiformes).

This 6-inch (15-cm) Indo-Pacific species is found in shallow tropical waters, often on coral sandy bottoms at depths of less than 100 feet (30 m). There it lies motionless, partly covered or camouflaged and thus invisible to its potential prey. One part of the body, though, is very visible—the rodlike first spine of the dorsal fin and its modified tip that looks like a small shrimp. The angler flatfish waves this rod and lure (called the "ilicium" and "esca," respectively) in the water until an unsuspecting victim becomes attracted by the "shrimp." However, this "shrimp" is no meal, as the would-be predator dramatically discovers when the flatfish sucks it into its large mouth in a lightning-fast move.

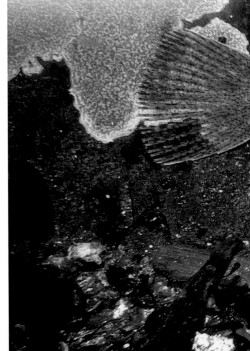

vetulus) is similarly fished from British Columbia down to California.

Among the Asian species the pelican flounder (*Chascanopsetta lugubris*) of the family Bothidae is one of the more unusual-looking food species. It grows to nearly 16 inches (40 cm) and occurs at depths of between 200 and 3,300 feet (60–1,000 m). It has a large mouth with a saclike throat, hence the name pelican. This huge gape allows it to feed on large prey.

The above is a small selection of the many species of flatfish that are consumed in various regions. Though markets and demands may vary, the vast majority of these fish are sold either fresh or frozen. Some, though, are dried, salted, or ground into fishmeal, while a few, such as the butter sole (*Isopsetta isolepis*) and the American Dover sole, are also sold for feeding to captive-reared mink on fur farms.

Lefteyes and Righteyes Compared

Apart from the fact that the lefteye and righteye flounders can, with few exceptions, be told apart—depending on which side of the head the eyes are located—there appear to be few other easily observed differences between the members of these families. Indeed, some scientists think that the righteye flounders of the subfamily Pleuronectinae resemble the lefteye flounders more closely than they do the members of the other subfamilies within their own family.

The fact is that at first sight, members of both the lefteye and righteye families look remarkably similar and share similar lifestyles. For example, the dorsal fin in both starts far forward on the body, above or in front of the eyes. They also both have their dorsal and anal fins quite separate from the tail, and so on.

Indeed, it is only when we start looking at smaller details, like the presence or absence of oil globules in the eggs and relative lengths of the pelvic fins, that distinct differences begin to appear. It is not surprising, therefore, that opinions differ among scientists on how these families should be identified, or if the subfamily of righteye flounders, which contains the European plaice, the halibuts, and around 40 other species, are really righteye flounders or special types of lefteye flounder.

⊕ *The dab* (Limanda limanda) *feeds largely on crustaceans and small fish, and can be found at depths down to 490 feet (150 m). It is native to the northeast Atlantic and the Baltic Sea.*

Longhorn cowfish (*Lactoria cornuta*)

Common name Boxfish and cowfish

Subfamilies Aracaninae, Ostraciinae

Family Ostraciidae (sometimes called Ostraciontidae)

Order Tetraodontiformes

Number of species 37 in 12 genera

Size 4.3 in (11 cm) to 21.7 in (55 cm)

Key features Body cubical or slightly longer and angular, encased in bony carapace or "shell" covered in thin, fleshy tissue; mouth small and partly beaklike; forehead may have hornlike projections; eyes located high on head; single dorsal fin placed well back on body, lacks hard spines; no pelvic skeleton or pelvic fins; coloration extremely variable and often bright: ranging from almost yellow all over to green with blue spots to deep-based colors highlighted with light spots

Breeding Most species have harem system of single male and several females; eggs released into water (often at dusk) and abandoned; hatching takes about 2 days

Diet Bottom-living invertebrates; also seagrasses

Habitat Mainly shallow-water reefs; some species found in seagrass meadows or sand, rocks, or rubble; Aracaninae members prefer deeper waters down to 660 ft (200 m)

Distribution Tropical, subtropical, and sometimes temperate regions of Atlantic, Indian, and Pacific Oceans

Status Not threatened

⊙ *The 18-inch (46-cm) longhorn cowfish (Lactoria cornuta) is found in the Red Sea east to Polynesia and north to Japan. It inhabits weedy areas near rocks or reefs at depths of between 60 and 330 feet (18–100 m).*

Boxfish and Cowfish

Ostraciidae

Boxfish and cowfish have some odd characteristics, with rigid, boxlike bodies and often horns attached. They also have a built-in ability to poison themselves.

THE BOXFISH AND COWFISH, ALONG with trunkfish, turretfish, and basketfish, form the family Ostraciidae. Strictly marine fish, they are most frequently encountered on shallow, tropical coral reefs, rubble areas, and seagrass meadows. Not all species are tropical or subtropical; the 8-inch (20-cm) striped cowfish (*Aracana aurita*) from southern Australian waters and the smaller *Kentrocapros aculeatus* from the western North Pacific are found in temperate waters down to 655 feet (200 m). The latter species, occurring at depths between 330 and 655 feet (100–200m), is therefore a strictly cold-water species.

Food Fish with a Health Warning
Some larger boxfish are excellent food fish, although several have been linked to ciguatera poisoning, caused by eating contaminated fish. Every year around 50,000 people are affected by severe digestive system problems, but the death rate is very low (less than 1 percent).

Comical Creatures
Most boxfish and cowfish attract interest because of their coloration, unusual body features (such as unfishlike "horns"), rigid boxlike body, and "comical" swimming style—all perfectly normal if you are a boxfish.

This comical effect is caused by restrictions enforced on the fish by their hard, inflexible body armor that does not let them bend or use their tail to propel themselves forward, as other fish do. Instead, they swim with their unpaired dorsal and anal fins, use their pectoral fins to balance themselves (they have no pelvic fins), and steer with their maneuverable tail.

⊙ *The hornlike projections and brightly colored scales of this longhorn cowfish (Lactoria cornuta) make it an attractive fish for the home aquarist, but at 18 inches (45 cm) in length it may grow too large for the tank.*

Toxic Boxes

Boxfish and their relatives are popular among aquarists because of their swimming style and shapes. But species like the longhorn cowfish (*Lactoria cornuta*), the yellow, black-spotted, polkadot, or cube boxfish (*Ostracion cubicus*), and the spotted, white-spotted, blue-spotted, or Pacific boxfish (*O. meleagris*) all grow too large, from 10 to 18 inches (25–45 cm).

More dramatically, they release a toxin (ostracitoxin) into the water if they are alarmed. In the wild this poison is unpleasant for other fish and, at worst, lethal—not even the boxfish themselves are immune. On a reef it can defend itself with this poison and can swim away, but in an aquarium the toxins can kill not only the other tank occupants but themselves as well.

⬿ *A spotted boxfish (Ostracion meleagris) can defend itself by releasing toxins into the water as a deterrent.*

Valentinni's sharpnose puffer (*Canthigaster valentini*)

Common name Puffers and porcupinefish

Families Triodontidae (three-toothed puffer or pursefish), Tetraodontidae (puffers), Diodontidae (porcupinefish or burrfish)

Subfamilies Tetraodontidae: Tetraodontinae, Canthigastrinae

Order Tetraodontiformes

Number of species Triodontidae: 1 in 1 genus; Tetraodontidae: 176 in 27 genera; Diodontidae: 20 in 7 genera

Size From 1.6 in (4 cm) to 48 in (1.2 m)

Key features Body elongated, almost spherical if inflated; roundly pointed snout, mouth at tip; fused jaw teeth project into beaklike structure: 2 fused teeth (porcupinefish), 3 (three-toothed puffer), 4 (other puffers); eyes high on head; body scaleless or short, pricklelike scales along belly (puffers), sharp spines (porcupinefish); belly with large purselike sac (three-toothed puffer); dorsal and anal fins set well back on body; no pelvic fins; coloration: variable, often brilliant, with spots and patches (puffers); belly "purse" has yellow ring circling prominent black "eye spot"; darker and lighter shades of brown (porcupinefish)

Breeding Spawn in groups in shallow nests in shallow beach areas after new and full moon; freshwater species spawn in pairs, male guards eggs or fry; eggs hatch in under 2 days or up to a month depending on species; planktonic larvae

Diet Invertebrates; also sea urchins, starfish, soft-bodied invertebrates, or other fish, and plants

Habitat Mostly marine: tropical or subtropical; or fresh brackish water; fine-grained to rocky bottoms; shallow water down to 1,000 ft (300 m)

Distribution Atlantic, Indian, and Pacific Oceans

Status IUCN lists blunthead puffer (*Sphoeroides pachygaster*) and Rapa sharpnose puffer (*Canthigaster rapaensis*) as Vulnerable

⬆ *This 4.3-inch (11-cm) Valentinni's sharpnose puffer* (Canthigaster valentini) *lives among coral in lagoons and reefs.*

Puffers and Porcupinefish

Triodontidae, Tetraodontidae, Diodontidae

When under attack, a puffer will inflate itself, making it extremely hard to swallow. The porcupinefish can do the same, but it is also covered in spines, making it an even more awkward mouthful.

THE PUFFERS AND PORCUPINEFISH, OR BURRFISH, are a group of nearly 200 species that belong to three closely related families—Diotontidae, Triodontidae, and Tetraoclontidae—which easily can be separated on the basis of their teeth.

A Question of Teeth

The Diodontidae have two fused jaw teeth ("di" means two), the Triodontidae three ("tri"), and the Tetraodontidae have four ("tetra").

The teeth of all families form a beaklike structure—a single fused tooth in the upper jaw and one in the lower jaw for porcupinefish (*Diodon* species); two fused teeth in the upper jaw separated by a suture (groove) in the three-toothed puffer (*Triodon macropterus*); and two fused teeth in each jaw, separated by a central suture in other puffers (family Tetraodontidae).

Dangerous Delicacies

In Japan there are establishments, called Fugu Restaurants, that specialize in pufferfish cuisine. Large specimens are easily filleted because the fish have certain bones reduced or lacking (especially in four-toothed puffers), no pelvic girdle or fin, and their tasty flesh is very popular.

The restaurants (under license and closely supervised) specialize in one of the 21 species in the genus *Takifugu*. Monitoring is necessary because puffers' internal organs are poisonous, containing a toxin (tetraodotoxin) that can either produce a druglike "high" but is not life-threatening (as in *Takifugu* species) or, in some other puffers, can actually kill people.

➔ *Parts of the Fugu puffer (*Takifugu niphobles*), such as the gonads and other viscera, are poisonous, but the fish is still used in the preparation of Japanese sushi.*

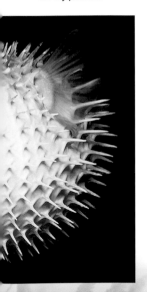

⊕ *If threatened, this blotched porcupinefish* (Diodon liturosus) *takes large gulps of water into its intestines. In a few seconds its body inflates until it is spherical, many times the original size, causing its spines to stand on end—an unwelcome mouthful for any predator.*

Tissues that are toxic can vary from species to species—for example, the skin, flesh, and testes of the torafugu or tiger puffer (*Takifugu rubripes*) are not poisonous, but its intestines, liver, and ovaries are. The smooth puffer's (*Lagocephalus laevigatus*) internal organs and skin are very toxic, as are the gut and muscles of the green puffer (*Tetraodon fluviatilis*).

However, the three-toothed puffer, the sharpnose puffer (*Canthigaster rostrata*), the eyespot or figure-of-eight puffer (*Tetraodon biocellatus*), and many porcupinefish are safe to eat; but the longspine porcupinefish (*Diodon holocanthus*) can cause "ciguatera" poisoning. In this case the fish itself is not toxic (as in tetraodotoxin poisoning) but becomes so if it eats fish or organisms that contain ciguatoxin. Thus it becomes a "carrier" of this poison.

The poisoning process begins at the bottom of the food chain when plant-eating fish eat algae containing ciguatoxin, acquiring some toxin in their tissues and passing it on when they are eaten by fish-eating predators, and so on. At every "link" in the food chain the concentration of ciguatoxin increases.

When people eat a ciguatoxin-containing fish, they have a high chance (73–100 percent) of being poisoned. In severe cases victims can die—fatalities range from 0.1 to 12 percent. In certain regions of the world the death rate is closer to 1 percent.

Species such as groupers (family Serranidae), moray eels (family Muraenidae), snappers (family Lutjanidae), and barracuda (family Sphyraenidae) are other fish that can also cause ciguatera poisoning.

Aquarium Favorites

The beaklike teeth of puffers and porcupinefish are linked to powerful jaw muscles that can act as an efficient crushing tool. In terms of their day-to-day survival the beak allows puffers to tackle tough-shelled foods such as snails, other mollusks, and crustaceans.

In species like the figure-of-eight puffer, the freshwater or giant puffer (*Tetraodon mbu*), and the green puffer their appetite for snails is used by aquarists to clear tanks of snail infestations.

However, their slow, unusual swimming movements, "dumpy" body shape, large eyes, and attractive body patterns make some puffer species popular among aquarists, such as the Malabar puffer (*Carinotetraodon travancoricus*). —the smallest puffer at 1.6 inches (4 cm)—the figure-of-eight puffer, the mosaic or ocellated puffer (*T. cutcutia*), the spotted Congo puffer (*T. schoutedeni*), and the red-bellied or redeye puffer (*C. lorteti*), ranging from 2.4 to 6 inches (6–15 cm) long. Even the giant puffer, growing to 26.4 inches (67 cm) in the wild, is popular.

Among marine species peaceful puffers like the sharpnose puffers (genus *Canthigaster*) and some *Arothron* species are popular. Sharpnoses are small (under 6 inches,15 cm), but the clown toado (*C. callisterna*) exceeds 9 inches (23 cm). *Arothron* species are much larger; the more colorful ones, like the dogface or black-spotted puffer (*A. nigropunctatus*), guineafowl puffer (*A. meleagris*), and white-spotted puffer (*A. hispidus*), are "substantial"—13 inches (33 cm) for the dogface, 20 inches (50 cm) for the other two. The giant of all puffers, the starry puffer or toadfish (*A. stellatus*), is 48 inches (120 cm).

Ocean sunfish (*Mola mola*)

Common names Molas

Family Molidae

Order Tetraodontiformes

Number of species 4 in 3 genera

Size 40 in (1 m) to 11 ft (3.3 m)

Key features Scaleless body relatively compressed (i.e., flattened side to side), almost circular, but slightly elongated in some species; head rounded; small mouth with 2 fused jaw teeth; tiny nostrils on each side of head; eyes small; gill slits are small openings at base of pectoral fins; no pelvic fins or true caudal fin; dorsal and anal fins long and spineless; pseudo-tail formed from last rays of dorsal and anal fins; coloration: drab bluish-brown on back, fading to lighter shades down sides and along belly; brighter in some species

Breeding Vast numbers of small eggs produced, especially by large female *M. mola* (300 million or more); eggs and sperm scattered in open water, then abandoned; larvae with body spines that initially increase in number and are later absorbed

Diet Mainly jellyfish and other soft-bodied invertebrates; also crustaceans, sea urchins, fish, and seaweed

Habitat Open sea, usually close to surface; some species dive deeper, from 900 ft (300 m) down to 2,200 ft (760 m)

Distribution Tropical, subtropical, and warm temperate regions worldwide

Status Not threatened

⊕ *The 11-foot (3.3-m) ocean sunfish (Mola mola) drifts at the surface while lying on its side or swims upright with its dorsal fin projecting above the water. It is believed the mola is the heaviest bony fish, up to 5,070 lb (2,300 kg), and with the most eggs (300 million).*

Molas

Molas look unfinished, with no true tail fin, but they have existed for over 12 million years. These gentle giants enjoy cruising surface waters and "sunbathing."

APPEARANCES CAN BE DECEPTIVE. OTHERWISE molas (or ocean sunfish) would not have been swimming in prehistoric oceans, as their earliest fossils prove. What is important is not what the fish looks like but how well suited it is for survival in its natural element. In this molas score high.

Tail of a Sunfish

When very young, during larval stages, four species, such as the slender sunfish (*Ranzania laevis*) and the ocean sunfish (*Mola mola*), have a true, though primitive, tail. As the fish develop to adulthood, the tail is absorbed and gradually replaced with a pseudo-tail (clavus).

The large dorsal and anal fins (located well back on the body), as well as the clavus, can propel the molas forward at some speed if necessary, although mostly they are used to move these large fish gently through the open ocean waters where they spend their lives.

Giant "Puffers"

Ocean sunfish look very different from pufferfish (families Triodontidae and Tetraodontidae) and porcupinefish (family Diodontidae). Yet they are related and belong to the same order—the Tetraodontiformes. The main characteristics that link them are their teeth and their larvae. For example, all have fused jaw teeth: two in the sunfish, two in the Diodontidae, three in the Triodontidae, and four in the Tetraodontidae.

In addition, the larvae show that they are related to the boxfish (family Ostraciidae). Mola larvae have spines on their bodies, the number increasing as the larvae develop. At an early stage they carry four body spines (also typical of puffers and porcupinefish). Later the number of spines increases, and they are distributed around the body (as in boxfish). As the larvae

① This ocean sunfish (Mola mola) is escorted by three pilot fish (Naucrates ductor) hoping to feed on scraps from this giant fish's food, but taking care to keep out of its way.

change into recognizable miniature sunfish, they leave their puffer-boxfish ancestry behind as they grow up to 11 feet (3.3 m) and weigh nearly 5,070 pounds (2,300 kg), like molas.

Gentle Sunbathers

For all their size and weight, ocean sunfish are gentle creatures that spend much of their time slowly cruising the surface layers of the world's tropical, subtropical, and warm temperate oceans. Often they lie on their side, looking as if they are dead or dying. While that may be true for some older or injured specimens, this unusual behavior is also typical of perfectly healthy individuals. They create an impression that they are "sunbathing," which may be why all four species are called "sunfish."

Despite its tendency to swim close to the surface, the ocean sunfish (also called giant sunfish, mola ocean sunfish, or headfish) can dive to over 900 feet (300 m). The sharptail sunfish (*Masturus lanceolatus*) goes even deeper—down to 2,200 feet (670 m).

Small Mouth

With its two fused teeth and small mouth the ocean sunfish feeds on jellyfish, free-swimming crustaceans, squid, mollusks, and plankton, as well as sea urchins and seaweed. The truncated slender sunfish (*Ranzania laevis*) eats mainly free-swimming crustaceans. In their turn juvenile ocean sunfish fall prey to larger fish and sea lions, while tuna (*Thunnus* species) and shark (class Chondrichthyes) eat larger molas.

Glossary

Words in SMALL CAPITALS refer to other entries in the glossary.

Abbreviated heterocercal term used to describe a HETEROCERCAL TAIL in which the upper lobe is less extended than in a typical heterocercal tail
Adaptation features of an organism that adjust it to its environment; NATURAL SELECTION favors the survival of individuals whose adaptations fit them to their surroundings better than other individuals
Adipose fin fatty fin located behind rayed DORSAL FIN in some fish
Adult fully grown animal that has reached breeding age
Agonistic any activity, aggressive or submissive, related to fighting
Air bladder see SWIM BLADDER
Ammocete larva filter-feeding lamprey LARVA
Ampullae of Lorenzini jelly-filled tubes on the head of sharks and relatives; responsible for detecting weak electrical impulses
Anadromous term describing a SPECIES that spends part of its life in the sea and part in freshwater habitats
Anal fin FIN located near the anus
Appendicula outgrowths from the umbilical cord of some sharks; appendicula enhance an embryo's ability to absorb UTERINE MILK
Aquatic associated with, or living in, water
Arborescent organ treelike modifications of GILL tissues found in air-breathing species like walking catfish
Atriopore small aperture in lancelets corresponding to the atrial, or exhalant, SIPHON in sea squirts

Barbel whiskerlike, filamentous sensory growth on the jaws of some fish, including catfish
Benthic occurring, or living, on the bottom
Brackish water water that contains salt in sufficient quantities to distinguish it from fresh water but not enough to make it sea water; brackish water is found in estuaries, mangrove swamps, and other habitats where fresh water and sea water mix
Branchiostegal rays flattish, riblike bones located ventrally behind the GILL covers and making up the floor of the gill chamber
Brood offspring of a single birth or clutch of eggs
Brood pouch structure formed from FINS or plates of a parent fish in which fertilized eggs are placed to hatch safely
Bubble nest nest of bubbles that harbors eggs or offspring of some fish

Camouflage markings or features of a creature that aid concealment
Carnivore creature whose diet consists exclusively of other animals
Cartilaginous formed of cartilage
Catadromous term describing a SPECIES that migrates from fresh water to the sea for spawning
Caudal fin "tail" FIN
Caudal peduncle part of the body where the tail begins
Caudodorsal term describing an extension of the CAUDAL FIN onto the back of the body; this fin contains RAYS but no spines; caudodorsal fins are found in catfish of the family Plotosidae
Cephalic shield head shield formed by bony plates, as found in upside-down catfish
Cephalofoil term used to describe the "'hammer" of hammerhead sharks; thought to provide lift and maneuverability
Cerebellum part of the hindbrain involved in the coordinated activity of muscles, posture, and movement
Cerebral hemispheres pair of symmetrical, rounded, convoluted tissue masses that form the largest part of the brain in many organisms, e.g., mammals
Chordata PHYLUM of animals having a single, hollow dorsal nerve cord, a NOTOCHORD, GILL SLITS, and a postanal tail; some of these characteristics may only be present in the earliest stages of development
Chromatophore pigment-containing cell whose shape or color can be altered
Chromosome tiny, rod-shaped structure in the cell NUCLEUS; chromosomes contain DNA, which carries genetic information
Cilium (*pl.* **cilia**) tiny, hairlike structure growing out from the surface of some cells; cilia are capable of whiplike actions and can facilitate movement
Cirrus (*pl.* **cirri**) hairlike or tentaclelike growth, e.g., as found on the nostrils, supraorbital area, and nose in some blennies
CITES Convention on International Trade in Endangered Species; an agreement between nations that restricts international trade to permitted levels through licensing and administrative controls; rare animals and plants are assigned categories
Claspers structures between the PELVIC FINS of male cartilaginous fish that allow them to clasp a female during mating, and that facilitate the transfer of sperm
Class taxonomic level below PHYLUM and above ORDER
Cloaca single chamber into which anal, urinary, and genital ducts (canals) open
Clone identical cell or individual derived from a single cell, e.g., an egg
Community all the animals and plants that live together in a HABITAT
Compressed term used to describe a structure that is flattened from side to side
Cone cone-shaped light-sensitive cell in the retina of the eye; cones are particularly sensitive to colors (see ROD)

Copepoda subclass of small crustaceans, some of which are parasitic; copepods do not have a hard carapace (shell) but have a single, centrally placed eye
Cosmoid scale type of SCALE found in many fossil and some primitive fish
Countershading color distribution seen in many fish in which the back is darker than the belly
Crepuscular active at twilight
Cryptic coloration camouflage-type coloration that helps organisms blend in with their surroundings; some species are cryptically colored at all times, while others, e.g., many squirrelfish, are cryptic during the day and more brightly colored at night
Ctenoid scale similar to the CYCLOID SCALE but with a toothed posterior edge rather than a smooth or wavy (crenulated) one
Cusp point or prominence, often on a tooth
Cycloid scale thin, flexible overlapping scale, roughly the shape of a human finger nail, found in modern bony fish and the primitive bowfin (*Amia calva*); the front edge of each scale is embedded in a special pouch in the surface of the skin; the back edge is free and smooth or wavy (crenulated) but not toothed as in CTENOID SCALES

Dendritic finely branched
Denticle small, toothlike scale found in sharks and some of their closest relatives (see PLACOID SCALE)
Depressed term used to describe a structure that is flattened from top to bottom
Detritus debris consisting of fragments of dead plants and animals
Dimorphism existence of two distinct forms
Dioecious having separate sexes (see HERMAPHRODITE)
Display any fairly conspicuous pattern of behavior that conveys specific information to others, usually to members of the same species; often associated with "courtship" but also in other activities, e.g., threat displays
Diurnal active during the day
DNA (deoxyribonucleic acid) the substance that makes up the main part of the chromosomes of all living things; DNA is the carrier of genetic information
Dorsal relating to the upper surface
Dorsal fin(s) FIN(S) on the back of a fish

Electrocyte electricity-generating cell, usually consisting of a modified muscle cell
Electroplaque stack or column of ELECTROCYTES; also referred to as electroplates
Endangered species SPECIES whose POPULATION has fallen to such a low level that it is at risk of EXTINCTION
Endemic term used to describe a SPECIES that is found in just one country or area

Endostyle longitudinal mucus-secreting groove found in the pharynx of sea squirts and relatives, lancelets, and lamprey LARVAE
Endothermic term used to describe animals that can generate internal body heat, e.g., mammals, birds, and certain fish like large tunas or some species of sharks
Erectile capable of being raised
Esca modified fleshy tissue on the tip of the first RAY of the DORSAL FIN (ILICIUM) in marine anglerfish; the esca resembles a small piece of "bait" that, when waved in the water, attracts PREY toward the anglerfish
Estivation dormancy or torpor during summer periods of heat and drought
Evolution development of living things by gradual changes in their characteristics as a result of MUTATION
Exotic term used to describe a SPECIES that is found in locations outside its natural distribution range, usually as a result of intentional or accidental introduction
Extant term used to describe SPECIES that are still in existence
Extinct term used to describe SPECIES that are no longer in existence
Extinction complete dying out of a SPECIES

Falcate sickle-shaped, as in the PECTORAL FINS of thresher sharks
Family group of closely related SPECIES, e.g., piranhas) or a pair of fish and their offspring
Fin winglike or paddlelike organ attached to certain parts of the body of a fish or other aquatic animals and used for steering, locomotion, and balance
Fontanel space or gap between some bones of the skull
Food chain sequence in which one organism becomes food for another, which in turn is eaten by another
Fry young fish
Fusiform body shape that tapers at both ends, i.e., spindle shaped

Ganoid scale SCALE found in most extinct ray-finned fish (Actinopterygii) consisting of a thick enamel-like layer underlaid by a dentine layer and a basal bony layer
Genus (*pl.* **genera**) group of closely related SPECIES
Gill organ by which a fish absorbs dissolved oxygen from the water and gets rid of carbon dioxide
Gill raker bristlelike extensions on the gill arches of filter-feeding fish; used for trapping suspended food particles in the water as it passes from the mouth via the GILLS and, subsequently, to the exterior through the GILL SLITS
Gill slit slit between the GILLS that allows water through
Gonopodium modified ANAL FIN of male LIVEBEARERS used to inseminate females

Habitat place where an animal or plant lives

Harem breeding "unit" consisting of a single male and several females, as in boxfish

Hemoglobin pigment that gives blood its red color; hemoglobin is used to carry oxygen around the body

Herbivore animal whose diet consists exclusively of plants

Hermaphrodite organism having both male and female reproductive organs

Heterocercal term used to describe a tail (CAUDAL FIN) in which the upper lobe contains the tip of the vertebral column (backbone); in such fins the upper lobe is usually considerably larger than the lower lobe

Holotype specimen on which the scientific description of a SPECIES is based; also referred to as the TYPE SPECIMEN

Hybrid offspring of a mating between two different SPECIES

Hydrostatic organ organ used in controlling flotation or buoyancy

Hypertrophy excessive growth as a result of an increase in cell size

Hypocercal term used to describe a tail (CAUDAL FIN) in which the lower lobe contains the end tip of the NOTOCHORD; in such fins the ventral (lower) lobe is usually larger than the dorsal (upper) one

Ichthyologist scientist specializing in the study of fish

Ilicium first modified ray of the DORSAL FIN in marine anglerfish, usually located on top of the head and bearing a fleshy tip (ESCA) used to lure unsuspecting victims toward the waiting anglerfish

Inferior mouth mouth located below the snout

Interoperculum bone joined anteriorly to the preoperculum and posteriorly to the interoperculum ligament, which, in turn, is connected to the OPERCULUM (gill cover)

Introduced describes a species that has been brought from places where it occurs naturally to places where it has not previously occurred

Invertebrate general term used to describe an animal that lacks a backbone

IUCN International Union for the Conservation of Nature, responsible for assigning animals and plants to internationally agreed categories of rarity (see table beow)

Juvenile young animal that has not reached breeding age

Krill tiny, shrimplike crustacean

Labyrinth organ respiratory organ found in gouramis and their relatives; formed from modified GILLS and housed in a chamber in the top of the gill cavity

Larva first stage of some fish SPECIES; newly hatched INVERTEBRATE

Lateral relating to the sides

Lateral line organ series of small fluid-filled pits linked to tubes that, in turn, are linked to a common canal; the lateral line detects movements (vibrations) in the water

Leptocephalus elongate, highly compressed, ribbonlike LARVAL stage of some fish such as eels

Livebearer SPECIES in which males introduce sperm into the body of the female, resulting in internal fertilization; developing embryos are generally retained by the female until birth

Macula neglecta part of the inner ear of sharks and related fish; important in sound perception

Melanoblast cell in which melanin (dark pigment) is formed

Mermaid's purse term used to describe the hard, leathery egg cases of sharks, skates, and rays

Metamorphosis changes undergone by an animal as it develops from the embryonic to the ADULT stage

Microphthalmic having tiny eyes

Migration movement of animals from one part of the world to another at different times of year to reach food or find a place to breed

Milt fluid containing male sperm

Monotype sole member of a GENUS

Monotypic GENUS or FAMILY that contains a single SPECIES

Mouthbrooder SPECIES in which the eggs are incubated in the mouth of one or other of the parents, according to species; FRY may also be protected this way

Mutation change in the genetic material (DNA) that, in turn, results in a change in a particular characteristic of an individual cell or organism

Nape the back of the neck

Naris (*pl.* **nares**) alternative word for nostril(s)

Nasopharyngeal duct nasal opening (nostril) in hagfish; also called the nasohypophysial opening

Natural selection process whereby individuals with the most appropriate ADAPTATIONS survive to produce offspring

Nematocyst stinging cell of sea anemones, jellyfish, and their relatives

Neoteny retention of larval characteristics into the sexually mature adult stage

Neural spine bone extension on the upper (dorsal) surface of individual vertebrae (back bones)

Niche part of a HABITAT occupied by a SPECIES, defined in terms of all aspects of its lifestyle (e.g., food, competitors, PREDATORS, and other resource requirements)

Nocturnal active at night

Notochord "rod" of cells along the back during the early stages of embryonic development in chordates; the notochord is replaced by the spinal column in all but the most primitive chordates

Nucleus dark, dense structure found in living cells of higher animals and plants, e.g., not in bacteria; the nucleus contains the CHROMOSOMES, which, in turn, contain genetic information in the form of DNA

Nuptial tubercle small, whitish, pimplelike growth developed by males during the breeding season, usually on the snout, head, cheeks and PECTORAL FINS; nuptial tubercles are known in at least 25 families of fish

Olfactory relating to the sense of smell

Olfactory bulb outgrowth from part of the lower anterior margin of the brain; responsible for detecting smells; also known as the OLFACTORY LOBE

Olfactory lobe see OLFACTORY BULB

Olfactory sac highly folded "chamber" in front of the OLFACTORY BULB; sensitive to smells

Omnivore animal whose diet includes both animals and plants

Operculum bone forming the gill cover in fish

Orbital relating to the eyes

Order level of taxonomic ranking

Organ of Hunter organ consisting of ELECTROCYTES that generate powerful electric pulses

Organ of Sachs organ consisting of ELECTROCYTES that are capable of generating weak electric pulses

Osmoregulation control of water balance in the body

Osmosis passage of molecules from a less concentrated to a more concentrated solution through a semipermeable membrane

Otolith grain of calcium carbonate in the semicircular canals of the ear; vital for balance

Oviparity egg laying; eggs and sperm are usually released into the environment and external fertilization takes place; in sharks the term is retained, but fertilization is internal

Ovipositor breeding tube extended by a female to place her eggs in a precise location

Palate roof of the mouth

Papilla (*pl.* **papillae**) small, usually cone-shaped projection

Parallel evolution development of similarities in separate but related evolutionary lineages through the operation of similar selective factors

Parasite organism that derives its food, for part or the whole of its life, from another living organism (belonging to a different SPECIES); parasites usually harm the organism on which they feed (the host)

Parasphenoid long, ridgelike bone with two side "arms"; located on the underside of the skull; this bone forms the "crucifix" in the crucifix fish (*Arius* spp.)

Pectoral fin one of the paired FINS connected to the pectoral girdle

Pelvic fin one of the paired FINS connected to the pelvic girdle

Pharyngeal slit alternative term for GILL SLIT

Pharyngeal teeth teeth located in the throat area and used primarily for grinding or crushing food

Pheromone substance released by an animal in tiny quantities and detected by another of the same SPECIES

Photophore luminous organ possessed by many deepwater bony and cartilaginous fish

IUCN CATEGORIES

EX Extinct, when there is no reasonable doubt that the last individual of a species has died.

EW Extinct in the Wild, when a species is known only to survive in captivity or as a naturalized population well outside the past range.

CR Critically Endangered, when a species is facing an extremely high risk of extinction in the wild in the immediate future.

EN Endangered, when a species faces a very high risk of extinction in the wild in the near future.

VU Vulnerable, when a species faces a high risk of extinction in the wild in the medium-term future.

LR Lower Risk (before 2001)/**NT Near Threatened** (since 2001), when a species has been evaluated and does not satisfy the criteria for CR, EN, or VU.

LC Least Concern (since 2001), when an animal has been evaluated and does not qualify for CR, EN, VU, LR, or NT.

DD Data Deficient, when there is not enough information about a species to assess the risk of extinction.

NE Not Evaluated, species that have not been assessed by the IUCN criteria.

Phylum (*pl.* **phyla**) group of animals whose basic or general plan is similar and that share an evolutionary relationship, e.g., the Chordata

Phytoplankton see PLANKTON

Piscivore animal whose diet consists exclusively of fish

Placenta spongy, blood-rich tissue found in mammals and some fish, such as livebearing sharks, by which oxygen and nutrients are supplied to—and waste products are removed from—embryos during development

Placoid scale small toothlike SCALE, often referred to as a DENTICLE, found in sharks; it consists of a bonelike basal part embedded in the skin and a backward-directed free, pointed border or spine covered in an enamel-like substance; placoid scales do not increase in size as the shark grows; instead, they are replaced throughout life

Plankton term used to describe the generally minute animals (zooplankton) and plants (phytoplankton) that drift in marine and fresh water

Plica fold or wrinkle, e.g., on the skin or a membrane

Poikilothermic term used to describe animals whose body temperature matches that of the environment, e.g., most fish, amphibians, and reptiles; such animals are frequently—but inaccurately—referred to as cold-blooded

Polyp individual animal making up a colony, as in corals; polyps have a tubular body, usually topped by a tentacle-ringed mouth, giving the animal the appearance of a miniature sea anemone

Polyploidy process by which cells possess three or more full sets of chromosomes

Population distinct group of animals of the same SPECIES or all the animals of that species

Postanal tail tail whose base originates behind the anus

Predator animal that hunts and kills other animals for food

Preoperculum anterior bone of the gill cover

Prey animal hunted for food

Proboscis elongated trunklike snout or projection

Protandrous hermaphrodite hermaphrodite that goes through a male phase before becoming a female

Protogynous hermaphrodite hermaphrodite that goes through a female phase before becoming a male

Protractile describes any structure that can be lengthened by, e.g., being pushed out, as spiny-finned fish are able to do with their mouths

Race see SUBSPECIES

Radial muscle muscle associated with the FIN RAYS of the head (known as radials)

Range geographical area over which an organism is distributed

Ray small spine that acts as a support for the FIN membrane

Recruitment addition of new individuals to a population, usually by reproduction or by inward migration from another population

Refractive index degree by which light rays are "bent" as they pass from one medium to another, e.g., from air to water

Rete mirabile dense network of blood vessels found in certain animals; heat exchange can occur between blood across this network allowing, e.g., some sharks to retain body heat and maintain their internal temperature at a higher level than that of the surrounding water

Retina inner, light-sensitive layer of the eye on which images are formed

Reverse countershading type of color distribution seen in fish SPECIES that habitually swim upside down, e.g., some members of the Mochokidae; in these fish the belly is darker than the back, i.e., it shows the opposite color distribution found in normally COUNTERSHADED fish

Rod rod-shaped light-sensitive cell in the retina of the eye; rods are particularly sensitive to discerning shapes, especially in dim light (see CONE)

Rostral associated with a snout or ROSTRUM

Rostrum snout

Rugosity term used to describe rough or wrinkled tissue

Scale one of the usually tough, flattish plates that form part of the external covering of most fish species

Scatophagous term used to describe an animal that feeds on waste materials like sewage or feces; best-known fish exhibiting this trait are the scats

Scute platelike, modified scales found in some fish, including catfish

Semicircular canal fluid-filled canal in the inner ear; semicircular canals are set at right angles to each other, contain OTOLITHS, and are essential in maintaining body balance

Shell gland gland possessed by female sharks, skates, and rays; responsible for secreting the outer egg casing known as a MERMAID'S PURSE

Siphon funnel-shaped structure through which water can be taken in (inhalant) or discharged (exhalant)

Spawn eggs of a fish; the act of producing eggs

Species a POPULATION or series of populations that interbreed freely but not normally with other species

Specific gravity (**SG**) "weight," or density, of a liquid compared with pure water at 39.2° F (4° C); pure water has an SG value of 1.000, while the SG of seawater is around 1.020

Spiracle porelike opening associated with the GILLS

Spiral valve spiral infolding of the intestinal wall in primitive fish like sharks and rays

Standard length (**SL**) length of a fish measured from the tip of the snout to the CAUDAL PEDUNCLE

Stridulation vibration or rubbing together of two surfaces to produce a sound; in fish it usually refers to rubbing together of bones or fin spines, e.g., in some filefish and triggerfish

Stripping removal of eggs and sperm from ripe fish by the application of gentle pressure along the abdomen

Suborbital located under the orbit, or eye socket

Subphylum grouping of organisms sharing a number of characteristics in addition to those shared by members of a PHYLUM; examples of a subphylum are the sea squirts and relatives (Urochordata) and the backboned animals (VERTEBRATA), which together form the phylum CHORDATA

Subspecies subdivision of a SPECIES that is distinguishable from the rest of that species; often called a RACE

Substrate bottom of an aquatic HABITAT

Subterminal located underneath the end or tip, e.g., a subterminal mouth is one located underneath the tip of the snout

Suprabranchial chamber cavity or space above the gill chamber; the suprabranchial chamber houses the suprabranchial organ, i.e., modified gill tissues used by air-breathing fish, such as walking catfish

Supraorbital located above the orbit, or eye socket

Suture line along which two or more bones are immovably joined, as in the skull

Swim bladder gas-filled sac found in the body cavity of most bony fish; the amount of gas in the swim bladder can be regulated, allowing the fish to rise or sink in the water

Symbiosis relationship between two unrelated organisms from which both parties benefit, e.g., the light-producing bacteria that flashlight fish have in special cheek pouches (light organs); organisms that live in this manner are referred to as symbionts

Symphysis junction between the left and right sides of the jaw, i.e., where both bones meet and fuse at the front

Tapetum lucidum layer of light-reflecting tissue located under the retina; it amplifies the amount of light entering the eye and assists vision under poor light conditions

Taxonomy studying, naming, and grouping of living organisms; also termed classification

Tendril entwining, fiberlike extension on some shark and ray egg cases that allows the eggs to attach themselves to underwater objects like seaweeds

Terminal located at the end or tip, e.g., a terminal mouth is one located at the tip of the snout

Territory area that an animal or animals consider their own and defend against others

Thermocline zone between warm surface water and colder deeper layers

Tholichthys term used to describe the young of certain fish, notably the scats, for a period after hatching; these larvae have large heads in relation to the body and protective bony plates and spines

Thoracic describes the area in or around the chest (thorax)

Thunniform swimming swimming technique in which the tail beats rapidly from side to side, but the body remains rigid; this type of swimming is found in tunas

Tonic immobility trancelike state or hypnosis exhibited by many animals, including some sharks and their relatives

Total length (**TL**) length of a fish measured from the tip of the snout to the tip of the CAUDAL FIN

T-position position adopted by at least some *Corydoras* species during mating, in which the female aligns herself at right angles to her mate's body, with her mouth close to his genital aperture

Truncated term often used to describe a CAUDAL FIN that has a straight, or more-or-less straight, edge

Tubercle small rounded swelling, nodule, or protuberance, as found, e.g., on the body of banjo catfish

Type specimen see HOLOTYPE

Uterine milk nutritious secretions produced in the womb (uterus) of female sharks during pregnancy; developing embryos feed on these secretions

Uterus womb

Variety occasional variation in a species not sufficiently persistent or geographically separate to form a SUBSPECIES

Ventral relating to the underside

Vertebra any of the bones of the spinal column

Vertebrata SUBPHYLUM of the PHYLUM Chordata characterized, especially, by a brain enclosed in a skull (cranium) and having a backbone (vertebral column) enclosing the spinal cord

Viviparity alternative term for LIVEBEARING

Weberian apparatus series of four small bones connecting the swim bladder to the ear in some fish (superorder Ostariophysi), including the catfish

World Conservation Union see IUCN

Yolk sac source of nourishment for some FRY prior to and immediately after hatching

Zooplankton see PLANKTON

Further Reading

Allen, G. R., **Damselfishes of the World.** Melle, Germany: Mergus Publishers Hans A. Baensch, 1991.

_____. **Freshwater Fishes of Australia.** Neptune City, NJ: T. F. H. Publications, Inc., 1989.

Allen, T. B., **The Shark Almanac.** New York: The Lyons Press, 2003.

Bond, C. E., **Biology of Fishes** (2nd edn.). Florence, KY: Brooks/Cole (Thomson Learning), 1996.

Bone, Q., Marshall, N. B., and Blaxter, J. H. S., **Biology of Fishes** (2nd edn.). London/New York: Blackie, 1995.

Burgess, W. E., **An Atlas of Freshwater and Marine Catfishes: A Preliminary Survey of the Siluriformes.** Neptune City, NJ: T. F. H. Publications, Inc., 1989.

Campbell, A., and Dawes, J. (eds.), **The New Encyclopedia of Aquatic Life.** New York: Facts On File, 2004.

Dawes, J., **Complete Encyclopedia of the Freshwater Aquarium.** Richmond Hill, Canada: Firefly Books Ltd., 2001.

_____. **Livebearing Fishes: A Complete Guide to their Aquarium Care, Biology and Classification.** London: Blandford, 1991.

Ebert, D. A., **Sharks, Rays, and Chimaeras of California.** Berkeley, CA: University of California Press, 2003.

Ferraris, C. Jr., **Catfish in the Aquarium.** Morris Plains, NJ: Tetra Press, 1991.

Fort, T., **The Book of Eels.** London: HarperCollins Publishers, 2003.

Garrick-Maidment, N., **Seahorses: Management and Care.** Havant, U.K.: Kingdom Books, 1997.

Gilbert, C. R., and Williams, J. D., **National Audubon Society Field Guide to Fishes.** New York: Alfred A. Knopf, 2002.

Hamlett, W. C. (ed.), **Sharks, Skates, and Rays: The Biology of Elasmobranch Fishes.** Baltimore, MD: The Johns Hopkins University Press, 1999.

Hayward, P., Nelson-Smith, T., and Shields, C., **Collins Pocket Guide to the Sea Shore of Britain and Europe.** London: HarperCollins Publishers, 1996.

Helfman, G. S., Colette, B. B., and Facey, D. E., **The Diversity of Fishes.** Cambridge, MA: Blackwell Scientific Publications, 1997.

Keenleyside, M. H. A. (ed.), **Cichlid Fishes: Behaviour, Ecology and Evolution** (Fish and Fisheries Series 2). London: Chapman and Hall, 1991.

Kempkes, M., and Schäfer, F., **All Livebearers and Halfbeaks: Guppys, Platys, Mollys.** Mörfelden Walldorf, Germany: Verlag A. C. S. GmbH, 1998

Kobayagawa, M., and Burgess, W. E. (eds.), **The World of Catfishes.** Neptune City, NJ: T. F. H. Publications, Inc., 1991.

Kurlansky, M., **Cod: A Biography of the Fish that Changed the World.** Toronto: Vintage, 2003.

Lever, C., **Naturalized Fishes of the World.** San Diego, CA/London: Academic Press, 1996.

Lourie, S. A., Vincent, A. C. J., and Hall, H. J., **Seahorses: An Identification Guide to the World's Species and their Conservation.** London: Project Seahorse, 1999.

Love, R. M., **Probably More than You Want to Know about the Fishes of the Pacific Coast.** Santa Barbara, CA: Really Big Press, 1991.

Meinkoth, N. A., **National Audubon Society Field Guide to North American Seashore Creatures.** New York: Alfred A. Knopf, 1998.

Moriarty, C., **Eels: A Natural and Unnatural History.** Newton Abbott, U.K.: David and Charles, 1978.

Moyle, P. B., and Cech, J. J. Jr., **An Introduction to Ichthyology** (4th edn.). Upper Saddle River, NJ: Prentice-Hall, Inc., 2000.

Nelson, J. S., **Fishes of the World** (3rd edn.). New York: John Wiley & Sons, Inc., 1994.

Ono, R. D., Williams, J. D., and Wagner, A., **Vanishing Fishes of North America.** Washington, DC: Stone Wall Press Inc., 1983.

Page, L. M., and Burr, B. M., **A Field Guide to Freshwater Fishes (North America, North of Mexico)** (Peterson Field Guide Series). Boston, MA: Houghton-Mifflin Co., 1991.

Paxton, J. R., and Eschmeyer, W. N., **Encyclopedia of Fishes** (2nd edn.). San Diego, CA: Academic Press, 1998.

Pecl, K., Hisek, K., and Maly, J., **Fishes of Lakes and Rivers** (Magna Colour Guide). Leicester, U.K.: Magna Books, 1995.

Quinn, J. R., **Piranhas: Fact and Fiction.** Neptune City, NJ: T. F. H. Publications, Inc., 1992.

Reebs, S., **Fish Behavior in the Aquarium and in the Wild.** Ithaca, NY: Cornell University Press, 2001.

Sands, D., **Back to Nature Guide to Catfishes.** Jonsered, Sweden: Fohrman Aquaristik AB, 1997.

Spotte, S., **Captive Seawater Fishes.** New York: John Wiley & Sons, Inc., 1992.

Taylor, L. R. (consultant ed.), **Sharks and Rays: The Ultimate Guide to Underwater Predators.** London: HarperCollins Publishers, 1997.

Thomson, K. S., **Living Fossil: The Story of the Coelacanth.** London: Hutchinson Radius, 1991.

Watson, R., **Salmon, Trout, and Charr of the World: A Fisherman's Natural History.** Shrewsbury, U.K.: Swan Hill Press, 1999.

Wheeler, A., **The Pocket Guide to Freshwater Fishes of Britain and Europe.** Limpsfield, U.K.: Dragon's World, 1992.

_____. **The Pocket Guide to Saltwater Fishes of Britain and Europe.** Limpsfield, U.K.: Dragon's World, 1992.

Winfield, I. J., and Nelson, J. S., **Cyprinid Fishes: Systematics, Biology and Exploitation** (Fish and Fisheries Series 3). London: Chapman and Hall, 1991.

Useful Websites

http://www.asmfc.org/
Detailed information about the American eel. Click on Managed Species and then on American eel.

http://www.elasmo-research.org/
The ReefQuest Center for Shark Research. A very informative site covering all types of elasmobranchs, including chimaeras

http://www.fishbase.org/home.htm
An amazing website full of information even on obscure fish, with copious references to other sources

http://www.gma.org/herring/biology
Fact-packed pages on the official website of the Gulf of Maine Research Institute

http:www.mantaray.com
Closeup encounters with manta rays in Micronesia, including online video

http:www.si.edu/resource/faq/nmnh/fish.htm
A useful list of alternative references for all kinds of fish

http://www.ucd.ie/codtrace/index.htm
Material on cod biology and fisheries from a European-Union-funded project studying Atlantic cod stocks

http:www.ucmp.berkeley.edu/vertebrates/basalfish/chondrintro.html
Covers both living fossil and living species, with good links

Index

Picture credits

Abbreviations
AL Ardea London; BCC Bruce Coleman Collection; C Corbis; FLPA Frank Lane
Picture Agency; NHPA Natural History Photographic Agency; NI Nature's
Images; NPL Naturepl.com; NV Natural Visions; OSF Oxford Scientific Films;
PX Photomax; SPL Science Photo Library; S Seapics.

t = top; **b** = bottom; **c** = center; **l** = left; **r** = right; **i** =inset

Jacket: tl Corbis/Digital Stock; **bc** Ken Usami/Photodisc; **c** Corbis/Digital
Stock; **tr** Ken Usami/Photodisc; **br** Corbis/Digital Stock
Back Cover: Georgette Douwma/Photodisc

Title Pages: Frank and Joyce Burek/Photodisc Denis Scott/Corbis

9 Gibbs, Max/PX; **11** Blair, Jonathan/C; **14** D. Hall; **15** Gibbs, Max/PX; **17**
Gibbs, Max/PX; **19t** Freund, Jurgen/NPL; **19b** Grewcock, D. T./FLPA; **21** Lucas,
Ken/AL; **22-23** Naturbild/NPL; **27** Kuiter, Rudie/OSF; **29** Taylor, Ron/AL; **31t**
Freund, Jurgen/NPL; **31b** Freund, Jurgen/NPL; **32-33** Jeff Rotman; **35t** Rotman,
Jeff/NPL; **35b** Rotman, Jeff/NPL; **37** Rotman, Jeff/NPL; **38-39** Klapfer, Avi &
Rotman, Jeff/NPL; **40-41** Klapfer, Avi & Rotman, Jeff/NPL; **43** McDobald,
Trevor/NHPA; **44-45** Burton, Dan/NPL; **46** Morris, P./AL; **47** Siefert, Douglas
David/AL; **49t** Rotman, Jeff/NPL; **49b** Maufe, Conrad/NPL; **50** Rotman,
Jeff/NPL; **52** Keifner, Ralf /AL; **52-53** Jeff Rotman; **55** S; **57** Lanceau,
Yves/NHPA; **59** Daly, Sue/NPL; **61** Rotman, Jeff/NPL; **63t** Hall, David/NPL; **63b**
Douwma, Georgette /NPL; **64-65** Rotman, Jeff/NPL; **67t** White, Doc/NPL; **67b**
Douwma, Georgette/NPL; **69t** SAIAB; **69b** Plage, Mary/OSF; **70-71** Scoones,
Peter/SPL; **72** Heuclin, Daniel/NHPA; **73** Morris, P./AL; **75** Morris, P./AL; **76-77**
Hartl, Okapia Andreas/OSF; **78-79** Lucas, Ken/AL; **81t** Schafer, Kevin/NHPA;
81b Wu, Norbert/NHPA; **83** Zipp, Jim/AL; **85** Morris, P./AL; **86-87** Gibbs,
Max/PX; **89** Payne Gill, Mark/NPL; **89i** Hall, Howard/OSF; **91** Heuclin,
Daniel/NHPA; **92-93** de Oliveira, Paulo/OSF; **94-95** OSF; **97** Gibbs, Max/PX; **98**
Gibbs, Max/PX; **100** Petrinos, Constantinos/NPL; **101** Foott, Jeff/NPL; **102-103**
OSF; **105** Lucas, Ken/AL; **106-107** Ausloos, Henry/NHPA; **108** Freund,
Jurgen/NPL; **111** Morris, P./AL; **113** Bevan, Brian/AL; **114** Martin, Tim/NPL; **115**
Milkins, Colin OSF; **116** Foto Natura Stock/FLPA; **118-119** Gibbs, Max/PX; **120-**

121 Gibbs, Max/PX; **120i** 11/2/PX; **123l** Gatercole, Peter/OSF; **123r** Gibbs,
Max/PX; **125** NI; **126-127** NI; **129** Gibbs, Max/PX; **131** Morris, P./AL; **132**
Gibbs, Max/PX; **133** Gibbs, Max/PX; **135** Gibbs, Max/PX; **137t** Gibbs, Max/PX;
137b Gibbs, Max/PX; **139** Watson, M./AL; **139i** Gibbs, Max/PX; **140-141**
Gibbs, Max/PX; **142-143** Gibbs, Max/PX; **143** Gibbs, Max/PX; **145** D. Allison;
146b Perry, Philip/FLPA; **146-147** D. Allison; **149t** Deeble, Mark & Stone,
Victoria/OSF; **149b** Gibbs, Max/PX; **150-151**Gibbs, Max/PX; **152-153** A. N.
T./NHPA; **154-155** Watt, Jim/BCC; **157** Reinhard, Hans/BCC; **158-159** Lacz,
Gerard/NHPA; **160-161** Gibbs, Max/PX; **163** Gibbs, Max/PX; **164-165** Martin-
Bahr, Chris/AL; **166-167** Lutra/NHPA; **168** D. Hall; **168-169** Lucas, Ken/AL; **170**
Morris, P./AL; **172-173** A. K. E. Lindau/AL; **175** Morris, P./AL; **176** Swedberg, J.
E./AL; **177** Angel, Heather/NV; **178-179** Angel, Heather/NV; **181** Martin,
Tim/NPL; **182** Cox, Daniel/OSF; **183** Moose Peterson, B./WRP/AL; **184**
Bannister, Anthony/NHPA; **184-185** Clegg, John/AL; **187** Wu, Norbert /NHPA;
188-189 Wu, Norbert/NHPA; **190-191** Angel, Heather/NV; **193l** Wu,
Norbert/NHPA; **193r** White, Doc/NPL; **195** Image Quest 3D/NHPA; **197** Scott,
Sue/OSF; **198-199** OSF; **201** Freund, Jurgen/NPL; **202** Gibbs, Max/PX; **202i**
Morris, P./AL; **204-205** Shale, David/NPL; **208-209** White, Doc/NPL; **210-211**
Wu, Norbert/OSF; **210i** Shale, David/NPL; **212-213** Wu, Norbert/NHPA;
215 Gibbs, Max/PX; **217** Foott, Jeff/NPL; **218** Foott, Jeff/BCC; **219** Webster,
Mark/OSF; **221t** Wisniewski, W./FLPA; **221b** Fox, David/OSF; **222-223** OSF; **223**
Kay, Paul/OSF; **224** Wisniewski, W./FLPA; **227** Gibbs, Max/PX; **228** Gibbs,
Max/PX; **228-229** Freund, Jurgen /NPL; **230-231** Petrinos, Constantinos/NPL;
232-233 Scoones, Peter/NHPA; **233i** Shimlock, M. & Jones, B./NHPA; **234**
Freund, Jurgen/NPL; **235** Bromhall, Clive/OSF; **237** Douwma, Georgette/NPL;
239t Wu, Norbert/NHPA; **239b** Lucas, Ken/AL; **241** Dalton, Stephen/NHPA; **243**
Shimlock, M. & Jones, B./NHPA; **244-245** Pacific Stock/BCC; **244i** McDonald,
Trevor/NHPA; **247** Foott, Jeff/NPL; **248** Gibbs, Max/PX; **249** Gibbs, Max/PX;
250-251 Gibbs, Max/PX; **253** Gibbs, Max/PX; **254t** Gibbs, Max/PX; **254-255**
Douwma, Georgette /PX; **256-257** Foott, Jeff/NPL; **258** Taylor, Ron &
Valerie/AL; **259** Pacific Stock/BCC; **261t** Minden Pictures/FLPA; **261b** Bernhard,
Tobias/OSF; **263** Rotman, Jeff/NPL; **264-265** Taylor, Ron & Valerie/AL; **267** Wu,
Norbert/NHPA; **269** White, Doc/AL; **270** Gibbs, Max/PX; **271** Graner,
Florian/NPL; **272-273** Waller, Roy/NHPA; **275t** Gibbs, Max/PX; **275b** Gibbs,
Max/PX